tropical truth

tropical truth

a story of music and revolution in brazil

caetano veloso

translated by **isabel de sena** · edited by **barbara einzig**

alfred a. knopf  new york 2002

Library of Congress Cataloging-in-Publication Data
Veloso, Caetano.
{Verdade tropical. English}
Tropical truth : a story of music and revolution in Brazil / Caetano Veloso.
p. cm.
Translation of: Verdade tropical.
Includes index.
ISBN 0-375-40788-X
1. Tropicália (Music)—Brazil—History and criticism. 2. Popular music—Brazil—History and
criticism. 3. Veloso, Caetano. 4. Composers—Brazil—Biography. I. Title.
ML3487.B7 V4513 2002
781.64'0981—dc21 2002066147

For José Miguel Wisnik, David Byrne, and Silvina Garré

contents

acknowledgments

As I composed the growing pile of increasingly intractable fragments, Cristiana Lavigne would read them, point out connections, make editorial suggestions, and in so doing she rekindled the hope that I could write a book.

Rubem Fonseca (who helped Cristiana Lavigne solve a computer problem over an international phone call), read the manuscript in its organized form, made very encouraging remarks (also over the phone), and suggested (in fact imposed) three cuts, short and precise like the sentences that have made him famous. (Two of those instructions were immediately followed to the letter, the other—after much hesitation—only in part.) Both nearer and farther, Luís Tenório de Oliveira Lima in the seventies offered me a book by Miguel de Unamuno where I read the most moving observations ever made by a foreigner about the Portuguese language, and so changed my relationship to words.

Finally, and very much closer to home, toward the end of the fifties Rodrigo Veloso gave me a subscription to the magazine *Senhor,* which led to the discovery of Clarice Lispector, whose books Rodrigo started buying for me assiduously, as he did those of João Guimarães Rosa and João Cabral de Melo Neto. This endowed me with a depth of love for books that surpasses my superficial acquaintance with them to this day.

Thank you.

—C.V.

tropical truth

introduction

In the year 2000, Brazil commemorated not only the passing
of the century and the millennium but also the five hundred
years since her discovery. To this date, then, is attached an accumula-
tion of meaning not shared with any other country in the world. And
the flood of omens let loose at this juncture is closely allied with the
psychology of Brazil—a failed nation ashamed of having once been
called "the country of the future." In fact, those past expectations have
today taken the form of a resignation that underlies new frustrations,
but the magnitude of Brazil's disillusionment reveals that—fortunately
or not—we remain very far from a sensible realism.

As children we learned that Brazil was discovered by the Portuguese
navigator Pedro Álvarez Cabral on April 22, 1500. All other American
nations consider it enough to have been discovered together by Christopher Columbus in 1492. It was only Brazil that had to be discovered
later, separately. From the earliest age, as a child in Santo Amaro da
Purificação in Bahia, I had to ask: "Why?"

They could have said, for example, that Columbus did not sail farther than the Caribbean islands and that the continent proper was only
arrived at by the Portuguese eight years later; they could have told us
that what Cabral discovered was the existence of South America, of
which the Spaniards had not the slightest idea. But no: they say Brazil
appeared as an independent continent, a huge island in the middle of
the South Atlantic, a surprise for those Lusitanian sailors who, aiming
to follow the coast of Africa to reach the Indies, sailed too far west. That
such a vaguely defined event should be situated so precisely in the middle of the second millennium serves to force upon Brazilians a sense of
themselves as a nation both unsubstantiated and exaggerated. The
United States is a country without a name: America is the name of the
continent where, among others, the states that were once English
colonies united. Brazil is a name without a country. The English seem
to have stolen the name of the continent and given it to the country

they founded. The Portuguese seem not to have really founded a country, but managed to suggest that they landed in a part of America that was absolutely Other, and they called it Brazil.

The parallel with the United States is inevitable. If all the countries in the world today must measure themselves against "America," position themselves in relation to the American Empire, and if the other countries in America have to do so in an even more direct way—comparing their respective histories to that of their stronger and more fortunate brother—Brazil's case is even more acute, since the mirror image is more evident and the alienation more radical. Brazil is America's other giant, the other *melting pot* of races and cultures, the other promised land to European and Asian immigrants, the Other. The double, the shadow, the negative image of the great adventure of the New World. The sobriquet "sleeping giant," which was applied to the United States by Admiral Yamamoto, will be taken by any Brazilian as a reference to Brazil, and confused with the seemingly ominous words of the national anthem, "forever lying in a splendid cradle."

The papal bull that created the Treaty of Tordesillas, stipulating that lands yet to be discovered to the east of the agreed-upon meridian would belong to Portugal, leaving those to the west for Spain, explains the need for a new "discovery" and for its being Portuguese. But in school we learn—and Pero Vaz de Caminha's beautiful letter reporting to the king about the voyage reassures us—that *chance* impelled Cabral's fleet on to the Brazilian coast. And that is how we came to have this immense floating world, the namesake of a utopian island imagined in the European Middle Ages, and perhaps less unreal than the latter, this enormous no-place with the burning name. (Brazil is usually assumed to be derived from "*braza*," burning coal or ember.)

In 1995, the Brazilian daily *Folha de São Paulo* bore this headline: "World Bank Report Indicates Brazil Is the Country with the Greatest Social and Economic Disparity in the World." The article reports that 51.3 percent of Brazilian income is concentrated in 10 percent of the population. The wealthiest 20 percent own 67.5 percent of Brazil, while the 20 percent who are poorest have only 2.1 percent. It was that way when I was a boy, and it is still that way. As we reached adolescence, my generation dreamed of inverting this brutal legacy.

In 1964, the military took power, motivated by the need to perpetuate those disparities that have proven to be the only way to make the Brazilian economy work (badly, needless to say) and, in the international arena, to defend the free market from the threat of the communist bloc (another American front of the Cold War). Students were either leftist or they would keep their mouths shut. Within the family or among one's circle of friends, there was no possibility of anyone's sanely disagreeing with a socialist ideology. The Right existed only to serve vested or unspeakable interests. Thus, the rallies "With God and for Freedom" organized by the "Catholic ladies" in support of the military coup appeared to us as the cynical, hypocritical gestures of evil people.

The coup, carried out in the name of the war against international communism, had put in power a man called Marshal Castelo Branco, a military officer of the so-called American line of thinking, meaning that he, unlike those called "Prussians" (who yearned to be centralizing nationalists), wanted to wipe out the Left and corruption in Brazil in order to turn her over to the modernity of the free market. Almost all of us were unaware of those nuances back then, and even if we had been, it would have changed nothing; we saw the coup simply as a decision to halt the redress of the horrible social inequities in Brazil and, simultaneously, to sustain North American supremacy in the hemisphere. The trend toward establishing a political art, sketched out in 1963 by the Centros Populares de Cultura (Centers for Popular Culture) of UNE (the National Students' Union) became widespread in all conventional artistic production, and, in spite of repression at the universities and censorship of the media, show business fell under the hegemony of the Left. In a highly politicized student environment, MPB (Música Popular Brasileira) functioned as an arena for important decisions concerning Brazilian culture and even national sovereignty—and the media covered it accordingly. And it was at MPB's huge televised festivals that the world of the students interacted with that of the wide masses of TV spectators. (The latter were naturally much more numerous than the record buyers.) At these events, one could encounter the more or less conscious illusion that this was where the problems of national affirmation, social justice, and advances in modernization were to be resolved. Market questions, often the only decisive ones, did not seem noble enough to be included in heated discussions. Of course girls would scream "beautiful!" when Chico Buarque came onstage (and, with far less reason, started screaming the same at me), but the conversations and hostilities between the groups would focus as much on an artist's political attitude and his fidelity to national characteristics as on his harmonic or rhythmic daring. That it should be so was a luxury. As silly as this state of things could be, we were living in an exceptionally stimulating period for composers, singers, and musicians. And one thing rang true: the recognition of MPB's power among us. Everything was heightened by the instinctive rejection of the military dictatorship, which seemed to unify the whole of the artistic class around a common objective: to oppose it.

Elizabeth Bishop, the American poet who lived in Brazil between 1952 and 1970, praised the rallies organized in support of the military, explaining in letters to her friends in the United States that while those demonstrations had "originally been organized as anticommunist parades," they "were becoming victory marches—more than one million people marching in the rain!" And she concludes: "It was totally spontaneous, they could not *all* be rich and right-wing reactionaries." Today, when I read those words, I am even more astonished by the distortion of my own point of view at the time than by the author's (though, to be sure, hers was no less distorted). To discover her version of the coup d'état causes me some unease, but it is one more lesson, in these times when private virtues must be taken as the causes of public evils, to come to the realization that back then someone—a woman poet at that!—might thus sum up the military coup that sent to jail some of my finest schoolmates and professors: "A few brave generals and the governors of three important states got together and, after a difficult forty-eight hours, it was all over. The (favorable) reactions have been really popular, thank God." Apparently there was such a thing as right-wing good intentions.

In 1964 the Left consisted of every Brazilian who deserved to be one, and all human beings worthy of the name. Antônio Risério points out, in his essay about Bahia during the pre-1964 democratic period, that when the Austrian intellectual Otto Maria Carpeaux arrived in Brazil to escape Hitler, he had already noticed that here "almost everyone" was a leftist. My intention in this book is to tell and interpret the adventure of a creative impulse that emerged within Brazilian pop music in the second half of the sixties, whose protagonists—among them the narrator—wanted the freedom to move beyond the automatic ties with the Left and at the same time to account for the visceral rebellion against the abysmal disparities that tear a people asunder, even as that people remains singular and charming. And also to tell about the fateful and joyous participation in a universal and international urban cultural reality. All of this being an unveiling of the mystery of the island of Brazil.

After the bossa nova revolution, and to a great extent *because of it,* there emerged the *tropicalista* movement, whose aim it was to sort out the tension between Brazil the Parallel Universe and Brazil the country peripheral to the American Empire. A country which, at the time, was ruled by a military dictatorship believed to have been fostered by the anticommunist maneuvers of the American Empire's Central Intelligence Agency. *Tropicalismo* wanted to project itself as the triumph over two notions: one, that the version of the Western enterprise offered by American pop and mass culture was potentially liberating—though we recognized that a naïve attraction to that version is a healthy impulse— and, two, the horrifying humiliation represented by capitulation to the narrow interests of dominant groups, whether at home or internationally. It was also an attempt to face up to the apparent coincidence, in this tropical country, of a countercultural wave emerging at the same time as the vogue in authoritarian regimes.

The fact that MPB (Brazilian Popular Music) would come to concentrate the energy of this generation only confirms the power of the tradition that made bossa nova possible: in fact, MPB has been, for Brazilians as well as for foreigners, the sound of the discovery of a dreamt-of Brazil. Parenthetically, at this point one foresees a mutual discovery, whereby the heart inclines toward the Indian going aboard the alien ship of the great Pedro Álvares, whose feet barely touched American soil. The Indian was so bereft of fear that he fell asleep on board. MPB proves to be the most efficient weapon for the affirmation of the Portuguese language in the world, when one considers how many unsuspected lovers it has won through the magic of the word sung in the Brazilian way.

The movement that turned the tradition of MPB on its head in the sixties earned the name *tropicalismo*. *Tropicália,* a term first invented by the artist Hélio Oiticica and then given as title to one of my songs by Cinema Novo director Luís Carlos Barreto, from which *tropicalismo* was derived, is more than beautiful-sounding to me: it is even preferable, to avoid confusion with Gilberto Freyre's term *"Luso-tropicalism"* (something much more respectable), or with the study of tropical diseases. Furthermore, it is free from the *-ism,* which, precisely owing to its reductiveness, facilitates the circulation of the ideas and repertory created, conferring on them the status of a movement. The word, however, will appear more frequently in these pages with that ending, since this is no more than an effort to disseminate that gesture on an international scale. In any event, in spite of some personal protest, we have long accepted *tropicalismo* as the most operationally effective term.

I am a Brazilian, and I became, more or less involuntarily, a singer and composer of songs. I was one of the creators and actors of the *tropicália* project. This book is an attempt to narrate and interpret what happened. João Gilberto, my supreme master, in answering a question about me in one of his rare interviews, said that my contribution to Brazilian music was "an accompaniment of thought" to his own work. Well, this book reflects my conscious effort to carry out that task. In a way it reviews the theoretical and critical endeavors that I undertook as I composed and interpreted the songs, but was forced to interrupt due to the intensity with which I was injecting them in the music. This is not an autobiography, though I do not refuse to "tell myself" with some prodigality. It is rather an effort to understand how I passed through *tropicalismo,* or how it passed through me: because we, it and I, were useful for a time and perhaps necessary to each other. The tone is frankly self-complacent (and in any event a large dose of self-complacency would be necessary in order to accept this task). I promised myself that I would plan my life so as to be able to stay home for at least a year to write it. Unable to keep that promise, I ended up having to make use of breaks during recording sessions, the wee hours in hotels after a show during tours, the time off between rehearsals and the (few) unoccupied hours of my vacations in Salvador. This perhaps overexposed the double (and somewhat contradictory) tendency toward digression and ellipsis that confounds my thinking, my conversations, and my writing. I also allowed myself to slide between the narrative and the essayistic, the technical and the confessional (and to situate myself as mediator/medium of the spirit of MPB—and of Brazil itself) in order to deal with even a part of the world of ideas suggested by the main theme.

Despite all this, the reader will certainly find in the pages that follow a prose more expansive than this introduction. For a long time I hesitated to write this book, one of the reasons being that I was unsure whether what I might say—and the way I might say it—would not be too complicated for people who wanted to read a book on pop music, and at the same time too close to pop music for people who like to read complicated books. Still, without transcending this uncertainty—and asking myself, even as I eagerly wrote, who could be interested in such a book—I decided not to pay undue attention to the fear of seeming too pretentious or vague (or, who knows, too modest and precise), focusing instead on the fact that books are written for those who like to read books. I've found intelligent people all over the world who care about Brazilian music: maybe the anecdotes, confidences, and insights presented here will awaken the reader's curiosity and provoke more reading. On the other hand, an account of the experiences of a "pop star intellectual" from a "third world" country may shed an unexpected light on the adventure of the sixties, since this period—remote and dated only for those intimidated by the challenges that presented themselves then, or for those justifiably afraid to rise to such challenges now—remains unresolved in the eyes of anyone inclined to rise above the usual dismissive nostalgia.

From the depths of the dark solar heart of the southern hemisphere, from inside a mix of races that constitutes neither a degradation nor a genetic utopia, from the befouled and healing guts of the global entertainment industry, from the island of Brazil ever floating barely suspended above the real ground of America, come these words, translated, rising out of the mists of the Portuguese, limited in their powers but still serving to bear witness and to ask why certain relationships exist between different groups, individuals, artistic forms, commercial transactions, and political forces.

elvis and marilyn

I used to say that if it were up to me, Elvis Presley and Marilyn Monroe would never have become stars.

In the late fifties, there were very few kids in my hometown of Santo Amaro drawn to the American life of rock 'n' roll and its style—boys in jeans and boots, girls with ponytails and chewing gum. They hardly constituted even a minority, and apart from being exotic, they seemed to me rather dull. It wasn't that I held myself so much apart from them or bore them any hostility. It was more that they embodied a trend that was surfacing hesitantly among a few people I knew—and definitely not among the most intelligent or interesting.

But soon rock 'n' roll contests were the rage in Rio and Salvador, and American mass culture was all around us. While I liked Sinatra and Nat King Cole, preferred Louis Armstrong, and would soon be adoring Chet Baker, Monk, Miles, and Ray Charles, at the same time I was listening to Brazilian music, old and new, as well as Argentinian, Cuban, and Mexican music. Still, like everyone else in my circle I simply could not identify with the young contestants featured in magazines, much less with their longings to emulate the silver screen's high-school football heroes, cheered on by girls with pompoms. It wasn't that my friends and I found those who did "culturally inauthentic," or even alienated from our national or regional roots—back then we simply weren't thinking in those terms, though we were probably not altogether immune to a mild and naïve strain of nationalism. Rather, what we found objectionable—without yet being quite able to say it this way—was that these kids were imitating a dazzling style that had come at them without their knowing what it meant. We laughed at them, as though understanding we had it over them somehow. In fact what estranged me most from rock, and from that entire impulse toward Americanization, was that it reached me without carrying any trace of rebellion.

I remember something said to me by an older cousin when I was only six or seven. "My Daia," one of a number of relatives who lived with us (and whom I still see, every time I go to Bahia), was already around thirty, and so she addressed me in that tone—half-amused, half-irritated, casually sincere—one takes with children: "Sweetheart, I wish I could live in Paris and be an existentialist." I was curious: "My Daia, what's an existentialist?" And she said, now with evident exasperation: "Existentialists are philosophers who do only what they like, and they do everything they feel like doing. I wish I could live like them, far away from this 'narrow' life in Santo Amaro."

I now realize that My Daia's definition of existentialism—which no doubt was a pop phenomenon of the forties—had probably been inspired by the lyrics of a popular Carnival *marchinha* called "Chiquita Bacana":

> *an existentialist she was*
> *that's really smart*
> *everything she does*
> *comes from the heart.*

But in fact my cousin's knowledge of the matter went deeper. When I pressed her for more explanation, she—hardly suspecting I would never forget it—specifically mentioned "existentialist *philosophers*" as she tried to tell me that there were people in the world who held out the promise of a life with more freedom than was possible in Santo Amaro.

Revolt against the "narrow" life was hardly to be found among those of my schoolmates aping American rock 'n' roll singers. Their attitudes—an awkward climbing up the rungs of a borrowed ladder of values they could barely fathom—were, to the contrary, a clear sign of conformity. And I knew they had no idea of what really mattered to me.

Santo Amaro, where I was born in 1942, is a small town—some buildings date back to the eighteenth century, and many to the nineteenth—and by the middle of the twentieth, the glaring social inequities of the past had been muted. The lower middle class, who lived in the two-story colonial houses once occupied by landowners, as well as in the smaller houses that leaned against each other, barely set back from sidewalks lined with ficus trees, along streets paved with granite flagstones—my family belonged to this middle class: my father worked for the Postal and Telegraph Service—these families remained close to the semirural poverty of the maids and laborers who lived all along the outskirts of town. We had no real contact with wealth: the prosperity many local families had enjoyed from colonial times until the nineteenth century was the source of an architectural legacy now in the hands of government workers, priests, doctors, dentists, lawyers, and small businessmen, just as the vast sugar plantations, the traditional source of income in the region, little by little were transferred away from the *recôncavo,* the hinterland, to far larger properties centralized in other Brazilian regions. None of the profits were any longer spent in Santo Amaro, and none of the proprietors lived or had even been born there.

My life was peaceful among a large and loving family, in our pretty little town with its snug civic life. The house in Amparo Street, where my mother still lives, was the seat of the most important events of my formation. It was here that I was to discover sex, see *La strada,* fall in love for the first (and for the second, even more startling) time, read Clarice Lispector, and—most important—hear João Gilberto.

I was timid and extravagant. As an introvert, I abandoned myself to endless solitary hours perched on the branches of the guava tree in the yard or playing the piano in the living room, picking out by ear simple songs learned from the radio, their harmonies massacred by my limited grasp. My first public performance occurred at age eight, in a talent show on the radio. When I heard the orchestra playing the introduction to the "Toureiro de Madri," the *marchinha* I'd chosen, I started to sing in the wrong key and was immediately disqualified. Later, I would turn to oil paintings—at first, landscapes and houses, and later, abstract paintings, which I credited with great expressiveness.

As an extrovert, I talked to everyone in school, wore socks of different colors, and let my hair grow far past my mother's tolerance, only to shave it off completely. By my teens I was everyone's favorite singer in high school, but I remained—as I am even today—terrified of hitting the wrong note. So I fantasized about becoming a high-school teacher, to be among young people and explain things, to have an admiring audience, grateful for my knowledge.

I wasn't intimidated when I had to sing in public in the high-school auditorium: I could do a reasonable imitation of the Portuguese accent and vocal arabesques typical of *fado* singers, the beauty of the songs moving audiences to forget themselves and lavish me with ovations. Full of that deep sadness that the Portuguese bear with such resignation, *fado* is sometimes called "the blues of Europe." Some courage was needed back then for anyone to say he liked it, much less sing it; people didn't listen to *fado* much, although it was sometimes played by radio stations popular among Portuguese immigrants. There were many reasons why both the Portuguese accent and Portugal itself were, as a rule, considered ridiculous: having been a Portuguese colony, independent Brazil naturally rejected the old metropolis; but even more, Portugal, perhaps the most important European country at the time of Brazil's "discovery" in 1500, had by the beginning of the twentieth century declined to the lowest position on the continent. The Brazilians had developed a totally different accent, and the Portuguese way of speaking sounded old-fashioned. (Imagine how a British accent might sound to an American ear had England in fact proved to be not the greatest empire of the nineteenth century but a historical failure.) It didn't help matters that, at the very start of the twentieth century, Portuguese immigrants flooded Rio, and being mostly illiterate, very naïve peasants, became the butt of all sorts of jokes.

The concerts happened occasionally, to celebrate anything: the end of term, the evening before a long holiday, or for no reason at all. My classmates sang or danced; we all used microphones. My very first composition, at the age of nine, was a *baião:* in C minor, no words. Only later, when I was fifteen or sixteen, did I begin to write songs, although rather carelessly. And only after I was seventeen—that is, after bossa nova—did I begin to dream of composing really beautiful things, though even now I imagine I never got there.

It was not only seeing poverty up close that made me question the world before wanting to change it. The values and habits of mind taken for granted in Santo Amaro never seemed intuitively correct to me. There, for example, it was unthinkable to have sex with girls we respected and liked; middle-class black girls had to straighten their hair in order to feel presentable; "nice" girls and women would never dream of smoking; a thuggish-looking guy could lay boys and still be accepted in the male society at the corner bar where queers—or even those who appeared slightly effeminate to the regulars—were regularly abused; married men were encouraged to keep at least one mistress, while their women (wives or lovers) had to flaunt an adamantine fidelity, and so on. Obviously such hypocrisies were not limited to Santo Amaro or even to small towns in the interior. In the fifties, allowing for some variation by region, class, and culture, it was more or less the same everywhere. And although today those conventions appear superficially to have been abandoned, the fact that many people still perceive a looming social chaos only confirms that the underlying assumptions persist.

It was clear to me even then I would not share these values, but since they were so pervasive, and bound up with so many others I was barely conscious of, there arose in me a vague uneasiness, which I attempted to exorcise through little eccentricities and big thoughts. As a small child I had complicated philosophical intuitions. I was overwhelmed by the impossibility of proving to myself the existence of the world outside of me—or, for that matter, the existence of my own body. When I was seven or eight (I know it could not have been later, since this thought occurred to me when we lived in the post office quarters, as was the custom back then, before we moved to Amparo Street, when I was eight), I promised myself, with a kind of anguished pride, that I would grow up and cause a scandal inflamed by this certainty: if I couldn't get outside myself—as I still cannot—then there is nothing in the world, nothing at all, apart from my thinking. It occurred to me that denouncing this nonexistence of everything might be a way of forcing something to happen in the world.

I have many siblings—three girls and three boys were born to my father and mother, and they adopted two daughters besides. Our house was enormous, full of family, friends, schoolmates, the guests of our parents, older sisters, and cousins—everyone stopped by to chat, sometimes on a daily basis. The atmosphere, while calm and affectionate, was excessively introspective, a world closed in on itself, and the fact that my father worked at home contributed to the sensation. In this way our big house also seemed a world apart to all the people who came in from the outside. We ourselves seldom went out, not even to play at someone else's house as children do. But the happy and sensuous life of the *recôncavo* was to be found in the food (of famously high quality), in the sweetness of the people, in the samba groups that assembled for each holiday, as though their gaiety were not at odds with the somber habits that made our day-to-day life at once so frightening and reassuring. We would ask our parents for their blessing every morning and each night before going to bed. They would answer archaically: "God bless thee," "May God bring thee happiness," "May God bring thee good luck." We addressed them as "Senhor" or "Senhora," never using *você,* the familiar form in Brazil. We could not go to bed without praying. I heard not a few times that we would go to hell if we died in our sleep without having said our prayers. We saw entire families dressed in black mourning for a dead relative, and although our elders often said that true feelings mattered more than conventions, when our very dear aunt "Mother Mina," our father's sister, died (I sensed her agony one night when I heard her gasping for air, in the room Roberto and I then shared with her), months passed before we were allowed to play the piano, go to the movies, dance, wear colorful clothes, sing, whistle, or laugh in the house (much less in the street, where others could see us). In the house there was the saints' room, and in it a niche for the Crucified One and images of the Virgin, Saint Anthony, Saint Joseph, the dove of the Holy Spirit, and Baby Jesus. Another of our father's sisters, My Ju—who dedicated her life to helping my parents raise us, working the telegraph and handing her entire salary over to my father—would lead the prayers: thirteen nights for Saint Anthony, a month for Saint Joseph, the Month of Mary, and so on. And all this praying went on without music, even though there was music in other people's houses, and My Ju sang so well in the church choir.

Soon after we moved to Amparo Street—whose name means "protection"—I made a decision: I, who had already taken my first communion and went regularly to Sunday mass, would set myself apart by telling my family that I did not believe in God or in the priests. I did not make an official announcement, or even a clear statement, as I had heard my brothers say that this would be a terrible blow to My Ju. Rather, I told some of my older brothers and sister, My Daia, and then my father, always introducing the subject in a hypothetical tone. Oddly, my parents were unaffected. They, in fact, were the only ones who did not go to mass on Sundays, taking advantage of the opportunity to be alone on the only day my father didn't work.

My family's older generation and their friends had been educated with Francophile literary tastes, but American influences did not begin with rock 'n' roll. By the forties, American movies and music—a strong presence in Brazilian life since the twenties—started to dominate the scene. It was true that American music was always competing with the Cuban rumba, the Argentine tango, and the Portuguese *fado,* even as Brazilian music remained—as it still is—the most consistently popular music in Brazil. But Hollywood movies met with almost no resistance. I was learning some English at school, and its only use was for singing American songs. We knew that all over the world Frank Sinatra had been—and still was—an enormous star, and that Nat King Cole was, for a while, an even bigger one. Alongside the successful artists who presented their versions of regional music (at times extraordinarily well-conceived)—people such as Luiz Gonzaga, Jackson do Pandeiro, and Pedro Raimundo—there was also a place for someone like Bob Nelson, who sang songs from the American West in Portuguese, dressed like a cowboy and displaying his great talent for yodeling, which came to be known as *"tir'o leite,"* milk 'em—an ingenious adaptation that managed to mimic the sound of the activity so typical of the countryside. Santo Amaro was no exception in a world where the American cowboy was an uncontested mythic hero. And we were especially entranced with the great MGM musicals. We'd come back from the movies dancing like Gene Kelly and Cyd Charisse. Elvis Presley was just the latest American idol, only a little different—when his fans appeared, they seemed simply another part of our keeping up with American mass culture. His music seemed simplistic and commercial, and his looks were a bit odd—the first image of him I can remember was in a Brazilian magazine; there he was, with greasy black hair, surrounded by teddy bears—childlike, treacly, in fact a bit disgusting.

It may seem that the great Hollywood studios had no reason to fear European competition for the film distribution market in Brazil, but to my friends and me this undisputed logic of the market was not obvious. French and Italian films were regularly exhibited in Santo Amaro. So were Mexican films. I do remember a curious joke that was popular toward the end of the forties: you would call someone's attention to a (nonexistent) bit of lint on his lapel, thus forcing him to twist his face somewhat uncomfortably in the direction of his shoulder, bringing his chin close to the shoulder blade and making him peer downward. At this point the prankster would suddenly change tone and, having thus tricked his mark into posing à la Rita Hayworth, say: "Looks like Gilda . . ." The effect was even more comical if the victim was a man. And My Daia, whom we privately called Bette Davis, could sometimes be heard repeating, as if she were thinking aloud: "There never was a woman like Gilda." It would have been incredible to have known then, as I know now, that at the very moment when Marilyn Monroe was becoming a mythical figure, hardly any Americans even knew who Françoise Arnou and Martine Carol were. And even if, in spite of Maria Felix's extraordinary beauty, we could have perceived a slight inferiority in the Olympus of Pelmex—Películas Mexicanas, the major Mexican studio—it was inconceivable that one could discern any difference of quality or importance between American and European stars. Early in our adolescence, it was the revelations of erotic intimacy that attracted us to French cinema—a woman's breast, a couple lying together on a wrought-iron bed, the indisputable signs that the characters had a sex life—everything that could not be seen in an American film was offered in French films quite naturally. And we were lucky enough to have, at that time, no age-restricted ratings, since there was no government office with jurisdiction over minors in Santo Amaro. But as we grew older, Italian cinema interested us more and more because of its "seriousness": neorealism and its offshoots were offered to us through commercial distribution, and we reacted to those films with real emotion, recognizing the lineaments of our daily reality in those gigantic, brilliant images. One of the most remarkable events in my personal development was the screening of Fellini's *La strada* one Sunday morning at the Cine Subaé (there were morning shows on Sundays, and this was the best of the three theaters in town—the only one that ever had Cinemascope). I cried for the rest of the day, and couldn't eat lunch—and from then on we called My Daia "Giulietta Masina." Mr. Agnelo Rato Grosso, the stocky, illiterate mulatto butcher who played trombone in the Lira dos Artistas (one of the two bands in town), was taken by surprise when Chico Motta, Dasinho, and I caught him weeping as we left the movie theater after a screening of *I vitelloni,* also by Fellini. Somewhat embarrassed and wiping his nose on his shirt, he offered as if to excuse himself: "That movie is our life!" I remember Nicinha, my oldest sister, commenting that when the actors in American films spoke near a table where a meal was served, the cut would always occur before they were seen putting anything in their mouths and chewing, whereas in Italian films people ate—and sometimes even talked with their mouths full.

Before Hollywood put them under contract and introduced them to the American public, this is how European beauties like Sophia Loren and Gina Lollobrigida arrived in our world. Together with others barely noticed in the United States—Silvana Pampanini, Silvana Mangano, Rossana Podestà—they were adored as goddesses among us. Actually, we found more cause to lament than to celebrate when Italian actresses went to Hollywood: these simple, gorgeous girls apparently plucked straight from the streets of Naples now looked like greenhorns in the big city, given a makeover that did not suit them. (In the provinces, to the extent that one finds criticism, it tends, more than anything one might hear in the metropolis, to run against provincialism.) In any event, nothing could persuade us that Brigitte Bardot might be even in the slightest inferior to Marilyn Monroe, whether respecting the salary she merited or her status as a cultural icon. The names I chose to include in the songs I composed in the sixties (which, in keeping with the pop aesthetic, introduced the names of celebrities) were those of such European stars as Claudia Cardinale, Brigitte Bardot, Alain Delon, and Jean-Paul Belmondo. In the late fifties, while I was still dabbling, I interrupted my abstract paintings to do a portrait of Sophia Loren based on a still from the film *La donna del Po.*

As for Marilyn Monroe, since we were unconvinced of her stature as a goddess and unaware that being American was a sine qua non for global celebrity, we saw in her little other than vulgar commercialism. (My first experience of her onscreen occurred in Rio, where I lived for one year when I turned fourteen—she played a crazy babysitter.) She appeared to be just a stereotypical blonde who had become famous in the United States. By some great good fortune the period from the mid-fifties to the mid-sixties was the only time in Brazil when European movies were just as big commercially as those from America. That's why if we found Ava Gardner, Elizabeth Taylor, or Jane Russell wanting, we were inclined to renew our list of divas by searching among the Italian actresses like Loren and Papanini. Neither did rock 'n' roll fans talk much about women; some may have liked Marilyn, while others might have thought that liking her was part of the pose they wanted to strike. But no one ever told me "I'd die for Marilyn Monroe."

I was astonished by the pop artists at the São Paulo Bienalle of 1967. By that time, my first *tropicalista* album was ready, and I had become vaguely aware of the trend toward a consumer mentality and of the impact of mass media upon it; I wasn't sure how the role of the superstar was changing, but I knew without doubt that it was happening. I intuited this through newspaper articles and in conversations with friends, but at the time I had no sense of what was happening in the New York art world, or of the person who would give this trend its clearest meaning: Andy Warhol. In his portraits of both Marilyn and Elvis, I recognized at once that it was not the actress or the rock star that I was meant to be seeing but a visual image with a life of its own. In Warhol's Marilyn I saw how raw images would become comments on the world if only we would abstain from commenting upon them. It was as if Marilyn had lived only to be a character in Warhol's drama. We could go even so far as to say, paraphrasing Oscar Wilde on Balzac, that the twentieth century as we know it is a creation of Andy Warhol's. While I hadn't even heard Warhol's name at the time, I still have to credit him and friends of mine who had gone much further—such as Rogério Duarte and José Agrippino de Paula—for the development of my perception of what turned out to be a major cultural shift. The impact of figures like Marilyn and Elvis was indirect; my growing sense of what was to become the unprecedented force of mass media would eventually be expressed in *tropicalismo,* that brief, rebellious, and self-analytical movement of music and visual arts in Brazil of which I was part in the late sixties.

In the early eighties, Roberto Dávila, a television reporter who later became vice mayor of Rio, asked me to accompany him to New York to help interview Mick Jagger for a Brazilian television series. My presence was supposed to attract attention, since people like me are often referred to in the press as "the Brazilian Bob Dylan," or "the Brazilian John Lennon" or—more appropriately in this case—"the Brazilian Mick Jagger." While despising such idiotic classifications, I agreed to do it out of curiosity and admiration for Mick Jagger. What is interesting is that when I asked Jagger how rock had won him over, I also confessed my own initial distaste for Elvis, acknowledging that while he and I were both college educated and of the same generation, rock at first had seemed to me too simple and not very exciting; for me and for many other Brazilians, it was bossa nova's powerful appeal that had oriented us in a different direction. He interrupted me and said: "That's good. It would be very boring if there weren't different styles in different places, and music were the same all over the world." He didn't say this to be kind, but rather as a gentle reprimand. Still, his simple observation sounded natural to me, and absolutely correct. I felt then and still feel how auspicious it was that bossa nova emerged precisely when the friends of my generation and I were first learning to think and to feel.

When *Rock Around the Clock* opened in Rio, I heard it had provoked such excitement that audiences stood on the seats and damaged the theaters. So when the movie was shown in Salvador, at the Cine Guarany (today's Cine Glauber Rocha), I broke out in a cold sweat for fear of being possessed by an Irrational Power—as I had so often felt in *candomblé* rituals—until I realized that the film was merely a kind of American version of the Brazilian B films that drew the crowds each summer: those primitive but reliable comedies of Carnival, refreshed with new jokes, would introduce the *marchinhas* and sambas to which we'd be dancing at the next Carnival, just as kids in the States were doing the twist after seeing it onscreen. Those moviegoers who went wild in Salvador were aping the enthusiasm that the newspapers were reporting on from Rio—it was their way of identifying with that Rio audience, and, in turn, with Americans who, it was said, had done the same thing in the United States.

Rock seemed unoriginal to me as both dance and music. The only difference I could hear between "Rock Around the Clock" and "In the Mood" or any other twelve-bar blues arrangement was its stridency and somewhat awkward attempt to be more savagely rhythmic than American music had been up to then; even so it was far less rhythmically intense than Brazilian or Cuban music had always been. The dancing— with the boy taking the girl's hands and making her twirl, before pulling her between his legs, and so on—was unbearably like what had been seen in American films of the thirties and forties. And I was not alone in my lack of enthusiasm: although the Irrational Power that would take many years to reach me had already taken hold of a great many moviegoers, Cine Guarany was not even full. In fact rock 'n' roll had a relatively difficult time catching on either as a commercial phenomenon or as a cultural influence. It was dependent upon the kind of taste and economic power that allowed ready access to information about American culture—records, movies, magazines—in other words, an audience of reasonable affluence, but such people often maintained an elitism to which the whorehouse-edge of Elvis did not appeal. Such limitations notwithstanding, there were certainly some outstandingly original Brazilian artists who did connect to rock, and that connection eventually led to professional careers in the sixties, before what may be thought of as the second rock onslaught, this time via England—the entrance on the scene of the Beatles and the Rolling Stones, or what I prefer to call "British neo-rock." Still the press continued to treat rock as though it should have quite naturally enjoyed the same kind of social presence as it had in the United States. And even now, rock fans deplore the fact that a seamless transplantation never occurred, while nationalists object that any took place at all.

The *tropicalistas* decided that a genuine blend of the ridiculous aspirations of Americanophiles, the naïve good intentions of the nationalists, traditional Brazilian "backwardness," the Brazilian avantgarde—absolutely everything in Brazil's real cultural life would be our raw material. Genuine creativity could redeem any aspect of it and make it transcendent.

bossa nova

I was seventeen and still living in Santo Amaro when I first heard João Gilberto. A high school friend wanted me to hear a record that sounded strange to him.

"Caetano, you like crazy things, you have to listen to a record by this guy who sings totally off-key—the orchestra does one thing and he does another." He exaggerated how weird it was for him to listen to João, perhaps influenced by the title of the song, "Desafinado" (Out of Tune)—a false lead for those first listening to that composition in the summer of 1959. With its unexpected melodic intervals, the song required interpreters with extraordinary pitch:

> My love, if you say I'm out of tune,
> know I'm provoked into painful ruin.
> Unlike the privileged ears of people like you
> mine only hear what God allows me to.
>
> If you have to classify
> my behavior as antimusical,
> I will argue even as a lie
> that this bossa nova is natural.
>
> What you don't know, don't have a clue
> is that the out-of-tune have a heart.
> I photographed you with my Rolleiflex,
> it revealed ingratitude in every part.
>
> But you can't say that about my love,
> don't you know it's the best love you're going to find?
> You forgot, with your music, what really counts,
> inside those who are out of tune,
> at heart a beat with barely a sound,
> the beating of the heart of the out-of-tune.

Bossa nova overwhelmed us. And it delighted my intelligence to follow closely this radical process of cultural transformation, which led us to reevaluate our tastes, our heritage and—even more important—our possibilities. What João Gilberto proposed was a deeply penetrating and highly personal interpretation of the spirit of samba. He did this through a mechanically simple but musically challenging guitar beat that suggested an infinite variety of subtle ways to make the vocal phrasing swing over a harmony of chords progressing in a fluent equilibrium. And in so doing, he ignited the combustible elements of a revolution that was not only to make possible the whole evolution of Antônio Carlos Jobim, Carlos Lyra, Newton Mendonça, João Donato, Ronaldo Bôscoli, and Sérgio Ricardo—his generational peers—but also to open the way for emerging younger musicians such as Roberto Menescal, Sérgio Mendes, Nara Leão, Baden Powell, and Leny Andrade. One now heard with a new ear the explorations of those talented musicians who, since the forties, had been striving for renewal through an imitation of American music—"modernizers" such as Dick Farney, Lúcio Alves, Johnny Alf, or the vocal group Os Cariocas. Gilberto validated what they had created, legitimized their pretensions—but he also had it all over them in his command of the cool jazz idiom, which was then the cutting edge of musical invention in the United States. And, critically, he was able to achieve this in a way that reconnected with what was greatest in the Brazilian tradition: the singing of Orlando Silva and Ciro Monteiro, the compositions of Ary Barroso and Dorival Caymmi, of Wilson Batista and Geraldo Pereira, the illuminating style of Assis Valente—in sum, that whole world the "modernizers" had thought it necessary to leave behind as they pursued American styles, which were themselves, ironically, already dated. And by establishing a position from which to innovate while still enjoying the popular musical traditions of Brazil, imagining a different future with the past in a different light, João struck a chord with music critics, avant-garde poets, and the percussion masters of the *escolas de samba*.

How can one understand the immediate resonance, the profound and widespread cultural impact of bossa nova? The observer—particularly the non-Brazilian—must grapple with not only the extraordinary sociological momentum of the emergence of such a sophisticated kind of popular music in a country like Brazil but also—and more important—the great aesthetic subtlety and complexity of the music itself. At bottom the music of bossa nova, even in its incorporation of Brazil's deepest samba roots with America's freshest cool jazz, was quintessentially Brazilian and therefore carried tremendous historical valence. Put another way, bossa nova did not represent a grafting of a foreign branch on to an indigenous rootstock but rather the continuation of a process of innovation that had always been integral to an ever-changing samba. One frequently reads in the American and European press that the prime, fundamental move of bossa nova was to take samba out of the streets, to remove it from its life as dance music, and to transform it into a pop genre for the consumption of middle-class urban youth. After João's 1988 concert in New York, Julian Dibell, who knows a great deal about MPB and whose vision of it is often original and always intelligent, wrote a review in the *Village Voice* in which he tried to give the American reader an idea of the revolutionary dimension of bossa nova in the musical and social environment of Brazil. In this article he calls João Gilberto "Brazil's Elvis." The comparison, made almost as a joke, is very suggestive to a Brazilian mind, for what it makes conspicuous above all are the nearly diametrical origins of bossa nova and rock: bossa nova's revival of samba evolved from a refinement of musical tastes that was influenced by high-quality American songs of the thirties and by the cool jazz of the fifties; by contrast, rock in its essence was a rejection of all sophistication, and continually proves to be so whenever it seeks its own reaffirmation, as the wildly commercial and regressive style of music it was from the beginning. While rock was simplistic, repudiating the elegance and elaboration of a Porter or a Gershwin, with their symphonic orchestrations, Miles Davis, or Bill Evans, in João Gilberto one was witnessing an almost antithetical impulse, a continuation, rather than a suppression, of musical history: with him came the emergence into the light of that long tradition of sophisticated stylizations that was samba, a form which, from the early years of the twentieth century, had distanced itself from the drum beat of the Bahian *candomblé terreiro.* Likewise it had already been removed from the *partido alto* of Rio's slums, where the Carnival blocks were gradually being transformed into the street version of the Folies Bergère that the *escolas de samba* have become (which is by no means to disparage the percussion ensembles—*baterias*—that constitute the most impressive manifestation of originality and musical competence to be found anywhere in Brazilian popular culture).

Indeed the transformation of samba into an elaborate pop genre happened before the modernizers of the late forties and early fifties came onto the scene. It was first the theater—musical comedies, vaudeville—and then radio and the recording industry that fostered successive generations of arrangers, singers, composers, and instrumentalists who created a samba both tamed and refined, particularly from the thirties onward. By the time João Gilberto invented the beat that would become the nucleus for what was eventually called bossa nova, the dominant form was the *samba-canção*. Also called pejoratively *sambolero,* this is a type of slow ballad in which the samba rhythm is perceptible only to a Brazilian ear trained to recognize it in all its variations of stress and tempo. This samba modality had been evolving since Noel Rosa—and could be heard even in the ostensibly "cool" interpretations of Mário Reis, a singer with a small voice and undramatic style. Eventually it could be heard in the songwriting of Ary Barroso and Herivelto Martins, as well as Caymmi in the forties. One has only to hear Sílvio Caldas's recordings of "Maria" or "Tu" by Ary Barroso, or Pixinguinha's "Carinhoso" sung by Orlando Silva—all songs from the thirties—to know that the tamed and refined samba of the studios and musical notation had long been the dominant genre, with recordings of the more percussive brand of "street" samba or the *terreiro* variety being the exception rather than the rule.

In the fifties, singers like Ângela Maria, Carmen Costa, Nora Ney, Nelson Gonçalves, Cauby Peixoto, and Dóris Monteiro, to name but a few, made the off-season samba—as opposed to the dance sambas composed especially for Carnival *canção*—the mainstay of their careers. Nora Ney in particular, with her low voice and clear diction, founded an urban and nocturnal style, marked by an almost literary density inspired by a repertory of magnificent *sambas-canções* by Antônio Maria, Fernando Lobo, and Pernambuco. (Nora Ney, in a quirk of her career, was the first woman to sing rock in Brazil—"Rock Around the Clock," on Rio's Rádio Nacional.) *Samba-canção* was also dominant in the low-quality commercial recordings. But even quick-paced sambas—even those recorded for dancing during Carnival—had orchestral arrangements and vocal interpretations that distanced them from the primitive *batucada.* In sum: samba has been a pop genre for urban consumption since its "standardization" in Rio de Janeiro, a process to which theater, radio, and the recording industry each made decisive contributions. The commercialization of *escolas de samba* recordings has occurred only in the last couple of decades of the twentieth century, with the exuberant percussion of the rhythm sections. Initially considered only a tourist attraction, the annual recording of the *sambas-enredos* of the great samba schools of Rio has become a required item on the agenda of Brazilian recording companies, and also entails an obligatory expenditure in the unimaginably meager budget of the poorer Brazilian consumer.

Ultimately, bossa nova is responsible for the new inclusivity of the music industry, which has inevitably extended its tentacles toward "unrefined" forms of music, not only the street sambas of Rio and Bahia but a wide range of musical styles that previously had been approached solely from a documentary perspective. The "discovered" were as responsible as the "discoverers," for what was important was not so much the journeys of the bossa nova musicians who, looking for the roots of everything, searched the slums or the back country—discovering and bringing out people like Cartola and João do Vale, Zé Kéti, and Clementina de Jesus—as it was the confidence that those journeys engendered: without the self-assurance that bossa nova infused in us, making us feel capable of creating things wholly our own, we would still when working in the studios be leaving out the supremely inventive elements of Brazilian traditions: the tambourines of Mocidade Independente de Padre Miguel, the harmonics of Nelson Cavaquinho's voice.

To understand the impact of bossa nova on Brazilian musical interpretations, it is worth listening to two recordings of the *samba-cançao* "Caminhos cruzados" (Intersections), a composition by Tom Jobim from his pre–bossa nova phase. Just as bossa nova burst upon the scene, it was recorded by Maysa—a beautiful eighteen-year-old from São Paulo's high society who, with her wild green eyes and her smoky voice, was the overnight sensation of the bohemian set; she would also write a few simple and exemplary songs of her own, all *sambas-canções,* none of them ever forgotten. Some years later, "Caminhos cruzados" was also recorded by João Gilberto. João's interpretation is more introspective than Maysa's, and also markedly less dramatic, but if with her version the essential elements of the original samba rhythm were almost completely lost within the overall arrangement, and, particularly, in the inflections of her phrasing, in João's version one can hear—in the mind's ear—the big *surdo* drum of the street samba, beating with a relaxed bounce from beginning to end. It is a lesson in how samba can be wholly present even in the most seemingly improbable of forms; by radicalizing the refinement, it finds a way of locating the black man's hand beating the leather of the first conga in samba's birthplace (and this in the context of a string arrangement by the German Klaus Ogerman). As for me, I find in João's recording of "Caminhos cruzados" one of the best examples of dance music, and this is not an eccentric opinion: I really like to dance samba to this recording, and every time I do, I feel how delicious it is to dance samba and to know that João Gilberto is showing me the samba hidden in the *samba-canção,* which, had it not been for him, would forever pretend to be just another ballad.

In Santo Amaro João Gilberto would become a cult figure for those of us who used to gather in front of what we called "Bubu's Bar," so named for the fat black man who owned it. He had bought João's first LP, *Chega de saudade*—the record that launched the movement—and played it repeatedly. He himself liked it, and he knew that we were going there to hear it. We were a small group: four or five high-school students without money to buy the record ourselves. The atmosphere of a small religious sect permeated those listening sessions, as compared with the mass explosion that was rock in the United States. But this difference should not lead us to overlook the subversive generational character common to both phenomena, which is at the core of the argument made by that journalist in the *Village Voice.* On the one hand, almost all the testimonials of Americans who grew up with rock as the inspiration for their intellectual, political, and existential ambitions maintain the tone of a closed cult, an esoteric brotherhood, this in spite of the explicit commercialism common to artists like Chuck Berry, Little Richard, and Bill Haley; on the other hand, Bubu's taste for João Gilberto was only one sign that Chico Motta, Dasinho, Bethânia, and I were not alone in our enthusiasm for our new discovery: soon bossa nova would bring considerable weight to bear on our recording market. More important, even today whenever any of us sings "Chega de saudade"—still bossa nova's anthem—in any stadium in Brazil, we are accompanied by a chorus of tens of thousands of voices of all ages singing each syllable and note of the long and rich melody. This would not happen if one were to sing "Blue Suede Shoes," "Roll Over Beethoven," or "Rock Around the Clock."

"to hell with everything and i'll give you heaven": brazilian rock

After the waves of bossa nova, American rock, British neo-rock, *tropicalismo,* and Brazilian rock (BRock), there would be a resurgence of the sort of sentimental fare Brazilians of the fifties had referred to as "commercial music." But when it appeared in the late eighties and early nineties this came to be called *"brega"* (a Bahian slang word for "whorehouse," whose coinage was attributed, so the story goes, to a street in the red-light district of Salvador named for Father Manuel da Nóbrega: when the street sign broke, only the last two syllables of the priest's name could be read). Of the musicians whose taste had been deeply informed by rock, some would become the professional interpreters of a naïve style copied from Italian copies of the silliest American pop from the early sixties (for example, Cely Campelo, Tony Campelo, or Carlos Gonzaga). Others would be led to innovative solutions, whether fusions of rhythm and blues with samba (Jorge Ben), soul with *baião* (Tim Maia), or pop-rock with bossa nova and Italian song (Roberto Carlos). But a few names would remain forever connected to true rock 'n' roll, owing either to the authenticity of their devotion to the style or the aptness of their temperament. No one who knows rock's Brazilian history, who is interested in what happened here since that music appeared in the United States, would dispute my choice of names to exemplify this last group: Erasmo Carlos and Raul Seixas.

Erasmo Carlos was a typical teenager from Rio's working-class "suburbs." In fact, Tijuca, where he was born and raised, is a middle-class neighborhood adjacent to the center of the city; and it is only because the Zona Sul neighborhoods along the coast (though actually farther from the center) have acquired such cachet as to represent Rio itself to residents and foreigners alike that a central area like Tijuca could come to be seen and lived as a distant neighborhood. But the group of rock fans to which Erasmo belonged, including Tim Maia and Roberto Carlos, used to gather in front of the Imperator movie theater in the Méier neighborhood—and Méier is truly working class, even if it is the most affluent of the outlying areas connected to the center of Rio by a line of commuter trains.

Erasmo Carlos's artistic persona took shape and gained public recognition in the second half of the sixties, when he became part of the TV program called *Jovem Guarda* (The Young Guard). The program had a musical ensemble of the same name, and the lead singer was Roberto Carlos, a greatly talented and wonderfully charismatic figure. Even when bossa nova was at its peak, his sales were extraordinary; he sang the quasi-rock tune "Quero que tudo vá para o inferno" (To Hell with Everything), and when reprimanded by the ecclesiastic authorities, he composed by way of response "Eu te darei o céu" (I'll Give You Heaven). He was called "The King," a title he still holds and which no one would deny him, even today as he sings sentimental ballads to a middle-aged public. But in spite of his association with the rockers in front of the Imperator, Roberto was, like so many of our generation, an early follower of João Gilberto—he would record a single with bits of bossa nova songs—and his sensibility was formed at a far remove from pure rock. For his part, Erasmo, who was not only a leader of the Jovem Guarda but also Roberto Carlos's collaborator in all their compositions, never seemed sincerely attracted to anything beyond the world of rock. The straightforwardness of his singing, as well as the sexual energy of his stage persona (tall, heavyset, sturdy, with the unintellectual and unsentimental air of someone who lives the essential dramas of life with his whole body, that combination of postindustrial and prehistoric man toward whom rock has been aimed with such insistence everywhere in the world), made of him forever a figure of such imposing integrity that neither market fluctuations, the occasional ingratitude of new rockers, or even rock's lack of cultural prestige could ever shake him.

In the fifties I knew nothing of Erasmo and his friends, and when I moved to Salvador in the first year of the following decade, the cult of João Gilberto had led me not only to Ella Fitzgerald, Sarah Vaughan, and Billie Holiday, but also to the Modern Jazz Quartet, Miles Davis, Jimmy Giuffre, Thelonious Monk, and especially Chet Baker, whose vibratoless vocals and androgynous sound, even more than his beautiful and discrete improvisations on the trumpet, exerted a compelling fascination. By contrast hearing Elvis was like hearing the songs in *Rock Around the Clock* sung in a heavy masculine vibrato. His image, frequently in the press and in record-store displays, suggested a cross-dressed Katy Jurado. One time I did feel attracted to him: I happened to see a preview of *King Creole,* and I felt an excitement that was sincerely intimate and sexually diffuse, provoked above all by the way he danced (it was my first time seeing this). Ultimately though, he did not win me over: I would see the film in its entirety only in the late seventies, on television; and while it was indeed wonderful, by then the fate of rock in my life had already been determined.

While Erasmo, in Rio, talked with Tim Maia and Jorge Ben about Bill Haley and His Comets, in Salvador, Raul Seixas, a bourgeois Bahian teenager, was studying English and planning to put together a rock group. By the mid-sixties in Salvador, Gilberto Gil, Gal Costa, Maria Bethânia, Alcivando Luz, Djalma Correia, Tom Zé, and I had plans of our own and were rehearsing an anthology of MPB classics from the thirties to the fifties, masterpieces of bossa nova, and some original songs composed for our performance at the Vila Velha, a small theater built on an avenue of the Passeio Público. Raul Seixas was rehearsing American rock songs to sing, in English, at the Teatro Roma, a big, popular movie house located in Roma Square, a lower-middle-class neighborhood. Unlike Erasmo, Raul had intellectual and aesthetic ambitions that did not naturally attract record companies: he became known as a singer and composer only after the British neo-rock wave, particularly after and in part because of *tropicalismo.* Indeed the fact that Raul's music became acceptable in the wake of *tropicalismo* led us to become closer than would have ever seemed possible in the old days of Salvador, when, though I was aware of his band, Raulzito e Os Panteras, I was never inspired to go see them. But I don't believe he came to see our shows at the Vila Velha either; later on, in our frequent (and fascinating) conversations during the seventies, he would refer to himself as the "poor rocker" who had been snubbed by the bossa nova fans, the epithet tinged with a certain irony, given our mutual awareness that as a boy he had been much richer—or much less poor—than we were.

Our shows at the Vila Velha—which are my reference point for those early days—were a great success among an audience made up predominantly of college students and enjoyed some prestige in the local press. Raul's shows drew a large audience of suburban teenagers and received some friendly notices, but could hardly command the respect that our group of composers, musicians, and singers enjoyed among opinion-makers. Raul knew as much about us as we knew about him—perhaps more. And if his complaints about our snobbery were well-founded, or the aggressively irreverent tone in which he and his group used to reminisce about the "bossa nova guys" was justified, that too only brought us closer. We were the inventors of *tropicalismo,* after all, and if we made reference to rock 'n' roll in our songs, the effect was to invite Brazilian rockers and rock fans to join the company of the creators and consumers of quality music. Raul was grateful to us for that, and when he railed against the sugary poetry and pretentious music then cultivated under the banner of MPB, he could count on our enthusiastic support: we had already turned our guns against what remained of those elements in ourselves—and he knew it.

A curious detail remains with me after all those meetings, and it now seems more and more revealing. Back then, Raul was married for some years to an American girl, and he seemed to converse more typically in English than in Portuguese, even when everyone present was Brazilian. His English was fluent and natural, and to our ears it sounded perfectly American. But when he returned to Portuguese, he seemed to insist on exaggerating his Bahianness: his short *o*'s and *e*'s were conspicuously open, the music of his sentences almost a regional caricature, and he used the old-fashioned slang of our teens in Salvador. We recognized this same impulse in his records and live performances: everything that was not American was Bahian. In this sense, his choices had much in common with what was at the root of *tropicalismo:* his insistence on what was distinctive in Bahia, of what made Bahia different from Rio and from everything suggestive of a nationalist Brazil—his choice of a Northeastern identity was a threat to whatever a homogenized national identity could mean. I could not help remembering that I myself had uttered to a journalist in 1967, during the dawn of *tropicalismo,* a sentence that Tom Zé would soon use in a song resonant with the movement: "I am Bahian and I am a foreigner." In fact, we had understood that in order to do what we believed necessary, we had to rid ourselves of Brazil as we knew it. We had to destroy the Brazil of the nationalists, we had to go deeper and pulverize the image of Brazil as being exclusively identified with Rio.

But our Bahia was, after all, the primal Bahia, the Bahia-mother of Brazil. I remember my first encounter with that great artist from the state of Minas Gerais, Lygia Clark, and how much I enjoyed hearing her say that Bahia is to Rio as the Old Testament is to the New. Truth to tell, we wanted to see Brazil in such a way that it would emerge at once as super-Rio, international and São Paulified, the archaic pre-Bahia, the futurist post-Brasilia. And this ambition actually distanced us from Raul Seixas to the same extent that I already felt myself distanced from the rock fans in the fifties: the fascination with American things seemed foolish to me—and the distinctive mark of folksy Bahianness, of regionalism in its most restrictive sense, appeared superficial. When, in the sixties, Juracy Magalhães, an important politician who had already been governor of Bahia (and who became minister for foreign affairs during the dictatorship), declared that "what is good for the United States is good for Brazil," the phrase was repeated as the most infamous demonstration of servility of which the Left could accuse the Right. Today there are many indications that any attempt at nonalignment with the interests of the capitalist West would result in monstrous violations of human rights, and also that any nationalist project for economic independence would seal the country off from modernity. Such a reversal of impressions may seem to grant Juracy's dictum the status of common sense, but it is not enough to legitimize it completely, even in retrospect. In truth, the statement is still repugnant to me, perhaps more today than ever before: it leads to resignation, to laziness in the face of historical responsibilities for the destiny of one's own country. And it ignores the fact that between two nations there may well exist real conflicts of interest.

To have known rock as something relatively contemptible during the decisive years of our intellectual growth and, on the other hand, to have had bossa nova as the soundtrack of our rebellion signifies for Brazilians of my generation the right to imagine an ambitious intervention in the future of the world, a right that immediately begins to be lived as a duty.

bethânia and ray charles

When I was about to turn four, my youngest sister was born, and I chose for her the name "Maria Bethânia," after a beautiful waltz beginning with lines that seemed to me majestic and mysterious:

Maria Bethânia, you are for me
the lady of the sugar mill.

The song, by the Pernambucan composer Capiba, in Nelson Gonçalves's powerful rendition was big in the late forties. While my determination to name my sister was admired, no one really had the courage to give a baby such a "heavy" name. Since there were several suggestions, ranging from Kristina to Gislaine, my father decided to write them all on little pieces of paper. He folded them up, tossed them into my little explorer's hat, and told me to draw one.

It was the name I had chosen. My father assumed an air of resignation, and, as if commanding everyone to accept it, said, "There. Now it has to be Maria Bethânia." And he went to register the baby with that name.

One of my older sisters recently told a different version, in which my father wrote "Maria Bethânia" on *all* the pieces of paper. It's not out of the question. In fact, his expression betrayed a trace of humor. Although I take pride in the thought that he might have cheated to please me, I've always preferred to believe in the validity of the game: this intervention of chance seems to confer a greater reality upon everything that has since come to pass as if by magic. A whole book could be written about each of my sisters and brothers, but I am focusing on Bethânia because she is a singer and has had a major influence on who I am professionally and even on my style of composing, singing, and thinking.

Around the time that Bethânia was eleven and I was fifteen, we solidified the alliance born with the choice of her name. My sister Nicinha was already grown up and Irene was still a baby, Clara and Mabel were married, and Rodrigo and Roberto had left Santo Amaro for Salvador, so Bethânia and I felt more and more like accomplices. In our family she seemed to dramatize passionate and irrational regions that the rest of us tended to avoid—jealousy, rage, demands for attention, and everything capricious. And I played the role of interpreter in both senses of the word: as the one who explained and justified her whims and as the apprentice of her values, which I accepted as tokens of larger realities. When she locked herself in her room enigmatically, refusing to talk to anyone, I was inclined to regard this as an instance of what magazines at that time were calling *"juventude transviada,"* after the Portuguese title for the film *Rebel Without a Cause.* Gradually, I began to apply Maria Bethânia's teachings to the development of my aesthetic criteria.

Bethânia was going on fourteen, and I on eighteen, when we moved to Salvador to go to school. Santo Amaro did not have the junior—the *ginásio*—or the senior levels of high school—what we call *científico* or *clássico,* depending on whether one majored in the sciences or the humanities. My parents always sent the girls to Salvador to study in the *ginásio,* while the boys were sent in the upper years.

It may seem curious—and some of my friends at the time thought so—but I had no wish to leave Santo Amaro for a larger city. I remember Roberto, my older brother, railing against the constricted life one led there, always impatient to leave for Salvador, just as later he would be impatient to move to São Paulo. Emanuel Araújo, my classmate in high school who later became a well-known artist, expressed similar sentiments, even more vehemently—and he followed the same itinerary. Hercília, the girl I loved with all my heart, who looked like a modern queen of the European cinema, had developed a rhetoric of arrogant contempt for our hometown. Nevertheless, I remained convinced that if I wanted to see life change, it had to change from within—it had to start with Santo Amaro. (Going somewhere else, I held, would effect only a superficial difference that would relieve me of the responsibility of real, deep change. I still think that I can't do anything worthwhile without a perspective centered on Santo Amaro, that is, one that starts from within me.) In any event, I loved the place where we had all been born and learned everything we knew—even the suggestion of the nerve to change that we'd heard in João Gilberto's singing. But my attachment to Santo Amaro was nothing compared to Bethânia's: she simply refused to accept the idea of moving.

The prospect of living in Salvador was not unpleasant: the city I now love beyond all others in the world was already familiar to me as to any native of Santo Amaro; moving there posed no particular impediment. Salvador, which we called "Bahia," was in fact so close to Santo Amaro that my father was afraid the new highway being planned would turn our town into "just another suburb." A traditional *cantiga de roda* from Santo Amaro became our theme song in those days, as we left our parents behind and went to share an apartment in "Bahia" with Rodrigo and Roberto. A song I composed took the folk ditty for its refrain; the artless verses sounded so touching set in the melody in minor key, to the rhythm of a slow *marcha:*

> Good-bye, my Santo Amaro
> I'll be leaving you behind
> I'm going to Bahia
> I'm going to stay, I'm going to fly
> I'm going to stay, I'm going to fly.

It was unusual then for anyone from the backlands of Bahia to call Salvador by any name other than "Bahia," although today everyone uses "Salvador," as people from Rio do. Bethânia, however, refused even to *see* "Bahia." We would walk or take the bus to school every day; every day she would ignore me as I called her attention to a tree, someone passing by, a house. Quiet and sad, she could hardly stand to listen to Nicinha, who had come to take care of us. All Maria Bethânia would say was how much she hated "Bahia," how she longed for vacation so that she could go home. Our apartment had a view of the Tororó dam, always changing, enchanting me and Bethânia, who would spend her afternoons in silent protest, staring at it from the window. She became passionately attached to this water; the mysterious green of the dam would become her first bond of love to Salvador.

The university's president, Dr. Edgar Santos, had just created music, dance, and theater departments. Salvador was undergoing a period of intense cultural activity, and he invited avant-garde companies to visit, so that young people could see the most interesting experimental performers. The Italian architect Lina bo Bardi, who lived in São Paulo, organized the Museum of Modern Art of Bahia (we liked to call it

MAMB, for "mambo"), and we were able to see Renoir, Degas, van Gogh. In the small semicircular theater, Eros Martim Gonçalves, head of the department, staged Brecht's *Threepenny Opera* and Camus's *Calígula.* The film critic Walter da Silveira founded a beautiful cinema space and featured older films that were not often seen (*Citizen Kane, M, Monsieur Verdoux,* etc., as well as *Greed, The Little Match Girl, Metropolis, A nous la liberté, October,* etc.). When less ancient films were shown (*Nazarin, On the Waterfront*) they would be introduced either by da Silveira or someone he invited. I remember one night when the very young but already famous genius Glauber Rocha—who later led the Cinema Novo movement and became internationally famous for such films as *Black God, White Devil,* and *Antonio das Mortes*—spoke before the screening of De Sica's *Umberto D,* a touching, poetic look at the day-to-day life of a poor old man. He criticized its "maudlin sentimentalism" and contrasted it to the dryness of Rossellini, his favorite director among the neorealists. Yet I found the film dazzling. Every week we heard instrumentalists and teachers from the school of music, who also collaborated with the theater department; an actor narrated *Peter and the Wolf.* The director of the music school, Koellreutter, who had been Tom Jobim's teacher, was adventurous in his programs: not only Beethoven, Mozart, Gershwin, and Brahms, but also David Tudor playing compositions by John Cage on piano as part of a piece in which turning on the radio figured in the score. I still recall the wave of laughter that overtook the audience—and even the director of the school—as Tudor turned it on and we heard the familiar voice of the announcer: "Radio Bahia, City of Salvador."

For me this was a tremendously exciting world, but Bethânia had spent the better part of 1960 shut off from anything happening in the city, other than the changes in the green color in the waters of the dam. Still, one day she finally accepted my invitation to go out, and we went to the university to see Paul Claudel's play *The Story of Tobias and Sara.* The luminous Helena Ignez and Érico de Freitas were performing that night; they seemed to us celestial visions as they pronounced lines full of mysterious poetry (to this day Bethânia and I imitate to perfection Helena's voice saying: "I am the pomegranate!"). After that evening, Bethânia never stopped going out with me to concerts, plays, films, exhibits—and attending all the popular festivals that fill the streets of Salvador on saints' days. She was particularly taken with theater, and we soon became devoted fans of Ignez, Geraldo del Rey, and Antônio Pitanga. Bethânia determined to become an actress.

During the second year of our stay in Salvador, my parents came to visit. My father could not accept his daughter freely coming and going at night, but proposed a compromise: he would allow her to go out at night provided I went along to take responsibility for her. He was to take this more seriously than I had bargained for. I remember particularly leaving her one night at a place called Bazarte (a kind of combination bar, art gallery, and jazz club). I was tired and wanted to go home and sleep, while our brother Roberto also wanted to stay. To my surprise my father was very upset; I cried, and solemnly promised it would never happen again—and it never did.

It was Álvaro Guimarães, Alvinho, who launched both Bethânia and me as professional musicians. I had been told by friends that he was a talented director who had collaborated with the CPC (Center for Public Culture) and UNE (National Students' Union). From our first conversations I was impressed with him, even more so when he criticized the CPC and its theater as propagandistic and spoke of Glauber Rocha as a close friend. When he decided to stage a nineteenth-century Brazilian comedy, he asked me to compose the score. I refused, sensibly asserting my incompetence, but he replied that only I could do it. He had never heard me sing or play any instrument, but said that he had made up his mind when he heard me talk about the relation between João Gilberto's music and Dorival Caymmi's. Alvinho is like that. I ended up composing all the music and then playing the piano during the shows. Less than a year later, he decided to stage *O boca de ouro* by Nelson Rodrigues, Brazil's greatest and best-known playwright, and he decided to open with all the lights down and a solo voice of an unknown girl singing Ataulfo Alves's "Na cadência do samba" in the dark—Bethânia's voice, unamplified. Unfortunately the rest of the show was not up to the standard of the beginning (but then, how many in the world would be?) and few were there to witness that unexpected premiere. The cult of Bethânia's voice, however, began to grow among artists and bohemians in Salvador.

Whenever we went to the MAMB exhibitions, to the theater, the film club, or the French House to see art films, Bethânia and I began noticing the presence of a thin mulatto with glasses; and as he became ubiquitous we began referring to him with a certain intimate amusement. We were curious to meet him and imagined he would like the things that we did; his face was attractive. He was always alone and evidently had no idea that we were observing him. One day Alvinho Guimarães told me that he wanted to make a film, and naturally I was to do the soundtrack; but he also wanted me to collaborate with him in writing the screenplay. (In fact I did do the soundtrack for *Moleques de rua,* a film about Salvador's street children, and I used Bethânia's voice.) When I went to meet the friend he wanted us both to work with, it was he, the stranger we had been watching. I was elated. He had been a friend of Alvinho's for quite a while.

Duda, as Alvinho called him, smiled all the time, had enormous eyes behind those glasses, and could say very serious things on any topic whatsoever. Alvinho's conversations became more exacting in his presence. The three of us began to spend time together. Our conversations were always memorable—we talked about literature, film, pop music; we talked about Salvador, life in the provinces, people we knew; and we talked about politics. Politics was not our forte, but in 1963—with the students behind President João Goulart, pressuring him to move further to the left; and with Miguel Arraes, who was doing a splendid job as governor of Pernambuco, working closely with his lower-income constituency—we were moved to write political plays and songs. The country seemed to be on the verge of implementing reforms that would transform its profoundly unjust face and allow Brazil to rise above American imperialism. Later on we would see that such a transformation was not even close. And today we have good reasons to think perhaps it was not even to be hoped for. But the illusion was lived with great intensity—an intensity that would later serve as a catalyst for the military coup.

Duda—today known as the poet and critic Duda Machado—impressed me with his clear and precise thinking. I was beginning to consider him and Alvinho to be my mentors. I had seen *L'avventura* by Antonioni, and admired it. *La notte* was being shown; I found it beautiful. Some of the mannerisms and the dialogue irritated me, yet I praised the film, insisting that I still preferred Fellini to Antonioni. Fellini had enjoyed great successes with *La dolce vita, La strada,* and *Nights of Cabiria,* whereas Antonioni was seen as more "difficult," less sentimental, and visually more rigorous. Thus began the fashion among critics of trashing Fellini; I would have appeared more intelligent had I claimed to prefer Antonioni, but I held fast, disdainful of the critics' snobbery.

Duda heard everything and, without taking sides, came up with something totally different: "What you should see is *Breathless* by Jean-Luc Godard. Everything else pales in comparison." He even thought it more interesting than *Hiroshima, mon amour,* which I was crazy about.

So I went to see that first film of Godard's at the Capri Cinema, in the Dois de Julho Square. I came away amazed at the supple rhythm and the poetry of atmosphere; it was shot more elegantly than an Antonioni film, yet it did not seem so rigidly controlled. Duda read *Cahiers du Cinéma* and was always up-to-date and thinking ahead.

I was amazed that Duda could be right about so much and that he thought on such a high plane, far above my own. But I was able to introduce him to Chet Baker, perhaps even to Billie Holiday. And I played for him some recordings of Thelonious Monk as well. I felt more relaxed talking about bossa nova and Brazilian pop music in general: it was the topic I knew best. But if his opinion differed even slightly from my own, I would stop and reconsider mine.

Bethânia was pleased that I had met the person we had already befriended without his knowing it. And Duda was enchanted with Bethânia. Our threesome often became a foursome, and Duda began to come over to our house occasionally. Soon he and Bethânia would be spending time together by themselves. Yet Bethânia would never go out at night without me. Some friends found it unbelievable that a nineteen-year-old guy would go out all the time with his fifteen-year-old sister. But Bethânia and I were immensely amused by each other's company and, meandering through Salvador's cultural life in the early sixties, we made an unusual pair. She read Carson McCullers and Clarice Lispector, wrote beautiful prose poems, and made small wood and copper sculptures. She fell in love with the color purple and started to make her own clothes in purple satin.

I will never forget a scene that, told now, seems inspired by the Addams Family, although we had never heard of them at the time. During Christmas week Bethânia and I were waiting at a bus stop in the Piedade Gardens. The streets were swarming with shoppers. Christmas had never been quite our favorite holiday, but in Santo Amaro people liked nativity scenes, and we found these filled the windows of Salvador as well. Back home people would cover the floors in their houses with a thin layer of white sand and fill their drawers with sprigs of *pitangueira*—the native plant with a small red fruit of many sections, whose fresh leaves have an absolutely delicious aroma. This tradition carried over to Salvador as well, where even the buses during the Christmas season had sprigs of pitanga tied to the back. Obviously the extreme whiteness of the sand brought from the dunes was meant to suggest snow, while the pitanga leaves took the place of holly, but the impression was thoroughly tropical all the same. By contrast that other Christmas affected in Salvador, trees covered with cotton balls and "Jingle Bells" played in department stores, seemed thoroughly vulgar, and we started to lament it out loud, to the silent disapproval of the others waiting for the bus, their arms full of presents. Our complaints began in a soft, almost analytical tone, but soon built towards a crescendo of deliberate black humor, with one of us imitating Maria Muniz, an actress with a very dramatic style whom we had befriended. To express, for example, a distaste for cucumbers, she would yell emphatically: "If I could, I would KILL the cucumber!" Here, on the bus, it was Bethânia and I who shouted, "If I could, I would KILL Christmas!"

Bethânia did not appear to be the adolescent she was, but rather an experienced woman. With her enormous forehead and sharp nose, wrapped in straight purple satin dresses, she was frequently taken to be older than I was. Her exotic beauty was almost indecipherable. One can imagine the strange effect it caused on the peaceful citizens of Bahia to see us together. Once, at a bar close to the Castro Alves Theater, I introduced the film critic and future filmmaker Orlando Senna to her. He asked if she was my sister, which was odd, since back then no one thought we looked alike. But before I could answer, she injected with an absolutely straight face: "No. We are lovers." And she sustained this farce for a few very long minutes.

Yet we were sweet and happy and, just as we did in the company of our other siblings, we tended to feel ourselves the objects of other people's affections, whatever the group happened to be. We made friends among actors, directors, musicians, dancers, and painters. Soon, whether we were in an apartment or around a table in a bar, or in a tent in a street celebration, there was always someone who would ask Bethânia to sing some *samba-canção* by Noel Rosa or Dolores Duran, just to hear the unique timbre of her contralto. At first there was not even the slightest hint that she might become a professional singer, and those exhibitions of her voice went unaccompanied. But my mother had yielded to my request for a guitar to help me get over my longing for the piano we had in Santo Amaro, which could not be brought to Salvador. Little by little I learned to play a few chords, and soon I began to back my sister's singing, and she herself learned to play a little too.

To say that Bethânia took part in the cult of João Gilberto and bossa nova with us is no lie, but it hardly gives a very clear sense of how things happened. She had been with me, Chico Motta, and Dasinho in front of Bubu's bar listening to "Chega de saudade" in Santo Amaro in

1959. And she was with me and Gal and Gil in Salvador, as we sat around, singing softly, and listening to the harmonies Gil could play by ear after listening only once to recordings of João and Carlos Lyra. But she was younger than we were, and one could say that bossa nova came into being as she did, it grew up next to her. She did not have to struggle for it. But above all it was her temperament that set her apart. After all, Gal Costa was only one year older than Bethânia, and Gal found her style in bossa nova. We were friends with the people at the Teatro dos Novos, a dissident group in the theater department that João Augusto Azevedo had formed with some brilliant ex-students, such as Othon Bastos, who was to play Corisco in *Black God, White Devil.* They would lend us all kinds of records—jazz, French songs, Broadway musicals. If I preferred Chet Baker, my sister chose Judy Garland. In the midst of so many *bossanovistas,* she longed for the drama of the old samba, and while we led her to listen to Ella and Miles, she was more interested in Edith Piaf. Neither of us was hostile to the other's preferences, and as time went by, we discovered common ground in Billie Holiday. The extraordinary Portuguese *fado* singer Amália Rodrigues soared above them all.

One day an article in an American magazine quoted Ray Charles as saying that bossa nova was just the "old Latin rhythm" with more modern syncopation. The same week Carlos Coquejo, a critic and passionate lover of music, as well as a friend of João Gilberto's, said that Gilberto was not in the least interested in Ray Charles, and considered him "a folksinger."

I understood how the bluesman who brought together tradition and pop, whose singing was Nat King Cole's turned upside down (while Johnny Mathis was like the varnish on its polished surface)—I understood how Ray Charles could disdain what he heard as "bossa nova," and I could forgive him his complacent allusion to a generic "Latin rhythm." I could also understand the contempt on the part of the creator of bossa nova (a style so exquisitely restrained) for what must have seemed the commercial exploitation of a stereotype. What I found a little more difficult was to come to terms with the fact that I profoundly enjoyed both kinds of music.

Judy Garland and Edith Piaf seemed to me like specters of the past and did not affect me as profoundly as they did Bethânia; Billie Holiday was something new from the past—though cool as they come. But Ray Charles swept us off our feet and fed our appetite for novelty with a style that was completely different from João's, or from Jimmy Giuffe's,

Chet Baker's, or Dave Brubeck's. I remember spending one afternoon in our Salvador apartment listening over and over to "Georgia on My Mind" and crying because I missed Santo Amaro. These were transcendental nostalgias, the beauty of the singing infusing memory with a life more intense than the moments as they were actually lived, allowing them to be relived more truthfully the second time. Years later, I would find this effect luminously described in Proust as well as in Deleuze's critical commentary on Proust, and I would be moved to compose the song "Jenipapo absoluto":

> *To sing is more than to remember*
> *More than to have had it then*
> *More than to live, more than to dream*
> *It's to have the heart of back then.*

In time, I would read not only Proust but Guimarães Rosa, Stendhal, Lorca, Joyce; I would see the films of Godard and Eisenstein, listen to Bach, would see the art of Mondrian, Velázquez, Lygia Clark. And there would come as well a time for Warhol, a return to Hitchcock films I had seen before, a time for Dylan, Lennon, Jagger. But every time, I always returned to my passion for João Gilberto to find a base and reestablish a perspective.

It's possible that Bethânia liked Ray Charles as much as I did, but, unlike me, she did not commit herself to listening to him with such attention as to suggest a form of research. When the time was ripe for *tropicalismo*—in which various extroverted styles were yoked together, the cool style of bossa nova eventually appearing as one element more among them in the resulting song-collages—one of its first heralds was Bethânia (who had called my attention to the "vitality" of Roberto Carlos and his colleagues in Jovem Guarda); and one of the principal signs of the transition from what we were doing to what we were about to do lay in my taste for Ray Charles. This is not to say that one will find in any tropicalist product even a trace of his influence, or to deny that Bethânia seemed at first to embody a resistance to *tropicalismo*. But it is not in the realm of similarities that one should seek the reasons that these two names appear joined together here in this manner I've contrived to begin the history of the movement.

By the time the ideas that came together as *tropicalismo* began to be felt around us, Bethânia was already a star. It happened overnight. In 1964 I was spending my summer vacation at the country estate of my

friend Pedro Novis's family in the valley of the Iguape, between Santo
Amaro and Cachoeira. I adored Pedrinho and I was enchanted with the
place. But a few days after my arrival, I suddenly became obsessed with
thoughts of Maria Bethânia, imagining that she needed me urgently,
and that the matter was somehow connected to the shows at the Vila
Velha theater. Pedrinho was perplexed, but I felt compelled to leave,
although I had no way of getting back to Salvador, and slept fitfully.
The next morning Pedro's godparents arrived unexpectedly. They
planned to have lunch before continuing on their way to Salvador. I
decided to go with them, but Pedrinho would not accept my decision.
Knowing how irrational I was being, I felt paralyzed. But as I saw the
van pull away, I was all the more certain that Bethânia needed me by
her side, even as Pedrinho, still angry, remarked that I had missed the
only opportunity to act upon such a senseless idea. That night, at the
dinner table, Dr. Renato, Pedrinho's father, solemnly announced his
sudden need to go to Salvador and that he would be leaving tomorrow.
And so it was that early the next morning I left Iguape for Salvador, and
though once on the road I realized how ridiculous my situation was and
deep down inside wanted to go back, this was hardly something I could
even dream of telling Dr. Renato. Since the road went through Santo
Amaro, I decided to get off there and go visit my sister Mabel. My initial vacillation had by now toppled into utter skepticism toward my
own motivation, and I no longer wanted to go to Salvador. Surprised,
Dr. Renato stopped and said good-bye with an intrigued smile. When I
saw myself walking toward Mabel's house, I imagined that in fact
Bethânia would be there, and that this was the reason why I had not
gone on to Salvador. Mabel was stunned to see me at her door so early in
the morning. I asked her immediately if Bethânia was with her. Looking surprised, she told me that of course she wasn't, that Bethânia had
no plans at all to come to Santo Amaro. I relaxed—relieved, disillusioned—and decided to forget the whole thing once and for all. But
shortly after lunch Bethânia arrived, saying that she had decided to
come to Santo Amaro on a whim. During lunch we received a phone
call with a message for Bethânia: the producers of *Opinião,* the musical
theater show that was a great hit in Rio, wanted to invite her to go
there to replace singer Nara Leão. Nara herself had made the recom-
mendation, after seeking us out in Bahia, a story I will come to later on.
On this day of extraordinary surprise arrivals and departures, we left
together for Salvador, where a pair of airplane tickets was already

awaiting us. The next day—just as my father had wished—I was in Rio taking care of Bethânia.

In 1964 some months after the "revolution"—that's what the coup d'état that had brought the military government to power was officially called—*Opinião* had brought together a composer from the hills of Rio de Janeiro (Zé Kéti), a composer from the rural Northeast (João do Vale), and a bossa nova singer from Rio's Zona Sul (Nara Leão) in a small repertory theater in Copacabana, which combined the charm of nightclub bossa nova shows with the excitement of politically engaged theater. *Opinião* epitomized the trend among some of the *bossanovistas* to promote the fusion of modern Brazilian music with politically engaged art. Vinicius de Moraes himself, bossa nova's first and foremost lyricist, was involved in the effort; and around this time Brazil created perhaps the most graceful protest songwriting in the world (although I would now say that it has been surpassed by Jamaican reggae). *Opinião* was a form of theater that alternated music with passages read aloud from Brazilian and world literature, or texts written especially for the occasion. This kind of show became one of the most influential forms of expression in the subsequent history of MPB. The song "Carcará" had already become in Nara's version the climax of the show, the biggest crowd-pleaser, but with her dramatic knack Bethânia seemed to give it a new life. The song described the violence natural to a type of hawk common to the Northeast—the *carcará*—as it attacks newborn calves, and the song's refrain is "pega, mata e come" ("catch, kill, and eat it"), repeated at intervals with growing intensity. And the hint of a comparison—*"Carcará, mais coragem do que homem"* ("Carcará, braver than a man")—was sufficient, at the time, to enable the song to be heard as a vague but compelling argument for insurrection. To this day I consider that song very beautiful. It is composed in the minor key so common to Northeastern music—the original Banda de "Pífanos" from Caruaru always plays them in that manner—that seems to convey the landscape of the region, as well as the essential feeling of its inhabitants: a mixture of melancholy and steadfastness. I understood immediately that Bethânia would make of this song an extraordinarily effective number. And in fact, after *Opinião* reopened with Bethânia, the song gained a cult following among politically conscious audiences and then, with its release as a recording, became a huge success. But for those who were only beginning to know her then, Bethânia's debut was interpreted as signifying a narrow regionalism, a situation that surprised us at first and soon became a source of embarrassment and misunderstandings that have never quite been dispelled.

Naturally that was not something that the show's producers could have anticipated. They were a group of professionals and leftist intellectuals who, among other things, had to find an image for the star they had launched. And it is interesting to note that our first experience with the hype of marketing was occasioned by a group of anticapitalist artists. Nara was a typical girl from Zona Sul in Rio de Janeiro—white, pretty, and modern. She was also a bossa nova celebrity when *Opinião* was created: her appearance, in contrast with the two semiliterate black men who shared the stage with her, had been an integral part of the show from its inception. Bethânia, if we omit the selective public who frequented the Vila Velha theater in Salvador, was an unknown—and she was not a typical middle-class white girl. Her frizzy hair and indefinite skin color, her thinness, her high forehead above that strong nose, her contralto voice, and even her indeterminable age created problems for the director, Augusto Boal, and the writers and producers, Oduvaldo Vianna Filho, Ferreira Gullar, Paulo Pontes, and Armando Costa. They didn't know how to dress her, style her hair, or otherwise present her to the public. Fittings and style sessions were charged with anxiety. Yet between us there was a feeling that her integrity—our integrity— ought to be maintained at all costs. Stories like the one that appeared in her public-relations materials about her having been a left end on the Santo Amaro soccer team—with the emphasis on the "left"—were simply not true. The network had her hair tied back in a way that neutralized race, age, and personal beauty, giving her an air of somewhat sexless but dignified seriousness; the show's team created the look that later everyone thought had come with her from Bahia. For a long time Bethânia had problems getting rid of her image as a Northeastern protest singer, someone from the backlands. Yet she became—and is still today—the queen of Brazilian song, above all for the density with which she infuses ballads of intense love, although she is also a brilliant interpreter of other genres like the *escolas de samba* of Rio, the *sambas de roda* of Bahia, and on occasion the songs beloved in northeastern Brazil.

When we first met her, Nara had gone to Bahia for pleasure, but also in part as a kind of research project. She was an adorable creature of the type that only Rio's Zona Sul can produce. One could sense in her the enjoyment of a freedom that has been won with difficulty and determination. So all her gestures and words seemed to flow out of a direct and serious realism, but they always came out in a delicate and graceful way. Nor should we forget that she was probably about twenty years old at the time. Her name was linked to the birth of bossa nova (it was said—and is still said today—that the movement was born in her Copacabana apartment) and though she was not yet a star, in Bahia she was already a legend. Having heard about us, she arranged to meet us at a place near the theater. We talked and sang; Nara had been trying for some time to expand the thematic range of bossa nova and find a way for music to be involved with the social and political issues then being frequently and passionately confronted by the new Brazilian theater and Cinema Novo. The show *Opinião* itself was inspired by her attempt to draw attention to the samba from the *morros* in Rio and the music coming out of the Northeastern backlands—and to the new songs with a social content that she, more than anyone, encouraged composers to write. Among us, in Bahia, her presence turned out to be enchanting and enigmatic: she would ask direct questions in a very soft voice and speak of her thrilling interests in a skeptical tone that we interpreted (perhaps correctly) as a mixture of discretion and caution.

On the day she came to see us, we were going to hear a recording of the most recent in a series of shows we had done at the Vila Velha. Where *Opinião* had been given to explicit political or social references, our shows aimed to create a historical perspective that would situate us in the context of the development of MPB. We were picking up on João Gilberto's most penetrating intuition, rejecting the oversimplified and myopic vision of those who wanted to infuse our music with a false jazz-like modernization or to make it serve as propaganda, or who wanted to combine these dubious purposes. We did group shows, with individual numbers that emphasized our respective styles, but we already had plans for solo productions.

With Nara at our side that day, we tried to listen to the faltering tape someone had made, as we worked through the planning stages of a solo show for Bethânia. Given her stage presence, we agreed unanimously that she should be the one to kick off the solo series. Nara not only took interest in everything we were doing and saying, she offered Bethânia unpublished songs by samba composers from Rio. Thus, in her first show, between the *sambas-canções* of Noel Rosa and Antônio Maria, a *baião,* an old Carnival *marchinha* sung in slow tempo, and the new material we composed ourselves, Bethânia sang some of the central themes of the show she would eventually be invited to do, the show that would make her a national celebrity.

Faced with Bethânia's temperament, Nara would typically react with a good humor that only confirmed her own directness, but her tone was affectionate all the same and showed her to be profoundly understanding of the personal styles of others. She would say, for instance: "When I come to see you, Bethânia, I always think of lighted candles, red roses, and special carpets," and Bethânia would laugh at this portrait of a prima donna, aware that the eternal girl before her, for whom everything seemed simple and clear, knew herself to be a giant in the history of our music—as Brazil would always know her to be.

Nara's unselfishness can be understood partly in relation to the atmosphere of collective searching and genuine collaboration that characterized relations among the creators of MPB from the end of the golden age of bossa nova until the end of the golden age of *tropicalismo*—a communal spirit that is still a distinctive mark of MPB. But this is not to deny Nara's personal qualities, her spiritually aristocratic way of being practical and objective, the delicate shimmer of her anti-stardom. Of course she was, then as later, a true star, whether she was standing by Chico Buarque when he released "A banda," or by the *tropicalistas* in the first hours of the battle, or in her own right, first transforming and then rereading bossa nova. And even when she abandoned the profession to devote herself to her marriage and to her new life as a college student (with her girlish charm, she looked no different than her colleagues who were ten or fifteen years younger), Nara shone in Brazil until her death in 1989.

In spite of my enthusiastic participation in the shows at the Vila Velha—singing, playing a little guitar, and, most of all, conceiving and playing the part of "director general" (the musical direction having been entrusted to Gilberto Gil and Alcivando Luz)—it did not enter my plans to become a professional pop musician. Once I went to Rio with Bethânia, however, this fate became almost inevitable. Among the compositions of the Bahia group, the producers of *Opinião* chose for Bethânia my song "De manhã" as the best representation of her musical origins, and so it found its way into the show's repertoire before it became side B of the best-selling single "Carcará." Many enjoyed the song, which was eventually recorded by the most classical of Brazilian traditional singers, the divine Elisete Cardoso, as well as by the most popular of the jazzed-up offspring of bossa nova, Wilson Simonal. From then on, the illusion that music might be something transitory in my life would be repeatedly dispelled.

When *Opinião* moved to São Paulo, I continued to accompany Bethânia, but I was already making plans to convince my father to entrust her to Augusto Boal, the director of the show, whom I trusted. As it turned out, my father, who had never been a rigid sort of man, proved perfectly reasonable on the subject of Bethânia's nocturnal outings. In fact, he and my mother, though both born in Santo Amaro at the beginning of the century and having always lived there, never opposed the changes in worldly mores that naturally presented themselves when we were growing up, although they did resist—and would never permit their children to submit to—the vulgarity that sometimes accompanies such transformations. My father had met Boal, and he agreed to my proposal. But Boal had plans of his own: he was arranging to do a new show with Bethânia after *Opinião* closed, and this time she was allowed to bring in her own people. So I returned to São Paulo, where I lived through an experience that would prove difficult but very instructive.

The military government established after the coup of '64 can only be felt as nondictatorial in retrospect, when compared to the harshness of the regime that came to power after '68. In 1965 our objective was to find our own means of saying "down with the dictatorship," and long before the student movements that brought millions into the streets, artists, particularly in the theater, took upon themselves the responsibilities of protest. The poet and literary critic Roberto Schwarz, a Marxist intellectual, wrote an essay in 1968 that, in addition to being an attempt to interpret *tropicalismo,* describes the kind of complicity that had developed between the stage and the audience during this period, and shows how hegemonic the Left had been in the Brazilian cultural milieu. Augusto Boal was an exponent of politically engaged theater, but to me his *Opinião,* while extremely good, did not seem to improve upon our own Vila Velha shows, he was a brilliant man and he talked about the theatrical personality that most interested Brazilians at the time, Bertolt Brecht, with greater confidence and sincerity than I had ever heard before. Above all he had just opened his new show in São Paulo, which had charmed me—*Arena conta Zumbi* (Arena Tells Zumbi), based on the story of Zumbi of Palmares, the black slave leader who founded the greatest and most famous of the Brazilian *quilombos*—communities of escaped slaves. The idea of a free territory conquered by courageous ex-captives naturally lent itself to all kinds of allusions to the military government and its curtailment of our freedom. The glamour of the central character's heroism, underscored by the gracefulness of the music, opened up a kind of agreeable clearing in our minds. *Zumbi* was also a musical but, unlike *Opinião,* it was not a potpourri of various songs interwoven with texts interpreted by different singers; rather, it was an original play conceived with a composer, whose new songs were sung by the actors. *Arena conta Zumbi* was a jewel of economical means, a lesson in how to obtain effects with a minimum of props. Fernanda Montenegro, frequently considered the best Brazilian actress, has said that it was the most important show in the modernization of Brazilian theater. For my part, I liked *Zumbi* the way someone likes *The Sound of Music* or Disney's *Peter Pan,* not for its "message" but for the music.

The freedom to like *Zumbi* as I did at once brought me closer and distanced me from Boal. He commissioned us to compose songs especially for the show he planned to do with us. Its name would be *Arena canta Bahia* (Arena sings Bahia)—and he would work around familiar songs about Bahia. We were to come up with an idea for a script. I still consider it perfectly fair that he turned down the mysterious, strange children's story that we collectively chose as the basis for a play. Following Boal's suggestion that we use Bahian folk material as the starting point for a modern script seasoned with a heavy dose of social criticism, and hampered by the confusion of trying to write something as a group, we opted for an adaptation of a macabre story of a little girl who is buried alive by her stepmother; from beneath the ground, her hair sprouts silky blades of grass. Boal was very tactful: he said we were gravitating toward an excessively lyrical atmosphere and, laying aside our ideas for a plot, set about choosing from among the songs we had proposed a repertoire that would allow him to stage something consistent with his prestigious, politically engaged theater. But two things shocked me: he rejected many arrangements—admittedly full of clichés clearly inspired by Elis Regina's numbers for the São Paulo TV program *O Fino da Bossa*—and justified himself by saying, "You are looking for regional purity—that's why you react against these gimmicks. I have in mind a young urban crowd, whom I intend to reach, and who understand that language." The fact is that, in 1965, I collaborated enthusiastically on *Arena canta Bahia.* It was stimulating to observe Boal's masterful choreography, and I was very happy to be working with Bethânia, Gil, Gal, Tom Zé, and Piti, but I told them all that there was something fundamentally wrong with staging a musical about Bahia in which there was not a single song by Caymmi. All the

songs selected had in common a Northeastern bias that distanced them
from the specifically Bahian style—from the charm, the taste, the
worldview typical of the *recôncavo* and of the city of Salvador. True,
Bethânia's public persona was already associated with "Carcará" and
Northeastern protest music in general. I, however, dreamt of a role for
us in MPB that would be radically connected to the stance of João
Gilberto, for whom Caymmi was a national genius. Even though João
had been born and raised in the Bahian outback close to Pernambuco,
he laid the groundwork for the evolution of a type of samba that had its
origin in the *samba de roda* of the backlands and reached maturity in the
form of urban carioca samba—and he strategically rejected regional
exoticism. But the voice of a wailing cowboy or the strident small guitar of a peasant were closer to the taste I attributed to João Gilberto
than was an unsophisticated return to a noisy samba tinged with
jazzed-up percussion or pretentious compositions based on Northeastern scales. It hurt me to hear Bethânia's raw voice packed in samba-jazz
conventions from the Beco das Garrafas—that street in Copacabana
that was the birthplace of the style that eventually came to be associated with *O Fino da Bossa.*

Arena canta Bahia opened in a relatively large theater, the TBC, the
old stage of the Brazilian Comedy Theater, but our show did not even
come close to the success of *Arena conta Zumbi.* The difference in public
reception was deserved. Putting aside the sheer force of its originality,
Zumbi was really a kind of off-Broadway musical on the verge of moving to Broadway; *Arena canta Bahia* made us realize that a simple show
like the ones we used to do in the Vila Velha theater in Salvador would
have been a better calling card for us.

I remember the beginning of an argument with Boal over another
musical show that had just opened in Rio; our views were diametrically
opposed. It was the unforgettable *Rosa de Ouro,* which discovered
Paulinho da Viola (at age twenty-four) and Clementina de Jesus (who
was sixty), and brought back the veteran Araci Cortês. I was touched by
the show's poetic way of introducing authentic musicians of the most
refined carioca samba tradition; Boal thought it "folksy." Naturally I
was too timid to argue with Boal, whom I respected and admired, and
he was too unconcerned with my opinions to encourage a real discussion. But it seemed to me that to dismiss a show like that was to discard
a rare opportunity to see clearly the potential beauty to which we might
lay claim and had so far only hinted at. Furthermore, the nationalism of

leftist intellectuals, being merely a reaction to North American imperialism, had little or nothing to do with liking things Brazilian or—and this interested me even more—with proposing original solutions for the problems of humanity and the world from the standpoint of our own way of doing things. Their only solution was a given, and had arrived ready-made: to attain socialism. And to that end any trick would do. Any interest in a refined sensibility—whether we sought it in greater contact with our traditional popular forms, or in the experimental avant-garde—was considered dangerous, and a form of irresponsible deviance.

Discrepancies of taste and attitude between Boal and myself were but one factor making my stay in São Paulo an unhappy one. I was living in a city I thought ugly and inhospitable, a chaos of skyscrapers, of pollution and traffic jams, and I began to realize that infusing this culture with my own vision was going to be difficult. While Bethânia's rise to stardom had opened doors for me professionally, it did not necessarily mean that the sort of artistic interaction I had in mind would be possible.

My suffering aside, the experience with Boal would prove a rich one. It was an internship in sociability in a great cultural center, and I learned a great deal about stage technique as well. But the gaps of vision and attitude that first appeared between us in São Paulo were to increase and deepen over the next two years. When *tropicalismo* came to the fore, we assumed deliberately antagonistic positions, but at no moment did I lose sight of the greatness and importance of Boal and the Arena Theater. And I am certain Boal must have seen something in me, since he once proposed staging a political version of *Hamlet* with me in the title role.

And it moves me to think that Bethânia, by this time a very big success, would heed Boal's courageous decision that she share the stage with total unknowns. In fact, after *Arena canta Bahia*'s run, Boal also directed another musical—*Tempo de guerra* (Wartime)—with Bethânia leading the same Bahian cast.

I was the lone exception. Missing Bahia and my girlfriend who had stayed there (Dedé, a dance student whom I would marry two years later, right in the middle of *tropicalismo*), I left São Paulo and returned to Salvador—to live, to love, and to plan, if lazily, my future as a filmmaker or professor. My inability to set things up entirely after my own taste and ideas—a failure I have always attributed to my mediocre musical talent—made me dream again of a life away from music. This was the case even though by this time—precisely because of the problems I faced in São Paulo—it no longer seemed so troublesome to like João Gilberto and Ray Charles with equal intensity. Even as I wished that my old companions in music could also jump from one to the other rather than remaining stuck in a homogenized sub-pre-bebop, I was getting ready to be more receptive to Bethânia's next suggestion: that I pay more attention to Roberto Carlos.

bahian interlude

The months (nearly a year) spent in Salvador de Bahia were aimless and happy. Dedé and I would go to Itapuã and pass the whole day at the beach. Fernando Barros, a high-school classmate, had a summer house his mother didn't use in the off-season, and sometimes we would spend two days at a time there. Dedé's parents, who would not have approved, were given to believe by one of her friends that the two girls were traveling together—off to the island of Itaparica or in the outback. At night we would go to Abaeté to drink *cachaça* and beer, singing together under the full moon. We would make love in the dunes, at Nando Barros's house, at the beach. But I felt a bit anxious about the future. Music had insinuated itself as a profession. More to the point, it had imposed itself as the path to follow, now that Bethânia was famous all over the country and that samba of mine on her "Carcará" record was playing from every radio. Being a filmmaker would have depended on a willingness to raise funds—and to deal with an array of people, all of them under the pressure of a shared enterprise. I was not that kind of person. Being a painter had been decided against: I would have had sadly to choose between making objects for bourgeois people to hang on their walls and making objects that no one would hang anywhere. (Purely formal questions made no sense to me; I would have become a passionate defender of Abstract Expressionism.) João Augusto Azevedo, the theater director, and the actor Équio Reis showed me reproductions of Lautrec, Matisse, Picasso (the MAMB—where I had seen Degas and van Gogh—had been closed by the military regime), and I still admired the paintings of the Brazilian abstract painters Manabu Mabe and Antônio Bandeira, who had become very famous by that time. Mondrian was a special case. Those red, blue, and yellow squares and rectangles seemed to have been executed with a ruler, and I wondered whether this were an open road or a cul-de-sac, while recognizing those structures behind everything we called "modern": buildings, furniture, clothes—and behind the notes

Caetano Veloso, age 2. "As a small child I had complicated philosophical intuitions."

BELOW: *The house on Amparo Street. In the back row, from left: Caetano's siblings Nicinha, Clara, and Rodrigo, his parents (known as seu Zezinho and dona Canô), sister Mabel, Caetano, and cousin Mariinha. In the front row: Maria Bethânia, cousin Tânia, and sister Irene.*

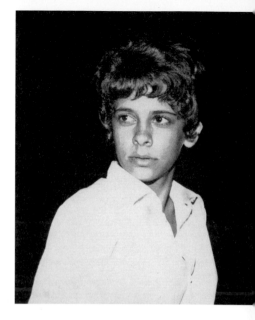

ABOVE LEFT: Chega de saudade *(1959), João Gilberto's first LP, launched the bossa nova movement. The title track remains its anthem. In Santo Amaro, João Gilberto became a cult figure for Caetano and his friends, who would gather at "Bubu's bar" to hear the record played over and over.*

ABOVE RIGHT: *Maria da Graça Costa Penna Burgos (later known as Gal Costa) at the time of the Vila Velha shows in 1964.*

BELOW: *Caetano's friend and musical collaborator Gilberto Gil, with Nana Caymmi, daughter of the legendary Dorival Caymmi, in 1967. "At times, through the years, I have heard Gil say, and been deeply moved by it, that when he met me he felt as though he were leaving behind a great loneliness: when he saw me he was sure that he had found a true companion."*

Gil, Gal, Maria Bethânia, and Caetano all released solo albums in 1966.
In Rio, the foursome would come to be known as "the Bahians."

ABOVE: *Caetano in 1966 with the poets Torquato Neto, left, and Capinan, right. Torquato later wrote the lyrics to Gil's* tropicalista *anthem "Geléia geral," and Capinan introduced Caetano to the work of the concretists.*

BELOW: *Os Mutantes, three Paulista teenage rockers. "When Duprat introduced them to Gil, he commented to me in a somewhat frightened tone: 'They're still kids and they know everything. It can't be true!'"*

ABOVE: *When TV festivals ruled:*
O Fino da Bossa, *Elis Regina's MPB
showcase on TV Record.* "TV Record
specialized in music as did no other
network in the world, as far as I know,
before the advent of MTV."

LEFT: *Before he applied his avant-garde
tastes to help shape* tropicalismo, *Rogerio
Duprat played cello for the Teatro Municipal de São Paulo.*

ABOVE: *A still from Glauber Rocha's 1966 film* Terra em Transe *(Land in Anguish). In that scene Caetano first recognized "the death of populism.* Tropicalismo *would never have come into being but for that traumatic moment."*

RIGHT: *Roberto Carlos, the King of Brazilian rock championed by the* tropicalistas *in defiance of the MPB party line, makes an appearance on the television show hosted by the outlandish Chacrinha (wearing a telephone dial). "Like some Dada experience for the masses, {Chacrinha} seemed at times dangerous just for being so absurd and energetic. This was the program that the domestic help would not miss."*

When the growing popularity of rock led to a slip in the ratings of Elis Regina's O Fino da Bossa, *TV Record called a meeting from which emerged a new show, to be hosted on a rotating basis, called* The Broad Front of Brazilian Popular Music. *To create an "antinationalist and anti-MPB scandal," Caetano and Gil dressed Maria Bethânia like a rocker and asked her to sing a song of Roberto Carlos's, playing an electric guitar.*

BELOW: *Caetano's favorite among the new shows was the one hosted by the American choreographer Lennie Dale, left, and Geraldo Vandré.*

Hélio Oiticica's Tropicália, *April 1967, the installation that furnished the name for the first* tropicalista *album.*

BELOW RIGHT: *Hélio Oiticica "enjoyed frequenting the* favelas *and admired figures who seemed to respond with violence to Brazil's unbelievable social disparities. Hélio turned himself into a kind of ambulating happening."*

BELOW LEFT: *Caetano in one of Oiticica's* parangolés: *"barely recognizable as clothes, impossible even to discern as autonomous objects, this assemblage of cloaks, capes, scarves, and jackets made of plastic, brocade, and netting was exhibited in such a way as to provoke in the viewer a whirlpool of thoughts and emotions about the body, clothing, beauty, invention, poverty, and freedom."*

played without vibrato in cool jazz and bossa nova. Lygia Clark's daring explorations had gone practically unnoticed: my friend Sônia Castro commented one day at the studio that the absolute abandonment into which painting as we know it had fallen made her question everything. I remember clearly Sônia's mention of the word "stone" in her description of some work of Lygia's she had seen in a vast group exhibition at the MAMB, which I, for some reason, had missed. I seem to recall that Lygia—who was finishing an abstract painting she found so beautiful it used to make her cry as she was painting it—wondered whether it would not be better to abandon oils, canvas, and brushes entirely; as an alternative, she proposed a work consisting of a "plastic bag full of water and a stone on top." It's curious that I should remember this, having no idea what Lygia could have been exhibiting in Salvador in 1963 and 1964—yet what Lygia eventually did create would have much to do with that description. But Sônia's comment fascinated me: I was, after all, the guy who liked "crazy things," and in 1971 would pay homage to Lygia's early installation art with a song: "If You Hold a Stone."

In any event, I was leaving it to chance to determine my future, and if I had not chosen music, in 1965 it seemed evident that music would choose me. I did offer some resistance, however. In the first place, after the season spent in São Paulo, I was loath to leave Bahia. Then there was my genuine musical modesty. I am capable of humility, but I am not modest by nature. I don't aim to underestimate myself or engage in deliberate self-effacement, least of all as a strategy to elicit the protests of others, nor am I embarrassed to recognize openly the value of what I accomplish. But I consider my musical acumen average, sometimes below average. To my surprise, it has improved with practice. But I have never become a Gil, an Edu Lobo, a Milton Nascimento, or a Djavan. If I am somehow able to work out musical syntax, it is only by virtue of that other intelligence that permits me to write relevant songs. Above all, I find myself singing: and it is my pleasure and growing competency as a singer that continue to furnish me with a justification for staying with this career.

Though singing forced me to confront my musical limitations, as in my early radio fiasco, my friends were pushing me toward music and toward Rio. Gil, as I said before, demanded my collaboration. One day in 1965, Solano Ribeiro, a young producer from São Paulo, came to Salvador looking for songs to enter in the first song festival there, which he was producing for TV Excelsior. Ribeiro wanted me to recommend young "undiscovered" talent, and he insisted on taking a song of mine. I thought it funny to be treated like someone who was already established in the profession. I gave him the song "Boa palavra" (Good Word), which I had composed using *samba de roda* refrains from the Iguape valley. The song made the finals and attracted the attention of some heavyweights in a memorable festival where Elis exploded onto the scene, singing Edu Lobo and Vinicius de Moraes's song "Arrastão." After this festival, producers at the other broadcasting company were also more receptive, and initiated a kind of programming that would transform television as much as music. The idea of song competitions (the "festivals") had been borrowed from the San Remo Festival in Italy, but in Brazil, after the success of this first one, it was to acquire different characteristics and carry a different sort of weight. Elis's performance had shown the owners of TV Record, Excelsior's competitor in São Paulo, how broadly appealing MPB could be with the Brazilian public, the scope of its potential audience as well as prestige; they invited her to host a weekly show, *O Fino da Bossa,* and asked Solano Ribeiro to produce similar festivals there. Gilberto Gil, who was living in São Paulo and supporting a wife and two small daughters, appeared frequently on *O Fino da Bossa.* MPB started to be taken very seriously in Brazil, in every sense: from the specifically musical aspects to the literary and the political, there was an aura of mission connected to the songs.

Significant though my success had been, my going to Rio was really a capitulation to Roberto Pinho's pressure. Alvinho Guimarães had introduced Roberto to me (it's amazing how Alvinho Guimarães seems to have introduced me to everything and everyone!), saying that he was a person with original ideas and a heart of gold. The assurance with which he expressed his opinions, realistic and prophetic at once, impressed me from the start. He had been a disciple of Professor Agostinho da Silva, a Portuguese intellectual who had come to Brazil to escape the Salazar dictatorship, and became a champion for the overthrow of the Northern-Protestant phase of civilization; his own paradoxical strain of left-wing Sebastianism (as that aspiration is called) seemed tempered by a lucid and open-minded realism, not the typical mystification. Still, it wasn't quite clear to me whether da Silva was involved in nostalgia for a Portuguese brand of medieval Christianity or an intuition of an inventive new path. I thought it was probably the latter, but was myself vulnerable to certain coincidences between chance and "revelations," which is only another way of saying that I was given to superstition. Roberto defended Jung over Freud (though he never convinced me). I was reading Mircea Eliade's *The Sacred and the Profane,* as well as Jacques Bergier and Louis Pauwels's *Morning of the Magicians,* both assertions of the continuities between the daytime world and other levels of experience, and a preoccupation with the imaginative life of Europe prior to the Enlightenment. We fantasized a future different from the Marxist and capitalist alternatives. (Later Pauwels's name would be associated with extreme right-wing publications in Europe, where obvious traces of fascist identification were not even disguised, next to the great Eliade's.) As for Professor Agostinho, he was interested in connecting Brazil, Africa, and the East, but never slipped toward any type of radical reactionary position: he loved to see in Portugal—the oldest country in Europe, created as a nation-state in the twelfth century—the promise of a spiritually ambitious future that would not deny technology. When he would say petulantly that "Portugal has already civilized Asia, Africa, and America, now it needs to civilize Europe," he was above all asserting his opposition to the superpowers. And although this succeeded in fascinating more than persuading me, what did convince me was Roberto Pinho's insistence that I should accept my destiny and go to Rio and São Paulo to make music, because great things would come of it.

I did not think his advice was prophetic. But combined with Alvinho's insistence, Gil's demands, Dedé's complicity, and Duda's agreement—and above all my inability to devise alternatives—Roberto's pressure seemed to be based on the anticipation of actual possibilities rather than on visions and revelations from another world. It's possible that he considered my songs more original and myself more intelligent than I would ever admit. Nevertheless, for a long time I remained in Bahia, without lifting a straw to prepare myself to go to Rio. I did not even give any thought to where I might live there until the Carnival of 1966, when Roberto introduced me to a Chilean graphic artist named Alex Chacon, who had come from Rio to Salvador to work with him. Alex immediately joined the effort to persuade me to move to Rio. I don't remember seeing him when I sang in Salvador. What could have made him so passionate? A conversation? Bethânia's recording of "De manhã"? I remember listening to him speak with comical enthusiasm about the madness of Carnival in Bahia. He was awed and kept saying that the little *bandolim* of the *trio elétrico* could only be played by the devil himself. Alex himself seemed like a little demon, very skinny and small, with quite lively eyes and the typically emphatic accent of Spanish-speakers. I asked him how he expected me to leave a place like

Bahia. At this point he changed his tone immediately and said that was not even an issue: he would offer me his place. He was married to a Brazilian woman whose parents had left them a large apartment on Nossa Senhora de Copacabana Avenue, practically on the corner of Santa Clara Street, where they lived, and they had no children. Almost two months later, spurred by Dedé—who had decided to move to Rio for me—I arrived by bus at the station in Rio de Janeiro, where to my surprise Sylvia Telles, the adorable singer, was waiting for me, holding her lapdog. She drove me to Alex's apartment and told me that, as soon as I was ready, we would go that same day to Edu Lobo's house. He was the great composer then riding the crest of the wave, and he greeted me that night with a sincere warmth and interest that I will never forget. In spite of the prejudices I encountered later, this is the image of Rio's hospitable welcome I have kept. And it will always be the measure of my gratitude—despite later fits of rage—for the city that João Gilberto calls "the city of Brazilians."

anguish

s far as *tropicalismo* owes anything to my actions and ideas, the catalyst of the movement may be found in my experience of Glauber Rocha's *Terra em transe* (Land in Anguish). Watching the film in Rio in 1966, my heart was pounding from the start; it opens with an aerial view of the ocean approaching the Brazilian coastline, against a soundtrack of the same *candomblé* chanting heard in his first film, *Barravento* (The Turning Wind). As the film continued, one powerful image after another confirmed my impression that unconscious aspects of our reality were on the verge of being revealed.

By that time Glauber was already on his way to becoming a leading cultural figure. While still living in Bahia he had already impressed European directors and critics; and *Barravento* was followed by *Black God, White Devil,* a film full of wild beauty that excited us with the prospect of achieving a great national cinema. This greatness was not a question of technical competency: such had already been the objective at Vera Cruz, a highly organized studio that produced well-made films through the mid-fifties. The São Paulo entrepreneur Franco Zampari had invited Alberto Cavalcanti, a Brazilian filmmaker who had enjoyed success in England and France, to answer the call of the Brazilian elite to return and create a film industry of high quality. Theirs was an attempt to overcome the primitive state of Brazilian commercial cinema, represented by the Carnivalesque comedies from Rio known as *chanchadas,* a successful formula introduced in the thirties.

The Cinema Novo movement that emerged in the early sixties—of which Glauber was always the leader in both theory and practice—was as much opposed to the conventionality of the more respectable films coming out of Vera Cruz as to the crudeness of the *chanchadas.* Glauber's *Revisão crítica do cinema brasileiro* (Critical Revision of Brazilian Cinema) advocated a cinema born of Brazilian poverty in the same way that neorealism had been born of the destitution of Italian cities immediately after the war. A call to arms for the young intellectuals of the Left,

Glauber's *Revisão* inspired their interest in cinema and drew their attention to films such as *Rio, 40 Degrees* by Nelson Pereira dos Santos, perhaps Brazil's most influential filmmaker; it was as much a rejection of the sensible people shooting reasonable scripts as it was of the hucksters selling entertainment to a semi-illiterate moviegoing public.

Black God, White Devil would be the most emblematic film of Cinema Novo. At around the time it was released, there were other good films with themes very different from those of the Vera Cruz being made, such as Ruy Guerra's *Os fuzis* (The Guns) and Pereira dos Santos's *Vidas secas* (Barren Lives), collectively inaugurating the movement; these had real technical quality among their many virtues. But *Black God, White Devil* went beyond this: it dared to soar above the industry's status quo and proscribed aesthetic. The film dealt with religious fanaticism in northeastern Brazil—and made clear allusions to Euclides da Cunha's book *Os sertões* (known in English as *Rebellion in the Backlands*), a unique hybrid of social-science treatise, history, journalism, and novel. *Black God, White Devil* portrayed the region's *cangaceiros,* those rural bandits made famous in Europe by the movie *O cangaceiro,* which won several awards at Cannes in the mid-fifties. The real-life *cangaceiros* were pretty impressive in their stylized Brazilian cowboy hats, medals, and jewels. Cruel and romantic, they were out to exact social vengeance in a land dominated by big landowners. Glauber was not afraid to take a sometimes heavy or awkward hand in his application of aesthetic principles learned from Eisenstein, Rossellini, Buñuel, and Brecht, while also drawing upon the French New Wave and incorporating mannerisms from the Japanese cinema, which we were just discovering. With a bit of Marxist ideology mixed in, his was an exuberant if somewhat deformed panorama of the epic forces driving our popular culture (in Europe, as in Brazil, it was justifiably described as baroque). Actually, the overall impact of the film comes closer to the genius of Pasolini's *The Gospel According to St. Matthew* than to anything. The photography without backlighting, the delirious sequences of raw images, the imposition of thought on the visual world—these were elements of both films, which were made in the same year. The difference is that *Black God, White Devil* was not based on the powerful starkness of a discrete text like Matthew's Gospel: instead, the author summoned up the entire imaginative space and particular problematic of Brazil. What appeared on the screen was the very desire of Brazilians to make a cinema. It wasn't so much Brazil trying to get it right (or proving that it could), but determining to fall short or succeed on its own terms. The Spanish filmmaker Fernando Trueba once told me that Brazilian films, even when they are bad, are never that bad, because there is always something wild that redeems them, a wildness one finds, concentrated, in the best films made in Brazil. This is a quality noticeable even to foreigners; it would not have been revealed but for Cinema Novo—and Cinema Novo would not have existed without Glauber. What purifies the bad and illuminates the good in Brazilian films of any period is the very flame that burns in *Black God, White Devil.* It is what made Glauber a master among his peers, quite apart from his critical influence on the culture of Brazil (despite, or because of, its polemicism). As *Land in Anguish* was being made, the buzz around what Glauber would do in the wake of *Black God, White Devil* was thunderous.

I had come to Rio in April or May of 1966 and, after living at Alex Chacon's apartment in Copacabana, moved to the Solar da Fossa, as that precursor of Rio's apartment-hotels was called. It was an old plantation house that had been converted into a series of apartments; as in a cheap hotel there was a front desk and a minimum of housekeeping. The apartments were strung along enormous hallways that encircled an inner courtyard. The owner (or the woman everyone took to be the owner) often sat at the front desk, with her bleached hair and a cigar. But one should not infer that this was a depressing dive. On the contrary, everything was clean, cheerful, airy, and forthright, the vision of the owner merely suggesting the eccentric elegance of a character in a German movie. Most apartments had a living room and bedroom, as well as a reasonably large bath, and were occupied by artists: musicians, poets, designers, and struggling actresses—people who had discovered a pleasant way of living for very little money in a stylish part of Rio. Dedé, who had decided to come with me, was living with her grandmother in the Flamengo neighborhood, but we spent as much time together as we could at the Solar.

The sobriquet Solar da Fossa (the real name was Solar Santa Teresinha) derived from the expression *"estar na fossa"* (to be blue, to be down and out), an "in" phrase among the Cariocas from Zona Sul. Used by fans of Bergman movies and psychoanalysis, *"fossa"* (literally, "cesspool"), in spite of its crude literal meaning, was applied to the modern *sambas-canções* sung by Maysa, Tito Madi, and Dolores Duran during the pre–bossa nova phase—it was very chic. The Solar da Fossa was well located: one could walk across the New Tunnel and in five minutes be in Prado Junior Street, the very center of cheap bohemian life during the sixties. Here the Cervantes Restaurant served great sandwiches with pressed French bread and an excellent draft beer.

I remember my walk from the Solar to the movie theater where *Land in Anguish* was playing. It must be said that I found the film even more uneven than *Black God, White Devil*. The lamentations of the main character—a left-wing poet torn apart by conflicting ambitions to achieve the "absolute" and social justice—were at times frankly subliterary. In addition, certain intolerable conventional shortcomings of Brazilian cinema—high-society parties staged unconvincingly, female extras encouraged by directors to enact deplorable provincial caricatures of sexy glamour, an overall lack of narrative clarity—these were all in painful evidence (though less intensely). Yet as in Glauber's previous films and a great many other Cinema Novo productions, suggestions of a different vision of life, of Brazil, of cinema, seemed to explode on the screen, overwhelming my reservations. The poet-protagonist offered a bitter, realistic vision of politics—in flagrant contrast to the naïveté of his companions—as he resisted the recently imposed military dictatorship. The film stages the moment of the coup d'état as a nightmare he has at the moment of his death: a confusing spectacle evoking at once Buñuel's *La fièvre monte à El Pao* (Republic of Sin), mixed with some of the bad habits of the New Wave and strokes of Fellini's *8½*. But that chaos contributed to the parodic force of the film. And the effect was not entirely a disservice to the character, even though his desperate attempts at maintaining a critical perspective on his political objectives while sustaining the will to carry them out—the kind of dilemma that would lead so many to madness, mysticism, or the trenches of the opposition—lead, rather gratuitously, to his death. It is touching to think, today, how such a series of events might provide, with slight variations, a succinct biography of Glauber himself.

The film naturally was not a box-office success, but it scandalized the intellectuals and artists of the Carioca Left. Some in the audience—leaders of politically engaged theater—jeered as the lights came up. One scene in particular shocked them: During a mass demonstration the poet, who is among those making speeches, calls forward a unionized worker and, to show how unprepared the worker is to fight for his rights, violently covers his mouth, shouting at the others (and at the audience), "This is the People! Idiots, illiterate, no politics!" Then a poor wretch, representing unorganized poverty, appears from among the crowd trying to speak, only to be silenced by the point of a gun stuck in his mouth by one of the candidate's bodyguards. This indelible image is reiterated in long close-ups.

I experienced that scene—and the indignant, heated discussions that it provoked in bars—as the nucleus of a great event whose brief name I now possess but did not know then (I would try to name it a thousand ways for myself and for other people): the death of populism. There is no doubt that populist demagogues are sumptuously ridiculed in the film: they are seen holding crucifixes and flags in open cars against the sky above the Aterro do Flamengo, a wide modern road by the sea, lined with landscaped gardens. There they are in their gaudy mansions, celebrating the solemn rites of the church and Carnival that touch the heart of the masses, and so forth. But it was their essential faith in the popular forces—and the very respect that the best souls invested in the poor man—that here was discarded as a political weapon and an ethical value in itself. It was a hecatomb that I was facing. And I was excited by the prospect of examining what drove it and anticipating its consequences. *Tropicalismo* would never have come into being but for that traumatic moment.

This assault on traditional left-wing populism liberated one to see Brazil squarely from a broader perspective, enabling new and undreamt-of critiques of an anthropological, mythic, mystical, formalist, and moral nature. If the scene of the poet and the worker that incensed the communists charmed me with its courage, it is because the images that came before and after it were trying to reveal something about our condition and ask questions about our destiny. A great cross on the beach overshadows a gathering of politicos, transvestites dressed to the nines for a ball, and Carnival Indians: one feels the presence of the grotesque and with it the revelation of an island always newly discovered and always hidden—Brazil. Among the multitude at the rally, a little old man is dancing samba, graceful and ridiculous, lecherous and angelic, happily lost—the Brazilian people captured in a paradox. One does not know whether they are meant to seem despairing or suggestive; political decisions are discussed on cement patios with black lines dividing the floor, asserting a denial of the comings and goings of the characters. The camera weaves among groups of four, five, six restless agitators, who express disagreement over tactics through their body language, all shot in black and white with enormous areas of light threatened by ominous, looming shadows. It was a political dramaturgy different from the usual reduction of everything to a stereotype of class struggle. Above all, here was the rhetoric and the poetics of post-1964 Brazilian life: a deep scream of pain and impotent rebellion, but also an updated vision, nearly prophetic, of our real possibilities to be and to feel.

Yet I might not have reacted as I did were it not for the determined intelligence and sensibilities of a unique intellectual who came into my life at the end of 1964. Two years later, he had already become a true friend: my fellow Bahian Rogério Duarte, who had moved to Rio the same year I arrived from Salvador.

In the early sixties, while still in Bahia, I heard his name frequently in conversations at the university. His tireless and unconventional intelligence had become legendary. He was known as a brilliant speaker who defended his sometimes shocking opinions with a force that scarcely failed to impress even those who questioned him. Though he had not even finished high school, he fascinated college students and professors alike. Equally legendary was his passion for a young woman—Anecir, Glauber's youngest sister. It was said that he would stand before her door in the Barris neighborhood for entire nights in mute serenade.

When I arrived in Rio with Bethânia in 1964, Rogério turned up at the Opinião Theater, and after the show we went out to talk. Nothing I had heard about him in Bahia could have prepared me for the impact he would eventually have on me. His voice was potent, his mind quick, and his ideas even more disconcerting than I could have imagined. There was about his sense of engagement something at once visceral and metaphysical that amplified the power of his arguments. Yet he was surprisingly kind and friendly. And by his affectionate and ironic way of dealing with us as fellow Bahians living in Rio, but slightly younger—we came to believe that he idealized our "purity." This did not prevent his bombarding our naïveté with blasphemous political tirades, however. He seemed to want to protect us from a certain bitter cynicism that life had already taught him, and at the same time to alert us to the dangers of an innocent adherence to the dominant ideology. I trembled to hear him declare that the National Student Union (UNE) building should really have been burned. UNE had been set on fire by rightist groups immediately after the coup of April 1964, an act of violence that revolted the Left as a whole, the frightened liberals, and all good souls in general. Rogério vehemently expressed his personal reasons for not joining the chorus of outrage: the intolerance that his complicated ideas had met with among the members of UNE made him see the group as a menace to freedom. He was able to detect the embryonic form of oppressive structures within the very groups that were fighting against oppression. The strange exaltation of our growing rapport overtook my initial shock at his heretical view. It was not long before I would discover that Rogério could express even fiercer hostility toward the reactionaries who supported aggression against UNE. This complete contradiction was for me proof of his soundness and rigor.

I did not know that Gobineau had by then formulated his infamous definition "Le brésilien est un homme qui désire passionnément habiter Paris" ("The Brazilian is a man who passionately wishes to live in Paris"). In fact, *tropicalismo* must be seen in part as a natural reaction to the old pro-French cultural orientation. And that reaction embodied an impulse that had been evolving slowly and anxiously in the Brazilian spirit, leading to a tender concern for constructing a sense of our own worth. But it also served the manifest desire of certain erudite producers of culture—and, being an extension of modernism, that desire was likewise a hallmark of the period. In fact the anti-French gesture was to be enacted in a way closer to mass culture, whether in criticizing that culture or identifying with it, or citicizing it by means of itself. The counterpoint to this development was the simultaneous emergence of a mass experimentalism that the avant-garde poet Décio Pignatari called *"produssumo"* (produsumption)—production and consumption merged in a single word. One could say that French culture was confused for us with erudite culture, and we wanted then to oppose to it American culture, which came to us primarily through mass culture.

Ironically, it was a French author who first suggested this project to me. Rogério talked about and sometimes read aloud from the works of the writer Edgar Morin, whose discussion of Hollywood stars and comic-book characters as figures within a new mythology opened my mind to a fresh grasp of pop art, an intense assimilation of Godard's poetic strains, and a total reevaluation of rock and American cinema. No less than Morin, Godard led me to pay attention to the poetry of American mass culture, to Hollywood, and to advertising. His films were—and still are today—my favorites of that period. Since the moment when Duda recommended that I see *À bout de souffle* (Breathless), I realized that I had not only found a new favorite in cinema but also that all cinema had to be reevaluated in light of him. *Land in Anguish* would be an awakening, but, in a way, what we wanted to do would be much closer, if possible, to Godard's films. *Vivre sa vie, Pierrot le fou, Une femme est une femme* are fundamental to the initial ferment of *tropicalismo*. And *Masculin-féminin,* with its scenes in a recording studio, its "children of Marx and Coca-Cola," its adolescent sexuality—I saw it as one more moment in our daily lives in São Paulo. Later, *La chinoise* and *Weekend* would serve as mature comments on the adventure that we had already lived through.

In fact, the connection to Morin would arise quite casually between Rogério and myself. At first our conversations—which would go on into the wee hours at the Solar, and often as not continue at his house in Santa Teresa, where I would then stay over—were about what was happening around us. Theater, cinema, popular music—as well as half-moralistic, half-psychological gossip—were frequent topics. At other times these conversations amounted to monologues delivered by Rogério on subjects as varied as Proust, Mozart, Heidegger, Villa-Lobos, and Lota Macedo Soares. I had not the least ambition to take any of them up myself; I was content to listen to Rogério speak about them. Although I read Sartre, Fernando Pessoa, Lorca, and Drummond, I believed that familiarity with the others was the responsibility of geniuses like Rogério or of great and wise scholars. But Dedé, who had found a job at a newspaper, had been asked to write an article about *fotonovelas* (graphic novels with soap opera themes); and having no formal training in writing, and despising *fotonovelas,* she did not welcome this assignment and asked Rogério for help. The arguments he used to counter Dedé's prejudices in relation to the literary form were based on his espousal of various theories about cultural manifestations often dismissed as trash. That is how Rogério led me to Edgar Morin; in fact, long before I met Zé Agrippino, Morin's ideas had stirred my imagination. But once Zé Agrippino finally appeared on the scene, revealing certain preferences for rock over MPB and encouraging the anti-French bite in the *tropicalista* taste, he only added to the excitement and provoked me to go even further.

In 1966, a few months before I saw *Land in Anguish,* Rogério had introduced me to a writer from São Paulo, José Agrippino de Paula. He told me that before he knew Agrippino, he had seen him walking in the street one day and, without addressing him or hearing him utter a single word, said to himself: "I have never seen such an intelligent man in my life." He approached the stranger, and that's how their friendship began.

Zé Agrippino turned the icons of American mass media into weapons against the intellectualism of our bohemian circles. But behind the iconoclast one could sense his appreciation for German literature (especially Kafka and Musil, but I think I also heard him speak of

Hölderlin, Heidegger, and Nietzsche) and literature in English (Joyce, Melville, and Swift, but also Kerouac, Ginsberg, and the other Beat poets). He impressed me when he boasted that he much preferred James Bond movies to *Jules et Jim,* Truffaut's delicate film so beloved of college audiences. Agrippino was not as eloquent as Rogério and never explained or justified his attitudes: he imposed his stony presence and let the conclusions fall where they would, like so many bricks, in the middle of the conversation. Being from São Paulo, Agrippino had a different perspective: to have been born in Brazil, for instance, was for him an accident, neither auspicious nor deplorable. He simply measured the advantages and disadvantages with lucid objectivity. That the disadvantages might outnumber the advantages did not bear upon his affection for the country: it was simply one discrete datum among others to be computed. He was to me, for a long time, a character of Rogério's. No doubt the anecdote of how they had met contributed to this impression. But he was also the radical embodiment of a favorite saying of Rogério's: "For me the problem with writing a novel is that I would not be content to be the author—I would want to be the character." Each man was nevertheless writing a novel. Rogério's would have been his literary debut had he not destroyed it before publication; Agrippino had already published *Lugar público* (Public Space) a year before we met, and his epic second novel would be entitled *Panamérica.*

Zé Agrippino seemed like a caveman, with his black beard and heavy gait. He never responded to smiles conventionally offered when people look at each other casually, and this habit made me uncomfortable at times. But he was not rude or lacking in manners, and when a smile did cross his face, it was real, irrepressible, and charged with the value of its rarity. His girlfriend, Maria Esther Stockler, likewise made no concessions to the rituals of petit-bourgeois conviviality. She, even more than he, exhaled an aristocratic air, and by her example offered a continuous lesson in true elegance, always showing how something ordinary—the length of a skirt, a gesture, a color—could achieve distinction. She was a dancer, and from a rich family in São Paulo. The two never kissed or even touched in public. They would just arrive and leave together. Rogério used to say, however, that when they occasionally stayed at his house in Santa Teresa, they would sometimes spend the entire night and day in the bedroom, without coming out even to eat. At the beach, the neat little Carioca girls would stare in awe, as Maria Esther's pubic hairs dripped with water below her bikini and down her thighs; she didn't shave her underarms either. Yet she was as majestic as a queen, while the others looked like chorus girls. Agrippino and Maria Esther read magazines in English and, unlike Rogério, used neither fashionable slang nor swear words. Physically Agrippino was a thoroughly Brazilian type, while Maria Esther looked like a pure Caucasian. They seemed to be foreigners, or people from another age (he the paleolithic, she pre-Renaissance)—both from the future.

Both Rogério and Zé Agrippino predisposed me toward a favorable opinion of *Land in Anguish*. Rogério had been Glauber's intimate since the days in Bahia, and he exerted a strong influence on the filmmaker. In truth I needed no encouragement to appreciate a film by Glauber. *Barravento*—which I had reviewed in a Salvador newspaper long before I met Rogério—had seemed to me extraordinarily beautiful, and I found *Black God, White Devil* the most exuberantly suggestive of all the Cinema Novo films. Glauber himself was already a mythic figure for me.

My third or fourth time seeing the film, Duda went with me. He had just moved from Bahia to Rio and was staying with me until he could find a place to live. It was the first time he'd seen it, and, objecting to the aesthetic unevenness, pretentiousness, and various failed efforts, he expressed a basic dislike for the film. His opinions were ones I myself might have held, had I never met Rogério and Zé. For a moment I felt awkward, wondering whether my own reaction wasn't only an attempt to please my new masters. Duda seemed so rigorous and genuine. But the fact is that I never talked about the film with either of my new friends; in this case, I had been searching alone. And it is also true that destiny brings us encounters that elucidate our intimate vocations.

If I identified with Rogério as soon as I met him, it was because my situation among my leftist colleagues at the University of Bahia had been similar to his among his friends at UNE in Rio; my reticent attitude in contrast to the political certainties of my friends provoked in them an ironic apprehension. I was one of those artistic types whom the more responsible among them liked to call "alienated." The first long article I ever wrote was a diatribe against José Ramos Tinhorão's book on popular music, a sociological exercise in which bossa nova was characterized on the one hand as being a cultural submission to the American model, and on the other hand as an undue appropriation of popular culture by the middle class. It was an articulate defense of the national ideology that circumscribed all value judgments by the Brazilian Left, the "national-popular" style demanded of every work of art and entertainment. I wrote the article for a college journal because I thought it intolerable that those ideas would be accepted without discussion by the more intelligent students in the university. I knew that bossa nova was something more—something precious to all of us—and I wrote in a confrontational spirit: I wanted it to be an effective form of intervention in shaping the views of the people with whom I lived. Politics itself—or what passed for it in the form of campaigns for the presidency of the student body, discussions in assemblies, and rigid opinions of public men whose names and faces I could barely remember—bored me. Of course, I cared about social justice and felt enthusiasm about belonging to a generation that appeared to have the potential to effect profound change. But such phrases as "dictatorship of the proletariat" meant nothing to me. I saw wretchedly unorganized poverty all around me, while the "proletariat" of the articles and speeches was always made up of workers in hard hats. The worker in a hard hat was a novelty in Santo Amaro, where I still spent my summer vacations. His image had made its appearance only recently as Petrobrás came into the area, to the joy of many young men who, in comparison to the life they would have lived without these oil-industry jobs, felt rich—with salaries that allowed them to renovate the facades of their houses, quickly destroying a large part of the architectural heritage of Bahia. This change I beheld not without some ambivalence: although I felt a loss of character in my city and missed the visual unity to which I was accustomed, I myself desired a modern house with wooden floors and even dreamed of moving into a new apartment, to be unburdened of the weight of the big old houses, stained by humidity, in which I had been born and raised; the impersonal air of an apartment seemed to bring elation and freedom into my life. I felt in some fundamental ways much further removed from anything petit bourgeois than were my critics: they never discussed topics such as sex or race, elegance or taste, love or form. In such matters the world was accepted just as it was. Among the poorest segments of the population, the status of a salaried worker was desirable and rare. I sincerely did not feel that the construction workers of Salvador, or the few factory workers one could identify as such, or even the comparatively numerous workers at Petrobrás—any more than the "proletariat" seen in films and photographs—could or should decide what my future might be. When the poet in *Land in Anguish* declared a lack of faith in the liberating energy of "the people," I heard this not as an end to possibilities but rather as proclamation of what I now needed to do.

useful landscape

Rogério moved from the Santa Teresa to the Solar da Fossa. Duda was staying with me in my apartment; across the hall lived the great composer, singer, and guitar player Paulinho da Viola and the lyricist and writer Abel Silva. I believe that Paulinho—the most profound and knowledgeable fan of traditional carioca samba—was the first person to hear a *tropicalista* song. I played "Paisagem útil" (Useful Landscape) for him as soon as I finished composing it. He nobly saw in it something different, something he could not really say he liked but in which he recognized integrity. And he told me all this almost verbatim, with an elegance that disarmed me: how was it possible that he could see what was new in that song and react with neither enthusiasm nor revulsion? Paulinho's response immediately defined the position he would consistently maintain toward *tropicalismo;* and coming as it did from a young man exactly my own age whom I admired passionately, it struck me as both reassurance and a bucket of cold water. Between "Paisagem útil" and "Alegria, alegria" (Happiness, Happiness), I would spend months pondering the power of what was taking shape inside me.

"Paisagem útil," the title an inversion of Tom Jobim's beautiful bossa-nova samba, "Inútil paisagem" (Useless Landscape), was composed to the rhythm of a *marcha-rancho*—a kind of slow and solemn Carnival march that had been the basis for elaborate parades at the time when the *escolas de samba* were still low-key and disorganized—with a melody that seemed to be a patchwork of musical phrases drawn from the Brazilian sentimental tradition. The lyrics describe in strong imagery the park of Aterro do Flamengo, a recent widening of the avenue along the beach in that neighborhood, echoing the nearly science-fiction-like effect of its modernist lines, with cars going by at high speed and busy people everywhere:

> *eyes open in the wind*
> *over the space of the* aterro

over the space, over the sea
the sea goes far from Flamengo
the sky goes far suspended
in slow and firm masts
a cold palm grove of cement
the sky goes far from the knoll
the sky goes far from Glória
the sky goes far suspended
in lights of dead moons
lights of a new dawn
that keep the grass new
and the day always breaking

those who go to the movies
who go to the theater
who go to work
who go to rest
who sing, who sing
who think about life
who look at the avenue
who hope to return
the automobiles seem to fly
the automobiles seem to fly

but now a moon comes on and floats high in the sky
a red and blue oval high in the Rio sky
the oval moon of Esso moves and illuminates the kiss
of the poor sad happy heart of lovers in our Brazil.

Paulinho's dispassionate reaction intimidated me at first, but proved to be paradigmatic of the kind of resistance that MPB would offer *tropicalismo.*

Bethânia, after taking some time off in Bahia to recover from the depersonalization that followed the success of "Carcará," had returned to Rio. In a strategy conceived together with the producer Guilherme Araújo, she was appearing in a Copacabana club singing the sentimental *sambas-canções* she had always liked, which she infused with dramatic power. This show became one of the great hits of Carioca nightlife, and Bethânia's earlier popularity increased, turning her into a genuine cult figure, well on the road to becoming the diva she is today. This was when she began to appear in a wig with straight hair, and also about the time she asked me to stop giving her advice about how to work or live. I was thus definitively relieved of the responsibility my father had entrusted to me, and for her, too, the emancipation was official. Consequently, although I saw her every night, our exchanges were different. Guilherme Araújo had put me in charge of the show—of making sure that everything was in order with Bethânia and the musicians, the sound, the lighting, and so on when it was time for her to go on. Dedé would accompany me but could not go in; being underage at seventeen, she would wait for me at the door. Edu Lobo would frequently keep her company in front of the club or nearby. Sandra, Dedé's beautiful older sister who had come to spend some time in Rio, was apparently the impetus for Edu's gallantry: she almost always came with Dedé, and soon Edu was courting her, not totally without success. The most important drummer in the modern history of samba, Edson Machado, was playing with Bethânia, as was the pianist Osmar Milito, among other musicians, all very good, all jazz-oriented, and all from the Beco das Garrafas. It was around that time that I learned how instrumentalists pejoratively refer to singers as "canaries" or "bells." If Bethânia no longer wanted my advice, she was now giving me advice of her own—a more conscious and explicit version of lessons about life she had always offered me. Our talks were less frequent, but they were more open and, for her part, more deliberate. And it was during one such occasion that she directed me to watch Roberto Carlos's show on TV.

I used to attend the interesting weekly MPB sessions in the Teatro Jovem, at the Mourisco, organized by Cléber Santos, who had alerted me to the possibility of living at the Solar da Fossa. During these sessions well-known composers would offer opportunities for undiscovered talents by providing unpublished songs for them to sing. There one listened to music and talked about making it, the profession, and the aesthetic problems of the post–bossa nova sound. Traditional samba musicians from the *morros* and bossa nova stars could meet onstage or in the audience. The evenings were hosted by such figures as the philologist Antônio Houaiss, who eventually became minister of culture in the nineties, and Sargentelli, a well-known show host who became famous in the seventies and eighties with shows for tourists. The emphasis was almost always on the defense of our national traditions against Americanization. Of course, my own inclination was to counter all this with the ideas that I was absorbing from Rogério and Agrippino. The attitude of Cléber Santos and the people at the Teatro Jovem was in itself a softening of the nationalist Left's orthodox stance, and no cultural or political debate could avoid resembling the caricatures of *Land in Anguish.*

All discussions, inside or outside the Teatro Jovem, were permeated by the idea of a popular national art, cultivated at the Center for Popular Culture of UNE since the coup d'état and fueled by the aesthetic demands of the harmonically sophisticated children of bossa nova. Bethânia, whose nonalignment with bossa nova left her free to choose a varied repertoire, told me explicitly that her interest in Roberto Carlos's programs—which she invited me to share—derived from the "vitality" that emanated from them, in contrast to the defensive atmosphere of respectable MPB.

There was an aura developing around songwriting that was both pretentious and responsible. In this connection I recall one night at the Cervantes Restaurant when the eminent film director Flávio Rangel recognized me sitting at a table near his (he was the sort of man who was familiar with emerging talents). Commenting on my songs "Um dia" and "Boa palavra," which he thought were excessively wordy, he yelled out in his squeaky voice and without the least fear of being thought absurd: "You have to read Ezra Pound, you have to read Ezra Pound!" I didn't quite know who Ezra Pound was, but I would hear his name mentioned with incredible frequency when, not long after this, I met the so-called concrete poets in São Paulo. But all the people present at my table as well as Flávio's reacted as if they knew it was a name worthy of reverence.

Elis's "Arrastão" had presented, in its television format, an immensely effective synthesis of the political ambitions of the nationalist-populist crowd and the experimentation of the crowd from Beco das Garrafas. Many songs were charged with this double valence— "Arrastão" was particularly strong, especially as sung by Elis. It was number one in the contest and became a hit, being pretentiously jazzy and politically "serious." In fact it was a great song by Edu and Vinicius de Moraes. Compared to Nara, Sylvia Telles, Carlos Lyra, and, above all, João Gilberto, Elis's style seemed emphatic and extroverted. But, contrary to what had happened to Bethânia, with Elis the drama and the broad gestures came back to MPB through television, not theater. She had a clear and brilliant voice, and her musical confidence was impressive. The song "Arrastão," which revisited Caymmi's favorite theme, a chronicle of the lives of poor fishermen, gave continuity to the developing stylization of Northeastern music by Edu Lobo. As I've mentioned, he was then *the* singer-songwriter, and was the young Carioca son of the Pernambucan Fernando Lobo, who had been an excellent, if not very prolific, composer of some masterpieces in the forties and fifties—including some together with Caymmi himself. Edu's songs brought to modern Brazilian music an epic dimension that was in striking contrast to the lyrical intimacy of bossa nova. But, although they also represented the resurrection of regionalist flavors, these songs were technically not a regression to the harmonic simplicity of pre–bossa nova folk melody. On the contrary, Edu was already then what he is to this day: an inventive composer of melodies and sophisticated harmonies with a powerful personal style. In "Arrastão," as in other compositions of his at that time, one feels the urge to leave the apartment for the wide open spaces, the desire to break out from one's own little world into a world in common with others, the move from urban anonymity to regional roots. All this was filtered through a polished technique of composition and took him closer to Hollywood than might have been advisable without threatening the richness and consistency of Edu's music. The way Elis sang "Arrastão" on television— punctuated by rhythmic, slick, dancelike movements—didn't miss a thing, even slowing down the tempo to half the pace, or the dramatic "belting out" of Broadway and Las Vegas. She succeeded in creating a tremendously effective style of presentation for sophisticated music on TV, which made her into a great star of high technical polish for the masses. Although I could not help but be enthusiastic about her obvious talent, I, a radical Joãogilbertian, was annoyed by the vulgarity of the pre–cool jazz effects and with the body language taught her by Lennie Dale, an American dancer who lived in Brazil.

Gil, who was living in São Paulo and supporting his wife and two small daughters with a job at Gessy Lever, the big soap and shampoo company, appeared frequently on the program hosted by Elis Regina, *O Fino da Bossa.* It was reminiscent of the famous college shows of bossa nova promoted by Walter Silva and was musically an imitation of the shows that were done at the Beco das Garrafas in Copacabana, where talents like Wilson Simonal, Leny Andrade, Edson Machado, and so many excellent instrumentalists had shone. The ambience of this television program, which enabled Elis to make the transition from commercial singer of inferior romantic pop to renowned performer of what then was called "samba-jazz," was propitious for a talent like Gil's. He was an inspired composer, a man with an exuberant guitar technique and a prodigious ear, which enabled him to improvise scats comparable to those of Ella Fitzgerald. *Fino da Bossa* made him very well known. Little by little, he was leaving the workaday world behind and was being drawn into the life of the artist.

domingo

I, who at that point could not imagine any other kind of life for myself than being an artist, saw the opportunity of making a record. And Edu, who had welcomed me affectionately since the day I arrived by bus from Salvador, expressed interest in my songs. Dori Caymmi, whom I had met in Bahia when he had gone on a tour of his father Dorival's old neighborhood, and Francis Hime, to whom Edu and Dori had introduced me, looked on my apparent promise with enthusiasm. They were naturally generous, and excited by the relative novelty represented by the Bahian group. People were talking about us. As admired as her shyness were the perfect pitch and the beauty of Gau's voice—that's how we spelled her nickname, until Guilherme Araújo changed it to Gal (most people still called her Gracinha). I suppose it must have been Dori himself—eventually the producer of the record—who persuaded João Araújo, at that time the artistic director of Philips (now PolyGram) and today the big man at Som Livre (TV Globo's recording branch) to make a record bringing together Gal and me.

We recorded in the morning. This, the schedule reserved for novices, was particularly inappropriate for me; I've always gone to bed late and am slow to feel totally awake. But although that aspect was frustrating, something about the record pleased me from the start—perhaps it was Dori's arrangements and his guitar, or Gal's voice in almost everything. I even liked my own voice in "Um dia" and, with some reservations, in "Coração vagabundo." While Gal and I were recording the album that would eventually be called *Domingo* (Sunday), Rogério and I were planning a repertoire for Gal that would reconcile the antagonism between MPB and Jovem Guarda, as much as it would transcend that other, deeper opposition between bossa nova and traditional samba, or even the broader one between sophisticated modern music (whether it be bossa nova, samba-jazz, neoregional, or protest song) and the standard commercial music of whatever origin (Argentine tangos, whorehouse boleros, sentimental *sambas-canções,* etc.).

Guilherme Araújo, who had fallen in love with Bethânia's expressiveness from the first night at the Teatro Opinião, was looking to move up from simple producer to true impresario, and he saw in Bethânia's group of friends a possible lineup commensurate with his dreams. Guilherme was a fascinating character. He had slight arms and narrow shoulders, and an overall ugliness that, taken with his apparent lack of modesty, provided every possible rationale to find him repulsive, yet he would in fact end up charming anyone willing to look beyond the first moment of encounter. There was a kind of nobility in the frankness and originality of his opinions about show business. He would repeat incessantly his praise of Bethânia, which was also a synthesis of his philosophy: "International, my dear. She is the most international of all the Brazilian singers." Guilherme, who had lived in Europe before he met us, liked to use this expression. We found it funny, but we understood what he meant: that Bethânia could be recognized internationally as a great artist, as great as Edith Piaf or Judy Garland, notwithstanding the fact that she sang in Portuguese and was from an "underdeveloped" country. For him, we, the other Bahians, were the confirmation of what he saw in Bethânia. We were "cool" and "modern" and we, too, could be "international." But though he did come to work with the whole group—and he has remained at our side, long after Bethânia disconnected herself from him—it always seemed to me that none of us ever impressed him the way Bethânia had.

He opened up an office in Copacabana to direct operations and began to make plans for his new artists. He invited Dedé to be his secretary. Guilherme felt sure about Bethânia and Gil, whose careers had by then taken off. But he could not envision the possibility of my getting up on a stage to sing and making a living at it. I would answer, with a growing confidence that would make him laugh incredulously, that I was sure I had such talent, but the truth is that he considered my only hope to be precisely in what I myself imagined doing: advising my friends, writing songs and scripts for their shows, liner notes for their records. As for Gal, he felt she really could make a living singing, and he foresaw a radiant future for her. Her beautiful voice and sweet presence were enough for us to see how she could become a new "yeah-yeah" girl, a queen of pop. As she liked to say, smiling at our reservations, she would not be just another commercial singer, but a new kind, with an intelligent repertoire. Dedé in particular, to whom Gal was almost a sister, was afraid that Guilherme would push her toward a degrading kind of vulgarity. Interestingly enough, Guilherme's plans for Gal were, finally, very similar to those that Rogério and I were on the verge of proposing. (I didn't mention these plans to Guilherme, afraid to contaminate the nobility of Rogério's project with what might prove just another form of commercialism.)

A discussion symbolic of these subtle conflicts took place over Gal's stage name. Her real name is Maria da Graça Costa Penna Burgos. Back in Salvador, we would write Maria da Graça in the posters and the programs for the shows at Vila Velha, and would otherwise call her Gracinha, or more affectionately, Gau. There were and are thousands of Gaus in Bahia: it is the term of endearment used for all the Marias da Graça or Graças out there. In fact, in the case of our Gal, Maria da Graça was only the name on her ID card and the one she used artistically; for all intents and purposes her name was Gracinha—that is how we would talk about her in front of strangers, that's how we would introduce her to new friends. Among ourselves, however, she was Gau. Guilherme thought that Maria da Graça would not do for a singer. He agreed that it was beautiful and noble-sounding, but it was more suggestive of an old Portuguese *fado* singer than a modern one. It was even less appropriate—and here he would smile diabolically—for the new queen of pop. He liked "Gau." We did too. First because it was her real name (and that mattered to us), and then because it was pretty and easy to remember; in Rio and in São Paulo it was not as common a nickname as it was in Bahia. But there were two problems: Guilherme thought it vulgar and "poor" for an artist to have only one name; and Gau, written like this, with a *u,* seemed to him a bit heavy and not very feminine. Since almost everywhere in Brazil Gal and Gau are pronounced the same way, we thought the spelling was insignificant. There was still the question of the last name. Gal Penna? Gal Burgos? Guilherme, with some justification, preferred Gal Costa. It sounded better than the other two. Knowing our intransigence in the matter, he did not dare go beyond her actual surnames. But I didn't like it. I thought I had already made enough concessions in accepting the *l,* so he should accept the single name: Gal, simply, was the best solution. But he insisted on the last name, and I responded that Gal Costa sounded like a made-up name, a brand name, a toothpaste, and, finally, that it wasn't feminine enough. Gal is, furthermore, the abbreviation of "general." And since General Costa e Silva had just come into power, replacing General Castelo Branco, Gal Costa would be the homonym of the second president under the despicable military regime. But Gal herself, who after all should have had the last word in the matter, accepted the name, and it has worked out very well with the pop image that was created for her.

It still annoys me today when I hear someone say that Gal Costa is an invented name and that her real name is Gracinha or Maria da Graça. Gal or Gau was always her name, more so than Maria da Graça, and only those who had not known her well would think that the name used by intimate friends was Gracinha. And yet that name, Gal Costa, more than any other, sounded like it had been invented. Now that everyone calls her Gal, I'm finally at peace with the whole story: it's her name, it's a Bahian name; as Guilherme desired, it is international and pop, but also personal and regional to the core. It is a deeply poetic find, made of happenstance and misunderstandings, which is an apt metaphor for the *tropicalista* drama.

Gal had come from Bahia, like myself, in the wake of Bethânia and Gil, to try to become a professional singer. She had never wanted to do anything else in her life besides singing. Gil had a degree in business management, and that was his profession. Bethânia had dreamed of being an actress, written short stories, and made sculptures. I had been a painter, had wanted to be a professor, and still wanted to be a film-maker. But Gal wanted to be a singer and nothing else. Dedé used to say that as a child Gal used the pots and pans in the kitchen to amplify her voice in her own ears, and thus gain better control over it, as if she were in a recording studio. All the young musicians were charmed by her voice, and the collaboration with them in *Domingo* was going very well. Edu composed a song for her "in the style of the Bahian group" (that was really quite a compliment, since what he normally composed was harmonically much superior to anything we did), a song called "Candeias," about the memory of a vacation in Pernambuco, and I still consider that song Gal's best interpretation on our first record. For me, everything happened in the studio—I was not overly timid—because I was already deep in new projects that distanced me from the material we were recording. Talking to Rogério and Agrippino, or in a discussion with Guilherme, listening to Bethânia's advice on Roberto Carlos, or listening to Roberto Carlos himself, seeing *Land in Anguish* and watching the absurd antics of Chacrinha, the outlandish TV personality, or while composing "Paisagem útil" and "Alegria, alegria," I sang the songs in *Domingo* with indifferent boldness. Still, when I listen to this record today, I am aghast at the slowness of my attack, and I'm annoyed at the mental sluggishness that it reveals. When I'm in a good mood I attribute it to the morning schedule of the recording sessions.

Domingo should have already been finished when Gil, who had quit Gessy Lever and moved with his wife and daughters to Rio, received an invitation from I don't know who in Pernambuco to do a series of shows in Recife. Guilherme went with him. When the two of them came back, Gil was transformed. Perhaps it was the many days he had spent away from his family—he was then still a novice in that sort of solitary voyage that excites the mind—that had made him more sensitive and receptive to the stimulus of Pernambuco's cultural character, to the suggestive of the singularity of our situation as Brazilians under a military government we loathed, to the contradictions of our professional projects. The fact is that he returned to Rio wanting to change everything, rethink everything—and, ceaselessly, he demanded from us an unconditional adherence to a program of action that he was sketching with both anxiety and impatience. He would talk about the violence of poverty and the power of artistic invention: that was the double lesson he had learned in Pernambuco, and he wanted to draw on it to chart a path for us. The vision of those miserably poor people in the Northeast, the gag imposed by the dictatorship in a state where political awareness had reached impressive maturity (Miguel Arraes's government had been the most significant example of someone listening to the popular voice until his arrest and deportation in 1964) and where the experiments of politically engaged art had gone the furthest, Gil's listening to the *ciranda* masters performing on the beaches, but above all to the Banda de Pífanos of Caruaru (a musical group composed of simple flautists from the interior of Pernambuco whose profound regional character fused with an inventiveness that fearlessly proclaimed its modernity—the cut that most impressed us was in fact called "Pipoca moderna" [Modern Popcorn])—all of these things had turned him into an exacting taskmaster. He said we could not continue on the defensive, nor ignore the business side of the industry in which we had inserted ourselves. Nor could we ignore the characteristics of mass culture whose mechanisms we could understand only by penetrating them. He said he was in love with a song by the Beatles called "Strawberry Fields Forever," which, in his mind, suggested what we should be doing and was similar to Banda de Pífanos' "Pipoca moderna." Both sounded experimental and delicate at the same time. Finally, Gil wanted us to hold meetings with our well-intentioned colleagues, in order to involve them in a movement that would unleash the truly revolutionary forces of Brazilian music, beyond the ideological slogans of protest music, the elegant chains of altered chords, the narrow nationalism.

None of that was exactly new to me, except in the sense that it was now coming at me relentlessly and all at once. Nevertheless it was surprising that it would be coming from Gil. The truth is that much of what he was talking about was already part of the unfulfilled plan I had made with Rogério for Gal, as it was in my "Paisagem útil," and in my conversations with Guilherme. Gil himself had been producing with Carlos Capinan a series of proto-*tropicalista* songs for the film *Brazil, Year 2000,* by Walter Lima, Jr., a lengthy science-fiction fantasy that had been profoundly influenced by *Land in Anguish.* But now Gil had come back with frightening clarity and vehemence—a transformation of sorts for someone who had always been more interested in politics than I and was ordinarily more adaptable and passive. Guilherme Araújo, having accompanied him to Recife, certainly took advantage of the time to motivate his artistic ambitions. Yes, Guilherme must not be seen simply as a sharply opportunistic impresario—actually, his entrepreneurial abilities, properly speaking, were actually always questionable, and yielded some rather disastrous results over time—but also (and especially) as a young man with a creative temperament, who saw in the Bahian group a possibility for realizing his dream of changing the face of Brazilian show business. He was, in fact, the co-idealizer of the movement. Gil seemed rather to have used that push Guilherme gave him as a catalyst and a pretext to express his own wishes. Suddenly, Gil was acting more like someone with a mission. Without a second's hesitation—and having already convinced me to pay as much attention to the Beatles as to Roberto Carlos—he sought out all our closest colleagues and those we most identified with, to set up meetings. Sérgio Ricardo, who had done the soundtrack for *Black God, White Devil,* and who was one of the most militant composers to come out of bossa nova (Carlos Lyra had moved to Mexico), turned out to be the most interested, and the first meeting was to take place at his house. I think there were only two, in fact. Capinan, Torquato Neto, Sidney Miller, Edu, Chico Buarque, and I, besides Sérgio Ricardo and Gil, were present at both. Perhaps Francis Hime and Dori came to one or the other, I'm not sure. I do remember this much clearly: Chico—bohemian and wary of programs—would get drunk and make ironic remarks about what he had barely listened to, while Sérgio Ricardo would misinterpret Gil's words. For instance, Gil's phrase "to be really popular" moved Sérgio to suggest that we do shows at the entrance to factories. Gil had an awful time trying to make himself understood. Whenever he mentioned rural music from Pernambuco, one could almost hear someone say that Edu was already working on that satisfactorily; and when he talked about the Beatles, some lowered their eyes, others opened them—all mouths were closed. He didn't dare speak about Roberto Carlos. And, after a tense pause, someone would say something just to show that he had understood it all to be a clever if somewhat dishonest strategy—and therefore destined to fail: to make music that was more commercial so it could better serve as a vehicle for revolutionary ideas. In the end, Gil did not give up trying to make himself understood, even though the others gave up trying to follow him. It was up to us to go it alone.

But who were "we"? Gil, of course, and I, and we would naturally count on Gal as interpreter and muse, as well as Guilherme, who would buy and sell our ideas. Bethânia? She had been one of those to pioneer the dislocations of *brega* songs, with the most aggressively lowbrow sentimentalism, and, at the same time, she had recommended Roberto Carlos: she was an obvious companion. But now things had changed. With Gil's return from Recife, all the scattered aims and fuzzy notions had gathered into a conscious and intentional project for a movement that demanded a kind of militancy. Gil and I both recognized Bethânia's ferocious individualism and capacity to understand the most complex of our ideas, yet we also knew she would resist involvment far more vigorously than any of our colleagues who hadn't understood a thing. In the end Bethânia would always know of our decisions (and indecisions), frequently approve of them, but remain on the sidelines, defending her individuality tooth and claw. It was her way of reaffirming her profound understanding of what we usually call "life."

The other two natural companions would have been the poets Capinan and Torquato. José Carlos Capinan was already respected and famous among the college students of Salvador before I entered the School of Philosophy. I remember the afternoon he was introduced to me, at Hélio Rocha's home. Hélio was a professor of sociology who became part of the Catholic Left and had a cultural journal called *Afirmação,* to which he invited young people to contribute. I had published an article on *Hiroshima, mon amour,* and I think Capinan had been publishing some of his poems there as well. The fact that Capinan was always called a poet had inspired in me an expectation of something nearly sacred; indeed the scrawny figure of a sallow, freckled boy from the backlands seemed angelic to me, or essentially artistic, as if he were the redeemed soul of the "yellow soldier" in Graciliano Ramos's *Barren Lives,* or a painted ceramic figure of a boy with a birdcage such as a Northeastern craftsman might make. I knew from the first moment I saw him that I would always like him, and that it would always be difficult for us to communicate, even though there would be no conflicts. There was no easy identification in those areas of personality that facilitate communication—and too much in those deeper and more mysterious regions: he had the suspicious aridity of the *sertanejo* who learns everything as if with great difficulty, and I, the sweet receptivity of a person from the *recôncavo,* who freely receives both his gifts and his sorrows; both of us, however, were in love with words and invisible images.

An activist in the CPC of UNE, Capinan was Bahia's revolutionary poet—"the engaged poet"—at the beginning of the sixties. I, who had as many misgivings about the political certainties that nurtured his poems as I had about the practice of making poems out of political certainties, whatever they might be, perceived in his personal aura—in what I knew of his work—something far beyond that role. In short, he seemed to be a real poet. At the time when *tropicalismo* was brewing, he was already living in Rio. Having been in hiding for some time to avoid arrest in 1964, he was incubating the poems that would eventually become his book *Inquisitorial,* in which the love of word and image overcomes ideological rhetoric. Capinan was never shocked by anything we said. Tinged with a caustic, almost sadistic wit, his conversations were nevertheless amiable, and never led to arguments. We were always left with the impression that he had understood only too well, which is to say he hadn't understood anything. In this way, our conversations with him, however peaceful, were somewhat tense all the same. And this sense grew at every turn as it became clear that his inevitable distance—and reflexive independence—was due to the originality of his personal project as poet, which developed alongside his activity as a lyricist of popular music. There was in him a purity that placed him above the fads, guile, and games endemic to our bohemian milieu. He would spend endless hours working on his poems, or reading the works of various other poets.

Most important, he wanted to call my attention to a book by two brothers from São Paulo—Augusto and Haroldo de Campos, the leaders of the concrete poetry movement that had emerged in the fifties. These poets would become key participants in the future of *tropicalismo.*

I never forgot the name of the author whom the brothers were trying to resuscitate critically: Sousândrade, the singular romantic poet from Maranhão whose *Inferno de Wall Street*—with its multilingual stanzas, purposeful attention to material aspects of the poem, and its hermetic and unexpected images—had anticipated and even surpassed some of the procedures of the modernists. Capinan showed me this book, and it made a lively impression on me, though without inducing me to stop and study it: I was too much caught up in the scandals that I wanted to unleash.

Unlike Capinan, Torquato Neto seemed to understand immediately what we wanted to say, and was always ready to discuss it. We related easily to each other, and our discussions were friendly. Duda had introduced him to me in Salvador, where he had come from his native Teresina to spend some time before going on to Rio. He was also busy with a notebook full of poems that might become a book someday. Torquato loved Carlos Drummond de Andrade, for most people the greatest Brazilian poet, a modernist of the second generation who started writing in the thirties and worked until the eighties; his poems were overtly Drummondian. They all seemed elegant to me, with a good sound, sensitive and sober, delicate and long—and they did not partake of the political naïveté of Capinan. The only thing he was missing was that sense of dedication that made Capinan a poet, perhaps a good poet, even if not a great one, but a poet. Torquato had the knack, but he did not study enough, he did not feel so seriously responsible for the poetry he produced, even if his ear for rhythms and rhymes was much more spontaneously sensitive than Capinan's, and even if his delicacy and imagination seemed more fluid.

We lived in the same world: communication between us was quick and fun. Unlike the Bahians, who had all developed some sort of critical attitude toward Rio de Janeiro, Torquato adored Rio like a traditional immigrant, who wants to distance himself rapidly from his original home and assimilate into Carioca life. Ana, the girlfriend whom he would soon marry, was an intelligent woman with a very strong personality. Although Bahian by birth, she had grown up in Rio and would say, laughing, that she hated the accent we had all brought from Salvador. Above all, it seemed to Torquato an endless miracle to live in the same city as Carlos Drummond de Andrade and Nelson Rodrigues. At times he would follow the two poets on the street, without their knowing it (or so he believed), and it would be as though he had participated in some clandestine rite. Sometimes he would confess his great desire to become a journalist in Rio, to write a column. He enjoyed directing all the taxi drivers who transported him around Zona Sul to take the beach route; then he would look them straight in the eye and say—as if it were lyric sensibility itself confronting the spirit of practicality— "because it is nicer." The Carioca taxi drivers, practical but poetic metropolitan men, pretended not to hear the wherefores, and Torquato would smile at me impishly, doubly satisfied: he had played his role as a folk character in the city, and he had reassured himself that the city was Rio de Janeiro. I loved him. There was no one else, not Duda, Rogério, not Capinan, much less Zé Agrippino—not even Gil, whose loyalty brought us together so easily without ever taking the form of an intimate and confessional type of friendship. He drank a lot, sometimes he was depressed, and he ended up committing suicide—after a series of botched attempts—in 1972, but "lightness" is the word that best describes the atmosphere that took hold of me whenever he came near.

He had formed a partnership with Edu ("Pra dizer adeus," a beautiful song they composed, became a classic), and from the middle of 1966 until about the middle of 1967 he had a close relationship with Chico Buarque, who by this time was already living in Rio with Marieta Severo. Chico was my pal from the drunken nights of São Paulo, before he moved to Rio. I was going to São Paulo to participate in the series of programs at TV Record. When my song "Boa palavra" won fifth or sixth place in the TV Excelsior festival, I made a few trips to São Paulo to collect the prize (it was something like a round-trip to Rome, or the equivalent in cash—and I wanted the equivalent in cash, because I was paying the rent at the Solar da Fossa with the unreliable royalties from "De manhã"), but I never received anything. Bethânia, who was already doing nightclub shows, had been invited to participate in a program at Record called *Esta Noite se Improvisa* (Tonight We Improvise). This was a competition between singers and composers in which a word was given and one of them—whoever first pressed the button at his feet, lighting up a panel—would have to sing a song with that word in it. Bethânia was unsure if she wanted to do this; although it would be a professional coup for her to appear on TV Record, she was not good at that kind of game, and she was afraid she would not be able to think of a single song. I tried to tell her it would be easy (in fact, it was a game we used to play around the table at the Cervantes, long before the program came into existence), and I suggested that we practice a little: I would try a word on her, and then she on me, always increasing the degree of difficulty, from common words, like *"flor,"* flower, and *"coração,"* heart, to more obscure ones such as *"lancha,"* motorboat, or *"considero,"* I consider. We were at a fast-food place near TV Record, where Bethânia had to go for a rehearsal. We laughed a lot, because while Bethânia hesitated, I could place any word in some song, and I could almost always sing the song in its entirety. A good-looking gray-haired man who was sitting on one of the high stools at the bar ended up bringing his lunch over and saying: "I'm Nilton Travesso, producer at TV Record, how are you, Bethânia?" and, tilting his face in my direction, asked "Who's he?" Travesso already knew about me because of "De manhã" and, once his suspicions were confirmed, that is to say, once I admitted to being Bethânia's brother, the composer, he invited me then and there to participate in the program. That same night I had my premiere on TV and from then on my knowledge of lyrics to Brazilian songs and my memory have been legendary. Chico Buarque was my greatest competitor, with one advantage: his repertoire was more extensive than mine and his memory equally fresh; in addition he was capable of inventing on the spot songs that sounded so good they seemed like jewels of our tradition. In the months following my debut we won various Gordini cars—which we would sell immediately without looking into whether we were losing anything in the transaction. And I became, in addition to being famous, very rich, by my standards. I ended up going to São Paulo almost every week.

The nights out with Chico and his friend the musician Toquinho were delicious, and São Paulo ceased being the detestable place of my first experience there. Guilherme, who by then divided his time between São Paulo and Rio (and tried to convince us that Rio was passé), had rented an apartment on Paulista Avenue, where I would stay. Chico had a car and knew everything about the city where he had grown up and gone to school. Sometimes he drank too much, and we would have to wake him up to take us back home. We were not afraid that he had been practically asleep before taking the wheel, because once on the road he displayed remarkable dexterity. Toquinho was a sweet and solid guy, very playful, but without guile, the typical Paulista who seems naïve in the eyes of other Brazilians. But Chico, with those beautiful green eyes that he would fix on us with diabolical hardness, was endowed with a sense of humor that was even more sadistic than Capinan's. At that time his good looks were extraordinary, at once angelic and demonic—nearly divine at any rate—but he did not seem to me sexually attractive, unlike Toquinho, who every once in a while sparked a vague and happy homoerotic promise, provoking me playfully to call him "my fiancé," without causing him the least embarrassment. In fact, girls were our most common topic of conversation. Chico would pretend to be jealous of me and his girlfriends, and in Rio he would even tell Dedé that I pursued them. One night he asked me along to the house of an old flame of his, whose parents disapproved of his attentions. She was coming back from Europe that day, having been away a long time, and he wanted us to serenade her. We were drunk, and I ended up climbing a tree in front of the girl's window, where I sang I don't know what old *seresta* song or a song by Chico himself. Dedé used to laugh at his stories, but she would ask me anxious questions when he left. The only time I betrayed Dedé was with one of those girls from São Paulo, and it was not a girlfriend of Chico's, but one of Toquinho's, and it was in Rio. And Chico hadn't even found out about it.

By then Chico was already a great star, with the enormous success of his *marchinha* called "A banda" in the Record festival of 1966, and he began to spend more and more time in Rio, until he finally moved there. Paradoxically, perhaps because we lived in the same city, we saw less and less of each other. Or perhaps it was that, even as he was gradually moving to Rio, I was spending more and more time in São Paulo. But I was still present at the first and pivotal encounters between him and Marieta, at a party at the Solar da Fossa. And after they moved in together, I visited them every once in a while. But Torquato got into the habit of visiting them assiduously.

It was not without suspicion that Torquato received the news, as it got out, that we were intent on subverting the MPB status quo. At that time, I was already professionally secure: the weekly appearances on *Esta Noite se Improvisa* assured me money and fame, and my song "Um dia" had won the prize for best lyrics in the same festival that made Chico famous. Around the time that Gil was organizing his meetings, Torquato had himself already seized upon the transformative ideas: the Beatles, Roberto Carlos, Chacrinha's TV program, direct contact with the real roots of Northeastern aesthetic expression—all of that had been digested and metabolized by Torquato with enough spontaneity to make us sure he really understood the program we were embracing. His uncluttered intelligence had allowed him to overcome all his initial resistance. From then on, his agreement with the project became organic and, if anything, worrisome. Such was his tendency to hew to the new principles as though they were dogma while despising the old ones with excessive ferocity. While Capinan seemed to hide in his heart of hearts his remaining fears about the antinationalist, antipopulist, or even vulgar risks of our undertaking, Torquato, showing that he truly understood the implications of those risks, seemed ready to become a somewhat intransigent herald.

I remember a revealing discussion with him. In 1967, people were talking about a Brazilian B movie that Glauber Rocha had liked, *À meia-noite levarei tua alma* (I'll Take Your Soul at Midnight), directed by the Paulista José Mojica Marins. In him Glauber sensed a primitive Nietzsche, although the production was a horror movie made on the sort of precarious budget typical of a small-town Brazilian circus. The director went around wearing the same black cape and long nails of the character he had created in the film (and in others afterwards). Marins was—in every sense—popular. In the film, he both exposed our poverty and attacked the religious conventions that were inimical to a bold individual will. The Catholic imagination appeared mixed with the pornography of terror, laughable visual effects, and dialogues on the edge of street language. Torquato insisted that it was pure charm on Glauber's (and my) part to show aesthetic interest in such a pile of trash. He did not believe I could see in the film a radical version of what Glauber had tried to do in *Land in Anguish.* But it was truly difficult, at the time, to admit to a critical posture that, soon after, would become commonplace. (It would be inspired again by the old black-and-white version of *The Fly, Freaks,* and *The Incredible Shrinking Man,* all of which delighted me at the Electric Cinema when I arrived in London in 1969; and Torquato himself to this day is remembered for his participation as an actor in *Nosferatu no Brasil* [Nosferatu in Brazil], a film made in the seventies by Ivan Cardoso, which gave rise to a cult of Mojica Marins and kindred figures, a cult defended ferociously by Torquato in the column he then wrote for a Carioca newspaper, wherein he conducted, on behalf of "marginal" cinema, a campaign against Cinema Novo with which position I could never agree.)

But Torquato was also close to me in his understanding that, while Capinan was willing and ready to become what used to be called—in the old days—a poet, the rest of us wanted to discover a new kind of poetry. In fact, I believed I was establishing a new way of being a poet that did not depend on the traditional rites of the trade. I was under the illusion that one could make use of the old habit of referring to the *sambistas de morro* as poets—and of the total adherence of Vinicius de Moraes, a genuine poet, to popular song—as a means of coming into direct contact with great poetry, through a combination of songs made with an eye to a public that would act upon the meaning of the words.

In reality, up until then I had never dared to think of being a poet: my experiments had been in drawing and painting, in critical prose (film and popular music), and in songwriting. "Poet" inspired too much awe, it was scary and embarrassing, and I had always shrunk from the idea. But the fact is that I already considered João Gilberto a great poet, in every sense, because of the rhythm and the musical phrasing he could intertwine with the sounds and the meanings of the words he sang. A revolutionary creator like Glauber Rocha—without the latter's faults, his heavy hand or awkwardness. On the same level as João Cabral and João Guimarães Rosa, but creating for a large audience, and immediately influencing the art and life of Brazilians. It occurred to me I could be a little like Glauber, a little like João Gilberto, launching that new set of ideas into the midst of popular music. And popular music is the Brazilian form of expression par excellence. Today I think the ambition to be "a little Glauber, a little João Gilberto" is ridiculous. But the absurdity was not in the overarching ambition—which, even when ridiculous, can be the motor and the sign of creative energy. The absurdity was in the fact that the very formula was all wrong. Fortunately, it was not possible to become "a little Glauber, a little João": that was just a silly way of acknowledging that I had to become myself.

bahiunos

Of course I did not see myself carrying out this poetic adventure on my own. The sense of a group was very powerful. When Rogério heard me argue passionately, he provoked me by saying I was only an apostle while Gil was the prophet; it seemed to me he was reading my innermost thoughts. I felt responsible for the great and beautiful task, since Gil and Gal (and even Bethânia, in spite of her cry of independence) would always need my advice, directly or indirectly, but the true poetic message would be delivered collectively—and beginning with Gil. It was never unclear to me that the group to which I belonged was made up of the four of us, whatever might happen. I had felt this way since the old days at the Vila Velha. Outside our quartet, I saw two distinct groups of people: the musicians who played with us there—Tom Zé, Alcivando Luz, Djalma Correia, Perna Fróes, Piti, Fernando Lona (and my friends) Alvinho, Duda, Waly, Roberto Pinho, and later Rogério, Agrippino, Guilherme, Torquato, and Capinan, mostly nonmusicians (although Rogério plays classical guitar and Torquato and Capinan ended up writing song lyrics), all of them interested in literature, poetry, cinema, history, and so on. I loved and admired them all, but they never meant to me what the four of us did. Duda and Waly, and Torquato, and even Rogério were more intimate friends of mine than Gil or Gal had ever been. But the vision I had of our common destiny, the certainty that we were comrades in the struggle to a degree the others would never experience, that's what bound us together. Perhaps it was only an intuition of the vocation for stardom—and how often, alas, many years after those heroic days, have I thought that maybe it was nothing more than an attraction to the emptiest of stardoms! But the truth of the matter is that I saw an intense light shining on us that did not seem to fall on the others. I did not experience what was happening to us as the fulfillment of my personal ambitions. My inner conviction was that once the point of no return had been reached, I would leave the three of them to their respective destinies—Gil, the authentic musician; Gal, the real singer; Bethânia, the true dramatic star of song—and I would find my way in filmmaking or literature. "In a year, a year and a half, I'll be free," I thought.

Money seemed to be coming in an avalanche. In fact there was not much: the Gordinis from TV Record, the pocket change from royalties. Up until then, I had lived more on what Dedé could earn in her various jobs than on the unreliable and parsimonious royalties, and the welcome assistance that My Daia would discreetly send me from Bahia. All of this covered my room in the Solar, the avocado shake with waffles for breakfast, cigarettes, and movies, enough since the day's main meal (whether lunch or dinner) was always at Dedé's grandmother's house. Forever unable to bring myself to care for money and therefore perpetually unaware of how it is made, I believed that *Esta Noite se Improvisa* had brought in much more than it had, so much that when I became a real professional I could go a long time without working. It never crossed my mind that it might be necessary or even desirable to lead a less modest life. I imagined that once our mission had been accomplished and I had separated myself from the others, I would study and work with Duda, or Waly, or on my own.

There were two intersecting groups: on the one hand, those who would eventually become the *tropicalistas* (among whom I count Torquato, Capinan, and Rogério—and soon would include a great number of Cariocas and Paulistas) and, on the other hand, those already known in Rio as the "Bahians": the four of us. Bethânia, with her refusal to be a militant, was the one who brought the pattern into the light. And deep down I was acting as the person who would always put *tropicalismo* at the service of the Bahians. The four of us were the center of my attentions: we were bound to become stars and I knew it if vaguely. In 1966 it seemed that the movement suggested by Gil was necessary to renovate MPB, but that great event would also be a kind of definitive launching of the Bahian group, with its peculiar set of interests. Since both necessitated a transformation of musical tastes, our appearance on the scene could occur only through a rupture. It had already started with Bethânia's explosion of popularity and the development of her complex public persona, beginning with the nightclub shows. In the late eighties, the Carioca journalist Paulo Francis would write from New York for a newspaper in São Paulo that, when he saw Bethânia singing "Carcará," having replaced Nara in 1964, he understood that Rio had changed and that from then on "those people" (the dread Northeastern contingent, whom he despised) were Rio. In the seventies, the Carioca newspaper *O Pasquim* would call us "Bahiunos," a slur upon the perceived unity of the barbaric invaders. But in 1966, people were already talking about the "Bahian group" with a mixture of fondness, curiosity, and suspicion: the term *"báfia"* was coined (a pun on "mafia") to characterize our alleged tendency to help each other out, which also earned us comparisons to the Jews, and, last but not least, there were rumors that inspired the term *"surubaiana,"* which could be a piquant way of referring to the fond way we treated each other, but which implied a sexual message that was feared (and perhaps secretly desired—*suruba* means orgy).

At this point Gal and I were not as famous as Gil and Bethânia, but we were almost finished with the record that would bring us our own prestige. In strictly professional terms, there was no need for any kind of launch (an expression that would have seemed to us strange at the time): things were going just fine. The movement Gil was trying to organize was actually a rather risky move for our careers. But for me, the sense of a mission made the movement a necessity—and brought a certain air of infallibility to the enterprise. If there was a risk, there was no choice but to face it squarely, if we wanted to be known for what we really were. True, we were already known—and it was not for what we weren't—but if we were to grow it would be only by following the course that encompassed the gamut of themes and problems eventually to be known as *tropicalismo.* I encouraged Gil's impatience, envisioning in my fantasy the break with MPB to be something cataclysmic. My thinking was continually engaged in the new shapes we were unleashing: I lived in a trance.

Zé Agrippino's book, *Panamérica,* was finally published. When he was interviewed by the *Jornal do Brasil,* he made a statement that Gil's music was an example of everything he did not like: "I'm from São Paulo. I've grown up among glass and concrete—I can't stand that sweet stuff, that Bahian stuff. I prefer rock to MPB. But I find the violence missing even in Brazilian rock." He claimed to be an urban man, from the modern world, and he didn't recognize himself in the Brazilian culture. I was intrigued by this attack, which seemed to be a secret appreciation of Gil as well as a provocation and a challenge to me. In the late eighties, Agrippino, by then retired and lonely, agreed to be interviewed by some young people from São Paulo who wanted to pay him homage, and in that interview he remembered the *tropicalista* Bahians, insisting he had never been much interested in "those people."

Panamérica had nothing to do with what I knew and loved as literature:

> It was darker in that dark corner behind the pile of cans, where Marilyn Monroe, Marlon Brando, and I used to get together. I lifted up Marilyn Monroe's skirt and made her sit on my erect penis. Marilyn moved up and down, and Marlon Brando excitedly masturbated, looking on as Marilyn went up and down on my organ. Cecil B. de Mille and Tony Curtis came back pushing the cart full of preserves. I, Marlon Brando, and Marilyn Monroe looked on impassively over the pile of cans as we waited for the director and the actor. The three of us were seen from the head up—our bodies hidden behind the pile of cans. Cecil B. de Mille passed by, accompanied by Tony Curtis, and we nodded at him, and then Marilyn started again moving up and down on my hard penis.

There is a scene in which the narrator, having killed the American military attaché, runs away and disappears among a group of tourists apparently visiting the statue of Christ of Corcovado—at least the description of the tour leaves no doubt that it is the Carioca monument. But, unlike the Hollywood stars, the great European politicians, the Cuban revolutionaries—and even the Statue of Liberty itself—all of which are mentioned without explanation, since their names already say everything, the Rio Christ is described with detailed objectivity (though with small and calculated distortions), as if it were something remote and imagined, while no mention is made of the name of the city or the famous mountain on which the statue stands. Every chapter consists of one paragraph, in which Hollywood celebrities, or well-known figures from politics, sports, or music, interact with the narrator. The language is repetitive, fast, impassive in the face of the enormities described, without subtlety or variation. The very graphic or diagrammatic aspect of the pages—a succession of identical rectangles formed by words that fill them almost completely, without a pause for breath, a blank space, a dialogue, a dash anywhere—produces the sensation of severe visual monotony, sustained by the exuberantly oneiric character of the narrative. The words engender visions: there is nothing beyond the surface. No concession is made to psychology or sociology, much less to any formalism or stylistic elegance. For someone used to the lacy and erudite prose of Guimarães Rosa, the dryness of Graciliano Ramos, and the hypersensibility of Clarice Lispector, *Panamérica* was both a shock and a challenge.

As with his reaction to *Land in Anguish,* Duda could not go along with such an adventure; evidently, he liked Agrippino's book even less than Glauber's film. But I took into consideration the radicalism of the project and decided it deserved attention. Besides, awed as I have always been by Agrippino's unique intelligence, I naturally suspected the fault lay with my own judgment long before I thought about his.

The great Brazilian scientist Mário Schemberg, a physicist and a connoisseur of literature, an extremely refined intellectual who was already in his sixties, wrote on the flap of the book that Agrippino had given us "a contemporary epic of the American Empire." Schemberg was a communist who also had an interest in Eastern wisdom (from the Mahabharata to Zen). "The emergence of new myths," he wrote, "is one of the most important aspects of the twentieth century. Its impact on culture has made itself felt with ever increasing amplitude, attaining traditional forms of artistic expression such as literature and the visual arts, after manifesting itself in cinema and comic books. . . . José Agrippino borrows the mythic figures from cinema, as well as the technique of narration through images . . . avoiding all psychological analysis. . . . He combines the minute description of the *Iliad* with an authentic fantastic imagination, akin to Gulliver's adventures. Homer and Swift are the two great literary influences in José Agrippino."

My conversations with Rogério had led me to find unsuspected aesthetic pleasure in comic books, a pleasure that I imagined was the inspiration for a poetic prose different in every way from the somewhat rustic style of Zé Agrippino. His characters were all myths of mass media, and the criterion for their choice was that the names would be internationally recognized as soon as they were mentioned.

In '67, the only comment I heard Rogério utter about the book— something he said at the Cervantes in front of the author—was that it did not belong to any Brazilian literary tradition, with the possible exception of the modernists Mário de Andrade and Oswald de Andrade. I, who at the time was not very familiar with Mário and knew nothing of Oswald, could not imagine that the latter would eventually be the connection between the *tropicalistas* and our most antagonistic admirers. No doubt, the later encounter with Oswald de Andrade's work, among other things, would contribute to my positive reevaluation of Agrippino's writing. In '67, his radical book filled my head with questions regarding literature in Brazil and Latin America, and literature in general on the periphery of the world economy. Those questions have not lost their relevance today.

In sum, *Panamérica,* which seemed to have come after *tropicalismo,* did not influence it. In fact, the book came close to inhibiting its emergence. And by expatiating here on the book, I am still asking the world what it was all about. Still, having rejected Gil's Bahianness from the perspective of a São Paulo native, without knowing that Gil wanted to be much closer to him than to the Cariocas, and having published a book that produced such an impact, Agrippino gave me a priceless point of reference by which to measure our own actions.

alegria, alegria

I t was already 1967 when *Domingo,* the record I did with Gal, was released. The reception was more enthusiastic than I had expected. The radical Joãogilbertist attitude, combined with an originality born more often of limitation than invention, impressed our colleagues who were getting tired of the jazzy gimmicks so common in those days. A drop of regional flavor (genuine or artificial) completed the charm of this modest record. Dori Caymmi was the producer, and for me it was he who made it possible for *Domingo* to be the first album of the Bahian group to achieve some freedom from the musical vices of the period. I had finally found some partial solutions to the problems I had tried to discuss with Augusto Boal when Bethânia did her first record.

"*Saudade,*" the famously untranslatable word (often loosely rendered as "nostalgia"), is a commonplace in Luso-Brazilian poetry as well as an emblem of the Portuguese language; in an unexplained accident of etymology, it traverses a semantic field that encompasses something peculiar about our way of being. Now I was beginning to leave behind *saudade* as a theme: most songs in *Domingo* are nostalgic for Santo Amaro, or for the pure good of an old poetic time; the cool-jazz influence through bossa nova is there, and quite consciously. But even while I was recording the songs on *Domingo,* I was already working on new things that would incorporate *saudade* differently in a future project— "Paisagem útil" and other proto-*tropicalista* songs, including "Alegria, alegria." In these the pop imagery and the rock sounds would be conspicuous, offering as contrast to the bossa nova style of *Domingo* a bit of the vulgar and the commercial.

The record company was responsible for the cover. Gal and I were taken to the Glória hills, near the center of Rio, to be photographed before the old church there, to give the impression we were in Bahia. The black-and-white photos were surrounded by letters and designs on the verge of melting—a typical sixties look—in loud blue and pink tones. I found it depressing, although I liked what I had written for the back:

My current inspiration is leaning toward paths very different from those I've followed up to this point. . . . I no longer desire to thrive on nostalgia for other times and places; on the contrary, I wish to incorporate that nostalgia in a future project.

In this I came close to offering a manifesto for *tropicalismo*.

At the Solar da Fossa, I showed the first copy of the record to Zé Agrippino and Rogério. Anxious to hear their reaction to my text—since I didn't have a stereo to play the songs—I was already preparing myself mentally to apologize for the illustrations when Agrippino turned to me and said: "I really like this cover, with these drawings and colored letters." I was surprised, but I was brave enough to say I disagreed. He looked disappointed, as if he were always being forced to backtrack because of the slowness of others. Rogério, who worked professionally as a graphic artist for a book publisher and was an eloquent theoretician of industrial design, intervened with very specific remarks that despite their technical nature amounted to saying that he didn't like the cover any more than I did.

My song "Um dia" was presented at the TV Record Festival of 1966. It was sung by Maria Odete (the same singer who had "defended" "Boa palavra" at the Excelsior Festival)—a young woman with a potent voice and precise ear. That night Guilherme Araújo had lent me one of his suits so that I would be well dressed, because the cameras occasionally spotted the composers sitting in the audience. Since the show was sold out when I arrived, I had joined the spectators seated in the carpeted aisles. I don't know whether that influenced the reaction of the audience to my fleeting appearance, but the fact is that to this day strangers in the street describe to me in vivid terms that moment when they saw me wearing a jacket, sitting on the floor, listening to the music, and hearing the news that I had won the prize for the best lyrics. One could say that since I became so famous in the intervening years, those people enjoy reliving with me the instant of that first appearance, as if it were an intimate shared reminiscence. But what is curious is that on the day after the program people were already coming up to me on the street to tell me about it—and in the same tone. To me what stands out is the power of television: a few seconds on the air and suddenly millions of people think they know you.

TV Record had a tradition of quality musical programming—veterans like Elisete Cardoso and Ciro Monteiro had been under contract since the fifties. Roberto Carlos's *Jovem Guarda* had appeared on Sunday afternoons as a teen show, presenting the "new" pop-rock. Elis's *O Fino da Bossa,* until then the most popular program and the flagship of "modern" MPB, was beginning to lose ground in the ratings. The rock-versus-MPB war was already old hat in the meetings of the Teatro Jovem, in the bohemian restaurants, and in the university quads. But now the debate had invaded the boardrooms at TV Record.

Elis, who had gone to Europe on vacation, came back to a frightening drop in popularity of her prime-time program, which was losing to the Sunday-afternoon competition. Paulinho Machado de Carvalho called a strategy session of all the most important representatives of MPB. In addition to Elis, he also invited Wilson Simonal, Nara Leão, Jair Rodrigues, Geraldo Vandré, and Gil. Vandré, a good-looking and charismatic Parahiban who was a radical nationalist, had been Carlos Lyra's partner and, in the previous year's festival he had shared first place with Chico, whose "A banda" was challenged by Vandré's powerful "Disparada." This beautiful song, masterfully interpreted by Jair Rodrigues (with the noteworthy presence of Airto Moreira on percussion, playing a donkey's skull, which we did not know was a trick that had already been used by a Cuban band in a Hollywood movie), was an updated and politicized *moda caipira* with a compositional perfection of epic scope and a tone ideally suited to its revolutionary rhetoric. The two songs tied. Gil as yet had no accomplishment comparable to Vandré's, but Elis had successfully recorded one of Gil's songs, and whenever he appeared on her program he demonstrated talent so exuberant as to assure anyone of his great future. When he was invited to participate in the meeting, Gil asked if I could come along. Paulinho agreed, on the condition that I not speak. I would go merely as a listener, as Gil's counsel.

Elis, accompanied by her husband, Ronaldo Bôscoli—the great lyricist and bossa nova agitator who by then was a TV producer—was naturally the center of attention. Everyone spoke with enthusiasm of the need to save Brazilian cultural "purity" from being destroyed by international pop-rock. Geraldo Vandré, overcome by his own eloquence, had tears in his eyes. Gil agreed with the heroic intentions, adding some reflections on the new mass media, but these were nearly unrecognizable fragments of his stirring speeches at the house of Sérgio Ricardo. Paulinho Machado de Carvalho listened to everyone, agreed with the general indignation, and, enlisting in the salvation army of the national identity, proposed that a new program should be created instead of trying to revitalize *O Fino da Bossa*. The Broad Front of Brazilian Popular Music (Frente Ampla da Música Popular Brasileira) had a more democratic leadership system, with responsibilities shared among the emerging stars, each contributing one program a month— the program, on the day and in the time slot of *Fino*, would air once a week. Four "slots" were created: one hosted by Elis, one by Simonal, one by Vandré, and the fourth by Gil.

The first night's program was Simonal's. A demonstration was planned, one more aping of political militancy: it was the Frente Ampla of MPB Against Rock, with banners and signs in the streets of São Paulo. After the strategy session, Gil and I had talked. It was clear to both of us that the new program was a nationalist circus, an attempt on the part of the station to find a conciliatory and commercially successful solution to Elis's problems on the channel. Gil needed to take advantage of the moment to launch the transformation that we had been envisioning. But I never thought it acceptable that he should participate, together with Elis, Simonal, Jair Rodrigues, Geraldo Vandré, and others, in that ridiculous and dangerous marketing ploy. Nara and I were the astounded witnesses, from a window of the Danúbio Hotel, to the sinister procession. I remember her commenting: "That's scary. It looks like a demonstration of the Integralista Party." She referred to the Brazilian fascist movement, an extreme group of Catholic-patriotic-nationalists dating from the thirties, some of whose co-religionists supported the military government.

We had to do something. I came to the conclusion that Gil's program should be turned into an antinationalist and anti-MPB scandal. Since the first pro-rock ideas had come from Bethânia, and she was the strongest among the four of us, I proposed that she break through the Northeastern earth-mother image that had been imposed on her, and appear in the program wearing a miniskirt, with an electric guitar, looking like a rocker; I further proposed that she sing "Querem acabar comigo" (They Want to Do Me In), Roberto Carlos's fabulous song of personal affirmation that she liked so much. To flesh out the performance, I wrote a text about Roberto Carlos for Bethânia to recite before singing. It was very literary—good for Bethânia, whose shows often included poetry readings of real feeling and intelligence.

Gil, Nara, and Torquato were not the only ones staying at the Hotel Danúbio to work on Gil's program. Geraldo Vandré and Lennie Dale, the American dancer who had taught Elis to dance in Beco das Garrafas, had also moved in. Lennie was collaborating with Vandré—they were friends—on the latter's program. Somehow, the text I had written for Bethânia fell into Vandré's hands. It spoke to Roberto Carlos's mythic dimension, his significance as gauge of the national unconscious, and how he was at that time, touchingly, the "face of Brazil." When Bethânia sang, after reciting the text, it would be clear what was to be shattered—and who wanted that result.

Vandré was furious. He showed up at Gil's door with goose bumps on his arms and howled that what we were planning would be an act of aggression against everything we valued, that my comments on Roberto Carlos might work in a sociological essay but not in a program where Brazilian music had to affirm itself against what Roberto Carlos represented. I tried to reason with him. But he was overwrought, and said that he would do everything he could to thwart our plan. He threatened to interrupt Bethânia's number and to make a scene. Gil tried to reason with him as well. His explanations did not alter Vandré's decision. We realized that the situation was risky. Bethânia, somewhat surprisingly, had agreed to go along with it. But she had no hint of what fury would possess Vandré. We could not let her go on without telling her what was happening—and she, once warned, might decide not to do it. The conversation with Vandré didn't exactly reach a conclusion. As we showed ourselves more and more conciliatory, he changed from the tone of command to one of begging. It was for the good of Brazil. I saw things fading. But I did not try to radicalize my position. After all, Gil had a program to do, and I didn't think it wise to throw the group into the fire (especially Bethânia) merely to be sure I wouldn't have to eat crow.

We went ahead with part of what we planned. I can't remember exactly, but I think that Bethânia did wear a miniskirt—a discreet one—though she did not have a guitar, and definitely did not read the text on Roberto Carlos, whose song I can't even remember if we included or not. What dulls my memory—and prevents me from checking with Gil or Bethânia—is the considerable obscurity into which Frente Ampla da Música Popular Brasileira fell, right then and ever after. With that kilometric title and without a central star, FAMPB proved neither a commercial success nor even an interesting cultural event for students. I have a vague memory of what happened on the stage of the Paramount Theater that month. I don't even know whether I saw all four programs. I remember nothing about Elis's.

Simonal's was light and swinging and pretty empty. Gil's was rather confused. I remember Torquato (who wrote the script with us) in the audience, somewhat annoyed with Gil's overly long vocal improvisations. The public did not know what to listen for, what to expect, and didn't understand anything. The program I liked the most, in the end, was Vandré's. He had rehearsed a heavily theatrical number with Lennie Dale, almost a dance, to accompany his beautiful song "Cipó de aroreira," which turned out to be crazy, with Lennie wearing very tight black clothing as he cracked a whip, eventually roping Vandré as in an Apache or tango number, or some scene with Rudolph Valentino. The lyrics to the song were very political, but the staging was so erotic that it would today be interpreted as S&M. I'm not saying this to suggest that they were being inadvertently funny, although that was true to a certain extent. Nor do I want to insinuate that there was a love affair going on between the two artists. But there was a certain humor they themselves encouraged in that respect (Lennie was gay but Vandré was not), and that gaiety pervaded the atmosphere (consciously, I imagine). Another unforgettable moment that same night demonstrates how narrow the "broad front" was. Vandré had invited Clementina de Jesus, the old black singer who, working as a house maid, was discovered at age sixty in Rio by Hermínio Bello de Carvalho and presented to the public in the show *Rosa de ouro* (The Golden Rose) at Teatro Jovem. Familiar with the old *lundus,* with a low and liquid voice and the face of an African mask, that woman was a treasure who had remained hidden in the life of a domestic servant, and her discovery, at that time already an event long celebrated in Rio, was profoundly significant for Brazilian music. It was the least obvious and the most intelligent of all the propositions offered by that series of programs. Well, the public at the Paramount Theater, young and Paulista, though mostly students and leftist nationalists, had no idea who Clementina was, nor were they prepared to hear samba delivered in such a pure and authentic state. When she appeared onstage, there was a frightened murmur, and when she began to sing, they hooted, and I heard some of the young people (of both sexes) scream, "Get lost, monkey!" Though intimidated and revolted, I stood up and screamed to those who would listen: "Stupid Paulistas, you don't know anything. Racist sons of bitches! Have some respect for Clementina!" and I left the theater. The interesting thing is that, in the seventies, when the legend of Clementina had finally reached São Paulo (in 1967 she was already a national myth but São Paulo, with its large industrial masses, has always had a life of its own), and at a point when samba was ebbing in the national market, she herself having been somewhat forgotten in Rio, would find refuge for some years in the great nightclubs of São Paulo specializing in samba, clubs that were the precursors of the commercial renaissance of the samba. My reaction that night at the Paramount Theater was violent but nearly unnoticed. I was already well known because of *Esta Noite se Improvisa* and my brief moment when "Um dia" was presented, but not enough to silence a noisy and disoriented audience.

Having taken up the task that Gil had so clearly outlined, I decided that we would launch our revolution at the festival of 1967. I started composing a song in my little apartment at the Solar da Fossa, with the aim that it should be easy for the audience to learn and, at the same time, absolutely clear in its presentation of the new attitude that we wanted to introduce. "Paisagem útil" no longer seemed to fulfill those two requirements. I thought the new song should be a version of a Carnival *marcha,* as "Paisagem" was, but not a drawn-out and erratic *marcha-rancho.* It had to be a happy *marchinha,* mixed up in some way with international pop, and bringing in through the lyrics the world in which this pop was happening. I remembered a song I had composed two years before in Bahia, "Clever Boy Samba," for a show that I was offered at the Anjo Azul Club, a refined hangout for artists and intellectuals in Salvador. The show never happened but the song, unlike others I had composed at the time, was full of allusions to all the "in" places in the city, the slang of the moment, and phrases from American songs and European movies. I wanted to create a song in tune with Anjo Azul's sophisticated audience, a portrait in the first person of a young person walking through the streets of Rio; the image of the city would surface from lists of products, personalities, places, functions. As the song progressed, I understood that, as with "Paisagem útil," what I might call a critical distance emerged—which for me is a condition of freedom—but there was also the joy inherent in things immediately to hand. This awareness of joy, thus situated, made me choose for a title the refrain "Alegria, alegria!" which the TV showman Chacrinha had borrowed from a good singer of samba jazz on his way to vulgar commercialism (though no less delicious for that): Wilson Simonal. It was a way of placing the listener simultaneously near and far from the vision of the world held by the character, who says in the song: "I'm going." Among the images, that of Coca-Cola seemed to define the composition: new and appearing there almost as if by chance, Coca-Cola assured that "Alegria, alegria" would go down in history.

Chacrinha (Abelardo Barbosa) was a radio showman who had gone on to make it big on television. A middle-aged man of little formal instruction and a heavy Pernambucan accent, he hosted his anarchic program with a hypnotic and fierce eccentricity. He ridiculed his guests without actually humiliating these poor, ignorant souls he occasionally interrupted with a horn similar to that of Harpo Marx. He did not merely affect to place himself on the same level as the guests but was really there, and, except for the horn, he had nothing in common with the angelic Harpo, being a paunchy mulatto with a voice both hoarse and strident. He would break into the musical numbers of famous stars and throw codfish to the audience. Chacrinha was a phenomenon of theatrical freedom—and of popularity. His program had a huge audience and, like some Dada experience for the masses, he seemed at times dangerous just for being so absurd and energetic. This was the program that the domestic help would not miss—and precisely the program that attracted the attention of Edgar Morin, who came to Brazil to study him. (Three years later, during my London exile, I ran into Morin at a dinner at the house of the then French cultural attaché, and when he found out that I was Brazilian, he asked me immediately, "How is Chacrinha doing?") "Alegria, alegria," his refrain for the season (he launched quite a few that found a place in everyday speech), became the title of the song I intended merely as an open-sesame but that became a much wider success and one of the most enduring of all my compositions. This is true within Brazil, while foreigners—who in this matter are closer to me—cannot see what all the fuss is about. Brazilians, in the meantime, never forgot it and never got used to the title, usually referring to it not by the first line or the last, nor even the near-refrain "I'm going," but by the more poignant phrase "without handkerchief, without papers," which appears twice in the long lyrics, in asymmetrical positions. The line that follows the phrase's second appearance— "Nothing in my hands or pockets"—was taken directly from the last page of Sartre's *The Words:* it was a private joke, weaving into this casual song a line from what was for me the most profound of books.

I imagined I would use a group already available in the rock world, possibly even Roberto Carlos's own band, RC7. It was made up of a brass section over a base of guitar, bass, drums, and keyboards, and came closer to the Motown sound or to James Brown than to a British neo-rock band. The decision to use a group already active on the rock scene reveals a lot about the *tropicalista* strategy, but also ultimately about its significance and even its limitations. Instead of working together to find a unified sound that would define the new style, we preferred to utilize one or more sounds that were already recognizable from commercial music, so that the arrangement would be an independent element that would enhance the song but also clash with it. In a way, what we wanted to do could be compared to the contemporary practice of sampling, and the parts we were combining were "readymades." This freed us from creating any sort of fusion, a musical mayonnaise that would be vulgarly palatable, but it also delayed our own investigation into the art of arrangement and performance—deplorable, particularly in the case of a great musician like Gil. To be sure, I was aware that we were being faithful to bossa nova in doing something that was its opposite. In fact, in *tropicalista* recordings one can find bossa nova elements dispersed among others of a different nature, but never an attempt to forge a new synthesis or even an evolution of the extraordinarily successful synthesis that bossa nova had been.

For the *tropicalista* premiere, the introduction of "Alegria, alegria" at the TV Record Festival, Gil, Guilherme, and I were all sure of the wisdom that a rock band should be brought in to accompany us. But before I could tell Guilherme about inviting RC7, he came up with an irresistible alternative. An old friend of his, Abelardo Figueiredo, owned a nightclub in São Paulo, O Beco, where he had under contract an Argentine rock group called the Beat Boys. The band members were young musicians from Buenos Aires who were very talented and familiar with the Beatles' work and whatever else one might wish. Guilherme, who had heard them casually one night at O Beco, suggested that I check them out. When I heard and saw them, I knew they were it. The look of these guys with very long hair, carrying colorful electric guitars, represented in the most strident way everything that the MPB nationalists hated and feared. The typical sound of British neo-rock, which they confidently reproduced, would be the last touch in my composition. The curious thing is, thinking like someone who was simply creating a collage, I didn't even plan to adapt my *marchinha* to the band's style. It was as if I believed that the easy superimposition of one thing on another would produce the desired explosive effect. The first rehearsals showed that such a superimposition would not be so easy, and the result—which turned out to be explosive for reasons very different from the ones I had imagined—exposes the naïveté of the solutions arrived at through a combination of my temerity and the goodwill of those young men. When I listen to that recording today, however, even though the pace of the studio version is depressingly slow and my singing too timid, I am touched by the intro, the veiled quote from the Beatles' "Fixing a Hole," and the final chord jumping out of the harmonic environment, itself so full of sudden shifts—in sum, everything that Marcelo, Maurício, Toyo, Tony, and Willie made possible and interesting in that tentative experiment that founded our movement.

Although it was arrived at lightheartedly, one aspect of the composition of "Alegria, alegria" says a great deal about the intentions and possibilities of the *tropicalista* moment. In striking and intentional contrast to the manner of bossa nova—a formal structure in which altered chords move with natural fluency—here the perfect major chords are oddly juxtaposed. This derived largely from the way we heard the Beatles, even though we (I even less than Gil) did not know them well. The lesson from the Beatles that Gil wanted from the start to incorporate was that of an alchemical transformation of commercial trash into an inspired and free creation, as a way of reinforcing the autonomy of the creators—and of the consumers. That's why the Beatles interested us in a way that the American rock from the fifties had not. The most important thing was not to try to replicate the musical procedures of the British rock group, but rather their attitude in relation to what popular music really meant as a phenomenon. Our point of departure would be what was actually at hand for us, not the sound of the four Englishmen. The Beat Boys felt at ease with this somewhat original material, though perhaps it was not faithful enough for Beatlemaniacs. In the seventies, Gil and I composed at least one song each in the obvious compositional style of Lennon and McCartney. These songs can be compared—not without some irony on our part—with the pastiches of Beatles songs that proliferate all over the world in the form of theme songs for TV programs. A case in point is the theme for *Sitio do Pica-pau Amarelo* (The Yellow Woodpecker Farm), composed by Gil for the television series of the same name, a program for children based on the work of Monteiro Lobato, the fascinating Brazilian author of children's books who was active from the twenties through the forties. My own "Leãozinho" (Little Lion) is a song of affection for a beautiful young man whose sign was Leo; he had played bass in rock bands since he was a boy—and he was a boy when the Beatles were at their height:

> *How I love to see you, little lion*
> *Walking out beneath the sun*
> *It makes my heart feel lighter, little lion*

Just to see you walking so
A glimpse of you is all it takes
To make my sadness go.

Lion cub, ray of light—
You're a captivating sight
When the sunshine lights on you
Color floods into my heart

I love to see you in the sun, little lion
Striking out from shore
The sunlight gleaming on your mane
While the ocean roars
I like to go down to the sea
And get my own mane wet with yours.

These songs were light and playful, using forms that had already become commonplace, unlike what we would be composing in 1966 and 1967, when we heard in the Beatles something we ourselves wanted to create. The *tropicalista* songs then are not like the Beatles songs—at least not to the same degree that those earlier ones are parodies of them.

I suppose it was the conductor Júlio Medaglia who introduced us to a contemporary music group—a collection of radical and erudite experimentalists (followers of Webern, Schoenberg, Berg, and admirers of Stockhausen and John Cage)—that he belonged to in São Paulo. Medaglia put Gil in contact with the avant-garde musician Rogério Duprat, who, in turn, put him in touch with the rock group known as Os Mutantes.

To introduce the as yet unnamed *tropicalismo* to the public at the festival, Gil chose a song based on *capoeira* themes adapted to the harmonic method of abrupt cuts (in this case far more enmeshed with smoothly harmonic phrases than "Alegria, alegria"), which supported the lyrics' strongly imagistic narrative: a crime of passion set amidst poverty, on a Sunday in Salvador. While my song alluded to movie stars (Brigitte Bardot, Claudia Cardinale), Gil's "Domingo no parque" (Sunday in the Park) was almost like a movie. Possessing a musical ability immensely superior to my own, Gil established a fascinating dialogue with Rogério Duprat and Os Mutantes, creating a hybrid sound composed of a rock trio with Bahian percussion (berimbau) and a large orchestra.

Os Mutantes were three teenagers from Pompéia, a middle-class neighborhood of São Paulo with working-class pockets and old abandoned factories, before it became famous as a breeding ground for rockers. They were two brothers—Arnaldo, who sang and played bass and keyboards, and Sérgio Dias Baptista, who played guitar—and a girl, Rita Lee Jones, who sang, occasionally playing drums and a little flute. The three were extraordinarily talented. If the Beat Boys had already become professionals with their competent nightly performances of tunes by the Beatles, Rolling Stones, or the Doors, Os Mutantes, who were still half amateurs, seemed not so much copies of the Beatles (much less of those other groups that were less popular or relevant), but their equals, creators on the same level. When Duprat introduced them to Gil, he commented to me in a somewhat frightened tone: "They're still kids and they play astonishingly well, and they know everything. It can't be true!"

They looked like three angels. They did indeed know everything about the British rock revival in the sixties, and they had the face of the avant-garde pop of the decade. Unlike rockers from the fifties, they were sophisticated and had a presence full of nuance and delicacy. Sérgio, who was only sixteen, displayed a truly world-class guitar technique. Rita and Arnaldo were childhood sweethearts, and everything around them tasted at once of anarchy and decorum. She was extremely beautiful, the daughter of an American immigrant and an Italian-Brazilian, which gave her an air in which freedom and puritanism commingled. The three were typical Paulistas—and to them we, the Bahians, seemed perhaps inherently malevolent; in an interview with the magazine *Veja,* on the occasion of the tenth or fifteenth anniversary of *tropicalismo,* Arnaldo stated that, at the time, they had feared we were going to propose group sex or something of that sort. All I remember is that because of Arnaldo, we had to avoid foul language when Rita was present. It is interesting to consider that one felt the bite of that tacit censorship despite the fact that we normally didn't swear anyway, and I myself grew up without ever having learned to do so with ease. It was, however, a pleasure, not to say extraordinarily amazing, to have them there. And the result of the collaboration with them—and their subsequent work as a group and as individual artists (Rita became and still is today the greatest female star of Brazilian rock)—was thoroughly exciting.

When the time came for the songs to be introduced, the events were as dramatic as we could have hoped but, naturally, often not in ways we had foreseen. The mere fact of my having taken to the stage with a rock group was predictably scandalous. Zé Agrippino, whom I had run into in São Paulo during rehearsals, asked me with something of an ironic smile (it was not his specialty) how the project of singing with a rock group was going. Most in the audience at Teatro Record that night perhaps did not know what was going to happen, but it was no secret, and possibly rumors had been circulating in the room before my appearance. As my program was announced, the Beat Boys made their entrance and set about plugging in their instruments and taking up their positions, as stipulated by the contract, surprising the audience with their long hair, their pink clothes, and their solid wood electric guitars. The angry booing abated only when I appeared onstage (which I did without waiting for my name to be announced) and the fury plainly frightened our hosts, the producers, and many in the audience. It was even more horrifying when people realized that we would not be wearing tuxedos, a tradition at this kind of festival, which my unexpected entrance abruptly revealed since I was wearing a brown checked suit and bright orange turtleneck (all borrowed from Guilherme). The brief silence that followed my appearance was interrupted by the voice of the presenter saying my name, and then, almost without pause, the guitars and drums of the Beat Boys attacked the introduction. The three perfect chords in strange relation, played on the electric instruments, imposed themselves, and my frightening entrance conquered the silence: what had been a tumult of booing gave way to fixed attention. And the song met with enthusiastic applause.

There was much talk after that of a rivalry between Chico Buarque and myself. He was the towering figure of national unanimity, the fabulous and seductive composer-singer and, for the students who filled the theaters at the festivals, the perennial star. He was also the great synthesizer of bossa nova's modernizing advances with the hopes for a return to the traditional samba of the thirties. As a lyricist, he was at once Vinicius de Moraes, Caymmi, Billy Blanco, and Noel Rosa; as a musician, he was a little Carlos Lyra, a little João Gilberto, a little Ataúlfo Alves, and a little Geraldo Pereira. His style in a certain sense was the opposite of Edu's (whose own star quality created a rivalry between them at the start of his career), and it was clearly the opposite of Elis's samba-jazz and the samba from Beco das Garrafas. All this made of him an icon, a status that his physical beauty, naturally elegant manners, and personal genius could only enhance. He was the embodi-

ment of the best of the best in the history of Brazilian music, and that is
how everyone saw him.

He had won the festival the year before the release of "Alegria, alegria" with a sweet old-fashioned tune called "A banda," a nostalgic
chronicle of the passing of a band through a sad street, the nineteenth-
century flavor bringing a momentary light to lackluster lives, and by a
seeming coincidence this also worked as a metaphor for the capacity of
Brazilian music to create happiness for a people with barely any other
source of joy:

> *My long-suffering people*
> *said good-bye to their sorrows*
> *to see the band pass by*
> *singing songs of love . . .*

"Alegria, alegria," with its exuberant embrace of life in the twentieth
century, its mention of Coca-Cola, its rock group as a backup, seemed
to present a screaming contrast to Chico's song. Naturally, and even
more so since I came to vie with him for preeminence in the pantheon
of national stars (at least in the imagination of the audience), I was destined to play the part of his antagonist. But what virtually no one ever
remarked—not even I, having up until now spoken of the origins of my
song in terms of only the Beatles, Gilberto Gil, and Franklin Dario—is
that "Alegria, alegria" was in part derived precisely from "A banda."

"A banda" was a minor work for Chico, to be sure, but useful to him
nonetheless as a foot in the door to a wider market through television—
a popularization of his lyrical persona, but the song hardly reflected
the compositional sophistication of which he was capable. I had imagined a similar role for "Alegria, alegria." The truth is that since "Alegria, alegria" was also a *marchinha* in a festival context, it was a sort of
anti-"Banda" but in a sense was also a "Banda" by another name. One
could quite easily exchange the first three lines of the two songs, and
not only because both triplets were made of lines of seven-syllables, the
most common meter in Brazilian oral poetry (and in Iberian poetry
generally). The words to "A banda" over the melody of "Alegria, alegria" sound particularly natural; both songs aimed at formal expectations deeply rooted in public taste—both are, therefore, equally
"old-fashioned"—and thus there is a kinship between the character
who says "Estava à toa na vida" ("I was hanging around") in "A banda,"

and the one in "Alegria, alegria" walking against the wind, "without handkerchief, without papers," that is, without the documentation relentlessly required by the state.

While everyone rushed to point out the potential rivalry between Chico and me, no one noticed the similarities between the two songs, except for the musicologist Geni Marcondes—who came close when he stated that the success of my composition owed more to its resembling the Lisbon *marchinhas* than to any rock aspirations—and Augusto de Campos, who saw each song as the inversion of the other. In any event, at the time that I was writing it I vaguely sensed that "Alegria, alegria" was, among other things, a kind of parody of "A banda," a chance to take shameless advantage of the festival and the opportunity it brought both to critique and to accept television as a phenomenon.

Augusto wrote some articles on our work that he published from time to time in São Paulo newspapers, on the spur of the moment. He later published them in his book, *Balanço da bossa,* together with essays on bossa nova by his erudite musician friends. I was proud of the way we had attracted their attention. But if, on the one hand, I understood and admired Augusto's partiality, on the other, the subtle differences between us did not allow me to adhere unreservedly to the stances he assumed.

I never took Augusto's discriminations as dogma. His own perception of an inevitable opposition between what we did and what Chico had been doing, for example, though basically correct, and elucidated in the most conscientious and balanced terms, never altered my special love for the style, the person, or the historical importance of Chico Buarque. We knew that a large segment of MPB had reacted negatively to what we were doing: Edu Lobo, Francis Hime, Wanda Sá, Dori, Sérgio Ricardo, and no one more than Geraldo Vandré—all demonstrated a certain irritation or disillusionment with us. We could not expect Chico to take a substantially different position. But *he* was different for us and therefore closer to us. My first lesson in how the press set their snares happened precisely because of this. A nice girl who came to interview me for *InTerValo* (the capital T and V indicating the publication's particular concern with television) asked how I saw the difference between Chico and myself. Excited by the opportunity—and believing that my entire disquisition would be published—I explained that what I did was to expose the mercantile aspect of the television singer, and that while Chico and I were saying many things with our songs, so far as television was concerned, I was the guy with the big hair and Chico the beautiful young man with green eyes; and that the more this game was exposed, the freer we would be in our songs and in our persons. A few days later the article appeared, quoting me as saying that "Chico Buarque is nothing but a beautiful young man with green eyes."

I didn't think I needed to call up Chico to explain (even before *tropicalismo* we did not see much of each other). I was not too worried: my confidence in our intervention turning out well for everyone was absolute; sooner or later, Chico and all the others would find out that we meant no hostility toward them and harbored no commercial ambitions for our project. I was more convinced of it then than I am now. Besides, as I have said before, Chico had been invited by Gil to participate in meetings intended to clarify our objectives and he didn't respond.

Today everyone in Brazil who writes about the events of the period takes particular pleasure in saying that there were two opposing sides in those festivals: one favoring us, the other favoring Chico. That's not how things were. We were systematically booed by Chico's supporters, but Chico was almost never booed by ours, who were never very many besides. Until we were imprisoned and exiled, the audience for those programs, mostly students, was consistently against us.

In 1969, when I would record "Carolina" in a tone certain to raise eyebrows, I clearly wanted, among other things, to relativize Chico's work, though that wasn't my primary motivation. If one thinks of the allusion to "A banda" in the lyrics to "Tropicália," of the suggestion of parody built into "Alegria, alegria," and of the reference to "Carolina" itself in the lyrics to "Geléia geral" (General Jam), the mere act of recognizing Paulinho da Viola's work implied a declaration of independence on our part with regard to the hegemony of the Buarquian style. Like Chico, Paulinho emulated traditional samba but, unlike him, he did so without bossa nova's filter. In effect, though less proficient and much less gifted as a poet than Chico, Paulinho was the miracle of our generation: he seemed not to have even heard of João Gilberto, Tom Jobim, or Lyra. Since he was young, he was ready to experiment and innovate, but these results would not emerge from post–bossa nova's aesthetic universe, as was the case with the work of Edu, Chico, Gil, Jorge Ben, or myself. This gave his songs a special charm. And our insistence on his importance also redefined the question of the return to tradition; our perspective was not the usual one, which saw Chico as the final synthesis of the dialectic of MPB composition in Brazil.

We were sure that Chico's creativity itself would profit from relativization and be stimulated by new challenges. The media naturally preferred to follow an imagined rivalry, and in this they were not wholly mistaken: Why should a journalist simply accept the professed good intentions in the celebrities he has helped to create? Much of the absurdity one reads in the newspapers is the unconscious voice of the agents of narrated facts, and not only the Machiavellian machinations of the newspaper owners, or the mediocrity of this or that miserable human being who needs to keep his job. But that doesn't mean that I should, for my part, submit to their sinister versions of reality. What we need is to be able to read newspapers with a psychoanalytical eye. To this day it is more voluptuous for a journalist to find a thorn in something I say against Chico (or vice versa) than to trace the contours of his widening productivity and our own, let alone to depict the maturing and deepening of our friendship. Chico was, at every turn, the most elegant, discreet, and generous of our colleagues. I know him well and have always known him to be this way, aside from being the virtuoso of rhymes and verbal rhythms. The image I had of him even at the time when our projects confronted each other was no different.

sunday in the park

The climate of opposition to the military dictatorship, equally powerful among filmmakers, theater directors, poets, and visual artists, inspired a name that probably sprung from the wit of rightist minds with denigrating intentions, yet was not always used in the pejorative sense by those to whom it was applied. I refer to the "Festive Left" *(esquerda festiva)*, an expression whose rough equivalent might be "radical chic," except for being less disagreeable than the latter (though also less intelligent, and more popular and generous), and preceding it in time. This is in fact an epithet we would have been happy to be able to apply literally, for instance to Cuban socialism. Unfortunately, harsh reality never permitted us to do so. (During the seventies, when the city government in Rome sponsored shows with Brazilian music and Patti Smith, it occurred to me how appropriate the expression "Festive Left" was for the Italian Communist Party—and how positive it was.) Naturally, within the time frame that occupies us here, we were working with a high degree of tension, and so when the various factions on the Left accused one another of being "festive," they meant "irresponsible and exhibitionist." But the pleasant connotation of the phrase was never completely lost.

TV Record specialized in music as did no other network in the world, as far as I know, before the advent of MTV. The programs were taped in an auditorium. The fad had begun with *O Fino da Bossa. Jovem Guarda,* which appealed to a different age group, at first grew without seeming to become a real contender. The success of "A banda" justified the launch of a program with Chico and Nara, a kind of cool reply to *Fino*'s Elis Regina–Jair Rodrigues combination. (Jair Rodrigues, a black Paulista with a high voice for a man and great musicality, who had no use for jazzy clichés, shared the program with Elis and did it brilliantly, singing duets of samba potpourris with lots of swing, but in the end one had the impression that the final responsibility was with

Elis, whose figure emanated an authority it seemed he neither cared to challenge nor needed to.)

Since what would come to be called *tropicalismo* intended to situate itself beyond the Left and to prove itself shamelessly festive, we felt immune to what others thought of us. I embarked on the adventure of "Alegria, alegria" as though fighting for freedom itself. Once the deed was done, I felt the euphoria of one who has bravely broken unbearable chains. Gil, however, aware of the power of MPB at the time and that we were adopting a drastic position in relation to it, feared there might be serious consequences—a thought that I, in my excitement, managed to avoid—and he panicked. The night we were supposed to present "Domingo no parque," he hid under the blankets in his hotel room (we were staying at the Danúbio, in São Paulo), trembling as though stricken with a sudden fever, and refused to go to the theater. He had separated from his first wife, Belina, a Bahian woman with whom he had two daughters, and was then beginning a romance with Nana Caymmi, the daughter of Dorival. Nana, who herself had sung Gil's "Bom dia" at the same festival to a booing audience, was making every effort to convince him to confront his destiny. Guilherme Araújo also intervened. The show was halfway through before Paulinho Machado de Carvalho arrived and finally managed to get Gil out of bed.

Gil's presentation was dazzling—Os Mutantes were an apparition from the future. There was a stimulating friction between the Afro-Bahian theme against other sound—Beatles + *berimbau* or Beatles × *berimbau*—and Rogério Duprat's beautiful orchestration gave it all an imposing, respectable air, carrying the audience light-years beyond the moment when, just the day before, it tried to boo "Alegria, alegria." And Gil himself, cheerful and extroverted as always, gave not the slightest hint of the dread that had overcome him only a few minutes before.

He was not willing to talk about it much in the days and months that followed this event. But, with all the deep insecurity of a man changing his life, leaving a marriage, and knowing himself to be responsible for a kind of revolution, Gil, for a brief and indeterminate moment, had bared an anguish that he would be better able to articulate a year later, when the terrible consequences were already a reality: "I felt we were messing with dangerous things."

I suppose the recording of my first solo album began with "Alegria, alegria," which needed to be ready for release as a single immediately after its introduction on television, as was expected of festival songs.

Not long after the 1967 festival I was already in the studio recording the new compositions that, in my euphoria, were bubbling up in my head. "Paisagem útil" would, of course, be included on the new record, as the older sister of the new family of songs. "Onde andarás" (Wherever You May Be), a *samba-canção*-flavored bolero I had composed at Bethânia's request while still in Rio, with lyrics by Ferreira Gullar, would be there, too, if only as a parody of a sentimental style considered corny even among those who loved and ennobled it. I had decided to include among the many cuts in the commercial-experimental category (or rock–avant-garde), a 100-percent pure interpretation of a classic tune by Dorival Caymmi, my favorite composer, and I chose "Dora," for while maintaining the desired contrast, this *samba-canção,* with its epic, veiled, and somewhat distant tone, confirmed the record's very aesthetic choices:

> *in the military band the brass play to announce*
> *that their Dora is going to pass*
> *come and see how beautiful . . .*

I remember Zé Agrippino grumbling when he heard me say that I wanted to record "Dora": "No! This whole thing has to be radical." But I never let myself be swayed. I invited Dori to make the recording with just the two of us, my voice and his guitar: Dori, my beloved arranger on *Domingo,* was the great composer's son and, above all, the finest bossa nova guitarist in João Gilberto's line except for João Gilberto himself. But Dori, who came to São Paulo from Rio to record, created many difficulties in the studio, exacerbating my timidity to an extreme. Several times we started, and he interrupted, claiming not to remember the harmony, or not to know what might be best, asking me again and again, in a tone I found intimidatingly ironic, whether I knew what chord to use in this or that passage. He left the studio before we could record even one complete version of the song, no matter how bad, saying, "It won't work, it won't work," leaving it unclear whether the fault was mine, his, or both of ours. Sad and ashamed, I forsook the idea of including Caymmi in the record that would launch the *tropicalista* movement.

To this day I don't know how to interpret Dori's attitude. I know that he belonged to a group of musicians who considered what Gil and I were doing a betrayal of elegant dissonance and civic cultural nationalism. But that had not prevented Dori from coming to São Paulo to record with me. Perhaps when faced with my insecurity he decided it wasn't worth it. Perhaps having agreed to do it at first, he thought better of it later, fearing he might come to regret the collaboration as a betrayal of his father's masterpiece. Perhaps he himself simply felt sincerely unprepared to record that song to his own satisfaction. Manuel Barembein tried to create a climate that would facilitate things, but to no avail: that recording session was frustrated utterly.

As for Barembein himself, he was not to be frustrated. He wanted me to include "Clarice," a song he loved that was not in the least *tropicalista,* and which I had composed with Capinan a year before. Since he understood the inclusion of "Dora" as just a relaxing break, the cut that would let the record "breathe," he felt easy about suggesting a substitute. At first I was determined to reject it. But then, depressed over the episode with Dori and touched by Barembein, who begged me to record "Clarice" "just for him," I gave in. (Months later, when the record was already released and arguments about it had broken out everywhere, Gianfrancesco Guarnieri, the great playwright and actor of Arena Theater, drunkenly told me at a table in Patachou, the restaurant on Augusta Street that we used to frequent, that even though he had been quite saddened by my having submitted to the commercialism of the multinational recording industry, he still loved me because I had retained a pure spot in my soul, a judgment he based on the presence of "Clarice" on my new record; little did he know this had been the only concession I had made to PolyGram.)

Whatever my relations with conductors, producers, or even the players, I had shown myself to be extraordinarily timid. My ambitions were much greater than my powers of concentration and leadership—and I was frightened to see something deformed emerging. Often in conversations with Gil about how happenstance, minor psychological quirks, and various imponderables—leaving aside, of course, the obvious technical and material poverty under which we live in Brazil—interposed themselves between what we dreamed of doing and what we were able to do, I heard him remark that "the spirit of underdevelopment" haunted the recording studios. Os Mutantes seemed in large measure magically immune to that spirit, and Rogério Duprat was too, though for different reasons. We still had (and have to this day) as our template and horizon the records of João Gilberto arranged by Jobim. Gil himself, with his incredible ear and mastery of the guitar, his pulverizing sense of rhythm, was a constant promise that the limitations of our environment could be overcome. And it seemed to me that the collaboration between Gil, Duprat, and Os Mutantes—of which "Domingo no parque" had been a foretaste—would, when carried through the cuts of the album they would soon make together, make up for my own frustrations. As I moved forward with the recordings of my album, I often thought that, in spite of all the shortcomings, maybe Gil and I should join forces to create something strong. Some years later, during our exile in the seventies, I would write in *O Pasquim* a comment on the release of the first Novos Baianos record: "The record, as usual, is not good. But on the other hand it is wonderful." This is what happened with ours.

tropicália

The other cuts on this record, an achievement I pursued with enthusiastic aims and depressing results, were all new compositions. One of them had taken me to the peak of excitement from the moment of its conception. I was thinking of an old samba by Noel Rosa, entitled "Coisas nossas," which enumerated typical scenes, characters, and cultural commonplaces from Brazilian life, tying them all together with the refrain "O samba, a prontidão e outras bossas / São nossas coisas / São coisas nossas" ("The samba, the readiness, and other bossas / Are our things / Are things of ours"); this followed the magnificent lead: "Queria ser pandeiro pra sentir o dia inteiro a sua mão na minha pele a batucar" ("I wish I were a tambourine to feel all day long your hand drumming on my skin"). I imagined a song that would be similar in theme and structure, except that—as with "Alegria, alegria" in relation to "Clever Boy Samba"—it wouldn't be just a satire.

Instead, it would be a moving portrait of Brazil at that time. With my mind racing at dizzying velocity, I realized (having already thought for some time of shouting out her name or brandishing her image) that "Carmen Miranda" rhymes with "A banda," and I imagined that setting the two side by side would somehow reveal the tragicomedy that is Brazil, the adventure, at once frustrating and brilliant, of being Brazilian. The word *"bossa,"* which had already appeared in that samba of Noel's from the thirties, seemed just right, and that it rhymed with *"palhoça,"* grass shack, would connect such phenomena as Elis's television program *Fino da Bossa* with a people who had barely left behind their rural roots. Carnival, the *tropicalista* movement itself (which as yet had neither that nor any other name), poverty and oppression, Roberto Carlos's Jovem Guarda—everything would carry an equal value— words, accidental rhymes; the ideas, oppositions, and analogies; the images, mirrors, prisms, and unsuspected angles. But I did not want the new song to be a mere inventory, like "Coisas nossas." Out of these elements—or others I had yet to consider—I would need to furnish a structure that would sustain a high level of tension as each concept was laid upon the next in this monstrous catalogue. The idea of Brasilia suddenly made my heart race: Brasilia, the capital-monument, the magical dream transformed into modern experiment—and, from the beginning, the center of the abominable power of the military dictatorship. I made up my mind: Brasilia, without being named, would be the capital of the freakish song-monument I'd raise to our sorrow, our delight, and our absurdity.

Well, that at any rate was how I felt in the throes of inspiration. The actual song I was able to compose does not thrill me as much as the vague image I had when it was no more than a possibility. But the song exerted all the same a strong pull on the popular music scene and on many of the most interesting minds in Brazil—provoking academic dissertations in which it was repeatedly termed "allegorical." It met with considerable popular success as well.

The arrangement was entrusted to Júlio Medaglia. I had divided the record's tracks among the three maestros of São Paulo's "new music" who were closest to us: Medaglia, Damiano Cozzela, and Sandino Hohagen. Rogério Duprat—who was in fact the most interesting among them—had appeared on the scene a little later, and beginning with "Domingo no parque" had remained more attached to Gil. On the day we taped the orchestral base of the song intended to be the most representative of any on the album, it still had no title; the drummer, Dirceu, had no idea of the lyrics, as these were to be recorded only later. Yet when he heard the introduction with its percussion, birdsong, and superimposed brass, he recalled Pero Vaz de Caminha's letter describing the Brazilian landscape at the moment of its discovery. The recorded version we used includes the discourse Dirceu improvised out of sheer playfulness, unaware that he was already being taped, much less how appropriate his oration would be to the theme of the song. "When Pero Vaz de Caminha discovered that the Brazilian land was fertile and green, he wrote a letter to the king: 'everything one plants in it, everything grows and flourishes.' " I then came in with the lines announcing a cubist landscape:

> Sobre a cabeça os aviões
> Sob os meus pés os caminhões
> aponta contra os chapadões meu nariz

Eu organizo o movimento
Eu oriento o Carnaval
Eu inauguro o monumento no planalto central do país.

(Above my head the soaring planes,
Below my feet the trucks and trains,
My nose head on with the highlands,
I lead the movement,
I direct the Carnival,
I unveil the monument in my homeland's central plain.)

This long song moves from the image of "a smiling child, ugly and dead" who "sticks out his hand" to a "swimming pool with the blue waters of Amaralina" and then to "five thousand loudspeakers" that "emit dissonant chords." These are always interspersed with lyrics that vary within a formula: "Viva a bossa-sa-sa / Viva a palhoça-ça-ça-ça" ("Viva the bossa-sa-sa / Viva the gra-gra-grass shacks!"); "Viva Maria-iá-iá/Viva a Bahia iá-iá-iá-iá"; "Viva Iracema ma-ma / Viva Ipanema ma-ma-ma-ma," and ending with Roberto Carlos's scream, "Que tudo o mais vá pro inferno" ("To hell with everything") and "Viva a Banda da-da / Carmen Miranda da-da da-da!" Clearly King Roberto Carlos's most famous phrase, followed by Chico's "A banda" and then Carmen Miranda's name (whose last syllable, when repeated, evoked the dada movement and, for me, blended its name with Dadá, the *cangaceiro* Corisco's famous companion, the last two being real personages and the central characters in *Black God, White Devil*), offered for any Brazilian who listened to songs a reeducation, however elliptical, in the tradition and significance of Brazilian popular music. Each refrain has its own constellation of references and associations. In addition to those already mentioned, we also have the title of the movie *Viva Maria* by Louis Malle, a film about women and Latin American revolutionaries, followed by *"iá-iá,"* which is how blacks in Bahia have always referred to their mistresses or masters, as well as any woman who might be above them (*"iá"* means "mother" in Yoruba); "Iracema"—an anagram of America, the name of the Indian woman who is the eponymous character of the beautiful nineteenth-century novel by José de Alencar—paired with "Ipanema" (a Guarani word meaning "bad water," famous throughout the world thanks to "The Girl from Ipanema" by Jobim and Vinicius de Moraes), bringing together beaches in Rio and Ceará, as well as uniting an Indian woman of the nineteenth century with a white woman of the twentieth, one giving her name to a beach (Iracema Beach, in Fortaleza, so named in homage to Alencar's character), the other taking her name from one.

It would require much patience (particularly on the reader's part) to extend this close reading from the refrain to the stanzas, which are longer but no less full of suggestiveness. Suffice it to say that this song without a name provided me with the justification for the record, the movement, and my dedication to a profession that at the time still seemed rather temporary: it was the closest I could come to what *Land in Anguish* had pointed toward.

During a lunch at someone's house in São Paulo I was asked to sing some of the songs I was recording. Luís Carlos Barreto—a newspaper photographer who had become a film producer after doing magnificent work as a director of photography (we owe him the extraordinary images of the masterpiece *Barren Lives* and *Land in Anguish* itself)—was impressed with that song, and when he found out that it still had no title, he suggested "Tropicália," citing the song's affinities to the work of a Carioca visual artist who had created an installation (not yet the term, but that's what it was) consisting of a winding path covered with sand, flanked by tropical plants and wooden walls, along which one was meant to walk barefoot before winding up facing a television screen tuned to regularly scheduled programs. The name of the artist was Hélio Oiticica, and this was the first time I had heard of him. Naturally I was unwilling to give my song the name of someone else's work. But the name "Tropicália" pleased me very much, and I was intrigued by the description of the installation. Guilherme Araújo liked it too. And Manuel Barembein, to whom I made the mistake of repeating Barreto's suggestion, fastened on to it tenaciously. Until I could find a better title the song would be called "Tropicália," and this in fact is still its name, since I never did find a better one.

The other songs on the record seemed like corollaries of one another. "Superbacana" (Supercool), featuring an enormous list of industrial products that used the prefix "super," was a tirade, at once bitter and amusing, about living in a peripheral country, and I recorded it with RC7, as I had dreamed of doing for "Alegria, alegria." "They" was recorded by Os Mutantes; "Maria," my only collaboration with Rogério Duarte, a mysterious and rather somber song about an imaginary child; and "Clara," a complex composition using the scheme of juxtaposed whole chords that Gil had began to use in "Bom dia." These songs were entrusted to Sandino Hohagen. "No dia que eu vim-me embora" (The

Day I Left), one of my rare collaborations with Gil, was done by the
Beat Boys. I think that "Paisagem útil" and "Clarice" were also orches-
trated by Júlio Medaglia. It seemed to me that the result was finally
still more uneven than *Land in Anguish.* I would not have had the nerve
to present it to a foreigner as an instance of the level Brazilian music
could attain. To me, it sounded amateurish (as it still does) and confused. But Glauber liked it.

At a gathering at the house of the architect and lyricist Marcos Vas-
concellos in Rio, we all heard the recording on a tape deck (the record
was already mixed but had not yet been printed), and Glauber became
exultant, quite credibly, in fact, over "Tropicália." He clearly recognized the connections with *Land in Anguish.* He was always very spontaneous, wanting to speak freely. The opportunity for genuine closeness
afforded by my new work revealed his seductiveness, the comically con-
spiratorial tone with which he demonstrated intimacy, and his childlike smile. Glauber's smile was disarming—his personal style could be
described as a mixture of Orson Welles and Marlon Brando, incorporating the visionary hired gun of the Bahian *recôncavo.* But he was fragile,
and dialogue between us was never easy.

The idea of a movement gathered momentum, and the media, naturally, needed a label. By its pregnant power, the word *tropicália* found
its way into headlines and conversations. The inevitable "ism" attached
itself almost immediately. Nelson Motta, a dear friend belonging to
that whole group of second-generation bossa nova in Rio, a lyricist
from our generation who was then beginning his career as a TV journalist, baptized the movement *"tropicalismo"* and, extracting from the
word itself a repertoire of attitudes, a folkloric wardrobe, capitalizing
on the stereotype of the old-time Brazilian gentleman in his perennial
white suit and straw hat, taking cough syrups with odd names, lan-
guishing under a palm tree—he inaugurated in a naïve and unpretentious way what would come to be a long series of typical interpretations
of the movement's character. It was in fact a declaration of support for a
trend that was rejected by all of his (and our) colleagues in Rio. As for
me, having resigned myself to "Tropicália" for lack of a better option—
and thinking that the song in the end would not be much affected by
the title—I didn't swallow that *tropicalista* syrup. The old-fashioned or
folksy images annoyed me—unlike *tropicália,* which was a new word,
tropicalismo sounded worn out to me. I had already heard it with a different meaning, perhaps connected to the Pernambucan sociologist
Gilberto Freyre (which later proved to be the case). At any rate the

word seemed to exclude some of the elements we wanted most to stress, above all the internationalizing, antinationalizing ones, those that proposed a necessary identification with the whole urban culture of the West. It was a measure of consolation that the newspapers called us "hippies" or "rockers" and our music "pop," and that some intellectuals connected us to the avant-garde, ranging from John Cage to Godard. But the definitive commentary about the *tropicalista* label that had just been attached to us was made by Dr. José Gil Moreira, Gilberto Gil's father: "I'm a tropicalist," he said laughing, "since I've been a specialist in tropical diseases for decades!" In fact, the entry "Tropicalista" in the *Aurélio Dictionary of the Portuguese Language* states: "1. The author of treatises on topics related to tropical regions. 2. A specialist in diseases from those regions."

"Alegria, alegria" was a popular success. Because of my statements in his support, Roberto Carlos invited me to sing on *Jovem Guarda*. I went on to make startling appearances on Chacrinha's program, singing "Tropicália" and "Superbacana," in addition to "Alegria, alegria." I finally moved to São Paulo, and I married Dedé. The ceremony took place on the twenty-ninth of November 1967 in Salvador, and became, in spite of ourselves, a public event. We were to marry in the São Pedro Church, Dedé wearing a short pink dress with a hood of the same color (a design by Ana, Torquato's wife), and I wearing a suit with an orange turtleneck, the look Guilherme invented to avoid the tuxedos everyone wore on the TV shows. I was also to carry a big yellow flower in my hand. The ceremony was supposed to be a secret. Dedé's family and mine kept the strictest silence. On the morning of the twenty-ninth, however, when we left in Dedé's father's car and headed for Sete de Setembro Avenue, we ran into a monstrous traffic jam. We arrived at church very late to find out that all the congestion was caused by a throng of schoolgirls in uniform who were cutting class to see me get married. Someone (Dedé always thought it was Guilherme Araújo, although he always denied it) had tipped off a radio announcer, who had been broadcasting the time and place since early morning. It was extremely difficult to enter the church, and even once we were inside, things did not improve. The multitudes of girls in uniform filled the church, taking over all the pews, the aisles, the pulpits, the altars. As though in some bad dream, they sang "Alegria, alegria" and tried to come near me. Those who managed would grab snatches of my hair and some even attacked Dedé. My mother, always so serene, fainted. Bethânia was hit in the head. I wanted to leave, but I couldn't make my way out. The priest asked for silence and respect, but all in vain. Even he wanted to cancel the ceremony, but he could see no way for us to leave before he could calm the girls. He decided to perform the marriage anyway. Many men report a certain anxiety at the precise moment of wedding. I felt a great anguish. Dedé and I had always agreed we would never wed. But she believed her mother, who told her that she "would die" if Dedé were to live with me in São Paulo without benefit of clergy. Since I had no intention whatsoever of parting from Dedé, I agreed to go through with it, although I was not convinced, as she claimed to be, that it was all the same whether we married or not. The nineteenth-century São Pedro church was comparatively somber, but the teenagers seemed to multiply like lascivious angels in a Bahian baroque church, as I entered adult life by way of a compromise whose weight took the form of a sacrament.

At age twenty-four I looked like an adolescent. And in fact I felt even more like a teenager than I looked. Someone said that men who set their minds to what is faced in childhood produce profound works, while those who revisit indefinitely the questions and illusions of adolescence are fated to wander the labyrinth of repression, sexual definition, and the fulfillment of the will to freedom. I find myself in this latter group. The whole wave of the sixties was an elevation of adolescent personalities or persons of adolescent style. But owing to the deep influence of my father, I had developed a genuine obsession with integrity. When we met, Dedé was sixteen, and I was twenty-one. One of the first things she asked me was whether I was "in favor of free love." Of course I was, but that's not what I said, or at least I didn't say it quite so directly. I was touched by the naïveté of her question. I say "naïveté" not in the sense of an absence of sexual motives on her part, since the attraction was clearly mutual, but she was plainly unaware of the complexity of the possible arguments against the idea of free love. And I played the devil's advocate. It was a good way to start our relationship. Ten years later, when we were still together, I took note that "love and freedom are still our theme." We were happy in each other's company. My considerable femininity ensured a perennial companionship, and we remained ever a couple of sweethearts, an inseparable pair. I, who had known the dark splendor of a great passion in Santo Amaro, a passion that has never left me but whose greatness was nourished in large measure by its impossibility, had finally found genuine love, which nourished itself on what was lived in its name, and not on what was denied. It was a joy of the body, alive and serene, and it was also a youthful happiness of social success (to have a girlfriend!) and psychological maturity. Dedé was the right person for that experience. She was very beautiful in an unconventional way, though she was not exotic. Her personality was truly original. Intrinsically modern, very open and clearheaded, she was intellectually attracted to the literary and artistic milieu. As I've said, she was studying modern dance at the university, but her lack of discipline was greater than her talent and she abandoned it. In 1966 we decided that she would come to Rio to be near me, but with no plan of marriage. Faced with what she presented as merely a stratagem for persuading her mother to move to São Paulo (in Rio, she lived with her grandmother), I had to make clear to her that if I accepted the ritual I would feel responsible for it. Anything else would be cynical. She, naturally, tried to make light of my scruples: women are less afraid of marriage than men. Now here I was in this overcrowded church, like someone who had taken the wrong path down the labyrinth of life.

I don't know how we got out of there. We had planned a party afterward, just for family and some close friends. It was supposed to be a secret, like the ceremony itself, and now I couldn't imagine it happening. We had chosen a restaurant, hidden from the street behind a hill with no other houses, amid some foliage, surrounded by verandas, and a staircase that led to the beautiful beach that was always deserted. It occurred to me that anyone able to discover what was to take place in the church would have even less trouble finding the restaurant on the beach. But Tom Zé, who was in charge of this secret lunch, assured us that everything would turn out perfect. It did. We went down to the beach and to the restaurant, the intimacy of the occasion unviolated by the uninvited. The day was beautiful, once everything had calmed down, and I thought only how lovely Dedé was and how happy I was to be married to her—a happiness that lasted as long as the marriage.

Appearing on Roberto Carlos's program was a very significant border crossing. The antagonism between MPB and rock was so apparent in the hostility of the former toward the latter that a great composer-singer like Jorge Ben had been put on the *Fino da Bossa* blacklist just because he appeared on the *Jovem Guarda* program. But Jorge Ben, who had exploded on the scene in 1963 with a very personal version of bossa nova, different from that of the founders and different from what was done in Beco das Garrafas—simplified and

Africanized—was by this time already doing a fusion of samba with R&B that was unacceptable to the MPB crowd. In fact, after his song "Mas que nada" took off worldwide in the version recorded by Sérgio Mendes and Brazil 66, Jorge Ben was ostracized by the more prestigious figures, and only Roberto Carlos offered him refuge. In a song of his from this period, he announces that "Eu sou da linha Jovem-Samba" ("I'm in the Young-Samba line"), an attempt at making a peace (and synthesis) between Jovem Guarda and MPB, which never got beyond that one song.

Gil had been an ardent admirer of Jorge Ben since our days in Bahia. One night, during a nightclub show in Salvador, he said that he had stopped composing and would never again sing any of his own songs because there was a new guy by the name of Jorge Ben who did everything Gil thought he himself ought to be doing—and so he did an entire show of Jorge Ben songs. I liked Jorge Ben for his originality and energy, but I could not agree that a musical talent like Gil's should be silenced out of reverence for him. Above all, I found it scandalous that Gil, who had a better ear for harmony than I, should abandon it all on account of a music infinitely more primitive than his own. I attributed it in part—and perhaps I was not totally wrong—to matters of race. Jorge Ben was not only the first great black composer since bossa nova (a role that could be Gil's), he was also and most importantly the first to make that blackness the determining stylistic element, initially in his musical and personal style and through some little hints in his lyrics. Later it became very open: he mentioned the American black movement, African heroes, and so on. Back then, in his beginnings, he already presented some African words and slices of legends. Of course we always had magnificent black singer-composers, and talking about being black or dark occurred not infrequently in the lyrics, always in a light, slightly comic way, never inviting any kind of political or even social perspective. Jorge Ben brought a tone of black consciousness to Brazilian pop music. Gil felt that something new concerning this issue was arriving with Jorge.

Jorge Ben's recording of "Se manda" (Get Lost) summed up all our ambitions. It was a hybrid of *baião* and *marcha*-funk, sung and played with a healthy aggression and a naturally pop modernity that filled us with enthusiasm and envy. It's not that Jorge Ben created fusion, nor could one say that he had gone from bossa nova to R&B. In his version of the new samba (*samba esquema novo,* New Style Samba), his originality was in playing like someone with an ear tuned to rock guitar and black

American music. And in part that's what had happened. The direct thematization of negritude—which, in Salvador, had impressed Gil all the more strongly, since he had always avoided doing it at any level— came through in the guitar beat and the half-blues, half-Afro phrasing, more so than in the occasional African or pseudo-African words or explicit references to black experience in his lyrics. What he was doing now was using the electric guitar in a way that simultaneously brought him closer to blues and rock and yet revealed clearly the essence of samba. What had been latent in the initial stages was now awakening and gaining depth during the period when he was relegated to exile in the *Jovem Guarda* show. A most characteristically rooted Carioca, Jorge Ben had been in self-imposed exile in São Paulo for several years. His engagement to the beautiful Paulista Domingas could explain that decision up to a point, but he was clearly also motivated by the lack of prestige into which he had fallen in Rio, and therefore in Brazil in general. São Paulo was a vast and neutral ground where it was possible to be a moderate success without depending on nationwide recognition. But what we were most attracted to was not so much the stylistic mixtures that he brought together as the atmosphere of genuine physical happiness that his presence in the panorama of Brazilian music had established. *Saúde* (health) was the word that most commonly appeared on our lips when we talked about him. It was becoming and would remain the key word for us. José Agrippino and Rogério had already used it to speak of literature (in fact, Rogério had spoken of *Panamérica* as a book that was too healthy to be good literature: "You're too healthy," he had said to Agrippino. "Maybe literature needs a little more neurosis"), giving it a connotation that I captured and immediately incorporated. Health emanated from his figure, the timbre, the ideas of Jorge Ben. His very attraction to the American pop scene was already for us a sign of "health." The North American pop scene (and the homage paid to it by the British creators of neo-rock in the sixties) was only one of the elements that, in this *tropicalista* turnaround, we had stopped considering "vulgar," in order to claim it as "healthy." "Se manda," with its happy aggressiveness (summarily and without incrimination, the lyrics tell the wife to get lost because she has been unfaithful), and its musicality, exposed the crude traces of *samba de morro* and blues in a composition with a Northeastern feel; it was the embodiment of our dreams. Jorge Ben, without attempting an artificial or homogenizing "fusion," came through with a strong, original sound, confronting a body of issues from the opposite end, that of the finished treatment, while we were groping and coming up with varied and incomplete solutions. Gil and I chose "Se manda" because it was extraordinarily successful, and also because its Northeastern flavor brought it closer to us as Bahians, but what I have said here about that song applies as well to the entire LP, *O bidu,* and to all the work of Jorge Ben in the late sixties. Jorge became a symbol, a myth, a master for us. Gil, who had admired him without restraint from the start, took Jorge's musical procedures as one main source of inspiration for his own guitar explorations and arrangements; and I, who since that time have often imitated something of his way of writing poetry and singing (and recorded a good number of his songs), once wrote that if we *tropicalistas* had, in our eagerness to turn Brazil inside out, made "a descent into hell," "the artist Jorge Ben is the denizen of that utopian country beyond history that lives within all of us, that we all have the duty to build."

2002

Dedé and I moved into an apartment in downtown São Paulo, on the corner of Ipiranga and São Luís, which had been found by Guilherme, who had lived in Rome, in Paris, and in Germany, and had a very broadminded idea of what it meant to live well. Perhaps by that time the idea of living in the center of a city was already taking on the meaning it has today: something outdated and a little dangerous. But Guilherme saw the advantages of comfort and price and ignored prejudices. I'm not even sure there were any advantages attached to the location chosen, such was my alienation from practical matters. Dedé went to see it with Guilherme, approved it, and in a sense I was taken there. The building, in which he had also found an apartment for himself, was one of those early residential skyscrapers of São Paulo, with solid walls, marble lobby, and elevators with large golden friezes. The overall effect was more antiquated and dignified than ostentatious. And the apartments were spacious and full of light. Guilherme took up residence on the eighteenth floor, and we moved to the twentieth, flat number 2002. Across the street was the tall Edifício Itália. It was delicious to live in the heart of a big city, among skyscrapers. Our apartment had an open balcony, where I could sit and look at the sky and the traffic below, feel the wind, and scare Dedé for fear that I might fall. The first month went by without our deciding on furniture for the living room and dining room. We had bought a bed and other things for the bedroom, a refrigerator, and a stove—and, naturally, a stereo, which was in the room that became known ever after as the "stereo room." The rest of the flat consisted of immense empty spaces where it was marvelous to be. The floor reflected the light that came in through the windows, and we would sit on it to talk, sing, read. I was already so used to living in an apartment without furniture—and thought that was a very good way of taking care of the issue of style—that I protested to myself when someone turned up with some suggestions for decorating the rooms.

It was a guy called Piero. He was Italian and lived in São Paulo, an intelligent young man. I think he was a visual artist. It all began with his saying that he knew the owner of an acrylics factory, and he could design original furniture for us and have it made and assembled at that factory within a short time and at a relatively low cost. Dedé and I thought it weird—the idea of having acrylic furniture—but little by little he persuaded us. The result was that Piero filled our rooms with transparent furniture in varied colors (all psychedelic). He also bought two enormous armchairs of clear, inflatable plastic, and, in the wide hallway that separated the living room from the dining room, he placed a kind of fiberglass mannequin, a life-size female figure, naked and bald. Over that statue he hung a stream of colored lights, the wires dropping down at different heights; they were connected to the stereo in the other room, so that the lowest notes lit up the blue lights, the medium notes the green and yellow ones, and the high notes the red. Above the hallway he hung two meat hooks. The table we ate on—the only idea that had actually come from Dedé and me—was a Ping-Pong table, with the net stretched across it. All we asked—timidly—was for Piero to stop when he started painting the windowpane across from that table, which he wanted to transform into a hippie stained-glass window—very maudlin. Described in this way, the apartment might sound like a real monstrosity, amusing only from the distance afforded by our memories. But in fact we never stopped Piero from continuing, because we liked what we saw. And to this day I see its charm.

Before we had any furniture, the only idea of interior decoration that had occurred to me (aside from the Ping-Pong table) was to cover the walls with an eye-catching ad from the street, an image of a pretty girl playing tennis against an immense blue sky. It was an advertisement for sugar—the text somewhat enigmatically said only "Sugar moves"— and it was the very vision of that health we talked about so much. Because of the conversations with Rogério and Agrippino, Morin's writings, and the *tropicalista* enterprise, I had for some time been paying attention to advertisements, although I was an eternal and deep-rooted anticonsumerist (I hate to buy). I started to go into supermarkets just to look at the cans and the piled-up packages, to explore multicolored aisles with their science-fiction ambiance and mystical decorativeness. That "health" in anonymous everyday life, that "health" of seeing the beauty in the total and unique surfaces of things, the "health" of the market, that's what I saw embodied in the sexual beauty of the girl playing tennis in that ad. The tennis game, on the other hand, reminded me of Godard—to my mind the true poet of such things, in a way that Agrippino, in his antilyrical radicalism, could never be—because of the opening images of *Pierrot le fou*, where two girls play tennis, accompanied by a narration about light in the paintings of Velázquez.

What Piero was doing was not based on any plan of ours, nor was it even inspired by our taste, but it was fun, different, delicate. It was becoming mysteriously our own, in a way that eluded our control. The light coming in from the windows fell on the acrylic armchairs, making their edges shimmer. The colors would have been strident were the material not translucent. As it was, they soothed the eyes and the spirit. The meat hooks, which could be seen from the entrance door, were an aggressive touch (today they would seem like a punk reference), breaking the sweetness that transparency lent to the acid colors. The fiberglass mannequin—neutral or colorless, translucent without being transparent—was a good match for the large rooms, giving everything a spacious air, as if this were a sculpture exhibition installed with no sense of visual discomfort. As for the lights connected to the stereo system, they bore not the least resemblance to those ingenious panels one found in go-go clubs. These were common lightbulbs, of the size one would use in ceiling fixtures, and they hung from their normal wires. Draped over the head and shoulders of the mannequin, they resembled nothing so much as a half-eaten bunch of fruit of different colors. When they were turned off (as they were, most of the time, even at night), they seemed just one more element of the fiberglass sculpture, giving the modern and stripped-down effect of an art object that purposefully reveals its wiring. And the musical effects we eventually discovered with them were far from the elemental rhythmic pulse of colors responding to the bass, so common in nightclubs. Most startling was the effect that Mahalia Jackson's voice produced when she sang "Summertime" or "Sometimes I Feel Like a Motherless Child" a cappella. Every so often we would turn off all the lights in the house and listen to Mahalia's voice, its timbre sustaining a yellow and red glow for a while, interspersed with blue flashes, before giving way to blues and greens, rising and falling in intensity, wavering like will-o'-the-wisps, until they faded, together with the last words and notes, into the silence of total darkness.

Nineteen sixty-eight, a year remembered in many parts of the world as violently meaningful, visited upon our group everything that would justify the mythology that has grown up around that time. Rhodia, a clothing manufacturer, invited us to participate in a show that, they told us, the company produced annually, featuring important artists as part of a major national fair organized by the textile industry in São Paulo, the Fenit. The show would be called *Momento 68.* There was the hint of a promise that the company might sponsor a *tropicalista* TV program. They lured us with a script written by Millôr Fernandes— the famous humorist, journalist, cartoonist, and playwright who was already a big name in the early fifties—to be directed by a respectable theater director and performed by two great actors. We found out that the show would include a ballet choreographed by Lennie Dale and a fashion show. When the rehearsals began, Gil and I noticed that things were a little strange. Not only were our numbers to be breaks in the fashion show, but the texts to be used were atrociously out of synch with our style and everything we were interested in. The costumes we were supposed to wear were horrendously styled (not even the white *tropicalista* suits were omitted) and the quips of the two actors were silly. But we had signed a contract, and although we considered the whole thing ridiculous, we enjoyed the camaraderie of the dancers, choreographer, actors, and, in spite of the limitations imposed by the producer, the models. The director had no time for talk, but he was kind and flexible. We figured out a way to keep going. But I was amazed at the absurdity of the situation: the "counterculture" themes were approached in the chatty manner of a social club, and there we both were onstage. It was the superficial journalistic vision of the era—a grotesque version of what might be called the "narcissism of the times." But that was the show that allowed us to leave Brazil for the first time. After the fair in São Paulo, *Momento 68* was to go to Rio, then Lisbon, Buenos Aires, and Montevideo. There was a rest period between Portugal and Argentina, and Dedé and I agreed to meet in Paris. From there we went to London. Gil went from Lisbon to Madrid with some of the dancers. It was moving to see Lisbon, pleasant to see Paris, and intriguing to see London. On the way back to Brazil, I can't remember what it was that the producer said that provoked us to quit the show in a huff, swearing at him. Gil went along with my decision. We didn't go to Buenos Aires or Montevideo. I was relieved and laughed my head off. They didn't sue us for quitting halfway through the run: I think my pretext had something to do with their not confirming their agreement to sponsor our TV show. Since this show claimed to be a synthesis of the essence of 1968, and since it attempted to realize this pretension in a manner both alienated and false, my recollection is vague, but the show now seems like a different 1968, virtual and parallel, phantasmagoric, a squalid reality closed in on itself.

concrete poetry

The reaction of leftist students was openly unfavorable, and many fellow musicians turned up their noses at us. Yet the media, while critical, found in the garishness of our shows (and the discussions they generated) a full serving of material to meet their daily requirement of idle reflection, sensationalism, and intrigue. In our case—and it is so more often than we might imagine—it was precisely the shows' venality that saved them from narrow morality and petty convention. We appeared in the magazines that covered television, in general-interest publications, and in the columns of daily newspapers, and we were frequently quoted by reporters interviewing other artists. There were a few episodes of grotesquerie, such as one involving the producer and TV host Flávio Cavalcanti, a figure of sensationalist conservatism who led a show in which the "jury" evaluated songs while he made inflammatory speeches of moral reprobation or sentimental praise. Cavalcanti, in his imaginative deviousness, found among the opening words of "Alegria, alegria" the phrase "sem lenço, sem documento" (without handkerchief, without papers), and he pointed to this as an encoded acronymic allusion to lysergic acid—and thus an incitement to drug use. His discovery compelled him to reenact a gesture he would typically perform on such occasions, one that had established his reputation for being both comical and sinister: he smashed a copy of the wicked record.

Many other rejections followed that one, but fortunately they were always more elevated. The point was usually our supposed "commercialism" and particularly our lack of respect for what were supposed to be the aesthetic principles of the Left. Yet *Manchete* published an interview with me in which I stated that "when I first heard João Gilberto, I had the desire to make music. After that, a kind of politically clichéd A-list samba with a slick feel became popular, and it was reduced to becoming ideological: the defense of the purity of our traditions against all the trash that was for sale. I felt lost: I had never thought of music as a product, and I did not consider *O Fino da Bossa* to be the salvation of our traditions. . . . I refuse to disguise my technical limitations beneath the costume of regionalism."

The fact that these lucid passages stand out from the prevailing banality in that magazine, which had the largest circulation of any in the country, only exacerbated my frustration with the cuts we had prepared for the eventual record. I had wanted to create an object that would be conceptually strong, whose artistic effect could not be improved upon, but the low production values were impossible to ignore. I had to accept that the daring of the ideas would be the only element of acceptable quality in the whole enterprise. I don't mean to say that I despised the commitment or the ability of the producer, Manuel Barembein, much less that of the arrangers (Medaglia, especially, did exceptional work). Yet while conscious that the final unity depended on my leadership, I recognized it was not within my power either to enable or to require these collaborators to achieve something that would transcend all provincialisms. How could I do so, when I of all people was precisely the most timid, the one who felt most disarmed in the studio. In any event, the result, little as it pleased me, did manage to hit the mark, at least respecting the foremost aspirations of *tropicalismo.* The angry reactions in the auditoriums and universities were proof of that.

But it was not the negative reaction that called attention to us. The intentionally provocative aspects of the music itself, as well as the carefully articulated outlines of our ideas, which found their way into the interviews I gave, caught the eye of the poet Augusto de Campos early on. Before *tropicalismo* had taken name and shape, Augusto heard Maria Odete singing "Boa palavra" at the TV Excelsior Festival and then, having read my contribution to a polemic on popular music in the *Revista Civilização Brasileira* (wherein I insisted on the importance of João Gilberto and advocated a "return to the evolutionary line" the latter represented), he wrote an article entitled "Boa palavra sobre a música popular" ("A Good Word on Popular Music"), in which he greeted my arrival on the MPB scene as an auspicious event. Alex Chacon, full of enthusiasm, showed me this article in Rio. This was before I had seen *Land in Anguish,* before Rogério had introduced me to Agrippino, and most important, before Bethânia had made her elliptically suggestive comments about Roberto Carlos and Jovem Guarda. Surely for that reason—but also because the name of the author was unfamiliar to me, and I had met with no reaction apart from Alex's—the article seemed to come from another planet. I was prepared for Augusto's critique of the emphatic style, resurgent at the time owing to the appearance on the scene of sociopolitical themes and the "protest song"; and as for my return to traditional samba and Northeastern folklore, my declaration cited by Augusto in the article ("Only the return to our evolutionary line can give us a proper basis for creative selection and judgment") echoed a long article I had written in 1965 for a student publication in Salvador, in which I attacked the hidebound nationalists who—theoretically led by the sociologist José Ramos Tinhorão—were trying to diminish and even annul the advances of bossa nova. But the critical stance Augusto delineated concerning Roberto and Erasmo Carlos was nevertheless unacceptable to me: I had concluded the article published in *Ângulos* by opposing a responsible faction of Brazilian youth—the same ones I would want to win back from the claws of the retrograde nationalists and shepherd toward bossa nova's evolutionary line—to another faction made up of "some young girls as suburban as Emilinha Borba, and boys whose idols fall somewhere between the Beatles and Francisco Carlos"; thus I identified the entire Jovem Guarda crowd with the least prestigious mass idols on Brazilian radio in the fifties.

What I find truly incredible today, as I reread Augusto's article, is that I could have in the very moment of *tropicalismo*—having by this time already overcome my prejudices against Jovem Guarda and come to establish, as Augusto had, a link between João Gilberto and Roberto Carlos—somehow failed to grasp, even in my heart of hearts, the prophetic aspect of the ideas he expressed. To be exact, if I had accurately read the conclusions Augusto derived from my interview, his article would have been the true catalyst of my turnaround. In fact, neither *Land in Anguish,* Edgar Morin, Guilherme's insinuations, nor even the conversations with Rogério and Agrippino ever came close to presenting such a complete vision of the issues we would be facing with *tropicalismo.* No one after Augusto, until *tropicalismo* hit the streets, would touch with so much precision upon the most urgent questions of popular music at that moment. His article said, for example, that the "nationaloids" were advocating a

> return to the square old samba and the tedious anthem of sym-
> phonic-folksiness. . . . Things were at this stage when, without
> knowing it, Jovem Guarda and its leaders Roberto and Erasmo
> Carlos arrived to illuminate this reality and the mistake it
> implied. While MPB—as though ashamed of the step forward it

had taken—was going back to retreads of the old standards and folkloric inspirations, foreign music (popular as well, but based on a less artificial and less refined folk music—the urban folkore produced in every city and shamelessly reworked by all the modern technologies) was able easily to attain the popularity that MPB was seeking with such strain and populist affectation. The epitome of the paradox is the news that in Recife there have emerged ballads recounting the meeting of the King of national rock with the Devil, glossing the theme from Roberto Carlos's song "To Hell with Everything." Most people have not understood that rock has undergone a transformation in its Brazilian translation, and is not, at its best, simply an imitation of imported rock. I have had the opportunity to observe . . . that, when it comes to interpretive style, the two Carloses are much closer to João Gilberto than many contemporary singers of typical MPB (and João Gilberto, in turn, has much more in common with Northeastern singers than do singers of protest songs).

Augusto's lucidity concerning MPB is even more surprising when one considers that the detachment of his tone corresponded to his actual condition: he was not just a poet with an erudite background but also—in part because of the nature and amplitude of that erudition as well as the radicalism of the poetical experiment to which he was dedicated since the fifties—a figure as much on the margins of mainstream Brazilian intellectual life as he was on those of the artistic-journalistic world where MPB was discussed and made. He seemed to know how firmly to confront the crucial issues, but he had quite evidently never been part of the crowd in which the Festive Left operated and in which the gossip circulated, an experience that would have given his language the currency that might have won me over upon my first reading him.

But perhaps I forgot this article precisely because it is so tight, almost schematic, and with a kind of ready course I could not have followed without having found the way on my own. As I say, my reaction to the article had to do more than anything with my failure really to absorb it; and so—since I was unable to disagree with his more daring proposals, had no idea of the importance of the author, nor could find a single acquaintance of mine who had read it—I simply considered it nonexistent. And just as his detachment had endowed Augusto with a discriminating gaze that could see only what was relevant to his schemes, my own involvement prevented me from taking a broad enough view—and thus from sharing his perspective. The defense of Roberto Carlos neither shocked nor excited me: it was a slightly uncomfortable topic that had been raised somewhat humorlessly by someone I did not know, who seemed to carry no weight in the balance of opinion. Nor was I enthusiastic about the sympathy expressed for my ideas (which, in the main, had been linked to those of Edu Lobo, whom I greatly admired but strongly disagreed with in matters of theory), since I believed no one was going to read it. I did not save that newspaper page for even a day. When, sometime later, Capinan showed me the book about Sousândrade and pronounced the names of the two brother-poets who had organized it, Augusto de Campos and Haroldo de Campos, I did not even recognize the name.

Augusto and his brother Haroldo, together with Décio Pignatari, formed the nucleus of a group of poets who, in the mid-fifties, launched the concrete poetry movement, a radical renewal of the modernist spirit of the twenties. These poets took a stand against the propriety of the antimodernists and anti–avant-gardists who had taken hold of Brazilian literature, first with the regionalist novelists of the thirties, and later with the poets of the so-called Generation of '45.

The concrete poets felt themselves to be in synch with European musicians like Boulez and Stockhausen who, in the fifties, had revived the radicalism of the Vienna school (especially Webern), and with the painters who were following the path of Mondrian and Malevich. They valued the physical aspect of the word, creating poems to be apprehended initially as visual artifacts—on the page the emphasis fell on typography, color, and white space. Passionately knowledgeable about the pioneering movements early in the century—Italian Futurism, Suprematism, Russian Cubo-Futurism, international dada, and so on (and with a certain antipathy toward surrealism)—they took a well-defined position with regard to modernism, the entire history of poetry, and the trajectory of the future. To this effect, they created what they called their *"paideuma,"* a canon of authors whose works were required reading for the new sensibility: Mallarmé (the first, with his "Un coup de dés," to think of the poem on the page as a constellation, and to use the whiteness of the paper as a structuring element); Ezra Pound (who gave them the concept of *paideuma,* his approach to Chinese calligraphy, and his monumental series of *Cantos,* elaborated in the manner of ideograms); Joyce (with his word-montages, the implosion of the "novel" as form in *Ulysses,* and the invention of a translanguage in *Finnegans Wake*); Mayakovski ("there is no revolutionary art without revolutionary form"); João Cabral de Melo Neto (the greatest Brazilian poet to emerge after modernism, who belonged, chronologically, to the Generation of '45 but who was opposed to everything they stood for, being a poet to see things with a lucid eye and express them in a dry and extremely rigorous language); e. e. cummings (who created isomorphic typographical gestures, making even punctuation marks protagonists in the poem); and Oswald de Andrade (the most radical of the Paulista modernists to emerge from the famous Modern Art Week of 1922); some baroque poets (and the British "metaphysicals," such as John Donne); and figures from Provençal poetry.

The appearance of the concretists provoked a scandal (*O Cruzeiro,* a magazine of wide circulation, talked about "the rock-n-roll of poetry"). Though they had the support of that giant of Brazilian poetry, Manuel Bandeira (who was older than the modernists, their precursor, and a master for all time), they found strong resistance among poets, literati, and scholars generally. But the level of the arguments they sustained was so high, their culture so vast, and their determination so unshakable that they became a tough bone of contention in the Brazilian intellectual milieu, commanding respect even where there was no receptivity. Consequently their enemies surrounded them with a wall of silence broken only every so often by some completely disproportionate aggression, while their friends were utterly steadfast.

When Augusto de Campos got in touch with me, he gave me as a present some issues of the journal *Invenção,* which he edited, along with Haroldo and Décio; they called themselves the Noigandres group, after a word from a Provençal poem appropriated by Pound for one of his cantos, a word that retains its indecipherable character even for the connoisseur whom the poet consults in order to unveil its significance. He mentioned the affinities he saw between what they did and what we were doing, and above all he spoke of Lupicínio Rodrigues. Lupicínio was a great composer, a black man from the deep south of Brazil—that is to say, from an area where it is thought that the whole population is white—who had become famous for his *sambas-canções* about unfaithful women and monstrous jealousies (in his greatest hit, "Vingança" [Revenge], he threatens the traitor with a curse that, decades later, would make Bob Dylan famous: "você há de rolar como as pedras que rolam na estrada / sem ter nunca um cantinho de seu . . ." ("You'll roll like a stone down the road / without a corner to call your own"). Lupicínio's melodies had a somewhat erratic character that gave them great dramatic efficacy and originality. Before writing the article in which he alluded to me, Augusto had written another, comparing *Jovem Guarda* favorably with *O Fino da Bossa,* and before that, yet another about Lupicínio's extreme poetry, his sometimes overly crude realism, and the unusualness of his melodic compositions, in particular the extraordinary effect that all this attained when the poems were sung in the surprisingly delicate voice of their author.

The curious thing during our conversation was that Augusto mentioned the article I had forgotten, and I was a little embarrassed not to be able to comment on it in detail. But I think there was a copy of it among the articles on Lupicínio and the issues of *Invenção* he gave me. I can't say there was true empathy between us. He seemed even more removed from my world than the tone of his article had led me to imagine. Almost all the characteristics of what in my milieu we call a *"careta,"* a square, could be found in that methodical man, so white, with his mustache and immaculate Paulista accent. Everything about him seemed to come from so far away and to be destined to remain unnoticed in a dark corner.

Although I felt the same estrangement upon meeting him as I had while reading the article, I saw in Augusto's very myopic eyes, and through the concentric circles of his greenish spectacle lenses, an unfading flash that came from a very precise point in his person, a flash of intact sweetness, defended with a crazy tenacity. It seemed to grant him a special right to look absentminded, as crazy people do, and also tied together the otherwise loose ends of his remonstrances of identification with what interested me. That thing in his eyes made him, suddenly, the least *careta* of us all.

Augusto's other articles, and above all some poems and introductory texts from *Invenção,* contributed to my understanding of the profound meaning of this rapprochement. One of those texts in particular—a quasi-manifesto written by Décio Pignatari—seemed to express exactly my preoccupations, and in a tone that would have been mine if only I could have written in it. There was something simplistic in Augusto's articles, which were for newspaper readers who saw pop music festivals on television, but this text by Pignatari, written as it was for the beautiful poetry journal that appeared at irregular intervals, was at once complex, suggestive, and extraordinarily convincing. It was a text for circulation among erudite people, but I, if I could, would have put it without any alteration on the back cover of my record. It was a defense of concretist principles against the socializing attacks of the nationalists. It was a critique of the folksiness that perpetuated underdevelopment, and an assumption of responsibility for what happens at the level of language on the part of those who work with it directly. He offered up the image of the fisherman, with a straw hat and a hammock on his back—the emblem of the publisher Editora Civilização Brasileira—to sound the alert that in developed countries fishing was done with sonar and well-equipped boats. And, in reply to the poet Cassiano Ricardo, a former modernist who had on occasion collaborated with them but now was fond of saying that he was waiting for them to "loosen the bow," Décio closed the article insisting that they, the concrete poets, would always keep the "bow tight" because "in the general Brazilian jam someone has to play the backbone."

The image of a tight bow and the expression "general jam" stayed in my mind, and we talked a lot about them at 2002. The latter found its way into a *tropicalista* lyric by Torquato Neto for a melody by Gil (and the title of a column Torquato wrote for the Carioca press in the following decade), and the image of the "tight bow" reappeared explicitly in a song of mine of the seventies and has remained a diffuse presence beneath the words of many of my compositions and declarations all these years.

2oo2, with its fiberglass doll and its clear acrylic furniture, was becoming more and more animated. Gil was always around. So were Os Mutantes and, naturally, Guilherme, who lived two floors below us. Zé Agrippino and Maria Esther would come by once in a while. Waly and Duda came from Rio and were living with us. And as always I listened to them. Duda was still a great influence on me. I thought that what I was doing was useful but intellectually minor compared with what they, being far more erudite and mentally adept than I, would do. Dedé used to joke with me, saying they were our consultants. We thought it great that the money I earned made it possible to keep a large apartment where they could stay while they were not making the films or writing the books by which our generation would leave its mark on Brazilian culture. We would talk and drink beer late into the night, and Dedé and I would feel proud that our house was host to those unforgettable feasts. The magazines, books, and articles that Augusto gave me would circulate among the members of this community. And the concretists also became frequent guests at 2002. Their visits, however, were always different from those of Agrippino, Os Mutantes, Gil, or even Rogério and Hélio Oiticica (to whom I was finally introduced, during one of my trips to Rio, by the marvelously attuned journalist Marisa Alvarez Lima): the concrete poets would call beforehand, and set a time; they went through all the so-called bourgeois formalities, while among ourselves we all came and went without warning, as though we lived in a commune. Such were the distinctive habits of the irrationalist romantics and the hyperrational offspring of the symbolists.

Little by little I started piecing together the fortuitous bits of information I had gathered regarding the concrete poets throughout the years. Dedé remembered clearly that her aesthetics professor, Yulo Brandão, had talked about them when she was studying dance in Bahia. But I couldn't remember ever having heard the expression "concrete poetry." I had remembered the name of Décio Pignatari from a conversation with Boal at a cast party for *Zumbi,* in 1966. But the names of the two Campos brothers were forgotten soon after they were heard, when Capinan showed me the book on Sousândrade. I remember being charmed when I saw a poem by e. e. cummings published in the cultural supplement of the *Diário de Notícias* in Salvador, which Glauber edited in the sixties. The translation into Portuguese must have been Augusto's, the only person as far as I know who has translated cummings in Brazil (with the rigorous supervision of the author, through an immense exchange of letters), but if his name appeared in print on that page I did not retain it. In the seventies I would hear Glauber say that he had "started out as a concretist," speaking of his first film. This was a short called *O pátio* (The Yard), the "formalism" of which, according to him, lost its fascination once he saw himself surrounded by the impoverished people in the fishing village where, soon after that short, he would make *Barravento.* But neither in the literary pages he published nor in his public statements did I once discover the meaning of "concrete poetry," much less the names of its creators. Nevertheless, I had been indirectly influenced by them since, at age twenty in Salvador, I began to make the connections between João Gilberto, cool jazz, João Cabral's poetry, Niemeyer's architecture in Brasilia, and the use of the Futura typeface on generous white spaces on the pages of the cultural supplement of the *Diário de Notícias.*

Now I began to absorb eagerly the meaning of the concretists' work. I liked to recognize in the poems the complexity they often seemed to lack at first glance. In all of them one felt the adventure of the radical abandonment of discursive syntax. And more, the critical arsenal they furnished the young reader of their publications, the translations (which Haroldo prefers to call "transcriations") of authors and works that seemed essential to them (some of Pound's *Cantos,* poems by Mallarmé, the British metaphysicals, the Provençal troubadours, excerpts from *Finnegans Wake,* cummings, Japanese poetry, etc.), and above all an alternative to the conventional Brazilian literary history that had deemed all works they admired to be peripheral and unimportant—all of this made their journal *Invenção,* the books they gave us, and their conversations a limitless source of stimulation and encouragement.

Haroldo and Décio did not exude the same sense of detachment that I always felt with Augusto. Décio in particular was someone we naturally felt close to. Haroldo, a rotund man with a metallic voice, whose Paulista accent lacked the Italianisms that marred Décio's, used to liven up the room with his exuberant blend of precision and bonhomie. He never let the conversation flag and he showed his command of the language and his immense erudition without ever seeming pedantic or making his listeners feel left out. Augusto, who had gone further than anyone without ever abandoning his objective and balanced tone, had led me to think that Rogério's brilliance, or Glauber's, or my own—since I could be eloquent if my interlocutor did not intimidate me—perhaps was rooted in a narcissism that obscured rather than illuminated the path to pertinent ideas and substantial discoveries. But I soon realized that things were not so simple. No doubt Augusto—like Capinan, like Cacá Diegues—seemed to lack that narcissistic pleasure of conceiving ideas and proffering words. (Never in his whole evolution had he heard the siren song of the romantic word "genius.") There was an undeniable indulgence in permitting the fruition of one's own ego in a group such as the one I was part of. But the excellence of the results—and even the worthiness of the objectives—can scarcely be derived from such an analysis. Augusto quite simply—and finally this is quite consistent with the concretist program—had no taste for rhetoric. It was no less curious that the one closest to me in that group of avant-garde poets should also be the most detached.

I began to frequent Augusto's house. In the stark living room of their home in Perdizes, the group was composed of Augusto, his wife, Lygia, and their son Cid, who was then still a boy. (Roland, the older son, was skittish and never took part in the discussions going on in his living room. Today he is an astrophysicist and researcher at the University of Brasilia.) Haroldo was nearly always present, accompanied by his wife, Carmen, and, more rarely, Décio, whose wife, Lila, did not come as often; and Torquato or Gil or some of the avant-garde musicians

(Rogério Duprat being the most assiduous), aside from Dedé and myself. Some of the visual poems, in large Futura type, were framed on the walls, as was a good reproduction of Seurat's *La Grande Jatte,* and a painting by Volpi, in addition to some works by the "concrete" painters of São Paulo, all of it evoking a sensibility at once open and meticulous. The taste for geometric shapes and the defined finish reflected a delicate rather than a neurotic mind: it was a lively and welcoming room, permeable and airy.

There we would listen to Charles Ives, Lupicínio, Webern, and Cage, and we would talk about the situation of Brazilian music and the festivals. We, the young *tropicalistas,* would listen to stories about the personages involved in the dada movement, Anglo-American modernism, the Brazilian Modern Art Week, and the heroic phase of concrete poetry. We would exchange ideas with great ease, the great differences in the extent of our knowledge (to say nothing of the mental aptitude for dealing with it) never creating cause for embarrassment. It is a particularly Brazilian experience that gives us reason to feel proud: in our case, the confusion of high culture with mass culture, which was so typical of the sixties, was able to bear substantial fruit and, in the undertow of the wave—when everyone felt the need to return to old labels—those of us involved succeeded, despite some painful episodes, in maintaining the dialogue, and the friendships survived. My understanding with Augusto de Campos, above all, perhaps because it was potentially the most difficult, has shown considerable resilience.

My tone as I write these pages must reveal to the attentive reader a combination of respect—near reverence—and a lack of ceremony toward serious topics, noble themes, and superior styles. This same mixture—sometimes in somewhat unbalanced measures—was already a characteristic of mine when, postponing my studies and a career as filmmaker, I played and enjoyed the part of TV idol, in the name of a passion for the "evolutionary line" of our popular music. My opinions on famous authors, sometimes expressed in an unrestrained manner, were received with benevolence by them: they were excited to see in us an incarnation of so many of their postulates. But they were never condescending, and the mistakes I (more than anyone) committed out of daring ignorance were always pointed out with kindness, however decisively. All the same, I was always far more extroverted and opinionated with Décio and Haroldo and the whole group of Bahians and *tropicalistas* than I was with Augusto alone.

The astonishing concurrence of our positions with their ideas—and the natural alliance against enemy attacks—postponed the clash of differences and the eventual disagreements. I will give an example that at the time had already occurred to me: the similarity signaled by Augusto, in conversations and later in an article written in 1969, between our work and the poetry of the Provençal troubadours. The emphasis was on the suitability of words to music. As to that, I had been, continued to be, and still am a Caymmian from the standpoint of João Gilberto. In Caymmi the sung word receives the loftiest treatment imaginable: always spontaneous, it nevertheless reveals the rigorous scrutiny it has undergone. Caymmi's songs seem to exist of their own accord, but the perfection of their simplicity, attained through precision in the choice of words and notes, is the mark of an exacting author. They are how a song ought to be, how good songs have always been and always will be. A Tuva song, a lied by Schubert, a Gershwin ballad, the "Dying Eagle" by Ives, must be compared with "Sargaço mar," "Lá vem a baiana," and "Você já foi à Bahia": they are all incursions into the essential reality of song. This is how João Gilberto understood Caymmi's "Rosa Morena," chosen by him as the thematic line on which to develop the style that eventually was called bossa nova. This is how João's great labor of modernization came to build on Caymmi's effortless modernization. At once impressionist and primitive, the greatest inventor of urban-modern samba, Caymmi weighs as heavily on the Joãogilbertian elaboration of bossa nova as Orlando Silva, Ciro Monteiro, American music from the thirties, and cool jazz—while possessing more gravity. Everything in João pays homage to him, from his sense of structure to his diction.

The way that João Gilberto heard Caymmi and cultivated the standard he set for the word as song—this is the selective filter of bossa nova; it is the source of the torque in Tom Jobim's music and the poetry in that of Vinicius. And it is all as exacting as anything I can conceive of in terms of the "art of combining words & sound," as Augusto explained the Provençal "motz el som" in Pound. This was also what Chico Buarque was searching for (and frequently found) in his pursuit of the beauty he divined in the lyrics of Vinicius: unlike what Edu Lobo or Marcos Valle were doing—and different from what Milton Nascimento and the Minas group would do some years later—Chico held on to the purity of that line, showing no tendency toward superficial trendiness, whether that of Beco das Garrafas or that of the Arena shows. He worked exclusively with the elements I had tried (almost always in vain) to preserve intact in our work, since Bethânia's record.

Behind the rivalry between Chico and me, one ought to look for an enormous identification. *Tropicalismo* came to put an end to the hyper-caution, and if there was anything to be careful about, it was exactly what Chico continued to cultivate and polish.

The first readings of the Provençal poets translated by Augusto revealed an impressive beauty and cleverness, but did not make it clear why, on the one hand, they were the acme of the sung word nor, on the other hand, why among us it was not Caymmi (or Chico) who came close to them but rather Gil and myself. Augusto was quite convincing in establishing the kinship between us and those poets, but that did not mean that our songs or theirs were better than Caymmi's respecting the "motz el som." Rereading the interview Augusto did with me in 1968, I was shocked by the comment he made that my song "Clara"—whose kinship with Provençal procedures is clear—had "a cleanness, a tight-ness one cannot find in Caymmi": those have always seemed to me to be Caymmian virtues par excellence. João Gilberto's cleanness and tight-ness were learned from Caymmi: they came from him. I cannot deny that, as the years go by, rereading the Provençal poets—and reading and listening to many other very different things—has made me under-stand better the sense of Augusto's evaluation. I have understood more and more clearly that, devoted as he was to evaluating continually a vast world of diverse experiments with words and sounds, he had devel-oped an ear with demands distinct from those I myself nurtured. But my opinion of Caymmi has not changed.

Now that the days we call heroic have passed, I have to submit all of my pretensions to a question: to what extent did my opportunity for shining as a great figure of MPB depend upon the drop in demand for quality incited by that same wave of supposed popularity that I helped to create? There was between the redemption Augusto offered and the rejection of our colleagues a void within Brazilian culture that could not be filled by popular success or by the scandalous notoriety that it brought us. Augusto at times used to say that Erik Satie, who could not compete with Debussy in harmonic invention, chose instead to turn the music inside out. And he concluded that, by the same token, the *tropi-calistas* had opted for the inside out of bossa nova.

The missing link turned up as if by magic. Augusto, who had gone to New York for some event connected to his poetry, spoke to João Gilberto, and the latter not only showed a total lack of prejudice towards the *tropicalistas,* but spoke with affection and interest about the group and its plans. The story of that encounter, by the way, was later to be told in what would be Augusto's only foray into prose narrative. It is a small masterpiece of concision that eventually found its way into his book, *Balanço da bossa,* the cover of which echoes the message to me that Augusto brought back from New York. It is a montage of photographs wherein João appears to be looking at me from above, as I sit onstage: "Tell Caetano that I'm keeping my eye on him."

Augusto's open defense of the *tropicalistas* showed not only how his feistiness had evolved, but also the limitations it had imposed on him. Many of those limitations were a conscious choice on his part. Thus he frequently said that he was not, could not be, and did not want to be "impartial." On the contrary, he had learned since the heroic phase of concrete poetry that he had to be extremely partial, and remained constant in his defense and appreciation of avant-garde attitudes. Augusto, Haroldo, and Décio themselves maintained an emphasis on experimentalism as a counterweight to conformity and the mediocrity it engenders. There was nevertheless something in Augusto's arguments that I believed pointed toward a problem in the whole avant-garde movement that for me had not been resolved—nor perhaps could be. This is the problem of progress in the arts.

There seemed to be a critical weakness in the assertions of Augusto and his friends among the avant-garde musicians when they attempted to insert João Gilberto in the lineage of Mário Reis, the popular thirties singer, whose small voice became fashionable with the advent of modern microphones. Mário sang almost as if speaking, in staccato, separating the syllables in regular relation to the rhythmic bars, with no ornamentation whatsoever. Of course I could recognize the superficial similarity to João, in the undramatic style, the small volume. But João is a singer of great legati, with a floating style of phrase and incredible rhythmic playfulness. His style comes from Orlando Silva, the great modernizer of Brazilian singing, whose powerful voice, always used with great delicacy, and vocal ornamentation made many listeners suppose, wrongly, that João was far from him. Undeniably, João also gives Mário Reis his due, and there is in both (as the filmmaker Júlio Bressane reminded me) an obsessive fidelity to the same repertoire, always revisited, and growing only in measured droplets. In a way, João is an anti-Mário: using his voice as one instrument among others; he is, like Orlando, a supersinger, while Mário, who refuses to let himself be swayed by melody, derives his charm from being an antisinger. All of which gave me to suppose that there was something superficial about the way those São Paulo avant-garde artists were listening to bossa nova. The very examples Augusto used to draw from the bossa nova repertoire made apparent a discrepancy in our tastes. I had always been more enamored of the reconnection João Gilberto established between the edge of modernity and the best Brazilian tradition—which is ultimately what made the great difference for bossa nova, in comparison to the somewhat silly Americanization of his predecessors in the forties and fifties (and some of his supposed followers from the sixties on). I saw in "Chega de saudade" the manifesto and the masterpiece of a movement: the mother ship. A samba with some traces of *choro,* immensely rich in melodic motifs, with a flavor so Brazilian it could be a recording by Silvio Caldas from the thirties (and with a flute intro inspired by a recording of Orlando Silva's), "Chega de saudade" managed to be a modern song while having enough harmonic and rhythmic daring to attract any bop or cool-jazz musician (as in fact it eventually did). On the other hand, the title and lyrics suggested a rejection/reinvention of *saudade,* that word so prevalent in and emblematic of our experience and our language. A lush composition full of uncommon commonplaces (to use Augusto's expression, or perhaps it was Décio's, out of context) and of novelties that sounded like atavisms—or experiments that seemed like memories—this song was a generous example of everything Tom, João, Vinicius, and others wanted to offer, containing all the elements that were elsewhere scattered. It was the prime mover of bossa nova, the map, the itinerary, the constitution. And yet Augusto, in a brief commentary, emphasizes the incremental variation of "colado assim, calado assim" ("so close like this, so quiet like this") as the only thing of interest in an otherwise conventional song. In fact, it is the moment when the melody in Jobim reaches for unusual intervals and Vinicius's lyrics move toward formal invention—the elements that produced "Desafinado" and "Samba de uma nota só" (One-Note Samba). But for Augusto, as for the São Paulo avant-garde musicians, these were the movement's "song-manifestos."

It must be pointed out, however, that Augusto did not dedicate himself to writing about bossa nova: his brief commentary on "Chega de saudade" appears in an interview done with Brasil Rocha Brito for an article. He wrote more about post–bossa nova: *Jovem Guarda, Fino da Bossa, tropicalismo.* And he did so in such an opportune and clear-headed way that, one believes, had he taken the time to write about bossa nova, none of its essential aspects would have escaped him. Actually, the mistake with regard to the issue of Mário Reis and Orlando Silva had already been addressed by José Lino Grunewald, the Carioca arm of concrete poetry, a poet who translated the complete *Cantos* of Ezra Pound, and who had been an aficionado of MPB from the thirties on. Augusto would certainly have listened again and again to Orlando, Mário, Sílvio Caldas, and many others, before sitting down to write. "The smokiness of João Gilberto," wrote Grunewald, "comes from Orlando Silva, not Mário Reis."

Years later, in the preface to a collection of translations of poets ranging from Ovid to Rimbaud, Augusto offered the image of poetry as "a family of ships wrecked and scattered, struggling in time and space." Elsewhere in the same essay he declares that "the old that was once new is as new as the newest of the new," as though to affiliate himself with a millennial lineage of avant-gardists, while always sensing that beneath the demand for progress lies a vision of all time, a transhistoric perspective, a view also advanced by the concrete poets, particularly Haroldo. This is no trivial discovery: with these texts so clear and enthusiastic, in advancing an aesthetic of the new, the concretist (Haroldo above all) would defend a synchronic, transhistorical vision. I wish to say it was not their passion for the new that attracted me, but this more profound aspect of their work. It was as if they cultivated an image of rage for the new as a strategy to engage their audience on a much more demanding level. When trying to understand modernist ruptures, the revitalization of tradition inherent in supposedly destructive tactics is readily apparent. Stravinsky and Schoenberg seem to intend not that we stop listening to Bach in order to listen to them, but rather that we become better listeners of Bach for having listened to them. In fact, all modernisms upon deeper examination show themselves to be a struggle against the imminent obsolescence of a past so beautiful as to be on the verge of banality. Never before modernism has art been so conservative! The artist, as supreme aristocrat, shows himself unable to submit to the dangerous vulgarization that seeks ready-made formulas anyone can use for the production and consumption of art. And this is done precisely to demonstrate that art is a terrible and difficult thing: one cannot be untouched by Velázquez, Mozart, or Dante. But the tension between this aristocratic attitude (which did not stop at negating even the work of the greatest contemporary artists) and the need of the modernist to affirm himself as the producer of new artistic objects of the first order (leading to a crossover with popular culture and a love affair with technology)—this tension is what produced the whole gamut of artistic movements at the end of the nineteenth century and the beginning of the twentieth—from the Impressionists to the Expressionists, the Constructivists to the Surrealists, Marinetti to Dada, Duchamp to Mondrian.

So it was that I, a mere singer on the radio, in the midst of such erudite people, was enlisted in a war that demanded the definition of such big issues. It excited me. It appeared that I was now really carrying out that mission of being a poet, only by means other than the printed poem. Augusto confirmed such an illusion when he stated that what was interesting about Brazilian poetry—the "new information"—had fled the pages of books and entered the voices of the music world. As even more of a provocation, he employed Pound's classification of the six different types of creators of literature—inventors, masters, diluters, "good writers without salient qualities," "writers of belles-lettres," and "the starters of crazes"—to announce that Villa-Lobos "diluted" his field, while dignifying Gil and me as true "inventors" in ours.

avant-garde

In the seventies, Breno, a friend of mine from Salvador and the son of Auto de Castro, my former professor of the history of philosophy, supposing it would offend my possible concretist ideology, told me he did not think that innovations or inventions in art were worthwhile. And he quoted someone or other who presumably said that Bartók was "the least innovative and the most original of modern musicians." Breno was still a boy then, a fact that heightened the wit of his having selected this quotation to demolish my likely arguments. In fact endorsing no ideology, I didn't respond to what he'd said, and chose rather to comment on the shrewd beauty of the quotation. And so we had a pleasant conversation. Then, many years later, I read a statement by Augusto de Campos to the effect that contrary to the advice of the philosopher who states that what cannot be said ought to be silenced (Wittgenstein), the poet should instead continue to "say the unsayable." As Décio Pignatari said in *Comunicação poética,* his wonderful manual for young people who are interested in poetry, "Here we teach how to make a poem, but not how to make a poet." If the concretists defend an objectivity that protects poetic appreciation against arbitrariness and irrationality, it is because they know that both are frequently enlisted in the service of those ingrained bad habits that result in the enslavement of the poet. When Augusto says, in his defense of the alleged "cerebralness" of the British "metaphysical poets" that the "true ethical function" of the poet implies a "refusal to let himself be transformed into an object, a jukebox for sentimental titillation," he is providing a clue for anyone with his wits about him to differentiate between the concretists' poetical creation and their guerrilla aesthetics, intertwined as these may be.

Nowadays many people ask themselves what modernism meant after all, and how Webern could possibly render Brahms obsolete, or how one should interpret the fact that John Cage—throwing I Ching coins and reading at random from *Finnegans Wake*—was considered the most

creative composer at the end of the twentieth century. I remember a
conversation I had with Augusto in Amaralina in the early seventies,
when I explained to him what was for me so impressive about Lévi-
Strauss's reasoning against atonal, concrete, or dodecaphonic music in
the introduction to *The Raw and the Cooked.* Augusto, though he listened with admiration and interest to the intelligence of the arguments, answered impassively: "That's all very well reasoned, but the
best musicians decide what's best for music. There is always something
that is understandable only to those who've got a hand in it."

In 1968, Augusto was impressed with Paul McCartney's
declared enthusiasm for Stockhausen. Yet in the years that
followed, as he was listening to the sweet and spineless pop produced
by Paul—music whose transgression was totally programmatic and
digestible following the spectacular growth of the pop market after the
Beatles—a man like Augusto, one can only imagine, must have been
filled with boredom and distaste. He must have felt the same toward
pop music, MPB, and the *tropicalistas.* Sooner or later we, the *tropicalistas,* in more or less noble ways, depending on the individual case, would
show signs of the essence of our chosen activity, which has always consisted in producing banal songs to compete in the market. (And in
Brazil the growth of this market means an advance on the national
scale.) Augusto keeps on fighting for unpopular music: Boulez, Stockhausen, Berio, Varèse, and Cage—and also Giacinto Scelsi, Luigi Nono,
Ustvolskaya, etc. The stubborn unpopularity of the most inventive
contemporary music is truly a mystery. Augusto's flash of euphoria
when he heard of McCartney's (ultimately undeveloped) interest in
Stockhausen in 1968 represented a fleeting hope of deciphering this
enigma. *Produssumo,* as I said earlier, was a word invented by another
concretist poet, Décio Pignatari, to define a period in which avant-
garde ideas had a place at the top of the pop-rock charts. One of the
most stimulating problems of the avant-garde, and a problem that
makes some of the most stimulating artists run from it like the Devil
from the cross—is its dubious position with regard to its intrinsic
ambition to become the norm. I have recently heard Arto Lindsay say
that the musicians and producers of the trendiest vogue in dance music
(techno) are voracious consumers of precisely the kind of music hero-
ically defended by Augusto. These young people are listening to Varèse
and Cage, to Boulez and Berio. And, says Arto, they don't talk about

anything else. What should we make of this? In the seventies, there was already an outcry of very conservative (and very useful) voices protesting "modernism in the streets." But will the collective ear adjust itself to postserialist or postdodecaphonic music? And what kind of world will it be, when such music sounds like music to "everyone's" ears? I myself can't say exactly why Webern's music (especially the most radical pieces) has always seemed to me indisputably beautiful. Might the techno-dance kids be an embryonic minority? What will happen to the tonal ear as we know it if unpopular music's failure with the public at large is overcome? When I first saw MTV in New York, I wrote an article entitled "Vendo canções" (See and Sell Songs), in which I ask more or less superficial questions but still point in the same direction. The procedures of avant-garde film, which were trashed by serious and commercial cinema alike, had finally found refuge in those snippets of rock 'n' roll film, which were at once erratic illustrations of the songs and ads for the corresponding records. Now I can't stand to watch rock videos for very long: the excess of images laboring to seem bizarre bores me, especially at the speed the editing presents them. But the question remains: don't the references to *Un chien andalou,* to *Metropolis*—and the undying kinship with Cocteau's *Blood of a Poet*—appear in a rock video exactly as Mondrian's designs flash across the skirt of a prostitute? Are "modernisms" and "avant-gardes" only now beginning to lose their rights to such labels?

I prefer to continue to love the advances made by all the modernisms and all their offshoots. In face of the surrender to Hollywood's laws of narrative, I still celebrate Godard. Before journalists who attack the French and German philosophers because they don't write with the Anglophile's (journalistic) "clarity," I praise Heidegger writing on Nietzsche and Deleuze on Proust. I salute the arrival of Arnaldo Antunes and Carlinhos Brown and Chico Science against those critics who bow (explicitly?) to the number of CDs sold or the intensity and duration of the applause in a concert hall. And I owe that strength, which for me means life, in great part to the concretists.*

---

*To say nothing of their having rescued from virtual anonymity the Baroque period and their rediscovery of figures like Sousândrade, Pedro Kilkerry, and Qorpo Santo, all of lthem more ambitious and inventive than many who had occupied the mainstream of Brazilian literary history. That academic tradition has always located our literary

beginnings withthe eithteenth-century's Minas GGerais poets of the "arcade" movement, while dismissing the seventeenth century, including the exuberant poetry of
Gregorio de Matos and the intricate sermons of Padre Antonio Vieira, whom Fernando Pessoa calls "the emperor of the Portuguese language." The concretists emphasized, to borrow the words of the North American historian Richard M. Morse, "a
new reading of American culture, no longer conceived in terms of a genealogical
imagery of branches, twigs, and buds that point to a gradual emergence of transat-
lantic 'identities.' " Here is the strength of synchronic vision. And of overcoming the
opposition of center/periphery.

anthropophagy

Antropofagia: cannibalism

This vision is the great legacy of the modernist poet Oswald de Andrade.

Oswald was, with Mário de Andrade, the intellectual leader of Brazilian modernism, a movement launched to great scandal in São Paulo in 1922, with a week of recitals and exhibitions that provoked awe, fright, and horror—and established the basis for a national culture. The painters Tarsila do Amaral and Anita Malfatti, and the composer Villa-Lobos, as well as other poets and writers like Menotti del Picchia, Plínio Salgado, and Cassiano Ricardo, were also central figures. While Mário de Andrade, whose name I heard constantly among my nationalist friends, had been the responsible, normative, and organizing figure of modernism, Oswald represented radical fragmentation, an intuitive and violently iconoclastic force.

My first real exposure occurred during the staging of a play of his by the theater group Oficina. I had seen their version of Gorky's *Petit Bourgeois* in 1965 and was charmed by the production. The style of the director, José Celso Martinez Corrêa, was more traditional and subtler than Boal's. I remember leaving the theater thinking what a problem it was that I should like this better than my dear *Arena conta Zumbi*. *Zumbi* was a step forward, but *Pequenos burgueses* took me back to the shows by Eros Martim Gonçalves's theater school and João Augusto Azevedo's Teatro dos Novos in Bahia, with a new sensibility that the more schematic *Zumbi* did not possess. The Oficina production was highly nuanced, very "European"—and it made Boal's *Zumbi* seem American, Broadway-like. And so it was that I went, full of great expectations, to see *O rei da vela* (The King of the Candle), Oswald de Andrade's play rescued by Oficina from the oblivion of thirty years. I did not, however, anticipate that I would find in this play both an elaboration of this sensibility and its complete negation.

Zé Celso, the director, was to become for me as significant an artist as Glauber Rocha. Like Glauber, he had an intense personal fire, but his knack for the finished product was something Glauber could not even dream of. His artistic confidence made it possible for him to let the spectator feel the space according to a profound poetics relating to the movement of bodies, the voices, the light. It is precisely the awkwardness in Glauber's work that often intensifies the aesthetic effect. Zé Celso produced these intensities with thorough control over the means. The play contained the off-beat elements and the anthropological gaze that distinguished *Land in Anguish.* The first act was done in Expressionist style, with the main antihero, Abelardo I, in his office, awaiting his debtors, who were kept in a cage and whipped by his assistant, Abelardo II; the costumes were dark, as was the makeup, with the exception of the two Abelardos, whose faces were painted white, like clowns. The second act was done in *chanchada* style: a stridently colorful panel consisted of a childlike cubist representation of Guanabara Bay in Rio. Here Abelardo I and his wife, Heloísa de Lesbos, are seen with her family: there is the fat mother listening to tales of her son-in-law's gallantries, the fascist brother, the younger sister with boxing gloves, the queer brother who bewails his family (and exclaims all the while that his "fate is to fish in the crags"), the grandmother to whom Abelardo dedicates verses by Lamartine Babo (the composer of sensational Carnival *marchinhas* from the thirties, when the play was written), the American guest (the first, and the most effective, instance of the caricatured imperialist agent who would be a constant element in the plays by CPC and UNE in the sixties). All this took place on a turning stage as the allusions to transactions of person, family, class, nation, and international economy alternated with dizzying agility and vivacity. The third act was operatic in tone. Heloísa de Lesbos, who in the first act had appeared with a cigarette holder, wearing a white outfit, and in the second wearing a futuristic silver bathing suit that made the actress (Itala Nandi) look like the robot in the film *Metropolis,* now took center stage in a long black dress to weep over the poverty into which Abelardo had fallen.

The play owed much of its visual impact to Hélio Eichbauer—who for that very reason has enormous importance in the history of *tropicalismo.* He was the young Carioca set designer who had studied in Czechoslovakia with Svoboda. The scenic coherence of each act was made possible only by the technical assurance and the inventiveness of this great Brazilian artist, whose work enriches our theater to this day, and with whom I have collaborated (I used his model of the set design for the second act of *O rei da vela* in the cover of my record *Estrangeiro*).

I had composed "Tropicália" shortly before *O rei da vela* premiered, and seeing this play was for me a revelation that there was indeed a movement afoot in Brazil, a movement that transcended popular music. In the program notes, Zé Celso dedicated the new production to Glauber and to Cinema Novo's responsiveness to the reality of the times, a quality he found wanting in contemporary theater.

If I had been rejected by the leftist nationalist sociologists as well as by the right-wing bourgeois moralists, at least I had won the support of—having attracted or been attracted to—the "irrationalists" (such as Zé Agrippino, Zé Celso, Jorge Mautner) as well as the "superrationalists" (including the concrete poets and the musical disciples of atonality). Yet as I was to discover in São Paulo between 1967 and 1968, there was one figure apparently connecting those two not always compatible groups: Oswald de Andrade. Oswald's imagery stimulated the imagination to be skeptical of nationality, history, language. Soon I would discover that his drama was the weak part of his oeuvre, and *O rei da vela* perhaps the weakest of his plays. Everything I had seen in that Oficina production was better said in his poetry, his novels, and his manifestos.

Before Zé Celso, the concrete poets had taken it upon themselves to resuscitate Oswald. An anthology of poems, with a long introductory essay by Haroldo de Campos, and an article by Décio Pignatari called "Marco Zero de Andrade": by these efforts they forced back into the upper ranks of Brazilian literature a figure who had been enveloped in silence, or remembered only as an "outdated" avant-gardist. When I told Augusto about the effect Oswald had produced in me, he felt encouraged to share with me Décio and Haroldo's essays, taking my enthusiasm as another confirmation of the affinities between the concretists and the *tropicalistas*. Through Augusto and his friends I became acquainted with Oswald's poetry—at once loose and dense and extraordinarily concentrated—and soon thereafter with his revolutionary prose fiction. Above all I surrendered to the shock of the "manifestos": *Manifesto da poesia pau-brasil* (Brazilwood Manifesto) of 1924, and particularly the *Manifesto antropófago* (Cannibal Manifesto) of 1928. These two texts of extraordinary beauty, both descended, like the European manifestos, from Marinetti's Futurism, were a rediscovery of and a new foundation for Brazil. Oswald referred to Brazilian literature as "the most backward in the world." It was not just to avoid saying this that he felt free to affirm, in the first manifesto: "Only Brazilians from our own time. The essential in chemistry, mechanics, economics, and ballistics. All fully digested. Without cultural encounter. Practicalities. Experimental. Poets."

The second manifesto develops and exposes the metaphor of devouring. We Brazilians should not imitate but rather devour new information from wherever it comes. In the words of Haroldo de Campos, this was a need "to assimilate the foreign experience into the Brazilian species, and to reinvent it on our own terms, with the ineluctable local qualities that will endow the resulting product with an autonomous character and confer on it, in principle, functionality as product for export." Oswald launched the myth of anthropophagy, bringing the cannibal ritual into the arena of international cultural relations. Father Pero Fernandes Sardinha's deglutition by the Indians becomes the inaugural scene of Brazilian culture, the very basis of nationality.

The idea of cultural cannibalism fit *tropicalistas* like a glove. We were "eating" the Beatles and Jimi Hendrix. Our arguments against the nationalists' defensive attitude found in this stance its most succinct and exhaustive enunciation. Of course we started to use it extensively and intensively, but not without attempting to rethink the terms in which we adopted it. I also attempted—and still do—to reread the poetry, fiction, and manifestos, keeping in mind the kind of works they were intended to defend, the context in which such poetry and such poetics emerged. Gil and I never lost sight of the differences between the modernist experience of the twenties and our electronic confrontations of the sixties. And if Gil, over the years, has withdrawn from this awareness of the "greater" implications of the movement—by which Gil means its correlations with what happened in theater, film, literature, and the visual arts—claiming instead that they were perhaps the result of overintellectualization, I myself have always been suspicious of the simplification with which the idea of anthropophagy, popularized by us, has tended to be invoked.

There are few moments in our cultural history that can vie with Oswald's vision. As I see it, it is a decision in favor of precision rather than a panacea to solve the problem of identity in Brazil. Oswald's limpid and cutting poetry is, in itself, the opposite of a complacent "choose your own cocktail of references." Anthropophagy, seen in more precise terms, is a means of radicalizing the demand for identity, not a denial of the question. We were sure that João Gilberto (who, in contrast to mayonnaise-style fusions—to borrow the expression of the Italian psychoanalyst Contardo Calligaris—created a new style, definite and fresh) was a clear example of the anthropophagist attitude. And we wanted to meet those standards.

It is worth the time here to comment on an unpretentious little book of Calligaris's, *Hello Brasil!: notas de um psicanalista europeu viajando ao Brasil* (Hello Brazil! Notes of a European Psychoanalyst Traveling in Brazil). This book formulates the most determined rejection of the anthropophagic wave, of which we, the *tropicalistas,* were the most effective disseminators. Calligaris says that his book was born of his passion for Brazil (and for a Brazilian woman . . .), a country that he had never considered until a professional invitation brought him here. And, being a psychoanalyst, he deduced the best way to help this newly beloved place overcome its failure as a national project was to force it to confront its fatal hopelessness. "Brazil is hopeless," wrote the American poet Elizabeth Bishop, without manifesting Calligaris's desire to help (though she too was here because she had fallen in love with a Brazilian woman). In Calligaris's book, there is, moreover, a pleasant tone as well as useful observations revealing a responsible and generous intelligence. The central thesis of what might provisionally be considered a "travel" book (as the author requests) illuminates the thinking of those who have taken up Brazil as a subject. The colonizer (who left the mother country in order to exercise, as it were, the potency of the father unhindered in the new land) and the colonist (the immigrant who, having come in hope that the colonizer would establish for him by some paternal interdiction a new nationality, finds only the enslavement of his body, which the colonizer confounds—as he does the bodies of black people—with the land itself which must perforce be drained to the last): these are two instances of the Brazilian mentality that inspires the expression (overheard by Calligaris at a time when it seemed even to Brazilians, an aberration and still a novelty—which does not exclude it from being, as he took it to be, a symptom): "This country is no good."

The very name of the country, Brazil, seems to him lacking in value: "The only name as far as I know that does not designate a remote ethnic origin, or a place, but rather a product of exploitation, the first, now completely extinct." (Namely, the wood.) Thus, everything in Brazil—from the young man who touches your butt during Carnival in Bahia (leaving it unclear as to whether he is after sex or money) to the foreign debt; to the children who are treated like royalty or murdered in the streets, to the *blocos Afros* who search, in the absurd Egypt of their songs, for the origin that will give meaning to their existence—everything is explained in relation to the lack of the name of the father, of a "national signifier." "Anthropophagism," as Calligaris prefers to call it, would have emerged as a solution to this problem. And it is harshly criticized by him for substituting the digestive tract (the end of which everyone knows too well) for the ONE that Brazil never succeeded in making. And with that substitution, in the end, would come a suggestion on the part of the colonizer to the colonist to take as the national ONE the enslaved body that offers itself: Brazil would thus be exotic not only to tourists but to Brazilians as well.

Of course all this is related to *tropicalismo.* But if Brazilian psycho-analysis had a João Gilberto the conversation might take a different turn. Calligaris's book provocatively reveals a courageous wish to know the body and soul of this country. One must admire his interpretation of the cynical treatment of historical figures (especially King João VI, forced to leave Portugal for Brazil when Napoleon blockaded Great Britain, his staunch ally—only for his courageous fidelity to be reduced in schoolbooks to "King João had debts and commercial interests in England"; he becomes known in Brazil as the "runaway king"), as of the resulting Brazilian vision that the "only motor of human action could be the appetite for a direct enjoyment of things." The provoca-tiveness and the courage to go so far in removing the blinders from Brazil are qualities that bring Calligaris's book closer to *tropicalismo* (which he does not cite) and to anthropophagy (which he tears apart). But one is tempted to ask what Calligaris would make of the fact that this anthropophagy, triumphant when he arrived, has been, of all the modernist contributions, the one to meet with the greatest resistance, in fact total rejection, having been repressed from the twenties until the sixties. And also this: if those values of the sixties are to be discred-ited—the conservative psychoanalytic realism of Calligaris's book con-tributes much to this purpose with its assault on Paradise Now and the pleasure principle—perhaps he should reconsider the diagnosis. If anthropophagy was such a bad symptom, apparently Brazil has power-ful antibodies against it, since it has been the greatest failure of the modernist movement of 1922, and common sense has continued to penalize it, whenever it attempts a return whether in concretism, in *tropicalismo,* and so on. But being a realist—Oswald was, too—I wel-come the conservative backlash. That is why I accept the provocation and value this book, so friendly and so discordant. I understand that, being a psychoanalyst and having arrived in Brazil at the end of the neo-anthropophagic vogue unleashed by *tropicalismo* (the last gasps were apparently being drawn in the milieu of psychology), the author reacted quite naturally to what he heard: it could have remained unsaid in the Brazilian unconscious for all time, but it was "said"—and the analyst arrived just in time to hear at least the echo.

In *tropicalismo* (in the wake of anthropophagy), there is a tendency to make Brazil exotic as much for the tourists as for Brazilians. No doubt even I myself reject what seem to me ridiculous attempts to neutralize the strangeness of this Catholic tropical monster, in the hunt for the crumbs of ordinary international respectability. Of course I recognize that a headdress of bananas is not particularly useful when worn by a nuclear physicist or a classicist born in Brazil. But "Brazil" can liberate the creative energies that will enable the proliferation of research (or the invention of new disciplines) only if Brazil refuses to feel intimidated by itself, and if it places its narcissistic pleasure above sensible submission to the international order.

When *Orfeu do Carnaval* (known in English as *Black Orpheus*) opened, I was eighteen. I laughed along with the entire audience and together we were shamed by the shameless lack of authenticity the French filmmaker had permitted himself for the sake of creating a fascinating piece of exoticism. The critique we Brazilians made of the film can be summed up in this way: "How is it possible that the best and most genuine musicians in Brazil could have agreed to create masterpieces to adorn (and dignify) such a deception?" It is well known that Vinicius de Moraes, the author of the play on which the film was based, left the theater irate, during a screening organized by the producers before the opening. The fascination, nevertheless, worked with foreigners: the film seemed (to people of the most widely diverse cultural backgrounds) not only a moving modern and popular version of the Greek myth but also the revelation of the paradisiacal country in which it was staged. By the time *tropicalismo* emerged, the film had already been forgotten in Brazil. But when we arrived in London in 1969, the recording executives, hippies, and intellectuals we met, all, without exception, would refer enthusiastically to *Black Orpheus* as soon as they heard that we were Brazilians. We felt a little embarrassed, but to accept the request to sing "Manhã de Carnaval" sometimes was a form of compensation. Even today there is no end of narratives about foreigners (rock singers, first-rate novelists, French sociologists, budding actresses) discovering Brazil, all touched by Marcel Camus's unforgettable film. Elizabeth Bishop, in her letters from Rio—possibly on

account of being a poet and having lived in Brazil for a long time—
made an effort from the outset to convince her American friends
(Robert Lowell included) that contrary to how it might seem to them,
the film was bad, though the music was worthwhile; but soon she distanced herself from Brazilians in her judgment, pronouncing the songs
in the film to be unworthy as well, because they were not the "authentic" music of the Carioca slums. Only Jean-Luc Godard, at around the
time when the film was released, would write a critique that was just in
every respect toward the filmmaking, the poetry, the Orpheus myth,
and the city of Rio de Janeiro—an article the *tropicalistas* would have
liked to sign. I found out about it only in the seventies, when I went
back to Bahia. In the meantime, the *tropicalista* critical revision of the
film would concern itself after all with a deepening study of the gaze of
the foreigner upon us—and the subtleties of love and war with exoticism.

I surprised myself by writing, for the introduction to this book,
about what Brazil is—for me, as for all Brazilians in my experience, it is
above all a name. (This is what made me think of the Italian psychoanalyst's book.) All Brazilians have the impression that the country simply has no practical sense. It is like a father with a good heart and an
honest reputation whom we respect but who can't make money or hold
a steady job, who wastes great opportunities, gets drunk, and lands in
trouble. And as for the name "Brazil," I find it beautiful for every reason, and have always entertained an integrated and satisfactory inner
sense of it. The Italian analyst says that it is typical of the Brazilian to
be named irresponsibly, without a symbolic connection, for instance, to
the saint whose feast falls on his birthday. But my name is Caetano
because I was born on St. Caetano's Day, in praise of whom my mother
causes a mass to be celebrated every year, even in my absence. I never
felt like an exception on this account. Santo Amaro did not have rich or
poor people, it was a well-planned town with its own style: everyone
felt naturally proud of being Brazilian. We thought the Portuguese
language was clear and beautiful. We would willingly say that French
(which we would learn in high school) was perhaps more beautiful, and
that Italian (which we heard often in movies) surely was too (the Spanish spoken in Mexican films seemed to us pretty ridiculous). We
thought English was easy as a subject of study because of the underin-
flected verbs, but we argued over the difference between how it is pronounced and how it is written, finding the sound of it more canine than
human, although hearing movies and songs in English involved us

more and more with the language. Almost everyone was visibly of mixed race. That the country might be poor was no reason for shame (although I rooted for it to get rich). We considered ourselves to be peaceful, affectionate, clean. It was unimaginable that anyone born here would want to live in another country.

Tropicalismo began in me as a painful experience. The development of a social, and then political and economic, conscience, combined with existential, aesthetic, and moral concerns that questioned everything, led me to think about the songs I composed and heard. Everything that came to be called *tropicalismo* was nourished by acts of violence against a taste that had matured steadily and was everywhere lucidly defended. Chico Buarque said that as a Paulista youth of the upper middle class he had felt attracted to Elvis and the urban folklore of "bad boys." Chico's rebellious episodes as a car thief reveal that identification. Bossa nova brought him to a maturity that transformed the earlier phase into his personal and artistic prehistory. I felt I lived in a homogeneous country whose inauthentic aspects—and the various versions of rock certainly represented one of them—were a result of social injustice (which fomented ignorance) and of its macromanifestation, imperialism, which imposed its styles and products. I heard and learned everything from the radio, but beginning in childhood, as I began to form a system of values, I would leave by the roadside a lot of rubbish, whose existence I condoned more than I would have acknowledged.

There came a time when, deep down inside, I did not even like the saxophone: I thought its timbre was vulgar; it had neither the nobility of the trombone or the French horn nor the respectability of the trumpet—and, on the other hand, it lacked the pastoral sweetness of the flute or woodwinds, or the heavenly softness of the strings. We had a piano at home, and we learned the rudiments of music from an old woman who could teach us about reading notes but not rhythms. Then came the national fad for the accordion. At home, everyone from my father to Bethânia—but me more than anyone else—thought that was an instrument in the worst taste (except when it was used by Luiz Gonzaga in the style of Northeastern music).

The drums always seemed to me an aberration: a grotesque concatenation of martial percussion instruments like a circus attraction, assembled with screws and bolts so that one man could play them alone. And

all this within the limitations of timbre of European martial percussion, harsh and bright, without the subtleties or the organicity of the
Cuban *tumbadora* or the bongo, the Brazilian *cuíca* and *atabaque* (when I
discovered the Indian, Balinese, Japanese, and many of the African
instruments, this opinion was strengthened). When bossa nova arrived,
I felt my needs met—and intensified. One of the things that attracted
me to João Gilberto's bossa nova was precisely the dismemberment of
the percussion (to be precise, there is no drumming in his records: there
is only percussion, played on a box or its edge, and later with a brush
on a telephone book). The absence of sax solos was also a great contribution.

Zé Celso liked to say that there was a strong masochist component in
tropicalismo. In fact there was something of a voluptuousness respecting
what previously had been considered contemptible. But I—who, as I
have said, had been in the habit of strolling among piles of cans at the
supermarket for the sheer aesthetic pleasure—did not surrender to that
voluptuousness without first subjecting it to close examination during
the waxing hours of my insomnia. And if, on the one hand, I'd had no
direct contact with American pop art (curiously Rogério had never
mentioned or showed me Warhol or Lichtenstein), on the other hand I
could not yet count on Oswald's anthropophagic formula. My early
adventures in sensibility took place in a great vacuum. Oswald's short
poems, extraordinarily far-reaching, beginning with the "ready-mades"
extracted from Pero Vaz de Caminha's letter describing the discovery of
Brazil, were an invitation to rethink everything I knew about Brazilian
literature, about Brazilian poetry, about Brazilian art, about Brazil in
general, about art, poetry, and literature in general.

For me personally, it was a way of reordering the literary figures I
admired. The cult of João Cabral de Melo Neto was not shaken. It must
have been a case of what Augusto says happened to the concretists as
well: Cabral's formal precision of construction found, for them and for
me, its complement in the Oswaldian openness to the "millionaire contribution of all errors." Guimarães Rosa's dazzling baroque prose did
not register the trauma either. But one could not say the same of my
admiration for Sartre or Clarice Lispector. It's not that Sartre's philosophical works and essays lost their luster in my eyes. But I remember
Rogério's reproach when I stated, at Solar da Fossa in 1966, that I
thought *The Words* was the best book ever written. (I read an identical
opinion years later expressed by Simone de Beauvoir, but she, naturally,
had her own reasons to think so. . . .) Rogério not only told me he dis-

agreed, he also identified in my judgment a distortion of perspective that denoted ignorance. I concurred without being able to understand his view. One might say that meeting Oswald gave me the proper perspective on that criticism. As for Clarice, I had idolized her since 1959 when I was still in Santo Amaro and read her short story "A imitação da rosa." In the early sixties I continued to read everything she wrote and had written, and my brother Rodrigo was always buying her books for me. When I went to live in Rio, in 1966, I got her phone number from the actor José Wilker and decided to give her a call. She seemed to be right by the phone waiting for that call, because she answered on the first ring. I started calling with some regularity. Her voice conveyed an immediacy of thought and feeling, and her words indicated a similar immediacy of perception. We never saw each other, but we kept up a telephone friendship that withered with her evident loss of interest when I moved to São Paulo. Today I love her books as I did when I was seventeen, but in the middle of *tropicalismo,* under the impact of Oswald, she seemed too focused on psychology, too subjective and, in a certain negative sense, feminine. This is the first time I say this, and perhaps I do so because I no longer think or feel this way (I don't need to think or feel this way). At the time I did not confess this change even to Augusto de Campos, who perhaps might have approved of the criticism.

In 1968, as a consequence of the murder of a student, Edson Luís, by the police, a large gathering of artists and intellectuals convened to demand an appropriate response from the governor of the state of Guanabara. I had come from São Paulo solely for that gathering. I was in the middle of a small multitude of notables in the waiting room of the governor's palace when I felt someone touch my shoulder and, turning around, heard the unmistakable voice, with its guttural *r*'s: "Hello, I'm Clarice Lispector." I was at a loss for words: we met just when my intellectual growth had drawn me away from her writing. She, who could now recognize me because of television and photos (when we used to talk on the phone one or two of my songs had been recorded by other singers, but I myself was still an unknown), understood immediately the nature of the situation and turned around naturally, leaving me standing there, feeling awkward and a little sad. Many times I think how significant it is that *tropicalismo* cost me, among other things, my dialogue with Clarice.

panis et circencis

Along with Mahalia Jackson, Jorge Ben, and the Beatles, our listening fare began to include the Mothers of Invention (one of Agrippino's favorites), James Brown, John Lee Hooker, Pink Floyd, the Doors. But we did not stop listening, again and again, to João Gilberto, and we naturally listened to everything by Brazilian musicians, whether they were close to us or not. Many who had been now withdrew, revolted by *tropicalismo,* but since most of them lived in Rio, it was hardly noticeable. We heard gossip, but we did not pay much mind. We were sure that no one's reputation would suffer from this episode. And we believed that in time all would see that our gesture benefitted everyone.

We had bought an old Victrola, the wind-up kind, and a spectacular collection of 78 records, mostly Brazilian. Even more than the stereo in the listening room, this gramophone was a kind of voluptuous oddity; and we used it with a particular aesthetic pleasure. This is how I came to know Orlando Silva's recordings from the thirties, the basis of João Gilberto's musical development and the object of his intense admiration. Since our days in Salvador, Bethânia and I had always been immensely fond of *Carinhoso,* an album Orlando Silva had done in the fifties, with new versions of his old hits. But we didn't know much about his early recordings, in comparison to which, much to our surprise, the record we knew was generally and unanimously considered worthless. I would never accept this excessive devaluation of that record from the fifties, but it was an event in my life when I first listened closely to the heavenly softness of the young Orlando, his inventive phrasing, and his miraculous musical grace. The underlying connection to João Gilberto's style was evident.

Orlando Silva—whom João Gilberto calls "the greatest singer in the world"—had enjoyed a kind of popularity in Brazil in the thirties without parallel in any other country. Yet he did so without becoming a national figure, as Gardel had in Argentina, or being associated with a particular genre, such as tango. (Samba, which by that time had become "the Brazilian rhythm" par excellence, never monopolized "Brazilianness" to the extent that the tango monopolized being Argentine.) Orlando had the type of success that Frank Sinatra would come to enjoy some time later, the kind that made girls swoon at the sight of him or try to tear off a piece of his jacket during his appearances in radio concert halls. Sometimes, in open-air performances, as many as sixty thousand people gathered to listen to him. A light-skinned mulatto, the kind that in Brazil is not even called a mulatto, very slender, Orlando was not the leading-man type. At best there was a mysterious air to his slanted eyes, and an intense natural virility beneath his exquisite manners. What made him irresistible was his singing. Of humble origins—a Carioca from Zona Norte, he had once worked as a trolley-car conductor—his more-than-obvious talent had been discovered by chance. He possessed a beautiful and powerful voice, yet he did not show it off. Rather, he softened the high-pitch notes that, when combined with his phrasing, his creative rhythmic pacing, and the clarity of his diction, made him a master of song. The softness of the stretched notes never attained the cloying, fluty half falsetto of the popular American tenors of the thirties: he was masculine and sober enough to avoid those outpourings. His sensibility was already very modern by nature, and he created an original, unique style. He was an excellent samba singer: his rhythmic playfulness and infectious variations made the melody float, and he never repeated the same tempo when he returned to the refrain; but it was really in the *samba-canção* and the *seresta*-style waltz that the fluency of his music fully manifested its charm.

João Gilberto took Orlando Silva—rather than Bing Crosby or Frank Sinatra, who had inspired Lúcio Alves and Dick Farney—as his model in creating a way to sing and play samba (which he did somewhat in the manner of cool-jazz singers and instrumentalists, though João himself, unlike his predecessor Johnny Alf or his successors of Beco das Garrafas, never played jazz). That he always credited Orlando as the most profound inspiration for the invention of bossa nova (in forty years, what interviews he gave were extremely rare—and always brief—but in nearly all of them he mentioned Orlando Silva)—all this, taken together with the fact that Orlando was at once a mass phenomenon and an artist of the utmost refinement, made him a key point of reference for anyone who sought to address the issue of art for the masses and at the same time meet the challenge of bossa nova.

It is not that Orlando was the greatest popular success for the longest period of Brazilian musical history—that honor goes to Francisco Alves (the King of Voice), his contemporary and one of his discoverers, a man with a tremendous voice, talent, charisma, but with a phrasing that was conventional and strained compared to Orlando's. But João Gilberto is not alone in paying perpetual homage to Orlando. The quality of his singing is more obvious than ever: of all the great masters from the past whose recordings have been reissued in remastered CD collections by the two independent labels—Revivendo and Collector's—Orlando's beat all sales records. I'd suggest to any lover of Brazilian music, anywhere in the world, to look to these Orlando Silva CDs from the thirties, in order better to understand and enjoy the mystery in the foggy sounds of the Portuguese language set across the Afro-Amerindian rhythmic landscape, while for Brazilians it is essential to listen to the extremely rare 78 recordings João made in 1952, in which he can be heard singing with such astonishing beauty, still immersed in Orlando's style but already recognizably João Gilberto.

Undoubtedly Orlando's modernity was subject to the stylistic advances introduced by Bing Crosby. Not that there are real individual similarities—Orlando used to define himself as a kind of mediator between the great voice of Francisco Alves and Sílvio Caldas's interpretation. He had created a modern Brazilian style of singing, with all of *choro*'s feints, the jiggle of *capoeira,* and the Latin feeling. When technical innovations, such as the electronic microphone, appeared in the United States and were used to good advantage by Bing Crosby and Charles Trenet, Orlando, a man of very little formal education, picked up on the possibilities and came back with a technique that was equally sophisticated. In the forties Dick Farney and Lúcio Alves, both wealthier and more educated than Orlando, consciously adapted Bing Crosby's style (and, by that time, also Sinatra's) to Brazilian music. But there is more of Bing Crosby in Orlando Silva—a greater sense of modern singing, greater naturalness, subtlety, swing, urbanity, a greater understanding of the microphone and of the world that produced it. But he is not, in any sense, an imitator of Bing Crosby's, and his grasp of modernity establishes a freedom of invention that transcends all issues of cultural derivation. João took up this spark of genius, and one must understand bossa nova through the profound meaning of that gesture—and its relationship to anthropophagy.

After Orlando Silva collapsed under morphine and alcohol, he spent many years not singing or being seen. Even though he took over the prime-time hour at noon on Rádio Nacional when he replaced Francisco Alves (who had died in a car accident on the São Paulo–Rio highway), his comeback in the fifties apparently only fueled the myth that he had "lost his voice." The truth is that few have aged with their ability to sing as well preserved as his was, but the memory of the miraculous sound of his young voice made anything short of that perfection seem like a disaster. His voice had become much lower, the softest high notes were gone, yet he still sang better than any of his contemporaries who were still active, and no one lamented their decline. In 1968, when we used to listen to him on the old gramophone in our São Paulo apartment, he was still alive and, in one of those TV Record festivals, we saw him share the stage for a few seconds with Roberto Carlos, one coming immediately after the other. This was a special appearance for both of them, since neither belonged to the MPB ambience or to what then was beginning to be called MPB: Orlando was the old guard, Roberto the Jovem Guarda. It was a very moving sight for a *tropicalista*.

Orlando's greatest competition on that old gramophone was Carmen Miranda. She is herself a *tropicalista* emblem, an overdetermined sign of the contradictory affections I had proclaimed in the lyrics of "Tropicália," the movement's theme song, and she emerged on those records as samba's reinventor. Full of freshness and amazingly dexterous, though she was not always careful or capable in the definition of some notes, she was nevertheless a wonder in the clarity of her intentions. The quick diction and the cheerful comic approach to the rhythm made her a master, quite apart from her historical significance. The fact that she had become a caricature as a result of her Hollywood success, something we had grown up a little ashamed of, made the mere mention of her name a bomb that the *tropicalista* guerrillas would, fatefully, seize. But to deploy such a bomb meant likewise the death warrant of that shame, issued as a challenge to the acceptance of American mass culture (and therefore of Hollywood, where Carmen had shone), acceptance as well of the stereotypical image of a sexually exposed Brazil, hypercolorful and fruit-full (which was the very image Carmen carried to such extremes)—an acceptance that had evolved because of our realization that both mass culture and that stereotype did (or could) reveal more far-reaching truths about Brazil than anything to which we had been previously limited. (In this sense, the photo of Carmen, her sex literally exposed, smiling in the arms of Cesar Romero, a photo I saw in *Interview* in the seventies, seemed like the subversive confirmation of some deeper meaning, as much of the caricature she had become as of the cul-

ture that made her famous.) Of course at that time, following her reign
as one of the best-paid women in American show business, and ten
years after the apotheosis that was her funeral in Rio, Carmen was more
of an absence than a reference in our conversations about MPB in
post–bossa nova Brazil. Though one could not say she had been forgotten—her films were still shown at times and with her camp image she
exerted the same fascination over some Brazilians as she did over so
many foreigners, from Wittgenstein to Ken Russell—her musical style
was not what brought to mind her work or persona. But the Carmen
Miranda who appeared in those old 78 rpm records excited our imaginations and elicited admiration—this was the substantiation of MPB as
a rich tradition, a potent aesthetic. Carmen Miranda's version of
"Adeus, batucada"—a masterpiece in the history of samba, and of the
Brazilian record—became the theme song of 2002.

There is a record—I can't remember whether we might have
heard it on the gramophone or the stereo, since we did have
some LPs of Brazilian and non-Brazilian oldies in the sound room—
that indeed rivaled the best of Carmen: this was "Camisa amarela" by
Ary Barroso, sung by Aracy de Almeida. Aracy, a legend then still very
much alive, was an explosive woman, a wild child. It was said that she
had been the favorite of Noel Rosa, the composer of carioca samba from
the thirties, a man of genius who had died at twenty-six, leaving a vast
legacy of extraordinary complexity. In her own way, Aracy had been the
vehicle for Noel's renewed prestige in the fifties, when he began to be
considered the greatest Brazilian composer of all time. His songs, interpreted by the marvelous Sílvio Caldas, Francisco Alves, Carlos Ga-
lhardo, Augusto Calheiros, and so many other greats, were our constant
cohabitants, the whole year we spent there, on the corner of Ipiranga
and São Luis Avenue.

Among the novelties of Anglo-American pop to which we were
introduced, two names, two styles, will forever be connected in my
memory to the atmosphere at 2002: Jimi Hendrix and Janis Joplin. Gil
especially was in love with Hendrix. In fact, he had felt such passion for
someone's music only twice before—for Jorge Ben and the Beatles, and
no one else.

I was stirred by Hendrix's modernity: his spoken-voice style of
singing, half-hidden behind the instrumental; his guitar style, half
blues, half Stockhausen; his outsider image—it all made him a symbol

of his times, and suggested that with Hendrix all fundamental themes could be radicalized. But there was too much confusion in his sound for my taste, too many cymbals, too much "jazz." I couldn't bring myself to like it as much as I liked the Beatles. I was more attracted to James Brown and his screams that tore in a clean rip over the lean swing of his band. Jimi Hendrix, in comparison, seemed important and serious, but naïve. James Brown's music was sheer entertainment, and aside from being simply more appealing, it was also representative of an American tradition of precision that interested me greatly. The styles created by blacks in that milieu that so venerates exactness were absolutely marvelous: there was in James Brown a charm that I find again in Stevie Wonder, Prince, and Michael Jackson.

Janis Joplin was the black white girl, the girl from our generation who, in the United States, synthesized freedom, adventure, and rebellion. This was the United States of an American fatally mestiza, fatally engaged, in all directions, with the nonwhites decimated or enslaved by colonization. She was also an exciting example of how a society of abundance, with its extremely high degree of competition, could produce artists who could combine the rough edge of the uncultivated with the most highly cultivated technical precision. We started watching the light show around the fiberglass doll as the bulbs followed the sounds of Janis Joplin's "Summertime." The musical inconsistency of Big Brother and the Holding Company enhanced more than detracted from the beauty of that girl's singing, which emerged like a nuclear force from the new world—of California college students, of Black Panthers radicalism, of opposition to the Vietnam War, and of show business suddenly transformed by neo-rock.

Bob Dylan was not a commercial phenomenon like the Beatles, but in Brazil he was better known than the Rolling Stones. The Stones could have their "Satisfaction" on the hit parades, but Dylan had his cult of admirers long before. I remember listening to an entire side of one of his records at Toquinho's house, around the time when he, Chico, and I used to hang out together in São Paulo, before I moved there. Toquinho wanted to know what I thought because it seemed to him insufferably boring—as I remember his emphasizing—to hear a record with all the songs sung and played in the same tone. To me it was interesting, that nasal voice and his coarse way of playing guitar and harmonica. But I found the lyrics incomprehensible and ended up bored as well. Once *tropicalismo* was established, though, I would listen over and over to his marvelous *Bringing It All Back Home.* To this day, this is the record of Dylan's that I find most moving. I still barely understood the lyrics, but the atmosphere, the voice, that studied carelessness, the general tone of his work were an inexhaustible source of interest to me. What made the greatest impression was the richness of texture, a sophistication attained with no apparent effort, in contrast to the Beatles. But I cannot say that I preferred Dylan to the Beatles, who, compared with the wordiness of Dylan's torrential songs, the rhetoric I could make out from what was intelligible in his lyrics (with my high school English), seemed more constructive and lean. The overt experimentalism of *Sgt. Pepper's Lonely Hearts Club Band* was closer not only to what we were doing, but also to the artists I admired, whether Godard, Oswald, Augusto de Campos, João Cabral de Melo Neto, James Joyce, Lewis Carroll, or e. e. cummings. Though the Beatles were obviously more naïve, in contrast Dylan seemed yoked to a romantic conception of the poet, without (explicit) incursions into metalanguage, atonality, or concretism. Yet to this day, I study Dylan's density. I now pay him more attention than I do to the Beatles—and I get more out of it. He is at once a central and a peripheral figure in the panorama of the sixties. At the moment when the British from their side of the Atlantic controlled the game with their version of rock, on this side Dylan was quickening the fountain from which the Beatles and the Rolling Stones had drunk, showing us where the source was and whence the energy pours out.

These were the relations we maintained, throughout the *tropicalista* period, with the stuff that was our bread and circuses: pop music. I suppose I was the one who decided we needed to do a record-manifesto, a collective record that would announce that our work was intended to be a movement. In any event, once the idea appeared, I took it over. I talked to Gil, to Torquato, Gal, Bethânia, Duprat. Gil had just done his own first *tropicalista* record with Duprat and Os Mutantes, a record that was much more consistent than mine, with greater musical control. But mine had produced a greater impact in "conceptual" terms, maybe because it was released earlier, maybe just because, in order to compensate for my strictly musical shortcomings, I have always had to be more "conceptual." I loved Gil's record for its focus and its pulse, its wealth of sounds highly suggestive of some perfect blend of traditional Brazilian elements with plugged-in music. I loved "Luzia Luluza," a song whose lyrics were vaguely reminiscent of the Beatles, because it dealt with the everyday life of a normal person—a ticket seller at a movie theater; it was constructed like the soundtrack from an American film, but it ended with Carnival. Gil appeared on the cover of the record—designed, like my own, by Rogério Duarte, but in this case in collaboration with Antônio Dias—wearing the uniform of the members of the Brazilian Academy of Letters, thus underscoring the irreverence.

I was hoping to be able to use Gil's, Duprat's, and Os Mutantes' musical dexterity as a vehicle for my own ideas. I wanted to hitch a ride, get a leg up: I was jealous of the quality of Gil's record. And if I didn't think it compared to, say, Jorge Ben's or Roberto Carlos's work, I certainly recognized that it was quite superior to my own.

Bethânia had commissioned a song for which she already had a title and most of the overall idea for the lyrics: "Baby" is what she wanted it to be called. And she insisted that the words should mention a T-shirt that said, in English, "I love you." She even said that the song should end with "Leia na minha camisa, *baby, I love you*" ("Read my T-shirt, baby, I love you"). It was a way of commenting, with Oswaldian love and humor, on the presence of English phrases in the songs everyone heard—and on the clothes everyone wore. I thought it was perfectly representative of the *tropicalista* aesthetic, and given Bethânia's contribution to the history, we agreed it would be included in our collective record, sung by her. Nara Leão, who from the start was clearly and totally free of anti-*tropicalista* prejudices, commissioned a song from Gil and me, the theme or inspiration of which was to be a painting by Rubens Gerchman called *Lindonéia,* a representation, in distorted lines of painful purity, of what looked like a photographic blowup of a poor girl who had been given up for lost; it was framed, in the kitschy style of suburban sitting rooms, under glass, decorated with flowers. Gil did the music, a bolero interwoven with rock, and I did the lyrics. Gerchman's painting, being a kind of melancholy chronicle of nameless loneliness done in a pop tone with metalinguistic overtones, was directly akin to *tropicalista* music, and we imagined that the song would heighten its poetical charge. The painting had not been influenced by *tropicalismo:* the painter had arrived at that point by solving problems of his own, in dialogue with pop art. Nor did we know the painting before Nara brought it to our attention. In fact, my having painted throughout my childhood and adolescence had only distanced me from the visual arts, with a mixture of disenchantment and shyness. Now it was *tropicalismo* that made me feel free to return, if only tentatively, to that area of artistic activity. My interest was reawakened by the 1967 São Paulo Bienal, when I first saw the American pop artists—and Edward Hopper—which gave me a new and more precise perspective on my wanderings through supermarket aisles and on the conversations I used to have with Rogério Duarte and Zé Agrippino. Of course, *tropicália,* the name, had come from Hélio Oiticica, with whom we were by then in contact, and we also knew Antônio Dias, who had done the cover for Agrippino's *Panamérica* in addition to collaborating with Rogério on the cover of Gil's record. Yet even at the height of *tropicalismo,* our contact with painters was occasional and fragmentary. It was only in the seventies that Hélio designed an album cover for us (Gal Costa's). Nara's suggestion forced us into a kind of interdisciplinary partnership without precedent in *tropicalismo.* The idea of including Nara on the group record seemed appropriate to me not only because she had established the bridge between us and Gerchman's painting, but also because it meant the fulfillment of Gil's initial dream that the movement would include the whole generation of musicians: Nara represented bossa nova and its origins. She had led the shift toward an engaged music and was therefore the personification of modern Brazilian music.

During one of my trips to Bahia (I could not spend more than two months in São Paulo without going to Salvador), I invited Tom Zé to come to São Paulo with me. He had been with us in the shows at the Vila Velha Theater, and when I began to frequent the artistic and bohemian milieus of Salvador, he was already familiar to college students and a figure of some prestige among the artists I knew. When we finally met, he captivated me with his *sertanejo* looks, his pseudo-ill-humored observations expressed in a rural accent that revealed rather than obscured the classical elegance of his educated and correct Portuguese. His physique was that of an elf; he had very lively eyes, which seemed to attest somehow that his diminutive frame was just the right container for an enormous concentration of energy. These signs of exceptionality were partly confirmed by his satirical songs, composed in a deliberately folksy tone. Consisting of long chronicles of urban life in Salvador, and portraits of characters both typical and peculiar, these compositions from his early phase were at once attractive and unsatisfactory, apparently for the very reason that they were out of step with the aesthetic interests of bossa nova. Unlike Gil and myself, Tom had studied in the Open Music Seminars of the University of Bahia, as the music school was called. This school, like all other art schools founded by Edgar Santos, brought news of the international avant-garde to Salvador, informing a whole generation.

With the *tropicalista* turnaround, I thought that the anti–bossa nova sophistication Tom Zé offered, the direct connection he insinuated between the rural and the experimental, would find a place in the world we envisioned. A musician as harmonically gifted as Alcivando Luz, who had also been an admirable companion in the Vila Velha, would not be able to forge ahead in that environment. I have often thought in these last few years that if I had been endowed with the talent and the temperament to do what Milton Nascimento and his friends from Clube da Esquina did in the seventies, rather than the *tropicalista* scandal, I would have invited Alcivando to come to São Paulo instead of Tom Zé. In *tropicália,* Tom Zé showed himself to be at home.

Initially, however, Tom Zé resisted the invitation, and I remember a conversation in which he told me it was a crazy idea. But when he was finally persuaded, the airplane trip from Salvador to São Paulo set the tone for his eventual contribution. The Caravelle of the Cruzeiro do Sul airline—a plane whose modern lines I loved, like a samba by Jobim or a building by Niemeyer—seemed as it flew through the blue skies liable to explode with the vibration of Tom Zé's presence. This became clear even to the stewardess and who knows how many passengers; it was not that he seemed nervous about flying, although his ostentatious unfamiliarity with everything happening on board made it seem (perhaps falsely) that he had never flown before—but his accent and his archaic expressions seemed to be an attack against the technological reality of aviation and the bourgeois comforts of consumer "services." He was telling me—and telling himself and the world—that yes, he was going to São Paulo, but that he would nevertheless remain tenaciously true to certain principles and traits of his character. This was his inventive way—bizarrely elegant, really—of dealing with his dread of change in his circumstances. He would refer to the plane as "this caravel," in a tone at once intimate and estranged, but behind that irony one sensed that this was for him a departure for another continent altogether. When the stewardess approached to ask what he wanted to drink, he answered dryly: *"Cachaça."*

Obviously, he knew that they didn't serve *cachaça*—a popular sugarcane brandy—on board. But the sincerity of his defiance exposed the absurd pretense of refinement within the cabin, the amorphous "internationalism"; there wasn't, for instance, a single black stewardess on any Brazilian airline back then. In response to the predictable answer of the stewardess—"I'm sorry, we don't have it"—Tom Zé started to take off his seat belt and, making as if to get up, said to me, not to her: "Then I'm leaving. Tell this caravel to stop." These words frightened us—even though we knew it would be impossible to fulfill such an absurd demand, we were unnerved by the determination with which it was made, the sheer imposition of his will. Of course Tom Zé didn't make a scene on the plane, but remained cool and aloof until the end of the flight, without losing his ironic, distant sense of humor.

The group record was a natural vehicle for the songs Tom Zé might have brought from Bahia or would compose in São Paulo. I had written, and given to Gil to set to music, the words to a song called "Panis et circensis." I thought I would use this as the subtitle for the record, assuming the title of the song would be the one arrogated from Hélio Oiticica's work for the movement as a whole (but, naturally, without the "ismo")—*Tropicália.* I hadn't bothered (and wouldn't have known where) to check whether "panis et circensis" was the correct Latin form. (In fact, the form in which the expression became famous is "panis et circenses," the last word being an adjective that, in the plural, denotes "circus things.") The intention was to superimpose on the pop collage of some trivial song lyrics—and now a record of pop songs—a Latin quotation (the bad Latin that Décio Pignatari in the seventies called "delicious avant-garde provincialism" and that now sounds full of "historical" charm). I have always believed in a kind of organicism in the assimilation of information, and I insist on the simple collection of culture, retaining from books, classes, and songs only what is congenial to me, and transmitting only what I have already incorporated. Once I said to Maria Esther Stockler, apropos of some allusions in a film I directed in the eighties *(O cinema falado):* "The only thing in there is what comes out in the piss." I remember Duda telling me in Salvador in 1965 about an interview in which Godard said that when he finished reading a book, he threw it out the window.

Panis et circensis, our record-manifesto, was released in 1968, and it included Nara, Tom Zé, as well as, obviously, the core group of Gil, Gal, Os Mutantes, Duprat, and myself. Bethânia, who rejected being involved with groups or movements, gave the song she herself had commissioned, "Baby," to Gal, and thus it became Gal's first great success. It was, in any event, a success thoroughly deserved since this cut, because of Gal's voice and Duprat's arrangement, turned out to be a masterpiece of *tropicalismo* (if that implies no fundamental contradiction in terms)—and the true fulfillment of Guilherme's dreams for Gal (and my plans with Rogério).

The happiness I felt in the studio upon hearing how well Gal's style fit the song (a mixture of bossa nova and rock that was somehow nei-

ther), and above all the charm and intelligence of Duprat's arrangement, led to a profoundly disagreeable episode. From the studio, we
went to celebrate at Patachou (so named for a French singer), a restaurant on Augusta Street we used to frequent. Geraldo Vandré, who was
sitting at another table, came over to ours and, observing our enthusiasm about the recording, asked Gal to sing the song. When he thought
he had heard enough, he interrupted her suddenly and banging on the
table shouted: "That's a piece of shit!" Gal shut up, frightened, and I,
incensed, ordered him to leave us. He tried to argue, saying that we
were betraying the national culture, but I wouldn't let him finish his
harangue. I continued to shout him away, but not before reproaching
him for his discourtesy to Gal, whose dulcet singing he had so coarsely
silenced.

Notwithstanding his natural combativeness and sadly ungenerous
nature, Vandré was only expressing openly what many felt about us: we
were altogether aware of the rejection of ideas and actions on the part of
the nationalist Left. One characteristic of *tropicália*, perhaps its own
indisputable historical success, was precisely the broadening and diver-
sification of the market, achieved through a dismantling of the order of
things, with a disregard for distinctions of class or level of education.
This healthy destruction of hierarchy lies at the heart of what some tire-
some critics have called the "cynical complacency of the post-sixties
period." It also explains the excessive "generosity" on my part that in
the seventies Augusto de Campos, on the one hand, and Glauber
Rocha, on the other, found so difficult to accept, pressuring me to be
less receptive and more discriminating. Several other friends showed
similar signs of impatience. João Gilberto himself, when we came
finally to speak to each other, wondered at my tolerance. Nevertheless,
it was our great effort, this second mission to overcome the market that
in its narrow vision controlled production and consumption of music in
Brazil, that made me not so much tolerant as sensitive to the virtues of
diversity. Vandré, trying to stop the current at its source—and this was,
after all, a demand imposed by MPB—proposed to Guilherme, our
impresario, that he try to dissuade us from entering the race. He
alleged that what Brazil needed was what he, Vandré, was doing
(namely, songs to "enlighten the masses") and that since the market
could not bear more than one strong name at a time, for the general
good of the country and the people we should put all our eggs in his
basket. Vandré did in fact make this strange proposal to Guilherme,
and I have often asked myself if this was not a model for the official

prestige enjoyed, in the name of history, by the insipid notables of communist countries.

Free of the red scare since our military enemies had taken power, we didn't see even the remotest possibility that Vandré's wish would come true. Indeed, we thought his reasoning was crazy, though we continued to admire what was admirable in him. I in particular, though I have always considered Chico Buarque Vandré's superior by far—musically, poetically, and ethically—much preferred "Disparada" to "A banda."

Gil was less enthusiastic than I about *Panis et circensis.* I suppose that, having made a record in which he explored so many sound combinations with Duprat and Os Mutantes, he wished to surge ahead in his musical investigations, and the group album would bind him to territories already explored. Moreover I, being the leader and, unlike him, delighted merely to be working with that whole group, was not about to exact his customarily impeccable standards of playing and production, and he lacked the energy (or was perhaps simply too modest) to demand them of me. Suffice it to say when the record was ready I was exceedingly proud—and Gil did nothing but complain about the brass being out of tune right from the opening song.

In order to understand these ruminations of mine, it is important to comprehend exactly who Gilberto Gil is to me. Sooner or later I would have to take stock of this figure—so central in this story and so close to me that, in a way, together we constituted a kind of entity—and it seems this is the best place to do it.

Around 1962 or 1963 I saw on TV Itapoan a young black man singing and playing the guitar like the best of the *bossanovistas.* His exuberant musicality, his perfect pitch, his rhythm and fluency thrilled me. It was exciting simply that someone so special could be nearby. Television created the illusion of distance, but with my heart racing I thought that, given the size of the city—and above all the number of people who together made up its art scene or even its middle class—it seemed likely that somewhere in Salvador I would run into this gifted musician with the happy smile and striking eyebrows. My mother, who always liked music, and always liked it that I liked music, had heard me praise him, and every time she saw him on television she would call me to see him. I remember with satisfaction how she would refer to him (she did this at least once and it made a deep impression): "Caetano, come see the black man you like." And this way of saying "the black man," with her tender smile, had—and *has*—an exquisite flavor that intensified the charm of the art and personality displayed by that young man on the screen. It was as if another charm had been added to the one I saw and heard, or as if the confirmation of this person's reality, conferred this way, as a kind of blessing, intensified his beauty. I felt happy that Gil was alive, that he was black, that he was who he was—and that my mother greeted all that in such a direct and transcendental way. It was evidently a great event, the emergence of this person—I could already see that he was a first-class musician, already one of the greats—and my mother celebrated this discovery with me.

I spoke about him to everyone I used to gather with at night. Almost no one watched television, and I myself had been lucky to see Gil because at home the TV would stay on in the dining room during meals. Surely the film criticism crowd—Orlando Senna, Geraldo Portela, Carlos Alberto Silva—had never heard of "Beto." Gilberto Gil is no less real a name than Gal Costa. Its euphony suggests a pop contrivance, rather like Diana Dors, Marilyn Monroe, or Brigitte Bardot— a pseudonym made up in an ad agency for a wannabe João Gilberto riding the crest of the bossa nova wave. It was in fact the inevitable choice among his four names—Gilberto Passos Gil Moreira—and it also turned out to be delicately beautiful on another level, nobler in the sense that the syllable *"gil"*—a Portuguese name with the archaic literary echo of Gil Vicente, the great playwright of the Portuguese medieval theater—repeated itself exactly and limpidly as if to prefigure, so I thought, the mysterious line written in the nineteenth century by Sousândrade in a poem I came to read only in '68: "Gil creates in Gil nightingale." In any event, I think Laís Salgado and the group from the Dance School had already seen him once or twice. Roberto Santana surely knew him personally. Santana, who belongs to a traditionally leftist family from the hinterland town of Irará, was a light-skinned mulatto my own age, a macho guy and very active, and he was friends with everyone in Salvador. He promised he would introduce me to Gil: "You don't know Beto? He's a good guy." Back then we didn't have the kind of slang everyone uses today, and to say he was "good," in a tone that indicated a slight semantic shift, could mean that the person had a good political stance or it could suggest talent or moral character. "He's cool, you'll love him." I was intimidated by the possibility of a real meeting: how could I interest "Beto"? And given my musical limitations and my lack of interest in soccer and other masculine topics, what would keep the conversation going? I feared a meeting that would result in minutes of awkward silence.

Roberto Santana introduced me to Gil by chance on Chile Street (I was walking around to Castro Alves Square as the two of them were coming the other way), and all three of us felt entirely at ease, each wanting to talk more than the other. Gil seemed as happy to meet me as I was to meet him. One could have said that he had been seeing me on some transcendental television and was expecting that meeting as much as I was. My praise of his technique and musicality led us to talk about the bossa nova masters (particularly João, Jobim, and Carlos Lyra), the object of our common passion, and the conversation (lacking guitars) did not require a test of my musical ability in order to stimulate Gil's interest: he delights in broad reflections that clarify the significance of music—which is not so common among musicians—so what I was saying was already worth a good chord sequence. At times, through the years, I have heard Gil say, and been deeply moved by it, that when he met me he felt as though he were leaving behind a great loneliness: when he saw me he was sure that he had found a true companion. I think that to prize in me a vision of the world that encompassed music, in which he was so gifted (while I could not then even imagine becoming a professional), a vision that seemed like an enlargement of his own, he created an image of me as the master and, much as the great see greatness in those they admire, he dismissed my shortcomings. Better yet: he interpreted them in such a way as to give them a finer meaning. He therefore saw qualities in my music then that no other musician of equal talent would have seen, and in this way he not only encouraged me, he also taught me everything that I could possibly learn, becoming himself truly my master.

It's not that Gil gave me lessons in harmony or guitar technique. But seeing him play and sing dispelled my inhibitions as nothing else could have done. And this made it possible for me to broaden my repertoire of chords and "chops" on the cheap guitar my mother had bought me, on which I had no hope of attaining any kind of mastery. Gil put the heavenly mystery of bossa nova's beauty within reach of my fingers—and I could permit myself to touch it only barely, fearing I could not scratch the surface without profaning it. Gil did not neglect to explain relations between chords, to describe how to position the fingers, or to teach me the harmonies of entire songs. On the contrary, he did it all casually, in the course of carefree conversations. Today it frightens me to think of the swiftness with which I progressed through the tonic/dominant/tonic basics and on to altered chords and the notion of internal voicings. I had no idea how much more "musical" I was becoming: it seemed that I was learning badly, in proportion to my noncompliant talent, this or that aspect of musical knowledge to which Gil by virtue of genetics had immediate access. To this day I think that the unbalanced way I handle music, as a composer and as a listener— displaying complexity where nothing but the simplest thing is expected, and naïveté where one would look for sophistication—comes from having refused to impose a method on myself, all on account of having no faith in my musical ability. I don't imagine I have ever progressed as much as I did in that time. But I would not be able to do anything in music today if Gil had not persisted in his faith at every turn, in spite of me. Gil drew forth from me far more music than I could have ever dreamt I contained.

Sometimes, despite my happiness at being closer to João Gilberto through what Gil taught me, I would fall into a state of crisis, feeling I had no right to make music. One of the most depressing things about a country so disoriented in relation to its own history—an incompetent country, to use Hannah Arendt's phrase for underdeveloped nations—is the disjuncture between the talents and temperaments of individuals and the roles they are called to play. There is a sense of waste and frustration, of which I have always been conscious and against which I have always felt incited to rebel. This was a central preoccupation of mine, as it was of *tropicalismo,* and it remains for me an unresolved problem. I suppose if I had lived in São Paulo or Rio I would have finished my philosophy degree, and perhaps that would have been a more appropriate route. Or if I had had the strength to begin making films before music took hold of me, who knows whether my generalizing mind allied with my ex-painter's eye (and the little bit of music that would always be there) would have made me more effective as a filmmaker than I can ever be as a musician. In any event, I experienced a fear—a fear that has not entirely died—that my entry into the history of our music would impoverish it instead of contribute to its greatness. The journalist Ruy Castro, in his book on bossa nova, refers to *tropicalismo* as having driven the first nail in the coffin of that movement synonymous with polish and refinement. My first impulse when I read this was to search my conscience again, but I came to the same inconclusive results. Before Gil left Bahia to go to São Paulo in 1965, a similar bout of searching moved me to tell him, from the bottom of my heart, that I had decided to give up music. Gil was emphatic: "Then I'll do the same." Unwilling to accept the possibility, he could not see any reason to go on without me. It was as though music itself were speaking to me. And I relented.

Gil is a dark mulatto, so dark that even in Bahia he is called black. I am a light-skinned mulatto, so light that even in São Paulo I am called white. Nevertheless, my eyes are much darker than his. At the same time, though we both came from the middle class, Gil, the son of a doctor and having only one sister, had known certain bourgeois privileges that I, the son of a federal employee with my seven brothers, could scarcely dream of. His father had a car, and he had gone to private schools, which by no means guaranteed a better education, but was certainly a sign of social status. Upon leaving the Marist Brothers school, Gil went to the School of Business Administration at the University of Bahia, in accordance with the station attained by his father. He felt perfectly at ease among his predominantly "white" colleagues of bourgeois extraction, properly speaking, and suffered no conflict on account of his left-wing ideas, which he in fact shared with a number of them. The School of Business Administration, obviously, was no den of communists. But Gil was more nearly a militant than I, who was studying at the School of Philosophy, with its departments of sociology, literature, and history, where the Left reigned supreme. In fact our political visions were essentially no different. We came together in music, but did not feel estranged in anything else: we welcomed the emergence of UNE's CPC—though our project was radically different from what the organization proposed—as well as the appearance of social themes in music lyrics, above all those by Vinicius de Moraes and Carlos Lyra.

Gil never seemed conscious of the fact that he was black. It was something that neither humiliated nor exalted him: he simply behaved like a free citizen. With his natural boldness his negritude seemed to correspond to the tone in which my mother referred to it. In the late sixties, especially under the influence of Jimi Hendrix, Gil donned the mask of the racially conscious black man, and this new persona revealed the latent pain and pride beneath the former veil. It had always seemed he saw no need to beat his breast and announce, "I'm black!" in protest against discrimination; he considered it enough to lead a dignified life and to affirm himself socially and intellectually, as his father had done. Now that he was embracing the "black is beautiful" wave of pop culture, he revolted against Brazilian social injustice in its racial dimension. It is emblematic of how deeply ingrained a problem this is in Brazil when one considers that Gil, the "black doctor's son" par excellence, could—at a time when the human landscape of the city of Salvador came to be dominated by poor blacks, and a decline in opportunities for this population to join the liberal professions followed inexorably from the growth of social inequality and the destruction of the public education system—that such a figure could become the mythic leader of the new black masses. It would come to pass that the petit bourgeois *bossanovista* of 1963 would be praised in the *blocos Afros,* the Afro-Bahian groups of the eighties and nineties, as Bob Marley's heir, the defender of his people.

Gil's change in regard to the question of blackness gave new meaning to his old love for Jorge Ben. And when *tropicalismo* took off, Ben's musical interests converged with ours. In the seventies, after our London exile, Gil would move even closer to Ben. Unlike me, Gil never liked Carnival, yet he wrote a song beseeching the *orixás* to bring the *afoxé* Filhos de Gandhi, his one childhood passion during Carnival in Salvador, back to life. This was a curious and extraordinarily beautiful Carnival group that had been formed in the forties by men, most of them black, attired like Hindus with white turbans, one of them dressing up as the Indian leader (complete with glasses and a walking stick), who would lead a cardboard elephant carrying a black child, also dressed up, and they paraded through the city—all to the sound of *atabaques* and *agogôs* straight out of the *candomblé terreiros.* Gil composed this song when he realized that only ten or twelve stubborn sons of Gandhi were left, too few to face off against the powerful *trios elétricos* groups (which by this time already played *frevo* with smatterings of progressive rock, glitter, and heavy metal, and whose vitality I myself had praised in a *marcha-frevo* from 1968, heightening their profile). One could say that the *orixás* heard Gil's request, because the next year the bloc paraded with more than a thousand members. This in turn prompted the establishment of new *afoxés* which—being already receptive to themes of racial affirmation—gave rise to *blocos Afros* like Ilê Aiyê and Olodum, who today are well known nationally and internationally for the vigorous originality of their percussion sections.

When Rogério used to say that "Gil is the prophet and Caetano only his apostle," it sounded true to me, especially because we never discovered anything of importance that did not begin in some mysteriously daring undertaking of his, which only after some time would be transformed by me into something more perceptibly coherent. It was that way with Jorge Ben; it was that way with *tropicalismo* as a whole; with our recognition of São Paulo's importance as the city about to take up a new position in the Brazilian imagination; with the compositional procedures derived from what we thought we heard in the Beatles, in Hendrix; with the recognition of Milton Nascimento's genius; and it was that way with the new pop culture of the city of Salvador. But this is not to say that I (or he) was always aware of this as our modus operandi, or that our natural divergence of temperament wouldn't reveal (or, more typically, harbor silently) our share of disagreements. If many times I felt I was reaping the rewards that were owed or denied him, there were also moments when I needed to unburden my mind and my attentions of the flux of his intuition and the obscurity of his spirit, which is quite stubborn, if extremely receptive. And he too must get tired of idealizing me.

Perhaps his reaction to *Panis et circensis* constituted a defense of his ego against mine (today I find the brass in the first song more obviously out of tune than I did then). When the record was ready, I was exultant, but what seemed to me a technical leap forward sounded to Gil like a step in the opposite direction. In any event, our friendship and partnership remained paramount. For Zé Agrippino, among the cuts on the album, only the title song by Os Mutantes, "Panis et circensis," rose above the limbo of underdevelopment. In fact Os Mutantes had already mastered the pop idiom, both in sound and visuals: the tapes and some of the clips made with them at the time seem like current MTV videos, and this distanced them from MPB as much as from rock and from *tropicalismo* itself. It's not surprising—they were young and had gotten their start in the heyday of British neo-rock, they were from São Paulo, the richest and least typical of Brazilian regions, and they were familiar with electronic equipment (the older of the two brothers being an imaginative engineer). But above all, they had talent.

Yet I felt that in "Baby" or in "Enquanto seu lobo não vem," there was something different and new—something fertile that ought to be judged by new criteria, not merely in comparison with Anglo-American productions. *Tropicalismo* took shape in MPB's history as a body of acts, among which the collaboration with Os Mutantes was one of the most auspicious, but the nucleus of *tropicalismo* was elsewhere. In the seventies, after my return from London, Rita Lee became Brazil's leading rocker, and Os Mutantes, without her, leaned toward progressive rock, ably sounding like Yes or Emerson, Lake, and Palmer. Serginho was always a virtuoso, and Arnaldo a good instrumentalist, a musician with a strong personal style. During this period Liminha joined the group. An exceptional bass player, he had worked previously with Ronnie Von, and later with me (today he is a first-rate producer on an international scale), and they formed a trio that raised the bar for the ambitions and the technical quality of Brazilian and Latin American rock, even if they never became a commercial success like Rita Lee.

The so-called progressive rock didn't attract us. We loved and admired the new Mutantes without sharing their enthusiasm for the kind of music they had elected to produce. And even Rita herself, when she went solo, with her poetry, her musicality, her wit and elegance, reinstated the old division between MPB and rock that *tropicalismo* had tried to overcome. The key to understanding *tropicalismo* is the word "syncretism." Everyone knows how dangerous this word is. And in fact we, the remnants of *tropicália,* take greater pride in having established a way to see, a perspective that nurtured the development of talents as disparate as Rita Lee and Zeca Pagodinho, Arnaldo Antunes, and João Bosco, than if we ourselves had invented a homogeneous and broadly acceptable fusion. We are Bahians. Eric Hobsbawm, in his comments on our "brief twentieth century," has written that, between the wars, "in the field of popular culture, the world was either American or provincial." (Curiously, the only exception he finds is sports, in which Brazilian soccer stands out as an art.) This is a reality that the *tropicalistas* would not wish to deny. Much less would we wish to confront it with melancholy. We recognized that joyfulness is essential to anyone who would participate in an urban and international cultural community. The template of nationalism seemed like a sad anachronism. We wanted to participate in the worldwide language both to strengthen ourselves as a people and to affirm our originality. Mere updating was not enough for us, above all because we saw—or imagined we did— that the opposition "American versus provincial" was about to be modified.

In the conception of *Tropicália ou Panis et circensis,* there was a quintessentially *tropicalista* plan: to record an old Brazilian song that had been discredited in every possible way. This was the hypersentimental "Coração materno" (A Mother's Heart), one of Vicente Celestino's greatest hits. (He was a melodramatic composer with an operatic voice whose brilliant career hailed back to the fifties, and included countless hits, operettas, and films.) "Coração materno" tells the story of a young peasant who, as a proof of his love, is forced to give his girlfriend his own mother's heart. The matricide takes place while the little old lady is kneeling at her prayers. The young man, after opening her chest and removing the heart, runs straight away to his lover carrying it in his hands. On the road, he trips and falls, breaking a leg. From the mother's heart, thrown some distance by the fall, comes a voice that asks: "Are you hurt, poor child of mine?" and, in a last pathetic touch, it exhorts him: "Come and get me, for I am still yours."

By 1967 Vicente Celestino was practically forgotten and his style—the exact opposite of what had led to bossa nova—was indefensible. The melody of "Coração materno," like all the others by Celestino, sounded to us like a pastiche of Italian operatic arias. The idea of recording this song occurred to me because it was a radical example of an aesthetic to which we felt vastly superior. But this story was, in many ways, far more archaic than it might seem. My first recollection of the taste police—aesthetic education in the form of humiliation or cultural snobbery—goes back to my earliest childhood, sometime between the ages four and six, when my brothers laughed at me for expressing admiration for Vicente Celestino, his melodies, and his great voice. Already back then, in the forties—at least within my own family—these melodramas were considered ridiculously vulgar. But I never forgot altogether Vicente Celestino's songs. I had learned to sing them almost before I could speak. To record "Coração materno," I didn't really need to relearn the song, I needed only to check the original recording to avoid possible mistakes.

While still a student in Salvador I had read the novel *Spartacus* for my course in classics. There was the drama of the peasant matricide narrated by a character from two thousand years ago, and even for him it was an ancient story. It surprised me at the time that this tale should have survived intact in all its details throughout the centuries. I never investigated whether the story was in fact already current in ancient Rome or had been inserted into the novel by the author. The fact is that this tale, which Vicente Celestino had used to move the multitudes as an example of motherly selflessness, the same story I would find again in Ann Douglas's *Terrible Honesty,* where it is related by the psychiatrist Frederic Wertham to explain the matricidal impulse as a result of the male child's need to free himself from a smothering maternal love, had proved to be representative not only of the sensibility of the Brazilian masses, but of the very nature of all popular culture.

Duprat's arrangement for the song is one of *tropicalismo*'s greatest triumphs. An excellent orchestrator, Duprat created the ambience of serious opera (though without omitting the suggestion of a Hollywood soundtrack), restoring dignity and lending solemnity to the abominable song, which emphasized my frighteningly sincere and sober interpretation. As for my singing, I admit there are in it profound influences heretofore unconfessed that colored my style, chief among them Sílvio Caldas (with his projection of "sincere" intensity) and the radio singer Roberto Faissal.

I am writing these words without the record at hand. In fact, it has been a long time since I've heard it. Just as I did not listen again to any of the *tropicalista* records, whether mine, Gil's, Gal's, or Os Mutantes', in order to write these observations, nor did I consult Zé Celso or any archivist to look for photographs of Oswald's *O rei da vela.* Maybe Heloísa de Lesbos's dress in the third act was completely white, not black. *Tropicália ou Panis et circensis* opens with a composition by Gil and Capinan entitled "Miserere nobis," and I find in its lyrics the embryo of the poetry that would flow from Minas Gerais in the seventies: the Catholic allusions, the noble images enveloping a political commitment that is more implicit than stated, a dignified diction. Always working at a far higher level than any of his followers could achieve, Capinan prefigured all the post-*tropicalista* "participatory" poetry. But it was Torquato who would write, also to Gil's music, the lyrics of what would for many become, even more than "Tropicália," the manifesto of the movement: "Geléia geral" (General Jam). It begins with a direct allusion to the poet, "o poeta desfolha a bandeira" ("the poet strips the flag"), then goes on to enumerate various signs of the tropics (bananas in the wind, sunflower heat) and of Brazilian life (*Jornal do Brasil,* Miss Brazil, Chico Buarque's "Carolina"), literally quoting Oswald de Andrade: "a alegria é a prova dos nove" ("joy is the acid test"). It popularized the phrase "geléia geral" (which, as I have said before, was coined by Décio Pignatari in the essay published in *Invenção* that had affected me so much), placing Brazilian folklore side by side with international urban lore ("ê bumba iê-iê boi, ê bumba iê-iê-iê," which juxtaposes the familiar words of a Northeastern folk dance with "yeah-yeah," the supreme metonym for rock 'n' roll). "Geléia geral" was Torquato's version of *tropicalismo.* For some it may have served as a kind of more accessible "Tropicália": but with Gil's lively melody underpinning its words, this song also offered Torquato's lyricism, the flow of his poetry and imagery, the not-so-hidden melancholy—and, of course, for me the very important affirmation of the movement's poetic dimension, inscribed in the attitude that precedes the decision to write poetry of great simplicity and not, as in the case of Capinan, to intensify poetic effects.

prohibiting is prohibited

It was around May 1968 that Guilherme showed me an article in the magazine *Manchete* about the students in Paris: in it was a photograph of a wall with a graffito that said "Prohibiting Is Prohibited." This was the phrase that Buñuel claimed the students borrowed from the Surrealists, and Guilherme thought it would be great to set it to music. But when he saw my cool reaction to his suggestion, he smiled with the stubborn air of someone who knows he is going to end up convincing me. I did not want our movement to be confused with the Paris movement, any more than I wanted Brazil confused with the world outside it—assuming what we were doing would one day be recognized outside (something I still hoped for, but much less than I had before my first record came out). But Guilherme didn't give up. Every day he would ask me for a song with that phrase. And finally he persuaded me to do it "just for me." Building on the ¾ bossa nova beat (or is it ⅝? Well, a ternary measure) that I had used in "Baby" and another song, "Saudosismo," I quickly composed a brief *marchinha* using a series of anarchist-flavored images, and I incorporated that simple and paradoxical phrase as refrain. When I showed it to Guilherme, he thought it all was "divine, marvelous," and so I felt I had fulfilled my obligation.

Near the end of 1968, Guilherme brought from Rio's TV Globo (back then an infinitely less important network than São Paulo's TV Record) an invitation for Gil and me to participate in its festival. This event was a pale imitation of the Paulista festivals, and all the more confusing on account of its striving to be "international," which is to say that it subjected the work of the best Brazilian composers to a judgment (by both the jury panel and the immense crowd that filled the sports arena of Maracanãzinho) informed by criteria so broad and amorphous as to be meaningless. Lacking both an interest in the event itself and a song to present, I told Guilherme to say no. But Guilherme once again refused to take no for an answer. Perhaps he had promised the festival producers that he would convince me to participate; or perhaps he thought the FIC (International Song Festival) was becoming a good promotional venue, or maybe he simply thought we shouldn't stay away from something that—though he himself didn't much like it—was nevertheless becoming, like everything else that happens in Rio, however vaguely, a media event with enormous national repercussions. Perhaps the word "international," which had become a leitmotif in his speech since he first heard Bethânia, struck some chord in his imagination. For whatever reason, Guilherme insisted we enter something in the TV Globo festival. My refusal was adamant. Then, suddenly remembering his own refusal to accept my earlier one, I thought of entering "Prohibiting Is Prohibited." I told him, in a tone verging on a threat, that I would select that song as a pretext for turning my entry into an event. Gil supported my decision. And we exchanged bands: I would be backed by Os Mutantes (a dream of mine) and he would appear with the Beat Boys, now rebaptized Os Bichos (the Animals).

We would introduce the songs during the elimination round in São Paulo, competing against other artists from the area. Gil decided to show off his knowledge of Jimi Hendrix's music (at the time completely unknown to the Brazilian public) by imitating in Portuguese the spoken-voice style of the great guitarist over a rhythmic-harmonic base in Brazilian colors, even as he retained the predominant blues base of his model. And all this would serve as an anarchistic provocation, since Gil's song took as its title the cliché of all leftist political meetings, "questão de ordem" (point of order), although it was subverted into "point of disorder," watered down and sugarcoated with a Beatlesy refrain, "in the name of love." It was, in any case, a far better song than my own, and fundamentally a much more radically innovative number. But "É proibido proibir" was transformed, with a little help from Os Mutantes and Rogério Duprat (who, though not responsible for the orchestral arrangement, directed the atonal introduction, reminiscent of Os Mutantes' concrete and electronic music), into a highly scandalous piece. My hair was very long and, left to its own rebellious curliness, seemed like a cross between Hendrix and his British accompanists from the Experience. I wore plastic clothing in green and black, my chest covered with thick necklaces made of electrical wires with the plugs hanging at the ends, and thick chains with animal teeth. The costume, designed by Regina Boni with tips from Dedé, had—like the meat hooks in our apartment—a touch of proto-punk that made our by-then-common (but still scandalous) bright African dashikis seem quite tame, and even outdid the science-fiction costumes Os Mutantes wore there right next to me on the stage—not to mention Guilherme's checked suit with its bright orange turtleneck, which he had taken care to retrieve from me following the premiere of "Alegria, alegria." After the long introduction—whose atonality and lack of rhythmic definition provoked some booing—I started to sing the silly lines ("The virgin's mother says no / And the TV ad / Was written on the gate") and do a kind of dance that consisted entirely of moving my hips to and fro, although not in the mechanical manner of the Elvis grind, but in the easygoing, sexy way one observes in Bahian women, or *morro* samba dancers, or Cuban men and women. Then, as if that were not enough, the singing and dancing were interrupted by a recitation of Fernando Pessoa's poem about Sebastian, the Portuguese king who while still a young man died in Alcácer Quibir in the final, hopeless crusade; his return is to this day conjured up in Brazilian popular rituals connected to the cult of the Holy Ghost, evolving into a myth to which intellectuals on both sides of the (South) Atlantic often return in order to signify the coming of a new era for the world—the "Fifth Empire" founded on Portugal's lost greatness. It is a poem from Pessoa's *Mensagem,* the book that had made such a deep impression on me when I was in college because of its power to dignify a myth that has so often been ridiculed. "Sebastianism" among us has become synonymous with delusions of grandeur, a quasi-consensual devaluation of cultural criticism. Our generation had been exposed to a boldly free version of this myth, in the person of a Portuguese professor, Agostinho da Silva, who during the golden years when the University of Bahia was under Edgar Santos's directorship had founded in Salvador the Center for Afro-Oriental Studies. His sights were set on transcending the phase in which the world found itself, under the leadership of the Protestant West (German philosophy, Marx, Freud, the United States, etc.), seeming never to let his thinking lapse into mere nostalgia for the medieval Catholicism of Portugal. On the contrary: despite his being a translator of Hölderlin and the Greeks, not only did his love for Luso-African or Luso-Asian syncretisms (or even Afro-Asian ones) seek the negation of the European conquest, but his ecumenism embraced various paganisms, anticipating a necessary transcendence of Christianity: the age of the Son would give way to the age of the Holy Ghost, as manifest in Marx and in technology. Something (or a lot) of this is what lies at the bottom of all of Glauber's works—and of all *tropicalismo,* in spite of its ironies.

Pessoa's poem is, itself, a jewel of Portuguese modernism—and a masterpiece of modern poetry in any language. To recite it on a television program, among electric guitars and surrealist slogans borrowed from French students, was for me a challenge, a most implausible spectacle in that atmosphere. To accentuate the contrast, I inverted the popular saying "the devil is loose," screaming "God is loose," as if announcing his arrival onstage in the guise of an American youth, John Danduran, who was obviously a gringo, tall, very white, wrapped in a hippie poncho, and without a single hair anywhere on his body (he'd had I don't know what disease), who howled and grunted unintelligibly. This was a surprise even to the festival organizers, who had not been informed ahead of time; and the audience, in the theater at Catholic University, made up predominantly of students who were pro-Left nationalists (meaning anti-imperialists), reacted with violent indignation. Many of the faces looked at me with evident hostility, and not a few punctuated the conventional booing with swearing and insults.

I can't say this really came as a surprise. I knew that I was being provocative. But *tropicalismo* had been out there for almost a year and it was perfectly foreseeable that there would come a time when boos would interrupt the applause for our daring combination of good musicianship and stage work. But the hatred (and there is no better word) that was stamped on the faces of the spectators was fiercer than I could have imagined. The jury, however, composed of people who were older and more educated than the public in general, took the positive aspects into consideration, and included the song among the finalists. But Gil's Hendrix experiment (which had met with similar, though not as extreme, disapproval on the part of the public) apparently offered the jury nothing they could recognize, and he was disqualified. Disturbed by the intensity of the public rage, I decided to withdraw from that round and to present the song again in the semifinals, thereby at least taking advantage of the opportunity to force the moment to its ultimate crisis: I would tell that audience exactly what I thought about their reaction and at the same time show the members of the jury that Gil's song had been disqualified on account of their backwardness and ignorance of the international pop scene (they were all too happy to approve clumsy imitations of familiar American or international styles or gimmicks, but it was beyond them to evaluate something well-made but from a different stylistic universe without the assurance that it had been approved "out there"), and then I would withdraw the song from the festival.

The speech I improvised (I was so excited on the eve of this second presentation that I was unable to prepare a coherent talk, the ideas racing through my head) had been inspired by the memory of those faces in the audience, by their rage and foolishness, but in the moment itself those faces disappeared almost entirely: as soon as Os Mutantes began to play the introduction, the overwhelming majority of those in attendance turned their backs to the stage in an unnerving demonstration, whereupon Os Mutantes had the wit promptly to turn themselves around, and began playing with their backs to the audience.

Instead of reciting Pessoa's poem I began to speak (bellow, actually), and practically all turned around to see what was happening. As the curiosity began to form on these faces—from which the hatred had not yet faded—my anger and confusion grew and, in a voice at once uncontrollably insecure and confidently prophetic, I said: "So you're the young people who say they want to take power! If you're the same in politics as you are in music, we're done for."

Gil, in response to my call, came onstage, and among the things thrown at us by the audience (mostly wadded-up paper, plastic cups, etc.) there was a chunk of wood about the size of a pack of cigarettes, which hit him in the ankle and drew blood. We left the theater a little frightened. On the sidewalk out front people were screaming. I was distressed. In a way, I understood for the first time the panic that afflicted Gil around *tropicalismo.* In my speech I had assumed a grand tone, but now I was afraid that I had gone too far. "God is on the loose" echoed in my head, and this fear at having evoked supernatural forces was a coded way of telling myself that perhaps we had touched certain deep structures in Brazilian life, at great risk to ourselves. Nevertheless, I felt proud. And when I got home, I was received with the warmest expressions of solidarity from friends whose tone of surprise and admiration flattered and intimidated me. Augusto de Campos and José Agrippino de Paula both called within moments of each other to offer their definitive approval. Even José Celso Martinez Corrêa came to my house— already packed with all the members of our inner circle—to offer more than support: he offered an analytical interpretation of the situation, a conversation I could hardly engage or even follow, in my frenetic exhaustion. The next day Dedé and I left with Gil for São Vicente, on the coast of São Paulo state, invited by an acquaintance of Gil and

Lennie Dale's to take refuge at his beach house, which he was placing at our disposal for a week. We needed to rest and put our heads in order.

Guilherme would soon come up with the plan to present both songs at a show in a Rio nightclub, concurrent with the Carioca finals of the festival. I proudly saw us in a sophisticated show that would run at the same time as the boring FIC program. I suppose it was then that the neophyte impresario Ricardo Amaral (a Paulista who began then to be "the man" to dominate the Rio night scene) proposed to Guilherme a *tropicalista* show with Os Mutantes, Gil, and me in his Boate Sucata (Scrap Box), in front of the Rodrigo de Freitas Lagoon. At the time this was already a "discothèque," without the name but with all the elements. And it was not the first one in the city: Le Bateau had already been around for some time. The show we did there was possibly the most successful *tropicalista* enterprise. At least it was the one that best reflected our aesthetic interests and our capacity for putting forth truly accomplished work. Unfortunately there is little good photographic documentation of what we did there, and no live recordings, although one can get an idea by listening to a recording of four of my numbers with Os Mutantes, released as a double single. I wore the same green and black plastic suit—and pushed the stage antics that I had been developing since "Alegria, alegria" even further—lying down, doing handstands, and elaborating on my Cuban-Bahian hip swing. But the most powerful part of the show was what Gil and Os Mutantes did with the musical material.

Gil's interest in Hendrix had extremely important consequences for Brazilian music. His guitar style, born out of bossa nova and reworked through his attention to Jorge Ben and his objective of reinventing the Northeastern *baião* and melody, found in Hendrix's avant-garde blues the key to what would constitute a new milestone in the history of the guitar among us, leading me to consider, as I have written elsewhere, that the genealogy might be Dorival Caymmi, João Gilberto, Jorge Ben, and finally Gil.

The performances in that show had the imposing freedom and independence of something new, its worth intrinsic, without anxiety or provincial lethargy. For that reason the show also represented our violent arrival on the Rio scene. Foreign artists who had come for the FIC would appear at the Boate Sucata to see us. I remember, for instance, Antoine, the French singer, on whom the show made quite an impression, remarking that it was "more important than *Hair,*" and then laughing incredulously because he had to explain to me all about the musical that had exploded on Broadway. An even more touching memory is that of a beautiful dark-skinned girl from Peru who, upon hearing me say that the Peruvian song she had presented had seemed the most interesting in the whole festival, told me about its composer, Isabel Granda, also known as Chabuca, and then sang to her piano accompaniment a song she thought was even better: "La flor de la canela." I never forgot the song or the composer, and a few years later I was quite shaken when someone told me—was it true?—that the beautiful dark-skinned young woman had died. People who were involved in Brazilian music also came to see the show and discuss it afterward— Wanda Sá wept to see our talents wasted in commercial venues, Francis Hime decided that our strategy was to pretend to join the system just to find a niche before eventually sneaking in a quality product; a few were simply hostile, others, more eloquent in their absence. The Cinema Novo people had the most affirmative reaction of all to our experiments, not surprising since they themselves had to face the facts of the market and were in constant contact with international cosmopolitanism. They were prepared to establish a dialogue with us about our work. This was also the case with young Cariocas who, though conservative, did not identify with the leftist nationalist student model. The visual artists who came were perhaps even closer to us than the filmmakers: Gerchman had inspired "Lindonéia," Antônio Dias had done the cover for Zé Agrippino's book, *Panamérica,* and Hélio Oiticica, who involuntarily had contributed the name of our movement, was present at the event itself. A work of his was displayed on the stage, completing the definition of our attitude toward the FIC, MPB, Brazilian culture, and reality in general: his homage to the slum bandit Cara de Cavalo, who had been shot by the police: a banner with a photograph of the dead body lying on the ground, and beneath that image the words: BE A CRIMINAL, BE A HERO. Many painters were experimenting with variations on pop art or with the questions it had raised, and Hélio Oiticica, who had come out of the "neo-concrete" group, was then attempting to create "environments" and wearable art. And high-society girls also came with their fiancés, husbands, lovers, and boyfriends. The audience was generally amiable.

One night, a judge who, for whatever reason, had come to see our show at the Sucata became incensed with Hélio's banner. Under a military dictatorship, it didn't take much to provoke a moralistic reaction to a work of art glorifying the misfit or criminal. Although the banner was only a meter long and was not present onstage or emphasized by lighting, the judge saw to closing down not only the show but the club as well. Ricardo Amaral was left trying to negotiate its reopening, while we waited, not too optimistically. The episode generated much talk, and soon enough would have terrible consequences.

divine, marvelous

Carlos Marques, a young Carioca journalist who had gone to the Amazon region to report a story, brought back for Gil a bottle of something he said was an indigenous sacred drink that produced dazzling visions and heightened states of consciousness. Gil took some on the same day that he was supposed to fly to Rio to pick up Nara, his two-year-old daughter, and bring her back to São Paulo. He says that when he arrived at the Santos Dumont airport, he came upon a group of military officers who were there to inaugurate some exhibition connected with the air force. The changes in perception caused by the drug were just starting to take effect, and he arrived back in São Paulo saying that he'd become aware of extraordinary things in the presence of those officers. It was as though he had understood in that moment the true meaning of our destiny as a people under authoritarian oppression, and at the same time he could see himself as an individual, alone, carefully carrying his small daughter, but also able to feel—beyond his fears and political inclinations—a love for the world in all its manifestations, including the military oppressors.

The 1964 coup—which the military dates to March 31 but which really happened on April 1, the day of fools—had caught me precisely at the moment when I felt ready for a politically responsible and socially useful action. Professor Paulo Freire, a left-wing Catholic educator, had created a very effective method of overcoming adult illiteracy, which involved concurrent education in social and political issues. It is important to point out that at the time no one would have deemed such a program political propaganda camouflaged as education. Indeed, with the exception of the reactionary forces that plotted the coup, there was a consensus that Brazil needed such "basic reforms," a vision shared by the federal government (which was deposed for that reason as well). The classes taught by Paulo Freire's teams were seen as instructive in the broadest sense, a means of preparing the general population for great social changes. Furthermore, the social and political implications of Freire's method entered the courses as subsidiary to the final objective, which was to teach adults to read. Yet the Brazilian social structure, entrenched since colonial times down to the unconscious level, reacted against the double threat posed by accelerated literacy and politicization of Brazil's poor.

The National Student Union (UNE) adopted the literacy program as their cause, and the People's Centers for Culture (CPC) supported teacher training. I had never identified with their sort of pamphleteering poetry and didactic theater, but given the clear objectives of the literacy campaign, I was immediately attracted to it. I had attended a meeting to train volunteer instructors when the news broke that a coup was going to take place that night, causing the work to be suspended. Some of the participants wanted to continue, arguing that it was no doubt an unfounded rumor. But the more experienced ones immediately canceled the meeting, advising us to go home while they investigated the possibilities of resistance. The next day classes were canceled, and rumors circulated of professors under arrest or being questioned, and of the whereabouts of missing students. Even more frightening were the tanks in the streets. I have a very vivid memory of the sensation I felt walking from the end of the line in the Nazaré neighborhood, where I lived, to the old faculty building of the university, in the middle of Joana Angélica Street. Looking at the tanks, I asked myself whether I had the courage to take part in a revolution, whether I was willing to lay down my life for the social causes I thought I supported. But at that moment—and from that moment on—I was not sure what "my life" meant. The silent streets, the tanks, everything seemed unreal. I felt fear and hatred for the army in the streets, with its soiled colors and anonymous air. I childishly wished it would all go away quickly.

When I was told at the university that some were predicting at least ten years of military rule, I felt a coldness inside. But people were telling funny stories—some of them true, like the one about our philosophy professor, Auto de Castro, who, having explained quite sincerely that he was not a Marxist but rather a neo-Kantian, forced the military to call Father Pinheiro, our professor of metaphysics and "general philosophy" (who in the seventies renounced his vows to become a censor), to explain what Auto was saying—and I somehow felt life went on.

On the night of that same April 1, 1964, I went to the Graça neighborhood to see Dedé and Gal. I used to go there frequently to listen to Gal sing and to get to know Dedé better. I wanted to date her, though she had a Carioca boyfriend. That night she told me she was not with him anymore. When everyone was going to bed, Dedé and I remained alone for a while longer and we kissed. I departed, leaving it open whether we would see each other the next day, which shocked Dedé, since for her the kiss had inaugurated a relationship. It had for me too, of course, but I wanted to preserve an ease in our subsequent meetings, leaving the decision of whether or not we were to be a couple to a more mature phase of our relations—and thus keeping a certain flair of freedom about it. In fact, from that moment on we stuck to each other. I was not in love, at least not in the way I had fallen in love with the girl in Santo Amaro years before, but I was very happy—and I was profoundly touched by the moment of the kiss. I arrived at the Biklour bar brimming with satisfaction, having contemplated along the way how delicious it would be to count on having a beautiful girl who would accept my caresses, which would become each time more intimate and daring. When Gil saw me, he said immediately: "You're going out with that girl from Graça!"

As I have said before, I met Dedé because of Gal—and Gal because of Dedé. But we did not see each other for a while after meeting. One night I went to the administration building to take part in a demonstration (or, more accurately, just to watch it) against the advice of the banker Clemente Mariani, a well-known Bahian millionaire who had hosted in his mansion the governor of Guanabara state, Carlos Lacerda, and who had been selected to give the inaugural address. Lacerda opposed then President Goulart's leftist regime and his reformist ideals. Having begun his public life as a communist, Lacerda had ended up by seeing that his own presidential ambitions were better served by switching to the international capitalist project—the American one— and he had thus become a relentless opponent of nationalism and "pro-labor" policies. Lacerda was the most brilliant of the Brazilian right-wing politicians, and his term as Rio's governor was nothing less than remarkable from an administrative point of view. He was a vibrant speaker, and well informed, and he was apparently much in demand among spinsters and widows. No doubt he had a plan for Brazil along capitalist lines, including collaboration with the United States in the Cold War. But even the sons of those ladies who were his followers thought he was abominable: he was the Left's number one enemy and, therefore, the enemy of students. The inaugural address that his friend, Clemente Mariani, was going to give that night was canceled because a youthful horde invaded the auditorium of the administration building and brought a young leader we were very fond of, a pitch-black man called Betinho (today a member of the PDT party, and known as Caó), who spoke from the middle of the auditorium. I ran into Dedé there, and it seemed delightful to me that she would be more of a participant than I was. She shouted slogans enthusiastically, and seemed to know everyone, while I stood on the sidelines, more impressed with her than with the demonstration. We all left the auditorium, and the rally proceeded to the municipal square, where the mayor, the Santo Amaran Virgildásio Senna, went up to the improvised podium and reiterated his support for the students and for President Goulart—and consequently his rejection of Lacerda's presence among us.

A few weeks later the coup happened, planned by Lacerda. Soon afterward, Dedé and I began secretly carrying I don't know what documents to Ernest Widmer, the director of the Free Music Seminars at the university, who, according to Laís Salgado (who had entrusted the mission to us), had shown great courage and surprising loyalty toward the leftist Brazilian students, although he was a Swiss avant-garde musician, whose political orientation was unknown.

The first military government was administered by a man who today is considered sensible and even brave, Marshal Castelo Branco, an ex-serviceman who wanted to see Brazil follow in the footsteps of the United States. The man he chose as minister of planning, Roberto Campos, was an economist with a diplomatic background who remains to this day a leader of the Brazilian Right. The minister of the treasury was Gouveia de Bulhões, but Roberto Campos's name was heard more frequently. Today we know much more about the CIA's involvement in arming Latin American military governments in the sixties and seventies, but at that time the Left tended to overestimate it. It doesn't seem that there was any direct American involvement in the Brazilian coup of 1964, as there was later in Chile when Allende was toppled.

During the next two days there was much talk of a resistance to be led by Brizola, the courageous governor of Rio Grande do Sul and brother-in-law of the deposed president. That brought with it some anxiety, but also served as an antidote to depression. To this day no one knows exactly why João Goulart failed to respond decisively to the coup, but simply retired to his hacienda on the border of Uruguay. The military came in, proffering assurances that theirs would be a brief and temporary regime, just long enough to get rid of communism, stabilize the economy, and put an end to corruption. Castelo Branco tried to follow that program, initiating the fad of military presidents elected indirectly to serve for limited terms. But by prolonging his mandate beyond the deadline set for elections in '65, he made clear that the military intended to stay in power and he destroyed the right-wing and center-right civil leadership—Carlos Lacerda included—who had collaborated in the coup. In 1964, we were unprepared for a full evaluation of the situation. Castelo Branco, who in retrospect was sensible and productive, seemed then the incarnation of evil: we did not yet know Garrastazu Médici, who would compel a reassessment of the honor. We little believed Castelo Branco's promise that his rule would not be long, and indeed a week after it was installed the military dictatorship already seemed firmly entrenched. In fact, the leading media had welcomed Goulart's fall. Demonstrations by the Catholic Ladies (the Family with God for Freedom marches) followed one another in Brazilian cities. Of course many average people commented sarcastically on those demonstrations, and antimilitary jokes were soon circulating everywhere. In our judgment no one believed a "truly" anti-communist Brazil had emerged in opposition to the imaginary Brazil we had lived in until then. It seemed to us rather that, aside from those directly interested in maintaining their privileges (the marchers and their backers), the majority of the population despised the military and submitted only out of fear. Of course, to a great extent, we were wrong. But it is also evident that the newspaper headlines did not translate the feelings of the middle-class people I knew, averse as they might be to communist ideals.

Between 1964 and 1968 the Brazilian cultural movement not only intensified, but took on even more markedly leftist overtones, bringing together writers, actors, singers, directors, plays, films, and the public in a kind of spiritual resistance to the dictatorship. Our premiere at the Vila Velha theater, for example, took place in the second semester of 1964. As I have said, Bethânia's national breakthrough happened with the musical *Opinião*, a pocket-size show presented by the nationalist populist Left. Cinema Novo emerged beginning precisely with *Black God, White Devil*, which was finished in 1964. Politics was never my forte. But I saw myself faced continually with the demands for political definition, in the realm of artistic creation as much as in that of individual conscience.

When I was seven years old, I commented one night at dinner that my teacher had told us communists were bad. My father—filling me with pride by addressing me as an equal—told me not to listen to that kind of talk, because communists, generally speaking, were intelligent individuals fighting for justice among men. His face seemed irate, but it was clear that his anger was not with me but rather with the teacher whose aim was to instill fear. That episode taught me to distrust anti-communists ever after. There was in my father's tone a complicity with greatness (a profession of faith in greatness, and perhaps a recognition of a vocation for it in me), and that, too, filled me with pride. And so I grew up seeing anti-communism on some level as the reaction of the mediocre against any particular greatness I might possess.

At the end of the war, my father was proud to have carried on his shoulders my brother Roberto, who was little then; he made him wave the flag of the Soviet Union during the parade (the Carnival of Victory) in Santo Amaro. He had done so to demonstrate pointedly his resistance to the reigning Catholic anti-communism—thus taking an independent position at the dawn of the Cold War. On the other hand, there was a photograph of Franklin Delano Roosevelt on the wall of our dining room. My father used to say that this homage—which lasted perhaps a few years—was owing to the fact that this American president had been a great defender of democracy, and so my father did not endorse the anti-Americanism typical of communist sympathizers. At the end of the sixties, during *tropicalismo,* the ideas of the New Left concerning sexual freedom, changing lifestyles, and so on, allied to the renewed prestige of Hollywood and rock, opened up a space in which it was possible to scorn orthodox communism. The "Big Party" was old hat, aside from being perennially hitched to whatever might be useful to Moscow where the internal politics of each country was concerned. The Cuban revolution, which seemed to promise a mulatto socialism in the tropics, minus the shadows of the European East, had not garnered in Cuba itself the support of the Communist Party. We believed, to paraphrase the Leninist saying, that "leftist ideology is the infantile illness of communism," and further, that the French, Brazilian, and American students, by identifying with Fidel against the Party, and by supporting Che Guevara against Fidel, would cure all the Lefts of the senile illness of orthodox communism.

In 1967 and 1968, when the military president was Artur da Costa e Silva, an ex-minister for the armed forces and Castelo Branco's rival, the rejection of the dictatorship overflowed the theater auditoriums, spreading out into the streets. The demonstrations increased, and student leaders appeared in the headlines. Of course May 1968 in France was a media event, and the Brazilian movement benefited from it. But I never quite understood how Costa e Silva, who was considered a hard-liner in comparison to Castelo, turned out to be so receptive to the demonstrations in opposition to the regime. In fact he soon gained a reputation for lacking intelligence, a careless man with a fondness for gambling. His wife, Yolanda, was actually an endearing woman for her atrociously bad taste. We, the *tropicalistas,* used to say among ourselves that she was the muse of the movement. I had a full-page color photo of her greeting Indira Gandhi when the latter visited Brazil. The contrast between the dignified, timeless style of the Indian woman and the vulgarity of the Brazilian first lady—in her multicolored dress, a look we used to call "fishtail," and her pantomime of a movie starlet—was so sharp we almost thought there must be something to be proud of in such extremes. Yolanda was "camp" itself.

A student called Edson Luís was killed by the police in Rio during a demonstration at the student cafeteria, and the resulting wave of indignation compelled the leaders of the students, religious groups, workers, and artists to organize a protest that drew more than a hundred thousand into the streets of Rio. Gil and I came from São Paulo to take part in it. There were some uncertainties as to whether the demonstration would be repressed or whether there would be violence. But the only noticeable presence of the mechanism of repression was an army helicopter that followed the demonstrators' movements from above. Some of the participants declared proudly that the oppressors had been driven back by the sight of the multitudes—the leading lights of Brazilian culture among them. After that protest, many smaller ones followed. In São Paulo one could sense a great indifference or even hostility on the part of the population, while in Rio it seemed the city supported the marches. Confetti would fall from the buildings in the center of town, and the climate was friendly, but this only provoked the military police to intensify their reactions.

During one of the long nights of conversation and beer at 2002, Waly, Luís Tenório (a friend of Dedé's from Salvador who would later become a famous psychoanalyst), and I had stayed up until daybreak, and we continued to talk nonstop until the sun was high. Suddenly, we became aware of a commotion in the street. Looking down from the twentieth floor, we saw that it was a student demonstration against the dictatorship. I decided to go see it at close range, and Waly and Tenório came along. The procession was moving along Ipiranga Avenue, and when it came to República Square, it was intercepted by police detachments in huge armored cars, whose appearance caused the students to disperse in all directions. Many were caught by the police and beaten.

My two friends remained at my side, quiet and tense. I was wearing an old European military jacket (a general's tunic) over my naked torso, jeans, sandals, and an Indian necklace made of big animal teeth. My hair was then very long, still a rarity at that time, and most observers found me threatening as I approached them. I questioned the by-standers, challenging their fearful indifference to (or perhaps tacit sup-port of) such brutality. But men and women still hurried by, scared of the demonstrators, the soldiers, me. I was sure that, under the cir-cumstances, I was untouchable, and I felt possessed by a holy wrath. In truth, no one would have known what to make of this strange appari-tion amid the upheaval, the confrontation between the students and soldiers. Anyone listening to me listened out of fear, willing to endure any outrage in order to escape. And outrage is what they heard. The sol-diers barely paid me any mind: I was moving against the flow of the students, my course a tangent, in fact, to the eye of the storm, and I did not appear to be one of the demonstrators. I yelled furiously, but no sol-dier ever came close enough to hear what I was saying. I ended up returning home, still scolding passersby as everyone dispersed and the tanks collected their prisoners. When I read those commentaries alleg-ing the narcissism of the protests in France that May—that the demon-strators were more theatrical than political—it occurred to me I had been right after all to accept Guilherme's invitation to make a song out of "it is forbidden to forbid." Now amid this strange descent into the streets, I was conscious of having enacted something—a serious and extravagant performance by the light of the sun, an improvisation of political theater, a poem in action. I was a *tropicalista,* free of ties to tra-ditional politics, and therefore I could react against oppression and nar-rowness according to my own creativity. Narcissus? I did feel myself at that moment above Chico Buarque or Edu Lobo, or any of my col-leagues thought to be great and profound.

It was in this climate of delusionary exaltation and conflagra-tions in the street that *auasca,* the hallucinogenic drink Car-los Marques had brought back from the Amazon, made its appearance. Following his own experience with it on the flight from Rio to São Paulo, Gil proposed we "trip" together. (At the time it was already common among musicians and becoming the fashion among followers of rock and *tropicalismo,* as well as the growing ranks of dropouts.) He came over to my apartment with a bottle and poured us each the amount that Marques ("Marx") had recommended: a little over half a glass. My first experience with a drug other than alcohol or tobacco had been a catastrophe. At fourteen, during the first Carnival I spent in Santo Amaro after coming back from my first year in Rio, Luís César, a friend from high school, suggested that we get high together using an atomizer of what was known as Carnival perfume. The atomizer was synonymous with happiness for me: the perfume was sold in little golden vials or small glass jars, and when it was sprayed on the skin it felt ice-cold and vanished within seconds; we could aim it at girls and hint at amorous passions—it held the aromatic suggestion of a dream. My father used to buy a little bottle for each of us (how he respected Carnival!), but many times I had heard him condemn the practice of using it as a narcotic and warn of the danger of cardiac arrest. Nevertheless, I would hear some of my older acquaintances (including my brothers) praising the marvelous "high." So when Luís César proposed the experiment, I resisted for a long while, but there came a point when my intense curiosity overcame my fear.

I inhaled a handkerchief drenched in the liquid, and in a second became the unhappiest person on earth. The whole illuminated night of the square in Santo Amaro was plunged into a darkness that seemed to be emanating from me, and a buzz in my ears, which oscillated but also seemed to grow steadily more intense, made me feel I was losing the world—and losing myself to the world. The most ferocious and childish fear of ceasing to be took possession of me in those seconds that seemed to last an eternity. An incommensurate happiness would take hold of me as I felt myself returning to life, but it was not enough to prevent me from falling into a kind of depression immediately following the high, spoiling both my Carnival of 1957 and the following days. I had visited a hell in which the unbearable absurdity of a disembodied spirit—a consciousness without a purpose—was in horrible evidence: I had always hated the idea that we continue to feel after death. So today whenever I hear someone tell of the spirits of deceased parents communicating with the living, I feel a solitary torment.

Gil, Dedé, Sandra, Péricles Cavalcanti, Rosa Maria Dias (then Péricles's wife), Waly, Duda, and I each had a dose of *auasca*. Everyone drank it immediately, while I hesitated; years after that experience with the atomizer, and a little over a year before that night, I had known an equally infernal suffering on account of marijuana, into which I was initiated along with some of my Bahian friends by a black American woman who had come to live in Salvador, a very interesting person, whose activities in the city we could never quite fathom. She had large quantities of weed of the highest quality, and she gave each of us a joint. Not knowing that it was too much, I smoked the whole thing, dragging on it and holding the smoke in as she instructed. When I finished the joint, still saying that I did not feel a thing, I got up to go to the window. In one blow, the light disappeared (it was daytime), my heart raced, my mouth dried up, and my body went numb—especially my legs. At the window the cobblestones below appeared to be glued to our third (or fourth) floor windosill. I understood that this was just the beginning. None of my friends—like me, all first-timers—had a similar reaction. Understanding my desperation they started to concentrate on taking care of me. I felt very far away, longing intensely for the very people who were right there with me. I felt a desperate longing for Bahia, for myself, for Dedé, for life. They gave me sweets, milk, orange juice. Nothing made me feel better. I suffered like a madman for about five hours. When I began to notice I was coming down, an intense love, there is no other word for it, began to take hold of me, toward the people who were there—each and every one of them—as well as the walls, the furniture, the floor of the house, and then for the neighborhood of Barra, and the world. But the interminable hours of anguish—the altered sense of time made them seem like millennia—left me traumatized, so that I promised myself I would never smoke that stuff again.

So now here I was, before the only glass of *auasca* that had not been emptied. I had listened to Gil's arguments as he tried to convince me: unlike marijuana, *auasca* did not cause a failure of light perception, numbness, drunkenness, or tachycardia. You would remain clearheaded and slowly begin to perceive things with greater intensity: lights, colors, textures, relations between forms, and sometimes things that were not "real," although they could be seen clearly. Wanting to free myself from fear, out of curiosity and the need to share, I raised the glass and drank it. At first it simply seemed to me that the Pink Floyd record Gil had put on was funny. Then the nylon rug in the sound room began to show its peculiar way of being: each neutral tone—straw, sand, ice, ash, and a thousand off-whites—said so much: the speed of vibrations that produced the neutral tone's appearance, the foolishness of man's pretense of imitating beauty, or the unity of the moment in which we found ourselves facing each other. I lingered over each object and marveled at how deeply I could understand it. I knew *everything* about that piece of wood appearing beneath the rug, as if understanding the *history* of every bit of matter. I was moved by the drama of all inanimate things: it wasn't as though they had a consciousness, but rather as though I were a consciousness that could pierce everything, including the deep consciousness of unconscious entities. Sometimes it seemed possible to perceive how molecules came together to form this or that perceptible effect: cloth, plastic, paper. I followed the workings of atoms, of chance and convention in the creation of recognizable forms.

The others started to move about in a way that attracted my attention. Sandra went in and out of the room with a serious expression on her face; her eyes were hard and she was frightened. I thought she looked like an Indian. Gil had tears in his eyes and was saying something about dying, or having died, I don't know which. Dedé circled the room saying that she saw herself in a different place. It made me very happy to see that the others were so clearly themselves. I closed my eyes. Colored points of light appeared in the unlimited darkness, organizing themselves in pleasant patterns. The points were more and more richly organized. The way they fell into place seemed both inevitable and chosen freely by me. I wished for this or that movement and it was immediately, fatally so. Circular forms composed themselves of beautiful luminous points dancing. And little by little I knew *who* each one was. They were many, of both sexes, all of them naked, and they looked like Hindus.

To say that those figures were dancing around in circles is to try to translate into ordinary language the sensation of absolute harmony those forms produced. I instantaneously alternated—opening and closing my eyes—between the observation of the exterior world and the experience of that world of images as it became each time more dense. In fact, gradually I could recognize things seen with my eyes closed as indubitably *more* real than my friends who were physically present in the sound room, more real than the walls or the rugs. The conception of space itself—the room in the apartment, the city, the world; the distance between people, the dimensions of the furniture— all was sustained at the price of an ironic recognition of its precarious conventionality.

Dedé called me over to the small carpeted veranda adjacent to the living room. She wanted to show me something amazing: São Paulo by night, seen from the window of our twentieth floor, under the influence of *auasca.* I don't know what she saw. It's obvious that we were expressing similar reactions without much explanation. What impressed me most was the sensation that the city was dead. Not that it was sad—

much less ugly. It was immense, metallic, brilliant even though dark (everything seemed dark) but, unlike Dedé, our friends, the apartment—even the nylon rug—and above all the Hindu angels I could see behind my eyelashes, it seemed to have no life. I returned to the sound room and to the celestial experience with my closed eyes.

Years later, when I read Aldous Huxley's *The Doors of Perception*, I quickly understood his observations on the role of color in the mind's validation of the reality of what it perceives. Black-and-white—or some monochrome—is the very sign of the representation, the abstraction, of irreality. Color, rather than seeming to us a mere attribute (as some of my friends who took issue with Huxley would have it), has the feel of reality as vision captures it. No doubt we automatically use color as proof of reality, among the other indicators that distinguish the real from hallucinations, illusions, and dreams. We come to an intuition of the evidence of reality. In the case of visions caused by *auasca,* especially because of color—and in spite of the fact of there being no verification through sound, touch, or smell—it was obvious to me that what I saw with my eyes closed was more real than what I saw with them open. But what does *more real* mean? I could see myself seeing what I was seeing and though I knew that it was all illusion, I was able to tell what came closer to absolute truth. There was no discounting of everyday reality: I knew myself, and mine, and the world, and my capacity to love was much enhanced in this respect. Rather, I had come into contact with a deeper and more intense level of reality. And the fact that I could love more what was thus represented contributed to the intensity of my love for common reality. I felt happy. But this happiness, though sweepingly felt, was nonetheless seen from afar, a mere aspect of that other world, less real than the one of the Hindu angels.

These were also recognized as my ancestors: *all* the people who ever existed, who might ever exist. These were also the people who actually existed. Unlike us, they had existed always and forever, the unending circle of their dance (this was a circle, though its limits could not be seen, and though it was not two-dimensional, nor was it a sphere) was a movement that brought the absolute closer. We were contingent, they were essential.

The dance of the Hindus described how the center of everything was formed: and without ceasing to be a multitude of naked dancers, it was also a face and a fountain. I knew that I was coming closer to the ultimate meaning of all things, as if I were literally seeing the face or source of God. Everything emanated perennially from that face. That fountain looked and knew. The angels were not simply lending their naked bodies that the pattern might come into being: their kind appearance, that quality of the color of their skin, the style of their movements, everything communicated the idea of face and fountain. They brought in their glances and gestures (it's important to remember that I felt I knew each one individually) the message of power, knowledge, inevitability, and the greatness of the face of the person-fountain.

There before that representation of the idea of God, I felt that shrinking of one who apprehends that the face of the Creator cannot be contemplated. The fact is, at that moment, I thought that perhaps I had gone too far. But my memory permits another interpretation of that moment when the effect of the *auasca* began to fade: I did not wish to stop seeing things; rather I wanted, all of a sudden, never to have seen what I just saw, never to have felt what I had been feeling. An overwhelming sense of exhaustion, combined with a great excitement, brought me to a state of despair. I decided to open my eyes and leave the sound room, where I had been nearly the whole time, and to go to the dining room. But the infinitude of complex mental processes this action implied paralyzed me. Then I was afraid of being mentally incapable of deciding to take ten steps. I understood, with the same clearheadedness with which I had come to understand everything I had seen under the influence of the drug, that I was mad. In short: I was no longer able to return whole—as when I had seen the angels and atoms—without losing the world, nor was I able to reintegrate myself into this world whose reality had been challenged. In any event, my mind was exhausted by the aesthetic, logical, and affective operations so spontaneously acted out. I felt the same longing for people and things I had felt from the perfume and marijuana, only this time I felt like a ghost in the shadowy periphery of life, I felt alive, all too alive, full of active nerves and in a state of uncontrollable disorder.

I yanked myself violently out of immobility, but realized to my dismay that this act of will did not return me entirely to myself. The suddenness with which I moved and the screams with which I tried to communicate what I was feeling worried my friends who, from that moment on—as they were all now coming down from their own trips—tried to calm me with caresses and reproofs. I remember Duda talking to me very seriously as if to ascribe to my capacity for self-control a moral responsibility. And Dedé saying little, making herself invisible, trying to find a moment when she might be truly helpful. In retrospect, I see them both being so characteristically themselves! I knew that I no longer knew who or what I was. I then asked Dedé to take me to the bathroom mirror. Seeing myself, I thought, would bring me back. But what I saw in the mirror—though in my recollection I know it to have been exactly my face, no more, no less—seemed an indecipherable image. For some hours I walked around the apartment, the intensity of the pain multiplying with the prospect of its continuation and the awareness of its already interminable duration.

Strangely enough, of all the friends present that day, only one comes to mind as being in some way connected—as agent or mere spectator—to the first moments of the hope of improvement. Waly Salomão, with his wide face, his genuine modesty belied by a meretricious egocentricity, his sweetness checked by his brightness and sometimes arbitrary reactions—all seem to have qualified him to welcome me back to life.

Waly had been introduced to me in the same way João Gilberto had: a classmate from college, Wanderlino, told me that since I liked crazy stuff, I should meet this marvelous fellow from his hometown (the city of Jequié, in the Bahian hinterland) who was a lot like me. He told me he would bring him to Severino Vieira (Waly went to Central School) to introduce us. Wanderlino had also spoken to him about me. After two false starts, we finally met. Waly was no disappointment, but while he appeared to find me pleasant, he betrayed no particular enthusiasm. Wanderlino, however, knew better: soon Waly and I had become friends, and we remain so to this day. His ability to surprise with unsuspected and revealing associations of ideas, his genuinely anarchic humor, his scary intelligence, and finally his immense energy, as destructive as it is enriching—all this I relish.

On the day of the *auasca* trip I understood clearly what I had always intuited: it was not to be an easy return. Seated with Waly Salomão on the small carpeted veranda, the sun already streaming in through the windows, I groped my way with the expectation of resigning myself to a provisional and precarious alliance with reality. I think the others, Dedé included, had gone to bed, reassured by the outward signs of my return to normalcy. Waly's face and its aura of sweet seriousness (the exact opposite of his usual persona) became associated for me with the moments in which a fragile happiness seems possible. Yet the quiet elation of returning to life was spoiled by the certainty that this recent experience would always represent a threat. In fact, for over a month I felt as though I were living a few inches above all creation. And for more than a year I suffered vivid flashbacks. In fact, something essential changed in me that night.

Of the four Bahians, only Gal had not yet attained stardom, in spite of her prestige among musicians and bossa nova fans. One afternoon I accompanied her to a rehearsal for an important program for TV Record—the sort of opportunity that at that time did not often come her way—and we discovered that her appearance had been canceled. I was incensed by the disrespectful treatment and made my own appearance contingent on hers. The producers were unmoved and so ended my relationship with the station.

I detested the cynicism of the star system, and bet everything on Gal's extraordinary singing. There was also an unresolved background issue—that of having our own weekly program on prime time. It was something that would have normally been expected to follow a success like ours. Elis, Nara, Chico, and the pre-*tropicalista* Gil himself had each moved into a prime-time slot, but the network's heads apparently didn't know what to do with the *tropicalistas,* although in the hallways there was talk of a program to be led by me. In a few conversations with Paulinho Machado de Carvalho, I noticed his uneasiness with the proposals I sketched out. They liked us, but that did not mean they were willing to put themselves at risk for our cause.

Gil finally decided to break with TV Record, and soon we received an invitation from TV Tupi to do our program there.

Guilherme's formula for expressing his highest praise was the expression *"divino, maravilhoso,"* divine, marvelous, which he not infrequently complemented with *"International!"* when his enthusiasm warranted it. We decided to adopt this phrase as the refrain to a song Gil and I were preparing for Gal to sing at TV Record's next festival—a gesture by which we also meant to pay homage to the grander aspects of Guilherme's personality. I should explain that at the time, participation in the festival did not obligate a performer to sign with the network. Gal could sing a song of ours and, even if it became a hit, she did not need to sign with Record and could instead come with us to Tupi. The song suggested the climate of student resistance to the dictatorship, and almost prefigured armed conflict in its violent imagery. The melody was, deliberately, pop at its sweetest, but the words were something else: They summoned a "girl" ("cuantos anos você tem?"—"how old are you?") to participate in something left unsaid but that required her to "a atenção para as janelas no alto / Atenção, ao pisar no asfalto, o mangue / Atenção para o sangue sobre o chão" ("watch out for the windows up above / Watch out, when you cross the street, the mud / watch out for the blood on the ground"), everything converging toward the refrain (which was explicitly announced in the lines: "Atenção, tudo é perigoso / Tudo é divino, maravilhoso / Atenção para o refrão"— "Watch out, everything is dangerous, / everything's divine, marvelous, / Watch out for the refrain"), which says: "É preciso estar atento e forte / Não temos tempo para temer a morte" ("You have to be strong and watch out / There is no time to be afraid to die").

Gal's vibrant interpretation marked a turning point in her style, incorporating new vocal sounds that included both Janis Joplin's grunts and the cries of James Brown. *Divine, Marvelous* would be the name for our program on TV Tupi, the oldest network in Brazil, as highly regarded as Record, but with no tradition of musical programming. At the time, TV in Brazil was not so big a thing as it is today. Few homes had TV sets, and there were almost none among the poor or lower middle classes. Early programming included high-quality theater with the best actors doing Shakespeare, Pirandello, Chekhov, and Nelson Rodrigues (the last of these being Brazilian). Even larger audiences were an elite: those who could afford a TV set. And that only in São Paulo and Rio.

Gil and I lined up Os Mutantes, Gal, and Tom Zé as regulars. Among our guests would be Jorge Ben, Juca Chaves (a satirical singer-songwriter who was initially confused with the bossa nova period, although he was actually the anti-*bossanovista* par excellence), and Paulinho da Viola (also not identified with bossa nova). It was with a certain detachment that I took part in the creative meetings, the rehearsals, and even the programs themselves: I knew the worth of each idea, of each decision, but was emotionally removed from it: *auasca* had delivered me to a kind of parallel universe. Here my customary interests and reactions obtained—the same inspiration, the same hard-on, the same insomnia—but somehow I was outside it all. Paradoxically, I felt very sad about this—a serene, stable sadness that could scarcely warm my existence. At times I rebelled, although I mostly maintained my composure, against the *auasca* and its visions. I regretted having taken the stuff. Sometimes I pondered, but not enthusiastically, the religious meaning of the experience. I remembered Rogério's theological quips—"I don't believe in God, but I saw him!" Above all I thought how ironic it was that I of all people should have coined the cry "God is on the loose!" joining it to a mystical Sebastianist poem by Pessoa. It was only as I became able truly to reintegrate myself in life that I could weigh the mystical value of what I had experienced, and of mysticism in general, against my genuine attachment to reality and my faith in

laws of the material world. While the world of visions could be dazzling, and even beneficial, the daily world, however relegated to an
inferior plane of reality was to be cherished and protected if the visions
woven by my own brain imposed themselves as more real than the
world itself, I was essentially losing both worlds. Even as I readapted
myself to the world of common sense, I was able to recover what was of
interest and dear in the "marvelous" world that had taken form within
me, but I did not yet feel calmly reinstalled in life. Indian illustrations,
until then virtually ignored (the closest thing to my visions then was
the cover to Jimi Hendrix's *Axis: Bold as Love*), were just coming into
fashion with the rise of the Hare Krishna movement. Reproductions
of mandalas (the rose windows of cathedrals, scenes from Esther
Williams's films directed by Busby Berkeley) and other images were
popular, yet I felt a sense of revulsion toward them. More than a year
later, already in my London exile, I was unable to look for long at one of
those images of Krishna without feeling hypnotized or on the verge of
hallucination. The fact that my mother looked Indian was, and is,
something to take into consideration. (When we were little, Rodrigo,
my older brother, used to say that she was the spitting image of the
actor Sabu.) In fact, I realized in London that many older Indian men
looked like my father (who was obviously a mulatto). I myself was often
taken for a Pakistani (which made me fear the skinheads).

While drugs such as *auasca* may perhaps enhance our capacities to
create decorative patterns, that creation may not be accompanied by
any heightening of our gifts for loving, understanding, discerning. No
one knows how extensive a repertoire of forms, structures, themes, and
operations we carry in our brains. I had read in Simone de Beauvoir's
memoirs that Sartre spent a year haunted by the lobsters and crabs that
were the residue of his mescaline trip. These crustaceans had not the
least symbolic value for him; nevertheless, they filled him with
anguish, particularly because they represented to him the loss of reason.

Yelling on television that "God is on the loose" while singing "Prohibiting Is Prohibited" was a gesture inspired by the discovery that
religion was just as repressed as sex. I myself had a Catholic upbringing. I attended public schools (the religious ones were all private), but
the director of my high school was a priest, Father Antenor. The inspec-
tor was Father Fenelon. And the director of the philosophy department
at the University of Bahia was Father Pinheiro. When I took my first
communion, I was frightened to receive the host. I had heard that God
would enter into my body, that a great peace would inundate me, that I

would be enveloped in the purest light. I wondered what those sensations would be like. They were described in a calm, friendly tone, but I escaped panic only by watching others go before me. Still, I would tremble as I received the host, but I felt no less disillusioned then to notice that nothing had happened to me. Why was I so afraid of God? I don't know. The fact is that I broke with religion too soon, without overcoming that fear.

Sunday mass, even if I chafed at the obligation, was neither uninteresting nor disagreeable. The Catholic liturgy is beautiful and exuberant—even more so when no microphones were used and the priest officiated with his back to us, speaking in Latin. And in Bahia *candomblé* was always present. People commonly said things like "my saint doesn't agree with his," or "I have a strong saint." We knew the names of Iemanjá, the goddess of the sea, the great Mother; Xangô, the god of fire and justice, the master of thunder; Oxum, the goddess of the brooks and wells, lakes and waterfalls, the vain and cruel queen of gold; and Oxóssi, my own orisha, the hunter, god of the forests. We heard those names in Caymmi's songs, but also in conversations with friends and relatives. And we would go to parties given in the Orixá's honor at the house of Edite, Nicinha's sister. I remember the first time I saw Edite possessed. I was still a boy and not allowed to stay to the end of the party. After the *samba de roda* something happened that I was not supposed to see. As I passed through the hallway on my way out, I ran into Edite dressed as an Indian, her eyes closed, being virtually dragged by two other women whose eyes were open. It was she, beyond any doubt, but her face had an expression I had never seen before: her lower lip protruded, her brow was deeply furrowed, her nostrils flared. She looked like an angry man. I was frightened by the evidence that Edite was and was not herself, and was concerned to know whether or not she was awake, what she could possibly be feeling. I was scared of finding myself before the unexplainable, scared to imagine myself in the same situation. This fear never quite left me. It figured in the anxiety surrounding my first communion, as well as in my first experiences with drugs.

The cult I had inadvertently witnessed at Sultão das Matas, in Edite's house, was and still is an example of the so-called Caboclo's *candomblé,* a variant in which the Yoruba pantheon appears mixed with indigenous figures. The Indian that appears does not issue directly from the original cultures of Brazil—although Tupi-Guarani words are used and there are some vestiges of the local. The *caboclo* is in fact closer to the persona first idealized by the Arcadian poets and then by the romantics, the generic and heroic Indian who came to symbolize the homeland in the struggles for independence and the fantasies of national affirmation. When Edite appeared before me, she was dressed like the clay figure of the *cabocla* carried in processions every year on July 2, the day commemorating Bahian independence. This is the type of *candomblé* predominant in the smaller towns of Bahia, while in Salvador the African liturgy characterizes the great *terreiros,* where it has been preserved nearly intact. When I moved to Salvador, I was hesitant to accompany the few friends who, out of cultural curiosity, sometimes went to Mrs. Olga at the Alakêtu's *terreiro,* to Opó Afonjá, or to the Gantois. Here too the fear of possession would prevent me from enjoying the ritual that so fascinated me: as a rule, I would run away from the place a few minutes after arriving, supposing myself to feel faint and interrogating every one of my nerves to reassure myself that I remained lucid and awake.

I don't remember whether I chose the title *Divine, Marvelous* before or after taking *auasca.* I suppose it was before. To have adopted a mainly (though not exclusively) intellectual atheism before facing up to my fear of God, while pursuing a public project that channeled the courage to take up religiosity—these were the ideal conditions for turning a single psychedelic experiment into a rich source of anguish.

When we left Brazil a year later headed for our London exile, our first stop was Portugal. My friend Roberto Pinho asked me to go with him to Sesimbra, where he was supposed to meet a Portuguese gentleman, the caretaker of a medieval castle perched on a hill, who was thought to be an alchemist. I recall some sheep with twisted horns nuzzling the old man as though they were pets, and a deep blue sea surrounding the stone ramparts. At one point Roberto asked me to sing "Tropicália" for the alchemist. I don't remember whether I sang or simply recited the words. I am sure that I imparted the lyrics in their entirety. When I finished, the gentleman looked at me with an exultant expression, and, even as Roberto winked at me conspiratorially, the man produced the most unlikely interpretation of "Tropicália" I had ever heard. Everything in the lyrics was taken literally and interpreted positively. "I lead the movement," for example, meant that not "I" but some force that was able to say "I" through me was organizing something; and "I unveil the monument in my homeland's central plain" was a clear reference to Brasilia as the concrete manifestation of a prophecy of St. João Bosco. And that was it. There was no trace of irony, no desire to denounce the horror we were then living. I don't know whether I had emphasized the passage that says "a child, smiling, ugly, dead, stretches out her hand" when I tried to explain that my motive for composing the song had been the opposite of vainglory, but I do know I tried to discuss the topic with him. But he, at first unable to conceive any reason for me to write such a song other than the happy certainty of Brazil's grandiose destiny, seemed not at all surprised when I protested; laughing at Roberto and saying repeatedly, "I know, I know," he concluded: "What do mothers ever know about their children?" I understood then that he was sure he knew better than I what my intentions had been. That was no news: I had already realized by then that songs have a life of their own, and others can find in them meanings unsuspected by the author himself. Nor was I surprised to hear that the song seemed to represent Brazil in a positive light. Above all, I was not unaware that every parody of patriotism is nevertheless a form of patriotism in itself—not I, the *tropicalista*, who would first love what he satirizes, and would not glibly satirize what he hates. But the fact that this man refused to consider that in my song I was describing a monster—a monster that had confirmed its monstrosity by turning its aggression toward me—this simply fascinated more than it irritated me.

I was not ignorant of the connection between my friend Roberto and that purported alchemist: Professor Agostinho da Silva, whom the reader may recall as the Portuguese intellectual who had organized the Center for Afro-Oriental Studies in Salvador. This heterodox thinker disseminated a kind of erudite Sebastianism linked to Pessoa, and my inclusion of Pessoa's poem during the premiere of "Prohibiting Is Prohibited" was not coincidental.

But I had not gone the way of those Sebastianists, either as a student or, shall we say, as a militant. I simply thought it was exciting that there would be people talking about the Kingdom of the Holy Spirit in a future civilization of the Atlantic at a time when most people around me were speaking about surplus value and proletarian theory. I knew the Fernando Pessoa of "Poem in a Straight Line" and "Maritime Ode." And also the one who'd written about the other Child Jesus and, naturally, the one who composed the little poem of the "feigner" ("The poet is a pretender / Pretending so completely / He comes to pretend what's real / The sorrow he truly feels"): these were poems that children would recite, that people read out loud to me, entire passages of which were repeated by heart and which I myself on occasion read in a copy belonging to some college friend. I was familiar with some apocryphal data about Pessoa's life. I classified those poems as modern Brazilian poetry (along with Vinicius de Moraes, Carlos Drummond de Andrade, Manuel Bandeira, and Cecília Meireles, and later also João Cabral de Melo Neto) and that was all the poetry I knew, aside from that of the blacks in Castro Alves, the Indians in Gonçalves Dias, and the gypsies in Lorca. With *Message* the Pessoa of the little poem of the pretender gained gravity. Each short poem was a labyrinth of forms and meanings and, most important, it did not seem possible to me that one could go deeper into the heart of the Portuguese language than in those poems. My favorite poet—the one I had read most extensively—was João Cabral. Next to his concision everything seemed diffuse and unnecessary. But with *Message* I felt I was in the presence of something more profound, in the treatment of the words, of each syllable and sound. Each suggestive idea seemed to be there out of a need arising from the Portuguese language itself: it was as though those poems had invented the language and were its ultimate justification:

> *All beginning is involuntary*
> *God is the agent*
> *The hero attends, multiple,*
> *And unconsciously*

> *To the sword found in your hand*
> *Your eyes descend:*
> *"What shall I do with this sword?"*
> *You raised it, it happened.*

The fact that this little book, the only one Pessoa published in his lifetime in our language, had as its theme the return to Sebastianism and the greatness of a deferred Portuguese destiny, lent enormous dignity to the people who cultivated those ideals and to their interests. So if while in Sesimbra I was at first startled to see my song "Tropicália" absorbed into a vision that annulled the song's critical intelligence, I eventually began to understand "Tropicália"—and to think of *tropicalismo* as well—a part of my own brand of Sebastianism. In fact, much of *Black God, White Devil* and *Land in Anguish* made more sense in this context. (And Glauber would later confirm this realization by confessing to me that "Sebastianism is the secret of Cinema Novo.")

As a child I had a dream I was taking a walk with my sister Clara along Purificação Square. It was difficult to walk, because the ground was made of long wooden slats suspended over an infinite void. Seated on a bench at the other end of the square was Norma, a girl with whom Clara was not on speaking terms. I thought it strange that my sister was going to talk to her. The benches, the trees, the houses, the church, everything was precariously suspended over the void. When we approached Norma, I heard every word of the dialogue between them, although I was small still and so treated as though I would not understand: "Norma, what do you want to tell me?" asked Clara. And Norma said: "I want to tell you I'm going to kill myself." I was awakened by some noise in the house in the middle of the night. I got up and asked what was happening, why everyone was up. No one wanted to tell me anything at first. But eventually I found out that Norma had turned up dead in the hallway of her house, next to the boyfriend who swore she had killed herself in front of him with a gun. Everyone suspected the boyfriend. I did not have the courage to say that I knew it hadn't been he. I was afraid, but I also felt very excited to have lived something supernatural. I was not very vehement when I finally spoke up: I was embarrassed to show off my excitement and had doubts as to how credible my story would seem. In time I would reassure myself that we frequently hear conversations while we sleep and as a trick to avoid waking up we create dreams around the fragments of what we hear. In fact, everyone in the house was talking about Norma's "suicide" (perhaps thinking that I, being a small boy, would not hear and, if I heard, would not understand, just as had happened in my dream). I did not, however, close the case, and pondered it for years to come: nothing like it ever happened to me again, even as my dreams provoked by events in the outside world multiplied.

Near the end of 1968, Roberto Pinho came to São Paulo solely to tell us that a friend of ours had gone into a kind of trance and had prophesied that the political situation in Brazil would become harsher by the end of the year and that Gil and I were fated to suffer the violent consequences. I attached great weight to Roberto's words—not that the mythology of the Sebastianists was gaining stature within me, but Roberto himself had an imposing personality—and I was distressed. A few days later, however, that distress was no longer just a memory.

The opening night of our program *Divine, Marvelous* was a great critical success, although I couldn't know how large the audience might have been. We created a set of bars and cages, and the stage was inside the biggest cage, in which Os Mutantes, Gal, and Tom Zé were singing; Jorge Ben was in a cage suspended from the ceiling. At the end, I came on screaming Roberto Carlos's hit, "A Lion Is Loose in the

Streets," and I broke the bars of timber made to look like iron, inviting the whole cast to take part in the destruction. The audience of young people were on the same wavelength and responded enthusiastically. In another program, we spread ourselves out somewhat like Christ and the Apostles in the Last Supper—reminiscent of Buñuel's *Viridiana*—but on the table there were only bananas. We would sing as we ate bananas. Os Mutantes carried out a mock funeral: a small procession, the placing of a cardboard grave marker with the inscription AQUI JAZ O TROPICALISMO, (Here Lies Tropicalism). The number of Catholic ladies who protested in letters from metropolitan São Paulo, as well as from the interior of the state, indicated that the program had a larger audience than we had suspected. What we were doing was certainly giving offense to some people, but we, proud and confident, remained unintimidated.

On December 13, 1968, a coup within the military government enacted Institutional Act no. 5, which revoked the right of habeas corpus, permitting the police to enter any house, establishing in effect a police state that would make the four years under martial law seem reasonable and amiable by comparison. I had been in Salvador for a few days and traveled to São Paulo precisely on that day, the thirteenth. I found out what had happened when I got home. I did not gauge the extent or depth of the changes announced on the television news. It was clear that the hard-liners had taken over. But we were justly looked upon with hostility by the noisier elements of the Left. Our sincere and secret sympathy for Marighella—the Bahian former Communist Party member who became the leader of the urban guerrillas in São Paulo—and for others who engaged in armed resistance, was known to neither radicals nor conservatives, though our admiration for Che Guevara had been suggested in the song "Soy loco por ti, América." The comedian Jô Soares told us he had heard a list of artists holding contracts with Record was circulating among the military (Jô worked at Record, where we had been until recently). The list included Gil's name and my own as possible subjects for interrogation. I imagined that at most they could ask us why we had participated in the March of a Hundred Thousand protesting the death of Edson Luís, the student killed by the police. Our reply would be that practically all Brazilian artists had participated.

We had already written a show to be aired at Christmas. As tribute to the great composer Assis Valente, who had committed suicide, and also to deflate all the rosy Yuletide sentimentality, I myself would sing the beautiful, sad song by that composer ("I thought everyone was a child of Santa Claus . . .") while pointing a gun to my head. And so I did. Originally a *marchinha,* the song is associated in Brazil with Christmas much as "Jingle Bells" is elsewhere (even if the words protest the fact that some receive Christmas presents while others don't). We stripped the song of its rhythm, presenting it as an adagio with the syllables of the lyrics obscured. The result (I saw it on video) was frightening. I felt proud of what seemed to be its "poetic" density, although in my heart of hearts I feared that perhaps, once again, I had gone too far. On December 27, Gil and I were arrested.

Guilherme Araújo had gone to Europe, where he was preparing for Gil's imminent appearance at the Midem, the annual recording-industry festival in Cannes. Guilherme, excited as he was by what would constitute the international premiere of one of the artists he handled, was shocked by the news of our arrest and proposed to the festival organizers that a protest be launched and a denunciation issued. They steadfastly refused to get involved, suggesting that if Guilherme wanted to organize a political protest, he should do so in his own name. He then accepted a suggestion to write a manifesto, which he signed and personally distributed to the spectators as they entered the theater. This brave gesture of defying the Brazilian dictatorship forced Guilherme into de facto exile, which would bring him even closer to us in later years.

After that, *Divine, Marvelous* led by Tom Zé went on for two or three more episodes; they were hoping we would come back to take the lead again. But we did not return.

narcissus on vacation

Day was breaking and I still had not fallen asleep when the federal police came to arrest me. The sound of the bell ringing at such an unexpected hour caused greater annoyance than surprise. I was lying under the covers and had just fallen into a state where surrender to sleep began to seem possible, the kind of state in which exciting projects, inexplicable fears, untimely elations—and my usual envy of Dedé who had, as always, drifted off so effortlessly by my side— were beginning to melt into sweet, acquiescent forgetfulness of everything, disguised as an illusorily clear image, a memory imagined to be true, or a deceptively precise idea. In sum, I was enveloped in the sensation of falling asleep and it was only the sound of the bell that made me suddenly aware this was finally happening. Since it wasn't the first time that night (I had already come close to nodding off a few times when internal bells had gone off—delight at the thought of finally falling asleep, fear of falling asleep, sudden awareness of the insufficiency of the image, idea, or memory that I had summoned up to induce sleep). I thought later, and still do frequently today, that if the police had not come to get me, I would perhaps have fallen asleep at that very moment.

Hilda, the maid from Paraíba we were so fond of, knocked at our bedroom door and, in confusion and embarrassment, told us that there were some men who wanted to talk to me. The feeling that overcame me when I walked into the living room and saw the policemen was simple impatience: I foresaw a nuisance that promised to last at least a couple of hours. There was something strange in the nervous way those men smiled at me, and their exaggerated kindness betrayed a promise of aggression. Soon afterward I understood they were waiting for my reaction before deciding how to proceed: any attempt at flight or resistance would have immediately been met with a dextrous violence barely concealed beneath a thin veneer of politeness. They said the military authorities wanted to ask me some questions and I, being much more naïve than they might have imagined, believed them. To them, it must have seemed unlikely that anyone would accept such a euphemism at face value, and while I tried to extract details about what was going to happen, they reluctantly gave up on the idea that I might resist an arrest. One of them made a suggestion that first seemed preposterous but then filled me with terror: "You'd better take a toothbrush." I asked for an explanation, but they didn't want to waste time.

Their repeated mention of planning to pick up Gilberto Gil at his house directly afterward reminded me that Gil might be asleep in some room of my own apartment. He was then beginning his relationship with Sandra, Dedé's older sister, who had come from Bahia to spend a few weeks with us, and we had gone to bed leaving the two of them alone in the living room. On the way to the bathroom to get the toothbrush, I decided with Dedé that she should warn Gil. I'm sure I asked her to advise him to return home and wait for the policemen there. Walking from our building to Gil's was only a matter of crossing Ipiranga Avenue and walking half a block. For some reason, it seemed to me that the police would be suspicious if one of those they had come for was in the other's house. But I'm not sure what motivated my advising Gil to go to his apartment instead of disappearing. In any event, Dedé went looking for him to deliver this message wherever he might be in my apartment, and he slipped out without the policemen even noticing our effort at communication.

Clearly neither Gil nor I had imagined we would be arrested. We were so used to the hostilities of the Left, so often accused of being alienated and Americanized, that when I saw myself before those policemen, I imagined they were taking me to talk to some officer in São Paulo, who would treat us like average young guys who were interested only in amusing the public.

When I decided to warn Gil, the suggestion that I take a toothbrush had already been made. And I was already scared. It was by no means a fear in proportion to what was really happening then, but it was enough to allow me to foresee moments of discomfort, which it was within my means to spare Gil. Nevertheless, until we were both arrested and in awful straits, none of that ever crossed my mind. It seemed perfectly natural that Gil should experience everything with me.

Outside Gil's door, the police were ready for the possibility that he might not be home or not come willingly. Inside the van that had brought me there, I was on guard not to give anything away, careful that no gesture, no look betrayed any knowledge that he was indeed home and would come peacefully. The sensation of directing a staged scene in which Gil would come to the van, both of us pretending not even to have seen each other the night before, made me extremely uncomfortable. Since our plan had been communicated through Dedé I had yet to see Gil since the whole thing started. Now, to see him appear at the entrance to his building made me feel as if I were the one who had brought the police. Being in São Paulo at that hour of morning exacerbated the vertigo; everything inside me asked what we were doing in that city, in that profession, in that life. Gil walking along the empty sidewalk toward the van; the men who had stayed behind to guard me, their comments a mixture of relief and disappointment that he had not resisted; myself looking through the glass—it all seemed to be witnessed from afar by a consciousness that saw with exaggerated clarity, yet was unable to give a shape to any idea: I would not allow it to occur to me that perhaps it would be better if Gil ran away and, deep down inside, I vaguely fantasized that I could prevent him from thinking of it himself.

We were in a sturdy van, with those men we had never seen before, whose like I had never imagined I would see at such close range. None of them wore uniforms, nor was the van marked as a police vehicle, all of which lent a sinister air to their resolute vulgarity. After riding around São Paulo for a long time we found ourselves veering onto a large road. When we asked for an explanation they told us rudely that we weren't entitled to ask questions. But they would talk among themselves without hiding the fact that we were on our way to Rio. Naturally they had shown me their badges at my apartment, but I only pretended to look at them: it never occurred to me to doubt the legitimacy of their visit. I was impatient for the whole thing to be over and, in any event, I would not have known how to verify the authenticity of a police ID. So we felt like the victims of a common kidnapping. Still, in a way, we were aware of participating in the precise moment when a new period began in Brazil, a time when people would fear the authorities and not the criminals, a time that would culminate in the seventies, with Chico Buarque's refrain: "Call the thief!"

As soon as we got on the road, I fell asleep. Whoever has read the opening sentences of this chapter may laugh and ask how this could be, given my long digressions about sleep (which I swear I have tried to keep to a minimum), or whether indeed it was Marcel Proust who was telling this story after all. Years before that morning, Rogério Duarte had told me that the first rule of good writing is not to imitate Proust. I had not yet read Proust back then, nor was I planning to do so. It was fascinating when I did, and I could not even contemplate the audacity of trying to imitate him. But it so happens that I like long sentences and, in fact, I think I could never express myself, even in conversation, in any other way. And the topic of sleep—of the difficulty of sleeping, of the subtleties of falling asleep, to the extent it is relevant to an understanding of all the aspects of my life—is fundamental to this particular episode. I fell asleep next to Gil, in the back seat of the federal police van, an irresistible and uncontrollably pleasant somnolence that, despite the hours upon hours I typically spent trying to fall asleep every night, was not exactly unknown to me. Many times in the early evening or late morning, having given up on sleep for the day, I would observe in myself the certainty of sleep's imminence coinciding with the deep desire for it. The equation of sleep and death is a literary commonplace. But it is uncommon that someone would confuse the two to the point of becoming unable to take pleasure in knowing that when tired and sleepy, having the time, space, and the necessary comforts, one could enjoy a long, life-affirming sleep. I was a baby who would not sleep. My mother tells me, and I remember it well, how I would stay up excitedly, attentive to everything that happened and, even more to the point, to everything that might come to pass. I have always found it difficult to believe that I, the one who is here lucidly, writing, talking, listening, acting, and thinking, could be unconscious within minutes, be seen without seeing, heard without hearing, present to others and absent to myself. For many years I attributed this attitude to my devotion to waking life, to alertness and consciousness. I used to say "Sleep—what a waste of time!" And though in bed I was occasionally overcome by an inconsolable anguish that would leave me icy cold, and more often, by a flood of anxiety that did not surface during the day, I never consciously attributed a morbid character to sleep. Rather, it seemed to me more "boring" than terrible. But I approached bedtime with something akin to terror. Ever since I was a small boy I have engaged, as though it were a vice, in long bouts of reflection: directed fantasies, plans, games of logic, delayed appreciation of acts and words, my own and others', and so on. In this way, I would never go to bed to *sleep,* but rather to hand myself over to an overly active "internal life." I remember how Rodrigo, my oldest brother, would sometimes fall asleep at the dinner table without finishing his coffee. And Nicinha, at ten at night, in the middle of Purificação Square during the festivities honoring the patron saint, nine nights of church service followed by profane revels in the streets, would delightedly comment that she was falling asleep and in her yearning for slumber could see her bed floating past her eyes. I would both envy and despise those people who were capable of enjoying the anticipation of something I felt as a burden. But the pleasures of sleep were not entirely unknown to me: at odd hours, or rather, when there wasn't any obligation to fall asleep, it has always been possible to enjoy the acceptance of rest, even as I wondered why this could not happen at a more conventional time. This is what happened in the police van, and I slept all the way, for the nearly five hours of the trip from São Paulo to Rio. There was only one interruption for lunch at a roadside restaurant, and even though Dedé, who had been following the van, was able to prevail upon the police to let us eat together at another table, my memory of this episode is dim, as though all my actions were the actions of a somnambulist. (This is even more remarkable when one considers that during the entire time of my imprisonment, I never suffered from insomnia—quite the opposite, as I will tell.)

I awoke when we arrived at the federal police parking lot in Rio. I remember almost nothing of what happened that day with any degree of clarity. I only know we stayed there until sundown. And that we started getting impatient to find out who was going to question us and when. The men who had picked us up simply disappeared. And the new faces we saw, laughing or rude, discouraged any questions on our part. I have a vague recollection of seeing a young woman I knew from Macalé's house (she had been my friend's neighbor in an apartment building in Ipanema), and what a disagreeable surprise it was to discover she worked for the police. It's possible that her job was merely clerical, but her presence there among the torturers, connected as she was to my "real" life, cast a dark shadow. As a matter of fact, I couldn't say whether we saw her on the day of our arrival or when we passed through the same building on our way out, two months later. I do remember it was thought there was something odd about her, involving bleeding all over her body during her periods. And this detail returns to me frequently to this day, embellishing the confused memory of the Carioca headquarters of the federal police, where Gil and I spent the day sitting side by side, first in a large room with busy agents, later in a smaller room, which though guarded by two policemen at the door was furnished with some cabinets, perhaps a desk, and was not a cell.

In the evening we were led to another car that would take us we knew not where. The first uniforms I saw changed the tenor of things in my head. I felt both reassured and more intimidated: on the one hand, I could see that the plainclothes policemen had not lied about being under orders from the military: we had not been kidnapped. On the other hand, the sight of the uniformed soldiers carrying large black guns, their dark uniforms, and, above all, their impenetrable expressions (the eyes and gestures of the federal agents seemed friendly by comparison)—everything contributed to a feeling of horror.

The civilians had disappeared. We were turned over to the soldiers, whose stern gestures and scowls made it clear that no dialogue was possible. The homogeneity of their clothing gives the military an appearance (and not just an appearance) of being an extrahuman entity. We were in the old Ministry of War building, the headquarters of Army I, right in the center of Rio, next to the Central do Brasil station, on President Vargas Avenue. I remember nothing about the intermediary stages before we were placed in a general's office. He must have held a high position in Army I—perhaps he was a powerful man in the new phase the "revolution" was entering. I remember being escorted by armed soldiers in an elevator up to the floor where the office was located. They left us in there without saying a word. They merely pointed to the chairs against the wall, where we sat down, again side by side. The room was large, carpeted, and furnished in a style that would merit the somewhat paradoxical description of austere pomp. In front of us there was a great table of jacaranda wood; the general was sitting on the other side. Our perspective was frontal yet remote—the table was at the far end of the room—so much so that the spectacle of the silent and solemn general behind his table took on a theatrical air. We were hoping this finally would be the interrogation, although we were already losing our minds with all the unexplained waits and had begun to surmise that our lives were being stolen from us. As a matter of fact, the general spent a long time staring fixedly at us, without saying a word or moving at all. If this were indeed the questioning, a considerable effort would be required for our voices to carry, given the absurd distance separating us. In my memory, the interval we spent staring at each other in silence seems endless. His first movement, barely perceptible, after this long silent confrontation (which, I am sure, did not last merely a few minutes) was to press a button that made a bell ring somewhere; there came a soldier to whom he spoke out of our earshot. Some more interminable minutes passed before two soldiers appeared, bringing dinner for the general on trays. Chicken. He calmly ate his meal before us, as if he were on a stage. The general finished his dinner, rang the bell again, the soldiers came and took the trays. He stared at us for a few minutes more, pressed the button again, other soldiers came in—who knows if they were the same ones who had brought us—and took us away. More than an hour had passed since we had entered that room. I have never been able to reproduce in my mind that general's face. It's interesting how memory can retain so many psychological attributes—and subtle details of behavior—of someone whose physical image has disappeared, as though the noun has evaporated and only the adjectives are left. I don't know whether Gil has a clearer memory of this man who had such strange contact with us. Nor do I know what purpose the contact could have served for the military. Were we in that room just to wait? Did the general want to get to know us? Was it merely a scene staged to unnerve us? Gil and I were unable to talk about it as we were taken in an army car from the old War Ministry building to the army police headquarters located on Barão de Mesquita Street, in Tijuca.

I was thrown into a tiny solitary cell, with only an old blanket on the floor, a latrine, and a shower almost exactly above it. I have a vague memory of the door or the bars that separated the cell from the small hallway. Sometimes it seems to me that it was a solid door, with a small barred porthole up above, and another, smaller one near the floor, through which the jailers could slide in the unswallowable food without being seen. At other times, it seems as though the part with the bars began at about the height of my chest and went all the way to the ceiling. The fact is that I remember only a solid metal door painted a grimy cream color, and the low porthole through which they slid the aluminum dish, or a tin of coffee. I remember being able to see the soldier on duty in the hallway. But not easily. Some effort was necessary to see just a little of what lay outside the cell. And that effort might be the asking of permission—the jailer could open the barred porthole at my request if it was justified—or on the order of something physical: since the barred porthole was high, I could look out only if I were standing on tiptoes and straining my neck. The general sensation was of being enclosed in a minimal space, with everything sealed, except for the one air shaft I remember clearly: a square window with bars, at the end of the cell, way up on the wall facing the door. Perhaps my confusion is on account of my having spent most of my time lying on the floor, and from there I could see only the solid door. But my recollections are clear respecting my rare dialogues with the soldiers (who were forbidden to speak to us) through the bars and, especially, the friendship that grew between me and an old communist whose face I saw once, just before I was moved to another prison. A friendship arose between us, based primarily on his discovery that I could sing "Súplica" (Prayer), the strange waltz in blank verse that had been such a hit as sung by Orlando Silva before I was born. This communication took place through the hall— his cell was between mine and Gil's. It was forbidden, and so depended on the goodwill of the soldier on duty. Given the distance between me and Gil, and our fear and suspicion, we said almost nothing to each other during the entire week we spent at Barão de Mesquita Street. On the very first night, after being in the general's office and placed in the cell, I fell asleep immediately.

I was woken up early the next morning by the harsh voice of a sergeant ordering me to stand. Someone slid a mug of black coffee through the porthole near the floor. I think they did a kind of roll call, or inspection of the prisoners, every morning. I'm certain they did it every night. A spark of hope that they might be calling me for the questioning emerged from within the dreamless sleep in which I had been submerged all night. But the sergeant or whoever woke me—was it only one man?—merely gave me a quick once-over and continued his ritual inspection, leaving me alone with that half-full tin mug of coffee and a rather hard piece of bread without butter. I have always thought it deeply illogical that I should have forgotten or confused the details of such a drastically limited reality. I spent a week in a bare cell, wherein each day the same gestures were repeated without fail, and yet I cannot remember with any clarity the look of that cell door or the exact actions of the jailers when they inspected us. But I believe in such circumstances it is the very paucity of occurrences and their regularity that end up eroding our usual perception of the passage of time and lead the mind to seek its defenses until one is allowed back into open space, a life rich with the diversity of the unforeseen events. I have heard former prisoners remark that, at some point, inside the cell, one doubts the reality of that unfettered life that memory tells us exists outside. I have recently read an interview with a brutal criminal in which he says that "sometimes I think I was born here, that I have always lived here, that the world outside, everything I lived, exists only in my head." This statement made me shudder, as the very same thought occurred to me and in the same terms while I was at Barão de Mesquita Street. The apartment in São Paulo, my marriage to Dedé, Bahia, the recording studios, the auditorium stages, everything seemed remote and without substance.

Sometimes I remember those days of solitary confinement as though they were a single day. After a long time—but what is "a long time"?— I started looking for myself in the person that slept and awoke in that loathsome place whose immutability imposed itself as proof that there wasn't, there had never been, any other. If seeing no one was the decisive fact contributing to this impression, another restriction, which lasted for the entire imprisonment, intensified it: having no access to mirrors. In fact, I did not see my own face for two months. I don't know after how many days I began my conversations with the old communist; or when that strange traffic in books I will tell of later began; or the walks in the sun (I know there were at least two of these); or the terse communication with the soldiers. All I know is that these small incentives were little by little encouraging me to believe that the world outside and prior to prison really existed, and more important, that I— the person who thought as "I"—was part of it. The first effort to recognize me in myself took the form of trying to cry: if I was indeed in such an awful situation, if they had separated me so abruptly from my wife, whom I had married only a year ago, if I could not see the apartment we had barely begun to settle into, if they threw me on a rough blanket and old newspapers, if no one heard my questions, surely to concentrate the mind on these matters would be enough to bring tears streaming from my eyes, to rack me with sobs and spasms. Not so. This intimacy between body and spirit that weeping conjures was not available to me. In retrospect, it's truly unbelievable what an absolute incapacity I had to sentimentalize. The old communist would ask me in his strong Northeastern accent to sing "Súplica," and soon my voice would carry the strange waltz to him, along the same hallway that had brought his message:

> *The steely cold of a dagger was her farewell to me.*
> *Not believing the truth, I asked and begged,*

My prayers died unheard, in vain
Against the cold walls of the apartment . . .

And that word "apartment," stressed and emphasized by the surprising lack of rhyme, stood out, unleashing a series of associations (the apartment in São Paulo—the first in my life—where I had heard and sung exactly that song in the nights immediately preceding my arrest), but these thoughts did not lead me to the expected emotions. I remained cold and aloof. Many times, once returned to freedom, I have been moved—and still am today—by the recollection of that scene: the old man asking me to sing, and the sweet, methodical way I used to sing for him. But at the time, in the cell, I could only *know,* coldly, that it was a moving scene. I felt something good toward the old man: the sincere and spontaneous desire to fulfill, as well and as quickly as possible, his singular wish. But I could not find empathy within myself: I did not see the charm of bringing a little beauty into the last days of an old communist, who was perhaps a veteran of prisons. I felt an arid friendship toward him, but I did not like myself. My voice echoed through the short hallway:

A torpor came over me and I was left in the dark.
I might have slept, who knows?
Through the open window the cold dawn
Shrouded my pain with a blanket of rain . . .

That drizzly rain we call *"garoa"* is one of the symbols of São Paulo, and its mere mention brings to the mind of any Brazilian the image of our largest city. So *"garoa"* and "apartment" in the same waltz sung at the request of a man who had not imagined I would know it and even less that I had been singing it frequently only days before, made "Súplica" the first theme song of this period in my life. But if I was able to recognize this so clearly, I still felt untouched by the recognition. Rather, I was moved to create a web of powerful superstitions that would follow me into exile and beyond. The waltz continued:

Hope, you died too soon.
Longing, so soon arrived.
When one leaves, the other's not far behind.
To cry? . . . if I have no tears.
Heart, why don't you stop?

You drank your fill of my cup of sorrows.
It's useless to resist, I have no strength left.
You know full well she is my life,
My sweet and great love.

And I saw in those words the announcement that it was no longer possible to have hope, that I would truly never see my apartment in São Paulo again (in fact I never did, and if I were to return now, that place I left behind, with its peculiar decor, would not be there). I even believed that having sung that song on the eve of the arrival of those policemen should now be interpreted as a kind of omen, or even an incantation. After all, those allusions to torpor, sleep, and cold, were they not proof that the lyrics referred to me? I continued to struggle in vain to open my emotions to the song or to the idea of the gift to the old man. But there was not so much as a single tear to prepare my spirit for what I hoped would flow freely from my invisible face.

I tried masturbation. Habituated to it since I was a boy and not having given it up after my—late—initiation into relations with women, not even after a marriage that was more than sexually rapturous, after some days in jail it occurred to me I would have to take on a deliberate attitude and make myself reach an orgasm quickly. It would be enough, I thought, to begin to think and then act. But I could not even get an erection. I remember how frightened I was by the neutrality with which my genitals reacted to my touch—a neutrality that became vexatious, corresponding to my mind's inability to welcome pleasure or desire, and once or twice I postponed the attempt. The days would follow one another without bringing any hope that my body and mind could even approach the routine miracle of sex, any more than that of crying. And yet, what a blessing it would be, the capacity to be ravished by sadness or pleasure but also, and perhaps above all, to have the physical experience of tears or an ejaculation! It seemed to me that if I could feel those liquids pouring out from me, I would be saved from the horror of my subjection, as though they were materializing in response to a momentary but overwhelming intensification of the life of the spirit. In fact, crying and coming are both, so to speak, experienced like an overflowing of the soul when it becomes denser and expands all at once, a paradox from which matter is exempt. Oftentimes, following my release, I have thought of this analogy between sperm and tears that came to me because of my experience of life in a cell of the military police.

Absent the mercy of weeping or sex, I felt as if I were dried up inside myself and removed from my body. The sensation of distance my mind had learned from the *auasca* experiment no doubt contributed to the effect. Many times, through the years, I have stopped to ponder how risky and unfortunate was the fact that this hallucinogenic trip was followed so soon by my arrest. And it seems typical—even emblematic—of the coincidence in Brazil of the harshest phase of the military regime with the high tide of the counterculture. This is in fact the backdrop to *tropicalismo:* though only partially intuited, it was the theme of our poetry. After we were released, we began to get used to the news of friends being taken from prisons to hospitals or from hospitals to prisons. We followed closely a number of cases of insanity and, as I have said, I definitely stopped doing drugs: I had barely escaped madness (I was saved by my father, as I will tell later). I was in no shape to take risks. The inside of a prison cell—the chill and narrowness that I had sampled in front of Gil's building awaiting his arrest—had become my only state of being. I fell asleep early at night, was always awakened by the soldiers, spent the entire morning on the blanket with my back against the wall and, in the middle of the day, after pushing down my throat a foul-smelling piece of meat and beans that tasted of dust, I would fall asleep again for I don't know how long, but would wake up again when the sun was still high in the sky. My inmate sleep was a sad and reliable sleep, from which I emerged without a trace of drowsiness.

I remember the old communist had planned a toast for New Year's Eve: he had figured out who was going to be on duty and assured us that with the help of this kind guard, we would at least get a swig of wine. I attached enormous importance to this, having always found extremely persuasive our family superstition that we had to stay up for the coming of the new year, lest a dark shadow cast itself on the season ahead. Without becoming emotionally involved in the celebration, I promised myself to stay awake as a way of saving my life, or at least to avoid perpetuating the misery I found myself in. The mere fact of beginning the year in jail was the worst of omens; to surrender to it in my sleep, without even an attempt at resistance, would be to consider myself dead, at least dead to the life I intended to repossess. But no matter how I tried to make sure I did not fall asleep, when the celebration took place—and it happened exactly as the old man had predicted—I was so soundly asleep that I did not hear Gil, the old man, or the guard calling me. There were few moments when we could talk to each other, but the old man knew how to take advantage of them: on the first day of 1969 they told me everything about the New Year's Eve party I had missed. Curiously, after I left that place, I invented a memory of the toast as if I had taken part in it: today I have a clear image of a glass of red wine being brought to me by the kind soldier, whose face I cannot make out behind the bars. The fact is that now, when I want to console myself in my insomnia, I think about how much worse it is to sleep when one doesn't want to than to be wakeful when one wishes to sleep.

As for my near-inability to tolerate the food served at the prison, on at least one occasion an officer misinterpreted my abstinence, taking it for an attempt to stage a hunger strike: after I heard him grumbling something to that effect through the bars, I would make an effort not to leave the meat and beans intact. Hunger strike? Any form of heroism or resistance could not have been further from my mind, concentrated as it was on its most immediate needs. Between the hard floor and the frayed, dark olive-green blanket that was my mattress, there were a few shreds of old newspapers, torn and yellowed. In them I would read again and again, without ever remembering them, snatches of interesting sentences, ads, meaningless headlines, fragments of news items and articles, in the relative torpor to which I had surrendered to avoid the despair of my confinement (with my back against one wall I could touch the one before me with my feet), or life without a foreseeable future. The sergeants and lieutenants who poked their faces through the high bars would tell us only, and unbidden, that every prisoner claims to be innocent. I would reread everything like an acritical automaton, without permitting myself to think whether it might be tedious or ridiculous. I can't describe how disturbing it was to read, in that same cell, a few days later, about a similar habit narrated in Camus's *The Stranger.*

One afternoon I saw the face of a man who was talking to me from up above, through the bars on the door. (Now I seem to remember with some certainty that the door was of a piece from the floor to about the height of my head, so that I had to stand on tiptoe, stretching my neck to see anything in the hallway, through the bars.) He spoke with a surprising frankness that suggested friendliness, and though unafraid, he seemed to be acting as though we had very little time. He was an army colonel who was in prison under suspicion of subversion or mere sympathy toward the communists. He told me, somewhat out of breath, that because he was a high-ranking officer, he enjoyed a few privileges, and among other things could circulate through the barracks. He was, however, not allowed to speak to Gil and me, who were incommunicados. Everything depended on whether the officer on duty was a friend of his, or even simply a tolerant person. He wanted to help me. He was in constant contact with Ênio Silveira, the owner of Civilização Brasileira, the publishing house of the intellectual Left. Ênio was also in the Barão de Mesquita prison, on a floor above ours, and in much better conditions. He had been able to receive many books, and even though Gil and I were forbidden to have them in our cells, the colonel would bring me some of those Ênio had obtained, or have them smuggled in. He warned I should try not to read them during inspection or mealtimes, when they should all be hidden under the blanket. The colonel came back at least once, bringing *The Stranger,* which he handed to me, no doubt with the guard's help, through the porthole for food. The second book was delivered in the same manner, only this time it was a soldier who furtively informed me he had been sent by the colonel and Ênio Silveira. The soldier brought *Rosemary's Baby.*

It's impossible to imagine a less appropriate pair of books to amuse a prisoner in solitary confinement. Still, the cold tone of *The Stranger,* its short, lean sentences evoking a direct and distanced vision, the book's formal and stylistic virtues, were able to produce a genuinely positive effect in me: the so-called aesthetic pleasure. It's incredible how this sense has a life of its own. I could maintain the most somber superstitious fantasies as I followed closely the fate of that man with neutralized passions, who kills for no reason, reads repeatedly a piece of newspaper in a prison cell, and becomes a stranger to his own death; I could be frightened by the precision with which something I myself was undergoing could be described in this book; I could even see in it a prophecy that nothing would change for me; but the ability to admire the text as such seemed to take hold with even but a thread of reason remaining. *Rosemary's Baby* perhaps did more damage. With its lively and conventional narrative, even more like Hollywood than the film it eventually inspired, this stimulating book turns out to be even more than a metaphor for paranoia: it is an incentive for its mechanisms. I have never reread either book since I was released. But I know that *Rosemary's Baby,* with its apartments, its competitiveness among artistic careers, its glamour and its descriptions of the adoration of evil itself, made me even more superstitious than I already was or was becoming, to the point of retrospectively influencing my interpretation of *The Stranger.* These readings, however, amused me and, even if only for the intensification of fear, they made the hours go by faster.

The sunbathing to which I had been told prisoners were entitled, and that therefore all facilities are required to provide, came somewhat late. I finally left my cell accompanied by a soldier carrying a machine gun pointed at my back. It was a most strenuous task for my mind to negotiate the inevitable excitement this fact caused, and to accept little by little that, despite the physical relief brought by my exposure to larger and more varied spaces, what I was witnessing was the reaffirmation of my confinement, rather than a genuine experience of freedom: prison had adhered to my body and would follow me everywhere. They let me out of my cell for a few minutes only so that I would feel more a prisoner than ever. The little soldier walking a step behind me with his machine gun as a permanent threat (I felt a steady kind of fear the whole time the barrel was pointed at me) would tell me not to talk, not to stop walking, not to get too far ahead of him or try to walk fast, lest he be forced to shoot me ("Don't make me do that," he said with notably false bravado). It was comforting, nevertheless, to see people moving around under the sun, going in and out of doors, even as the fact of all the men in uniform confirmed the nightmare the world had become since that daybreak in São Paulo.

Another man without a uniform was strolling in the prison yard. He was obviously a prisoner: his armed guard followed him closely, as mine followed me. Veering in my direction, attempting to draw near against his guard's feeble protest, he spoke to me, causing my guard great consternation: "You can't, I've orders to shoot." If I didn't panic it was only because of the assured and disdainful expression those threats met with in the face of my willful would-be interlocutor. He boldly called out my name and his eyes seemed to say: "No one is going to kill us, I know these scared little soldiers. Let's talk." It was Ênio Silveira. His resoluteness suggested he was familiar with prisons and jailers: his great stature, his easygoing and elegant demeanor, his assurance, seemed to impose themselves on those uniformed adolescents. He asked me if I had gotten the books. I said yes and thanked him with what I believe may have been a smile. He smiled himself, no tension apparent. It was the only time I saw him. He walked away followed by his guard, leaving the impression that he had done so because he had decided to, not out of obedience or fear. In fact, he made a subtle gesture to the soldiers, as if to say: "That's all right, I know the rules of the game, my sense of decorum permits me these little infractions, I have already told my fellow inmate the trivialities I wanted to tell him, now we can continue." The soldier responsible for me was much more nervous, I myself much more frightened than the famous editor. A few minutes later, I was back in my cell.

I don't know whether there was another sunbath. I remember a large yard, the intense light, and the heat. And those memories sometimes surface independent of the encounter with Ênio, as though one such promenade had been dominated by the encounter, and another might have elapsed given over entirely to silent observation. Perhaps everything happened during a single outing in the yard. If there were two, I don't know in which the old communist and I decided to get acquainted face to face. It pleases me to imagine that I was the one to feel emboldened and, before being led down the hallway (or, who knows, before being returned to the cell), I asked the guards to let me see him. But it is more likely that the suggestion came from him. However it came about, the soldiers granted the request and I saw the flat and nearly bald head of a man with eyes like an Indian; he smiled discreetly at me with that nakedly sincere air that enables the kindness and affection of Northeasterners never to seem maudlin. He was clearly a sturdy man. I can't remember what we said. I think he mentioned my career as a singer, thanking me for the many times I had sung "Súplica," and in some manner made it clear that he hoped I would not be in prison for long, although he knew he himself had a long stretch before him.

It seemed the old man's good wish was coming true when a soldier appeared with my clothes and shoes and then an officer ordering me to take a bath and get dressed to leave. I didn't think I was going to be set free immediately, but it seemed auspicious that they were taking me to be questioned. In fact, the notion of the interrogation had become an obsession. It represented the only connection with the last moments of real life I had experienced before entering the nightmare. Inside my cell I could hear them talking to Gil, probably giving him similar instructions. I showered, got dressed, and soon found myself next to Gil, in some place under the building stilts, standing against the wall, waiting for we knew not what. They told us with some force that it would go better for us if we did not exchange any words. And so, under the guard of officers and soldiers, Gil and I tried to communicate silently. We exchanged questions and messages of support, trying to shore up each other's mental integrity and patience. Finally we were thrown into the back of the van, and once they slammed the door brutally, we were left in utter darkness. When the car started they turned on the siren, and I took advantage of the din to speak to Gil undetected. Even so, we whispered to each other. We were in fact repeating the same questions we had exchanged wordlessly moments earlier, about which we had wondered since our arrest. The sound of the siren was so intense it seemed to come from inside us. It was a common noise in the city, though one we had previously heard only from afar as the herald that a sick or injured person, or perhaps a criminal, was being transported. To be shaken about inside the belly of the beast producing such a wail, in utter darkness, made us feel as though we were in the very heart of evil—and for the first time it occurred to me how painful it would be for the members of a good family to see their son or brother arrested for some crime. I thought about my father and mother. How many other parents would be walking on the sidewalk as the van passed by! How far from their lives would this strident whine seem, while I found myself immersed in its inscrutable center! My eyes popped out in the dark as the car proceeded, making sudden halts and noisy starts. Gil and I gave up trying to talk. The inexplicable duration of the noisy trip made us imagine that the policemen were driving around aimlessly, just to scare us. I don't remember having remarked on this to Gil, even after we were set free, but I am sure he was thinking the same thing. We were afraid. The car did not belong to the army or to the federal police. Maybe it belonged to the military police. It's more likely that it was the civilian police, as I remember two or three plainclothes agents sitting in front, which only made it seem likelier that—in this confusingly repressive system, without warrants, without questioning, but with so many different agencies involved—anything could happen to us and no one would notice. Soon, in fact, disappearances like this would proliferate in Brazil, and more and more parents would find their children in similar situations, or much worse ones.

We were ejected at another army police location, the military compound near the distant suburb of Deodoro, which may explain the length of the trip, if not the tortuous route apparently taken. In any event, I can't remember our arrival in the compound clearly. The plainclothes agents handed us over to our military hosts not at the door of some building, but rather in what appeared to be the barracks courtyard. It was the only time they used physical violence on us: handcuffed from behind, we were pushed and shoved along. The handcuffs were removed before we walked into the barracks. It was a modern, one-story complex; the main building, where the cells were, reminded me of the Ginásio Teodoro Sampaio, a high school in Santo Amaro. Just as had happened at the army police headquarters at Barão de Mesquita, they told us to take our clothes off, allowing us to keep only the briefs we wore, and we were taken to the cells. This time the cells were large and there were already a number of prisoners. The soldiers put me into the first one along the hallway and then took Gil to the one immediately next to it. When I saw the others in the same situation as myself, it seemed we would be able to talk as equals. And those people did not have the desperate or somnambulist aspect that I doubtless had. I don't think I wept, but it felt as though I had. I nervously hugged many of them as though meeting old friends. They reacted naturally and with great understanding, hugging me, too, and saying whatever they could to calm me. They were all apparently younger than I was. One of them, in a spirit of leadership, proposed that we recite the rosary all together, and he formed a circle with us in the middle of the room. He was the only inmate I made friends with, and whose name I would never forget even if this had not happened—and even if he had not gone on to become a great actor and an even greater cultural activist in Rio de Janeiro from the seventies on: this is because he had been baptized unforgettably as Perfeito Fortuna (Perfect Fortune). The majority of the youths with whom I would henceforth share the cell belonged to a neighborhood Catholic association connected to a leftist priest. I felt comforted by the idea of the collective prayer: it was their ritual way of saying that we were together in this and that in this manner we could do something. But the orison barely began. A sergeant or lieutenant who'd heard the sound of our voices praying came over and, furious, ordered the soldier on duty to open the barred door. As he swore he yanked the rosary from the hand of our leader. This group of youths in their barest underwear, not knowing exactly what was happening to them, thrown into a cell like so many loaves of bread in the oven, had for a moment acquired, through the ritual of the rosary, a human dignity, a composure that the brutality of the military officer smashed in a few seconds. Now they grumbled indignantly, whispering their anger against the tyrant. Some of them, noticing that I had been particularly hurt by the aggression, tried to console me, urging me not to be frightened, that our jailers were a bunch of clowns, and we would always find a way to preserve ourselves.

We stayed in this second headquarters of the army police for at least another week. As had happened during the first week, I never once saw Gil. Here there were no sunbaths. It was January in Rio, and worse, we were in the valley of the city's Zona Norte, where one finds a heat suggestive of science fiction: the water from the single showerhead seemed to be artificially heated, but we knew that it was only the heat of the sun upon the tank. The bathroom here was a tiny closed room, with a shower, a washbasin, and a toilet, adjacent to the cell proper, separated by a door which, naturally, could not be locked. I found out from my fellow inmates that Gil was staying in the next cell with various famous writers and journalists. Among them, Ferreira Gullar was particularly admired for his inspirational manner, his spirit of solidarity, and his talent for finding inventive solutions, even in the most hopeless situations. A young man had been transferred from their cell to ours—a skinny boy with glasses, whose Japanese eyes and nearly suicidal daring toward the officers had earned him the sobriquet of Sumidinha (Little Disappearance), a reference to a former prisoner, a nisei by the name of Sumida who, it was rumored, had been murdered by the military. The young man's eyes shone with admiration when he spoke of Gullar, and he told us about a system that Gullar had invented to permit written communication between the cells by means of strings that would carry notes from one side to the other over the water tank that served both bathrooms. The pen, which had been obtained through some stratagem I never discovered, and the paper, extracted from the ration of brown stock that passed for toilet tissue, were hidden atop the wall beside the tank, near the strings, and every time the need for communication arose, one prisoner would go into the bathroom while the others kept an eye on the bars for any officer or soldier. There was a signal of taps on the wall to announce that a note was being sent, and another to alert us that an officer was coming. Gil never sent me any message, nor I him. Sumidinha told us about a man who had difficulty getting about and who had been literally dumped from a wheelchair into the other cell because he had the same name as Antônio Callado, whom they were looking for. In spite of the other prisoners' insistence that this was not the writer Callado, whom they all knew well, the military held the lame man there for days, supposing that his colleagues were conspiring to deny his identity out of pity for him. The real Antônio Callado arrived while we were still there, and only then was his unfortunate namesake set free.

I come in my memory to that toothbrush the arresting officer recommended. It must have been with me the entire time, yet try as I might, I can't recall brushing my teeth in any of the three cells I was held in for two months. Nor do I remember seeing my fellow inmates doing so. No doubt I was brushing my teeth daily, since the first day at Barão de Mesquita. But I can't account for how the business of the toothbrush was handled at the moment of our arrival at each of the three prisons, when they would tell us to remove our watches, our wallets with whatever was in them (money, documents), and finally our clothes, with the exception of the bikini underwear, still something of a novelty back then (though all the young men in my cell wore them as well, no one preferring what by then were beginning to be called *"samba-canção shorts"*—which perhaps could be found in Gil's cell, as it was full of older men). Of course we can't remember "everything," but it is a curious thing how the memory makes its selections. Perhaps those merely mechanical daily gestures were forgotten even as they were carried out. By the same token, I have never been able to remember with any certainty whether there was a towel, either in solitary confinement or in the common cell. I am almost sure that at Vila Militar, where there were so many of us, we did not have towels to dry ourselves after showering. In any event, it would hardly have been necessary, as the heat was so intense that no sooner had we stepped out of the shower than we felt dry.

Though I felt considerably less unhappy than I had been in solitary confinement, sleep continued to come irresistibly. The presence of young people I could talk to was a great relief after a week alone. It's true that every once in a while we were told we weren't allowed to talk. But everyone, prisoners and guards, knew that this was almost impossible to enforce. Sometimes, when we were talking loudly, a sergeant would yell for us to shut up. Perfeito Fortuna, who reacted with humor to any kind of aggression, was not intimidated by those commands and would stage musical numbers and dramatic monologues, improvising the costumes with bedsheets. (There were bedsheets and mattresses strewn around the floor, and at least one bed we took turns sleeping on.) Sometimes he was the leading man, sometimes the female star. Many times I came close to laughing. Nevertheless, that sublife dragged on with no sign of relief: no one mentioned the questioning. On visiting days everyone could leave the cell to speak to his family on the veranda or in the large waiting room, everyone with the exception of Gil and myself, still incommunicado. Whenever they went to see their families, the youths would try to find words tender enough to console me. I would be left alone in the huge cell. But not even that made me cry.

One detail I do recall has made me weep countless times since my release: Dedé's exchanges with the officers on visiting days, which I overheard from inside the cell without her knowing it. She would insist on seeing me, always answering the threats of the officers with rage and courage. They refused to confirm even my captivity there, and neither they nor I knew how she had discovered my whereabouts. She claimed that an important person had assured her of her right to visit me. Apparently someone had, but without putting the order in writing for my hosts. At least once I know she was crying as she spoke. To hear Dedé's voice, its timbre full of turmoil and honesty, and to hear it without seeing her face, touching her skin, answering her—this, under the circumstances, was more than I could bear. Though unable to extricate me entirely from the madness I had fallen into, that voice, coming from a remote and unconvincing past I kept guarded in my memory, still had the power to move me. And this tenderness dislocated the lethargy that had become my protection. I felt the grateful urge to hug and kiss that little woman who was mine, the source of all possible good, and who was but a few steps away from me without knowing it, barely a wall between us. The first time I heard her voice, alone in the cell, I was frightened and couldn't believe it. Now that the stubborn repetition confirmed its reality, and even though I remained still, I did not know how to restrain my desire to leave that place, to free myself from those walls and restrictions, to lash out against my misery. Dedé, crying loudly, was telling the officers she would be back the next visiting day. And that shred of hope gave me the strength to forestall the imminent loss of control. A few minutes later, the other inmates would return to offer me their homemade sweets and news of Dedé. They saw her but could tell her nothing, not even that I was really there.

Thereafter sleep continued to be irresistible when it came, but did not come as frequently. Even before those afternoons when I heard Dedé's voice, the mere fact of her having been near was enough to make a difference. It's possible that I fell asleep as early as I had done in solitary confinement, but now even the afternoon nap was no longer reliable. As I have said of the various factors contributing to the perpetuation of that torpor, the first among them was always the absence of any sign that our situation could be resolved. In solitary I had given up masturbating altogether: the few attempts had left me a little frightened. In the common cell of Vila Militar I was not alone, and I had neither the occasion nor the inclination. One day one of the youths in the cell stated, in the middle of a conversation, that the military were putting something in our food, a *"substância broxante."* Today I think that must have been only a comforting myth. At least it was for me: I accepted it as a satisfactory explanation for my complete lack of sexual appetite. After fifteen days without sex, I had not so much as a wet dream. But then I have reason to believe that I was no longer sleeping so soundly at night. There was a third cell, reserved for common prisoners. All of us who were political prisoners knew that we were under the protection of an order against physical violence, to which some of the officers alluded at times with contempt and impatience. The irritation would sometimes take the form of black humor, when some officer would point his gun inside the cell, in protest against the benevolence of his superiors, and say: "If it were up to me, I would shoot the hell out of you." (Sumidinha, in his temerity, would dare the lieutenant or captain to carry out the threat.) The common prisoners were not eligible for such benevolence. The high turnover in the third cell was quite noticeable: prisoners would arrive during the night, others would go in and out the same day, several would leave through the hallway, under the threats of guards who would warn them never to dare cross their path out in the street. It was said they were thieves and lawbreakers from Zona Norte. Sometimes I was awoken in the middle of the night by horrendous screaming from down the hallway. There were interminable beatings and, more than once, I heard the voices of the torturers calling urgently for a stretcher. Sometimes in those voices one could hear surprise at the results of the treatment. Once, at least, I was nearly certain that the victim had died. Some of my fellow inmates insinuated that all this might be a pretense to frighten us, but such an insinuation was not convincing. Others lived off their hatred for the executioners, and the fact that those poor people could be beaten and even murdered without anyone knowing it. In reality, after my time at the army police barracks in Vila Militar I came to have a different idea of Brazilian society, an awareness of the exclusion of the poor and the descendants of slaves that mere statistics could never have provided. But were those infernal moans we heard at night at Vila Militar really those of common prisoners? The duration of some of those torture sessions to which I bore auditory witness leads me to suppose that perhaps, during the night, some of the militants from whom they wanted to extract very important confessions were dragged in. Perhaps the protractedness of those sessions was due to sadism pure and simple on the part of the officers. (They no doubt boasted of it: I remember that mixture of pride and envy with which they referred to the most feared among them, the *catarinas,* as they called the tall, blond soldiers of German descent who came from southern states, especially from Santa Catarina—hence the name—and who were famous for their rigidness and bigotry.) However this may be, the screams awakened me. I think if I had heard these same sounds in solitary, they could not have pierced my leaden sleep (some of the young men in the common cell did not wake up during those macabre nocturnal sessions). Today, however, I'm even more amazed that I could have gone back to sleep so easily once the howling had died down. Undoubtedly in Vila Militar I was less lethargic than at Barão de Mesquita, but the wakeup calls had not induced the sort of wakefulness that the cries of pain did now. Those of us awakened, at first silent and frightened, would exchange enraged whispers before returning to sleep without a drop of sweetness in our souls.

One day I thought I was going to die. A young soldier had appeared at the grate and was staring through the bars at me with a look of fear and pity. It was as though he knew of something horrible soon to happen but could tell me nothing about it. In a little while, the same soldier was obeying the order to open the barred door and I was following an officer and a sergeant to the wide porch through which I had entered on the day I arrived. The officer ordered me to walk straight and not look back. The group, made up of the officer, the sergeant, as well as a soldier pointing his machine gun at me, led me outside the building and then, receiving an order to turn left, I saw myself in the open air, walking along a road rimmed on my right by some smaller buildings, also belonging to the barracks, little white houses, almost all with their doors shut. The three did not speak much, and I can remember nothing they said, but the sensation caused by the solemnity of their tone is one I can still feel. It was clear they were not taking me to be questioned, clear as well that they were going to do something *physical* to me. I could read it in the rhythm of their actions and of their speech, even in the unfurling of the road before me, that they were going to do something violent to my body. I knew it was nothing to do with sex, or torture, or even a beating—it was evidently something simple and clean, a single gesture, something equal to this atmosphere, which, while grandiose, was not quite so heavy as to suggest they were going to execute me. Still, that is exactly what I thought when I came to the end of the lane, where there was nothing before me but the open door of the last small house, and the officer ordered me to stop and not look back. The blue of the sky was obscured by that green haze that forms when the summer air in Rio offers little to breathe and little to behold, a haze we love all the same since it gives us to know it is summer in Rio. I stopped in accordance with the order, and I felt an icy blow inside my stomach, in the center of my body, and suddenly my legs were not there. I didn't fall, however. I waited for a shot. I remained standing with a worthy steadiness that scarcely corresponded to the collapse I was feeling inside. The officer told me to turn right and go into the little house with the open door. It was the barracks barber shop. The barber, scissors and clipper in hand, stood there ready to demolish my famous head of hair.

My apparent indifference—which disappointed my torturers—followed naturally from the elation I felt when I saw that I was not going to die, a joy dampened only by the depressing ridiculousness of the whole thing. The officers lost their solemn tone and were erratically looking for a harsh or mocking one that they couldn't quite find; my strange mix of happy relief and measured disgust gave me a nonchalant air that confused them. The fear I had felt and the momentary happiness that followed had been equally regulated by emergency mechanisms activated in me beyond my conscious control. Besides, whatever the importance of my hair might be—we, the *tropicalistas,* were the pioneers of wildly long hair in Brazil, a step ahead of the Beatles model adopted by Jovem Guarda and Roberto Carlos, and here it was in January of 1969 and I had not cut my hair since 1967—in jail I could scarcely remember that I had long hair (and wasn't even sure I had a career as a pop singer). And so, the officers' anticipation, which had inspired such solemnity during the walk, was all on account of something that hadn't even occurred to me: the shearing of my hair was, for them a symbolic assassination.

The barber (I don't remember him wearing a uniform), though he soon understood there wasn't much room for humor, demonstrated much greater strength and independence than the officers. I felt a touch of tenderness for him—after all he signified life for me at this moment—and I remember our exchanging a few calm words. I don't know whether I had the courage to ask him to save the curls that were falling to the floor, but Dedé says to this day that on the first visiting day after that episode, Perfeito found a way to get a packet of my hair to her. She and I knew that according to Afro-Bahian religious tradition, one must gather any hair cut from a person and throw it into the sea. Dedé has a very vivid recollection of this, because having been denied permission to see me and having received the packet of my curls, she could assume only that I was dead. Equally unforgettable for her is that moment when, far away from me, she threw my hair into the ocean. I still have no idea how that exchange took place. But I am sure that for as long as I was in Vila Militar I knew nothing of the result. What I did not forget was the face of the young soldier—the one who surely knew what was going to happen—crying quietly when he saw me coming back with a crew cut.

The only other time I was outside that cell before leaving the army police barracks at Vila Militar, I thought the time for the interrogation had finally come. In fact, though it turned out not to be the interrogation I expected, it was an interrogation all the same. I think the officer on duty had left for the day, and the sergeant who relieved him decided to call me in. I didn't even know his rank: when I saw him order the guard to open the door and let me out, I thought he was an officer. He made me cross the small yard under the columns and led me into a room furnished like an office. There was a worktable covered with papers, an armchair next to the wall behind the table, and facing it, an ordinary chair in which he ordered me to sit. After seating himself in the armchair, he began to stare me down contemptuously before he finally started to talk. He was a corpulent man, ruddy and blondish, and, I immediately realized, a complete moron. He asked some questions about our having taken part in student demonstrations, his tone so stern that it soon became apparent this was not to be taken seriously. These first questions required no answers: the sergeant was simply scolding me. His manner, that of a school principal, indicated that his main purpose was to play at being in charge.

In fact he himself disclosed that he was a sergeant and that he had taken the initiative to question me because there were some things he would not tolerate. For example, was I friends with that scum who'd staged the play *Roda viva?* I replied that I was acquainted with many of those involved. He wanted to know whether I thought that was the right thing to do. "What do you mean, 'the right thing'?" I asked. "You think people can tolerate all that whoring around with the Virgin Mary?" he replied.

I was somewhat enraged at this but was able to hide it completely. His words reminded me of the day I arrived and saw the rosary being torn, amid an outburst of profanity, from the hands of some young men who only wanted to pray, and I thought it equally disrespectful that this idiot would use the word "whoring" so close to the name of the Virgin: it occurred to me that deep down inside he did not respect religious symbols and yet he was not ashamed to attack those who, bearing much greater love for the symbols and teachings of Christianity, would not yield to the hypocrisy he protected like a dog.

As he continued, my suspicions were confirmed: "Putting bobby pins on Our Lady! . . . I don't give a shit about religion, but we can't have this sort of thing. You think families go to the theater to see this?" Something of my indignation must have surfaced. I answered that I believed in the Virgin, but I had not found that scene offensive. To say that I was a believer was not entirely untrue: as I have described, I was in the midst of a kind of confrontation with my religious beliefs. In any event, I felt that I was representing the Catholic young men who were in the same cell with me; it was precisely because they believed in Christ and the Virgin that they would not accept the intolerance displayed by this officer toward the show.

Roda viva, the first play my fellow composer Chico Buarque wrote, deals with the rise of a pop music star and the ridiculousness and lack of authenticity that entails. In the old days it was referred to as his juvenilia, in the sense that it was a bit naïve. Yet it was written by an excellent composer, about whose beginnings and evolution there was nothing inauthentic. What had transformed it into a momentous event, however, was the direction of José Celso Martinez Corrêa. In this, his first work since the professional turning point that was his staging of Oswald de Andrade's *O rei da vela,* Corrêa took his violent, anarchic style to a new extreme, turning the play into a pop ritual and an opportunity to reveal the unconscious levels of what I might call "the Brazilian fantastic"—the zeitgeist. These revelations spared no one—neither the characters nor the audience. The young star has a wife more honest than his fans or his agent, and this wife is—owing to a cascade of images that appeared onstage (and in no way followed the directions of the script)—soon transformed into a kind of Madonna, yet without ever removing her housewife's hair curlers. This was the scene the sergeant had chosen to account for the hatred the military nurtured toward *Roda viva,* which had motivated them to invade the theater in

São Paulo, physically assault the actors and some of the public, and close down the play. They were not operating under orders. As a matter of fact the army never admitted—and I myself, who had attributed the attack to a right-wing terrorist group, the so-called Commandos for Hunting Communists, could not have imagined—that the military was involved in this episode. But when the sergeant called me he was acting on an impulse that culminated in this confession: "I was there. I was one of the guys who beat the shit out of that gang of sons of bitches."

The scandal born of *Roda viva* was caused by the savagery of its mise-en-scène. For instance, in a scene staged in the audience, the chorus portrayed a fanatical mob that wanted to touch its idol. Zé Celso ratcheted the fans' ardor to the point of cannibalism, and soon it looked as though out of the body of the singer who had disappeared into the crowd, there had emerged a liver (actually that of an ox) brandished by one of the admirers, as real blood splattered onto those in the audience seated in the middle of it all, near the aisles. Adaptations of familiar images from advertising or everyday life, drawn from television and from religion, were endowed with a physical presence felt as the threat of a nakedness that was deliberately neither erotic nor decorative, but simply carnal. In sum, everything in the show was relevant to the *tropicalista* work. This sergeant was telling me that our arrest was motivated by the very same logic (or illogic) that had made him beat up the cast of *Roda viva*—and he wanted very much for me to know that. Later I was proud that *tropicalismo* could have found such proof of its subversive power. After all, just as I had so many times convinced our opponents, the sergeant was revealing that we *tropicalistas* were the most serious enemies of the regime. But in that little room of the army police, I did not have the strength to feel proud: I was merely afraid.

Afraid and enormously tired. I had discovered the reason for our arrest, and at the same time—in a dialogue that proved to be no less exhausting than actual interrogation—that there would be no interrogation, since we were under arrest without anyone's knowing what for.

The days that followed were devastating. The cell, which up until then had been so full that at times we could not all lie down at once, began to empty out. Everyone was gradually freed, and I ended up alone, at least for one day and one night, perhaps longer, feeling once again as though time did not exist.

The move from the army police to the army parachutist head-quarters was quick and without incident. The area of the PQD, the abbreviation used among soldiers for the Parachutist Battalion, was also in Vila Militar, located a few kilometers from the army police area. We were taken in an army jeep or van and were able to see the road and feel the hot wind through the windows. The only surprise was that when we arrived at the barracks where I would be kept, I was separated from Gil, who continued on in the car. Afterward I would find out that he had been taken to another section of the PQD, but when they separated us I was afraid I would never see him again. I remember the gate opening onto a hill with white buildings of various sizes, the largest of which was at the top. The cell that awaited me was down below, on the road, next to the guardhouse. I would be staying in it alone, but it could not be called solitary since, unlike the one at Barão de Mesquita, this one had a bed with sheets and a pillow with a pillow-case, and the bathroom was a separate room with a toilet and a shower at a reasonable distance from each other, and a clean washstand. I think there might even have been soap. A door with iron bars separated this squalid suite, hot as an oven, from an entrance room that connected to the barracks and was always under guard by a soldier. As for my being watched, this soldier took his orders from a sergeant who was always nearby, and this sergeant took his orders from the officer on duty (generally a lieutenant) who, in turn, answered to the major commander of the headquarters. It was with considerable relief that I landed among the PQD, for this was considered an "elite" battalion, and a great rivalry existed between it and the army police. Though at night we could hear the screams of what were said to be civilian petty criminals at the army police headquarters, officially this place was intended for punishment of military personnel alone. The parachutists were, therefore, subject to arrest and punishment as carried out by these super-police. The parachutists were an elite by virtue of their specialty: they were proud of their rigorous training and of their daring free-fall jumps from air force planes. These officers and army soldiers even boasted about their physical beauty (many would tell me that this was an unofficial requirement for selection in the recruiting process), and they thought it abominable that they were subject to the brutality of the soldiers in the army police. Above all they feared and hated the *catarinas.*

The first PQD soldiers who talked to me made a point of assuring me that among them I would not be treated as I had been by the army police. They would ask questions that showed their eagerness to hear me speak ill of my previous hosts. And they wanted to emphasize the contrast. This gave me some hope.

But hope can lure us to an even more dangerous mental state than despair: this game of going from the worst to the less bad, without a prospect of resolution, proved a torment in itself. In fact, although materially I had begun to lead a more dignified life, many days passed with no one coming to say anything about the questioning, much less my freedom. Major Hilton, the commanding officer, came to my cell one night. His visit had been repeatedly announced by soldiers, sergeants, and officers who approached the bars during the day, and I was very anxious. But the major limited himself to the enumeration of the barracks rules, emphasizing his disapproval of the soft image the parachutists might perhaps have suggested. He left without asking me a single question. I came to feel I was being relatively well treated only so that I might better endure prison, that my term would last forever. This notion left me prey to a variety of superstitions that had been since my adolescence an almost innocent mental vice, but had burgeoned in dreadful form during my first two weeks at the army police prison. Here, with a few hours less sleep, with various antennae aimed toward the immediate future for any sign of freedom, the internal rituals multiplied and deepened, to the point where I would divine future events with inexplicable precision and believe that I could act to precipitate, evade, or alter them.

I had developed an increasingly complex system of magical signs and gestures, a monstrous capacity for the interpretation of the signs combined with a no less monstrous imagination for devising the gestures. On the day when the army police had taken me for the haircut, apart from the smallest details, I could make out the essence of what was going to happen, arriving at the adjectives, as it were, of the imminent act, without discerning the noun. I now perceived a system of numbers, images, and questions that, if read with enough skill held the clues to what was to come. A much heightened mental state—the result of the improvement in material conditions—contributed to the sophistication of this system. And while at Barão de Mesquita I feared only that "Súplica" and cockroaches might be a bad omen, here at PQD I began to attribute meanings to all the songs I sang or heard, and to perform mathematical computations based on the number of times I saw cock-

roaches or that a song was heard or sung. At first I would sing or whistle a song and a soldier would do the same. After I was able to obtain a
little transistor radio (lent to me by a sergeant and hidden under the
pillow every time the on-duty officer passed by), several songs—whose
respective divinational powers I would measure with every repetition—entered into my game, and in the end I was able to prophesy
with absolute precision the day, time, and place I would receive the
news of my freedom.

The ritual of sunbathing was observed with religious regularity
among the parachutists. I remember a young soldier following me,
with the barrel of his machine gun a few inches from my waist. He
would plead repeatedly for forgiveness, saying in his sincere and touching voice that if it were up to him, none of this would have ever happened to me. One day an officer approached and, ordering the soldier to
stop, initiated a pleasant conversation. He liked pop music. He recalled
several hits by Francisco Alves, the great Brazilian idol of the thirties
and fifties. Among them was a *samba-canção* he found particularly moving: "Fracasso" (Failure), and he asked me if I could sing it. Somewhat
flattered, I acquiesced. I liked this samba, with its sad melody in a
minor key, and as I sang it, just as I had done with "Súplica" at Barão de
Mesquita, I would reinterpret the lyrics as allusions to my situation.
Today I look back on this scene in the open-air courtyard of the PQD
headquarters with a mixture of humor and horror. Under the merciless
sun, with the barrel of a machine gun pointed at my back, I softly sang
for the officer on duty: "Why is it all I have left of that sad love story /
the painful story of a failure . . ." The word "failure" is heard seven
times in the course of the song, culminating with its insistent repetition in the high final notes:

> *Failure, failure, failure, failure after all*
> *For having loved you too much,*
> *For bringing me such pain . . .*

That word—as I repeated it in those circumstances, feeling all the
more vulnerable on account of the music's beauty and the weight of the
emotions its history awakened—turned into an evil incantation in my
imagination. Sometimes, alone in my cell, I would make an effort to
forget that song, but it would begin to sing itself again. It started playing an important role in the system I was developing, together with
"Súplica" and "Onde o céu é mais azul." The latter, "Where the Sky's

More Blue," was also a hit of Francisco Alves, a "samba-exaltation," a genre that had emerged during the Vargas period, praising the virtues of the nation: I had been singing it the night before my arrest.

The food here was a little better than at the army police headquarters, which is not saying much. With a bed and a bathroom, and suffering no particular mistreatment, I began to feel once again the pleasure of having—being—a body, and this brought forth, with the very first nights, the lineaments of erotic dreams. I was still too frightened not to wake up startled before ejaculation was possible. In the shower—the water here, too, was very hot because of the weather—I was astonished by spontaneous erections, feeling myself on the verge of orgasm. Since I had already resigned myself to zero libido for the rest of my life, this wonder brought me greater happiness than I was ready to bear. But masturbation had become the taboo par excellence in my internal system for controlling the future. A direct contact with the reality of sex—of life—literally in our hands to make or to abstain from making, masturbation reveals itself as a prefiguration of frustration. It's not so much that in a desperate moment, like mine in the prison, we succumb to the idea learned in childhood that masturbation is a sin. Rather I would say that before such moments we should better understand why such a particular idea of sin is attached to masturbation. In my system, the worst sign was to see a cockroach; the worst gesture (and I did not do it until I left the place) was to masturbate. On the other hand, to kill a cockroach (an almost impossible feat) meant that I was gaining ground toward freedom through suffering, just as hearing certain songs assured me of surprisingly good news.

Things really were improving. I think that by the second week Dedé was allowed to visit me. They would open the barred door and let her in. Everything was transformed. Not that we were left alone: the soldier was under orders to watch us and, in any event, since the door was made of bars, we had no privacy. But she would sit beside me on the bed and tell me about the world outside and about her efforts to obtain my freedom. She would listen to my confused story of the days I had spent without seeing her, and she would comfort me. She brought books and magazines (they were finally allowed here) and messages from friends, as well as a can of insecticide and—she insists today—Valium. The fact that I might have used this tranquilizer, which I came to know after my experience with *auasca,* leads me to think that my problems with sleeping had returned under these conditions of relative well-being. But Dedé herself seemed startled by my physical state. She found me terribly thin and, without warning me, went to Major Hilton's house—in Marechal Hermes, a suburb in Zona Norte next to Vila Militar—to demand that I be given better food. I suppose that Gil had, in the barracks where he was detained, the right to eat the same food as the officers, because that's what Dedé demanded for me. But—as with the privilege of having a guitar in my cell, for which I had petitioned the major many times without success—this right was accorded Gil on account of his having been graduated from the university, while I had not been. Dedé, however, found out that better food would be served me only for reasons of health. One day (duly prefigured by the appearance of a cockroach that I killed with a blast of insecticide), the major had me brought in and started shouting threats of the severest punishments if what my wife had claimed were false; she had insolently visited his house once again to request that I be given food from the officers' mess on account of my bout of tuberculosis as a teenager. She maintained that I had scarred lungs, and so he had ordered an X ray: I would be in trouble if those scars did not materialize. I was quite frightened — Dedé had not warned me about this. The next day, after I had been taken to the X-ray lab, the major, who was not a brilliant man, said to me with great seriousness: "Congratulations, your wife didn't lie."

The magazines brought by Dedé frequently had photos of half-naked women, pretty actresses, models, stars. The proximity to Dedé was often accompanied by a series of erections that, given the satisfaction of being next to her, were more like spasms of pleasure than the anxiety of desire. But many times, alone, having those photos of women at hand, I had to make a great effort not to masturbate. I would dream at night of unknown women, and would always wake up close to orgasm, my heart racing. I never loved women so intensely and exclusively as when I was in the parachutists' barracks. Women seemed to me the embodiment of happiness. Never had men seemed so disgusting and repugnant. My sexuality had died in solitary at Barão de Mesquita but had now totally rebounded, toward women. One month spent among the military was enough to make me reject in disgust any man as a possible sexual object. One day Dedé brought me the magazine *Manchete* with photos of Earth taken from outside the atmosphere. These were the first in which the entire globe was visible, and there was a strong emotion provoked by the confirmation of what we had until then known only through deduction and abstract representation. I considered the irony of my situation: a prisoner in a tiny cell, I looked in admiration at images of the whole planet, seen from the wide open of space. Years

later, back in Bahia, I composed a song I am still very fond of today—
"Terra" (Earth); its lyrics begin with allusion to that moment . . .

A not-so-young sergeant once offered, with a tact I thought very
moving, to provide me some moments of total intimacy with Dedé. He
was a black Bahian man, of humble origins, who told me he would
never make it past sergeant because he hadn't had any formal instruction (and was no longer the right age anyway). I always feel a certain
pride when I recognize in the gesture of this sergeant—which revealed
a kind of respectful fascination with sex—a characteristic of the people
of Bahia. He offered to make sure, during the days when he was on
duty, that no one would come near the door of the cell during Dedé's
visits. And so it was that he exerted his authority over the soldiers
(who, in this case, seemed to obey willingly). Since the road that led
down to the offices (and to the mess, which was called "the casino") was
rather long, the sergeant had enough time to warn us and to regroup his
forces in the event an officer was coming down the hill. I had Dedé with
me, in a way I had thought would never again be possible. These brief
encounters were tender and intense—and they saved me, restoring my
nearly shattered equilibrium. But the sergeant was either denounced or
had been caught and was arrested, a fact communicated by Major
Hilton when he came to bellow that from that day on Dedé would
never be permitted in my cell again. The visits now took place under
careful surveillance, and I could talk to her only through the bars. The
Bahian sergeant was imprisoned, and I never saw him again.

Among the books I read in the cell at PQD, two left an indelible
mark: one was a collection of poems by Jorge de Lima, and the other
John Steinbeck's *To a God Unknown.* The latter completed, in a way, the
work of *The Stranger* and *Rosemary's Baby;* it made me even more superstitious. Jorge de Lima's poems were equally mystical, and I felt myself
even more fully imprisoned. The image of my sister Irene would appear
to me frequently to save me from these shadows; she was fourteen at the
time and was becoming so lovely that I would sometimes mention Ava
Gardner when speaking of her beauty. But even more glorious was her
happiness, exploding at every moment in sincere and spontaneous peals
of laughter. Even without the guitar, I wrote a song about her, and
started to repeat as if it were a rule:

> *I want to go, people.*
> *I'm not from here.*
> *I've got nothing.*

I want to see Irene laugh.
I want to see her laughing.
Laugh, Irene, laugh, Irene, laugh.

It was the only song I would write in prison. I didn't think of publishing it: it seemed incommunicable. But to my surprise, Gil would find it beautiful and, once it was recorded, not only did it become a hit, but Augusto de Campos published it in a version that emphasized (again to my surprise) its visual aspect as a poem, in particular the palindrome of its refrain: "Irene ri."

One day, confirming one of my meticulously constructed premonitions, Major Hilton called me in. When I entered his office I understood this at last was going to be the interrogation: he was sitting at his desk with a solemn air, and there was a clerk next to him. I think that aside from the soldier who had followed me in with his machine gun, there were two others, guns strapped to their backs, each like a statue on either side of the major's desk. I obeyed the order to sit down in the chair across from him. I listened to his introductory speech in which, briefly put, he declared himself to be an implacable inquisitor: everything would be cleared up for better or for worse. He wanted no doubt to convince me that it would be for the worse. He then proceeded with the first questions. I thought it only natural he would begin by asking my name, age, nationality, etc. But I never dreamed he would ask me the date of birth, occupation, and civil status of every one of my brothers, brothers-in-law, and nephews. The majority of the latter were still small children and I felt I was involved in a sinister comedy when the major insisted upon precision in all data. I even fantasized that perhaps they wanted to use the children as possible weapons of intimidation, in case a more complex kind of psychological torture were necessary, because the major wanted me to tell him what degree of affection existed between me and each of them. Many hours were spent detailing things like the life of Layrton Barreto, my sister Clara's husband, and Antônio Mesquita, my sister Mabel's husband. Needless to say, the same happened with my parents, and with Dedé and her family. The fact is that this first day of questioning passed without moving beyond such minute inquiry into the activities of parents and in-laws.

From then on, I would go up the hill daily, followed by my guard and his machine gun, to answer the minutely detailed questions of the major. I glimpsed the possibility that things would sort themselves out when the major broached what must have been the formal justification for my arrest: the episode at the Boate Sucata involving Hélio Oiticica and his banner paying homage to Cara de Cavalo. As I previously related, Cara de Cavalo was a famous criminal from Rio, whose romantic legend had flourished following his murder by the police. Hélio Oiticica—who enjoyed frequenting the *favelas* and admired such figures who seemed to respond with violence to Brazil's unbelievable social disparities—had made a banner with the image of Cara de Cavalo lying dead in the road. It read: BE A CRIMINAL, BE A HERO. The judge had succeeded in closing down the show and the club. The measure had seemed to us out of all proportion, since Hélio's banner was only one element among the show's many preposterous and shocking touches. The mere existence of this show already had shock value in itself, given that it was staged on the margins of the International Song Festival, from which our compositions had been excluded, provoking a scandal. The story of the Sucata's closing because of Hélio's banner spread by word of mouth and, seizing upon the word "banner," a radio and television presenter from São Paulo decided to create a fantasy version of the facts, in which we appeared wrapped in the national flag and sang the national anthem interspersed with swear words. The presenter, Randal Juliano, was a demagogue in the fascist style who courted the dictatorship by attacking artists. This kind of bluster was common in his programs, and since we had not listened to his jeremiad against us, we attached little importance to what we were told. Now Major Hilton was informing me that this man had explicitly asked the military to punish us, and that the tirade had produced the desired effect in the academy at Agulhas Negras, the prestigious school for army officers.

Naturally, I answered that I was surprised the officers had not tried to verify those accusations, which, given the chance, I would prove false. The major seemed furious, since he was not willing to admit that the reason for my imprisonment for over a month might not be valid. But he assured me all the same: "If you prove your innocence, I'll release you immediately." He asked whether I could produce any witnesses to confirm my version of the facts. I replied firmly and quickly that I could and gave him the names: Ricardo Amaral, the owner of the club, and Pelé, the disc jockey. Both had been present at the show every night. The major said he would take measures to summon the witnesses, and that he would call me back only when the hearing was scheduled. And so it went. Two or three days later, I went up the hill to hear Amaral, the famed Paulista impresario of Carioca nightlife, and Pelé, the elegant and lively fellow who, like so many other blacks in

Brazil at that time, had taken the name of the great soccer player, and who had become a fast friend. It was interesting to know that those two denizens of Zona Sul's night life would come to a hearing at seven or eight in the morning at the opposite side of town, in Zona Norte. They were sitting back to back, both with their backs to the chair that awaited me, an odd arrangement to prevent any communication through signs or gestures among us. I thought it very strange to hear their voices without seeing their faces, but I was extremely pleased to see the impact of their words—a little nervous but simple and clear all the same—on the major: both of their versions corroborated mine in every detail, confirming without a shadow of doubt the truth of what I had been saying all along. At the end of the hearing, when I was allowed to, I said good-bye to Pelé and Ricardo, and saw in their expressions an insecurity I had never imagined possible in either of them. The major looked me straight in the eyes and, with that solemn and not too intelligent air of his, partially repeated what he had said about the X rays: "Congratulations. You told the truth." But, more important, he added: "I'm going to request your release today; you'll be free in two or three days."

Irrespective of what the major had said, it was to the interpretation of my signs that I attributed the news of my imminent release. But in truth I queried my erratic oracle only because I already knew that such a clear and fair interrogation did not correspond with the absurd way they had made me wait for it. The irrationality of what had been happening to me—and had inspired me to create that system of signs— was proof that it would be silly to believe that a stroke of reason could change things.

They never again opened the cell to let Dedé in. The only person who entered it, aside from the soldiers who came to take me to the hearings, was a young lieutenant called Paulo, a very handsome man who had grown up in Marechal Hermes and dreamed of the glamorous life in Zona Sul, where all the artists lived. He obviously knew he was very beautiful and asked me to introduce him to film directors and agents once I got out. He said he wanted to be an actor or something like that. He was visibly fascinated by me, by my fame, the colorful world of my profession. He would walk freely into the cell because, being a lieutenant graduated from the academy, he had, apart from his authority over sergeants and soldiers, special privileges. But he did not inform his superiors of these visits, which were forbidden by the major. When the major told me he had found out about them, his voice was full of bitter disapproval, as though I were responsible. I felt somewhat relieved to be free of the dazzled lieutenant. Another presence, however, seemed to me more sexually threatening: an officer, I think he was a captain, who was said to have completed some antiguerrilla course in the United States (and for that reason wore a special red badge). He posted himself every day before the bars, staring at me for long wordless moments. He walked around with a slender rod in hand, and I think often wore dark glasses, though not always, since I seem to remember his frozen, piercing eyes. In the two previous barracks, where I had no clothing at all, I had grown accustomed to spending the day in my underwear, nearly naked; and in PQD, although I do seem to have had some clothes, I continued the habit because of the heat. But this captain's gaze made me want to get dressed. I felt enormous repugnance for his coldly masculine manner, and faced with his enigmatic expression, it was as uncomfortable to look at him as to look away.

One day Major Hilton called me, somewhat embarrassed that so many days had passed with nothing more said of my release, and he told me that he was going to summon the radio presenter Randal Juliano so I might confront my accuser. A few more days went by, during which time the inscrutable captain was absent only once, and again the major sent for me to say, sincerely disillusioned and sad, that he had been told Randal Juliano would not come without further explanation. Then he confessed to me, perplexed: "I don't understand what's going on. You should have been released. This is shameful." I was taken back to my cell and no one said anything further. This is when my system of signs really took off—I put all my energies into it. I became a fortune-teller of remarkable import. Years later, while commenting on the case of Thomas Green Morton, the paranormal who could bend spoons, make coins appear, send telepathic messages, and predict events, with my psychoanalyst, Rubens Molina, the latter told me that all those things seemed to him horrible symptoms—what could lead a young man to *need* to accomplish such wonders?—and I, instead of remarking on the perversity of psychoanalysis in aiming to reduce everything to a particular system, thought that Molina had actually got to the heart of the matter: I knew how far despair could take us. In the last ten days I spent at PQD, I trusted only the signs that I myself had chosen to inform me about my future. One day they came for me and, as it had been predicted and the expressions on the soldiers' faces confirmed, it was not the major who had summoned me. It was the captain, they told me, who wanted to talk to me. I trembled as I walked up the hill. The signs had not predicted any kind of catastrophe, but the fact is that, no matter how enslaved to it we may be, we never fully believe in magic; living in reality, we are compelled by its perennially brutal freshness, its senselessness.

When I arrived at the door of the captain's office—he occupied a special position by virtue of his U.S. training and had an office to himself—I thought I was going to faint. He told me to come in, ordered the soldiers to leave us alone, and locked the door from the inside. After staring at me for a long time, exactly as he did near the bars of my cell, he asked in a clear voice—calm, understanding, overwhelmingly human, even sweet: "Do you feel you have been treated unfairly?" I promptly answered, with a firmness unmatched by my mental state: "Yes, sir. I do." And I felt an immense relief: as had been presaged, no physical violence would be inflicted on me. He walked back and forth for a while, looking serious but not hostile, and said with sincere sadness: "I understand." His eyes, which he had averted, looked at me again with the old coldness. "But are you naïve, or perhaps you think you can make fools of us?" he went on, displaying a little intellectual vanity in citing the names and ideas of Freud and Marcuse (by contrast, the names of Marx and Lenin were uttered more dryly, without the sense of excitement), and he laid out his entire sophisticated explanation of *tropicalismo.* He alluded to some of my statements to the press in which the term "deconstruct" had appeared, and using it as the keyword, he denounced the insidious subversive power of our work. He said he understood clearly that what Gil and I were doing was much more dangerous than the work of artists who were engaged in explicit protests and political activity. In sum, he showed himself to be much more attuned to the real motivations for our arrest than Major Hilton, implying that he had always known that the stories about the flag and the anthem were false, and therefore that my having proved my innocence was irrelevant. There was nevertheless a strange atmosphere of complicity between us: we could laugh at the major and his naïve principles and his Minas accent. We could discuss Marcuse's concept of surplus repression. But without adding any information about what the less educated military officers planned to do with me, not even asking me to say what I thought about what he had said, the captain dismissed me with a courteous air, unlocked the door, and called the guards to escort me back to my cell.

Alone again, I thought how this conversation with the captain had been but a more refined version of the one I had with the army police sergeant. Both had summoned me out of the need to show off. Both confirmed a theory I would have used to justify my work politically to my leftist opposition. Both left me without hope: in fact, if the motive behind my arrest was no particular act but rather a vague intuition on the part of the military that something in me was essentially hostile to them, there was nothing that could be done to effect my release. All that was left was to count my cockroaches, sing my cheerful songs, and make my calculations. And all signs, at least, started to say liberation was at hand.

There was a lieutenant by the name of Oliveira who never missed a chance to humiliate or insult me. When he was the officer on duty, he allowed me no privileges, and he began to demand that I do interminable and unnecessary rounds of cleaning in my cell and bathroom. But by now any one of the other officers would let me go out in the afternoon to the door of the building where the waiting room, my cell, and my bathroom were, and sit in a chair by the gate and gaze at the road in front of the barracks. It was a desolate view, but I sucked in the outdoors with my eyes, as though I could draw the whole wide world back to me again. The silent act of inhaling the landscape of freedom—so miserably represented here by a stretch of road and the hot, opaque haze of Deodoro—was adopted as though it were a ritual obligation, and the songs I heard then were computed with double value. "Hey Jude" by the Beatles, everything heard daily on the hit parade—"F comme femme," songs by Roberto Carlos, a *samba de partido alto* by Martinho da Vila—were the strongest indication of my immi-nent release. If the melodic phrase that is repeated in that triumphant tone at the end of "Hey Jude" was heard suddenly—because the radio was turned on, or its owner had unexpectedly changed stations—at the exact moment of a deep inhalation, while my eyes were glued on the turn of the red dirt road shimmering in the heat, this was an anticipa-tion of my luminous and joyful leaving. I went even so far as to predict that I would be informed of my release at the top of the hill, after mid-day but before sundown, while in the act of eating something. My pre-dictions were exact. I would say: "If I spray insecticide on that cockroach and it is able to run away without dying, there will be a three-day delay in the release"; or: "If 'Hey Jude' is whistled by a soldier outside my cell, this will give a much weaker push toward freedom than had the same song been sung by the soldier; if, however, it is heard on the radio before sundown, the delay will be reduced by twelve hours," and so on. I knew I should not whistle any of the beneficial songs—that would weaken them. It was good to sing them—like a prayer—but, as omens, they had much more value if heard by chance. I interpreted signs concerning the time and place of my receiving the news of the release as an announcement that it would find me during lunch at the officers' "casino" (where I had continued to take my meals since Dedé had succeeded in proving my lungs were scarred), at such and such a time (I was precise) on the next Wednesday afternoon. I barely remembered it was Ash Wednesday, and refused to complain that I could not be in Bahia for Carnival. That one—in 1969—was the Carnival of "Atrás do trio elétrico" (After the Electric Trio), my *marcha frevo* that popularized those musical groups typical of Bahian Carnivals and spurred their development, the consequences of which are notice-able today in, among other things, the success of Bahian Carnival music and the phenomenon that came to be known as "*axé* music." But during those sultry afternoons in the barracks I did not think about how the streets of Salvador would be crammed with people and that my *mar-chinha* was a leading hit: I only did my calculations.

At times, when I had long been free again, I surprised myself, horri-fied, surrendering to nostalgia for a remote time and place that I recog-nized within seconds to be those days at PQD. At those times I did not long for the suffering per se, or even for that excitement of premonition (which I now abominate with irritation), but for a certain balmy, sweet abandon, something hidden in the intimate sense of one's body. I attrib-ute this feeling to the fact that after a certain point, at PQD I was already waiting for liberation. (Today I consider another factor at least as important: I had started to gain weight after a few meals in the offi-cers' mess.) The heat, the space limitations, and the dependence on orders from above caused the days at PQD to blur in my memory with Santo Amaro and my childhood, at which time, too, I was slowly saving my life. But the strange happiness I derived from those longings—at times set off by hearing a song I had often heard there but had since forgotten—would give me pause, and I would live the nostalgia of those moments the way women live the nostalgia for pregnancy. There were times in the barracks of the parachutists when I still did not know the happiness of imminent liberation, yet no longer felt the terror of seeing the nightmare begin, time when I reached that zero degree of being in which I simply existed.

On Ash Wednesday during lunch at the "casino," I was waiting, with a disturbingly tranquil certainty, for the arrival of the major's emissaries with the release order. Yet I did not give myself permission to believe. The premonition was so daringly precise that even I considered it ridiculous that this event should take place. I was afraid of it, but I so hungered after freedom—and had dedicated so many of my rituals to obtaining it—I felt nearly free already, and was therefore brave enough to surrender my magical powers. It was with a kind of cold awe that I saw the prediction fulfilled. I was still chewing the last forkful of what was left on my plate when two officers who had entered approached the table I was sharing with lieutenants and captains and ordered me to get up and gather my things to go: "You're going to be freed." The signs had told me that I would receive such an order "while I was eating," and even that I "would not finish the meal." Just as in action films, the denouement came at the last minute, when I was already afraid lunch would end without a summons. When I saw the officers walk in, I wanted to laugh. In fact, I laughed to myself, a bit uneasy at the radical experience of loneliness such a situation provokes. But the happiness of knowing I was free, the prospect of being alone with Dedé, seeing my parents and siblings again—and Gil—these were greater than the anguish of a soul trapped in a system. I was free, and that's what mattered, and if I had entered into some supernatural pact, we would see about that later.

But was I free? I left the remaining food on the dish and followed the officers. I collected my things in the cell, listened to the good wishes of the sergeants and soldiers—and even the major—and was soon sitting beside Gil once again in a van that took us from Deodoro to the central precinct of the federal police, in the heart of the city. We remained there longer than on the day they arrested us. We spent the night there, without receiving any more information. A high-ranking officer—I suppose it was the highest officer of that organization in the then state of Guanabara—came to talk to us the next day. He told us he'd received orders to escort us to Salvador personally and would therefore be driving us to Santos Dumont Airport, where we would be put on an air force jet. The fact that I was still under arrest had considerably devalued my system, which on the one hand gave me a measure of relief, but on the other revived my insecurities, which included a fear of airplanes.

But an intolerable impatience took hold of me, and this was greater than any fear. The little jet had technical problems that made takeoff impossible, and we were forced to return to the federal police. Hours later we were summoned again, and again the chief drove us to the airport, where we boarded a Brazilian Air Force plane, similar in every way to a commercial plane and full of plainclothes passengers, including women and children who were the relatives of air force officers. Aside from the chief of the federal police, another officer (or two others?) boarded the plane with us. As before, Gil was separated from me, each of us sitting next to one of them. (In my memory, I was handcuffed to the federal agent during the entire flight from Rio to Salvador.) This indeterminacy of our situation (were we free or not?) the indecisiveness of the trip itself (a whole day waiting, then a little jet that would not take off, before flying now among the military families—to say nothing of what might be awaiting us in Salvador) left me exhausted. As the plane pierced great clouds, I felt myself in a limbo, between fear and pain, unable to believe that any kind of simple motion could be accomplished. Tied to that man at my side, seeing that eternal cold color through the window with the rounded corners, I was afraid of dying, believed I was already dead, dreamt of the hope of happiness I had felt for just one day. I finally understood that my happiness was not an illusion when the plane started to prepare for landing, and I saw Salvador emerge through the clouds. My legs trembled, and the buzzing in my ears I have heard since adolescence seemed to rise above all the airport sounds. Air force officers who had been waiting for the plane were talking to the head of the federal police who had brought us, and I noticed they were arguing. The air force military officers took us by the arm, against the protests of the policeman. We were thrown into a cell at the air force headquarters in Salvador, where the behavior of sergeants and lieutenants was much closer to the arrogant brutality of the army police than the relative courtesy of the parachutists. This time, however, we were put together, Gil and I. We tried to talk—and how strange we were to each other!—but the shouts of the officers silenced us. This was the last blow to my waning strength. The small finger in my right hand went to sleep—and this anesthesia would last for months, disappearing only gradually. We spent a few hours there. It seemed the air force in Salvador had received orders to arrest us in December and no countermand had come since, so they were beginning everything from scratch. They did not even know we had been under arrest the whole time in Rio; that was the reason for the argument between the policeman and the air force officers. When it was finally decided that we could go, many offered their sadistic regrets that we would not be staying.

The chief of the federal police in Rio took us to Salvador's central precinct and turned us over to a colonel, Luís Artur, the head of the federal police in Bahia. After his colleague left, Colonel Artur asked us some questions about the March of a Hundred Thousand, showing us pictures from the newspapers in which we appeared among the demonstrators. He also confessed to us some uneasiness at the whole business of having received us directly from the hands of the highest authority of the federal police in Rio, who had come personally but without the requisite official papers documenting our status. He asked us whether we had anywhere to go in Salvador. We said we did, and he told us to take a taxi and go. Before we went, he asked us to sign a big ledger and informed us that we were categorically forbidden to leave the city and had to present ourselves to him on a daily basis or we would be sent back to jail. "Confinement" was the word he used to differentiate the prison regimen to which we would submit for future infractions from the one to which we had submitted before. It was night: when I walked out with Gil, I felt lost. I didn't know whether I would have the strength to walk. I didn't recognize the city, didn't know whether to consider myself free or not, or whether I would still know how to live. Gil insisted on accompanying me home. I suppose he must have noticed the state I was in and wanted to take care of me. But it is also plausible that he wanted to postpone his own arrival at his aunt's house—the aunt who raised him—and to have first some contact with my family, to which he always attributed a kind of spiritual value.

When we arrived at my parents' house on Prado Valadares Street, we found only Nicinha, my eldest sister, who had stayed home to watch the house while the others went to the airport to wait for us. Gil sat on a chair and was very quiet, with a half smile across his lips. I felt an absolute stranger to myself. I knew Nicinha was Nicinha, but I didn't exactly recognize her. Nor did I recognize the house. The photographs on the wall—of my brothers, of my parents—seemed to be not only of strange people, but of strange things. Even so I knew that Bethânia was Bethânia, and Rodrigo, Rodrigo. I felt the same desperate longing for myself, for my world, for life, that I had suffered during the *auasca* trip—only without even being able to tell myself that I was under the influence of a drug and that it would pass. I ran from one part of the house to the other, and Nicinha was unable to restrain me. I remember seeing a tear on Gil's childlike face, but I could not stop even to try to keep him in my heart. Freedom had come, but I was no longer there: I had waited too long. For a moment I was sure that it was all over, that I would never come back from the hell into which I had fallen. Then I heard voices and footsteps on the stairs and saw my father and my mother appear before me. My father looked at me as if he understood exactly what I was feeling—as no one else could—and he said, speaking as he never had before in front of my mother, in a steady, half-wry voice that brought me back to the house, to love, to problems, to life: "Don't tell me you let those sons of bitches get to you!"

tough luck 69

When I think of the number of people who died in Brazilian prisons after 1968 (a small number compared to the
Argentine and Chilean victims of the following decade); when I think
of those who were tortured, or those who were exiled in 1964 and were
able to return only after the amnesty of 1979, I realize that my two-
month prison stint was an episode hardly worth mentioning. Many
who suffered worse treatment—or who were arrested more often and
for longer periods of time—skim over the topic, often in a tone of indifference. Gil's own memory of life in prison is neither as bitter nor as
recurrent as mine. Having understood early on that something like this
could happen, and being more mature than I was, unlike me he did not
feel annihilated and was therefore at least able to transform his experience into something useful to his own development. In jail he found
the opportunity to attain a kind of asceticism; he stopped eating meat
and began learning about macrobiotic food and Eastern systems of
thought. The latter have literally transformed his life: his body, his
skin, his temperament all changed for the better. My only discovery
was that suffering is absolutely useless. But the many pages devoted
here to my prison experience have their place all the same because this
is a chronicle of the *tropicalista* experience from my very personal perspective. If nothing else, they serve to reveal how psychologically and,
even more, politically immature I was.

After four months under house arrest in Salvador, Gil and I were
invited to leave the country. This awful event came as a result of Gil's
conversations with Colonel Luís Artur, chief of the federal police in
Bahia, to whom we had to report every day during this period, and
whose goodwill Gil had won owing to the apparent affinity between his
new religious interests and the colonel's spiritualism, a belief not
uncommon in the Brazilian military. Forbidden from making public
appearances, we could not make enough to support our families. And so
toward the end of the month Gil started pressing the colonel to inter-

cede on our behalf with his superiors in Rio and Brasilia. Since our arrival, the colonel had been complaining of our having been handed over to him without any official paperwork to document our "case" or even our arrest, and he was determined to help us. But his repeated requests that we be granted work permits finally met with the suggestion that we leave the country. It seems that having arrested two rising stars of MPB and shorn their famous hair, before subjecting them to an unjustified prison sentence, which would have doubtless turned them into even more ferocious enemies than initially supposed—and enemies with influence over public opinion at that—the military had no idea what to do with us. Exile, imposed with the same rude informality that had characterized our arrest, seemed an intelligent solution to them.

We had no money to cover the airfare, much less to cover our living expenses during the first few months, and so the colonel persuaded the highest authorities to allow us to do a concert in Salvador to raise enough money, assuring them that we would not take advantage of the occasion to incite the crowd. Gil and I were living with Dedé and Sandra in a small rental house in the humdrum beach neighborhood of Pituba. A young man with thick lips who played guitar really well came by one day. Everyone thought he looked like Mick Jagger. His name was Pepeu Gomes. He must have been about sixteen then, and he was a prodigy. His brothers were also good musicians. Carlinhos, the older one, played bass. Jorginho, who was then a boy of fifteen, already sounded like a professional drummer. Together with some friends, these members of a large and humble family of the Garcia neighborhood had formed a rock group called Leif's, whatever that meant. We rehearsed with them the numbers we were going to play at the Castro Alves Theater before leaving Brazil.

This was a time when hallucinations, fantasies of other dimensions, and various kinds of mysticism were all the rage. Gil was not only in the sway of eastern religions but interested in stories he heard about UFOs. Aside from drugs and politics, the occult and other esoteric topics attracted almost all our acquaintances. Everywhere one could find the fear of darkness mixed with the elation of freeing oneself from the chain of causality. I truly loathed this perennial hunger for novelty and miracles. Since I was very vulnerable, in a childish way, to my own fantasies, I reacted aggressively against this fad: "You guys adore things that don't exist. Fine, I like only what exists!" I would yell in the middle of conversations about astrology, theosophy, macrobiotics, and tarot. Roberto Pinho's Sebastianism à la Pessoa (which, in an utterly fascinating way, included religious homage to *candomblé*) was also encouraged in this climate, and I tended to reject it out of fear. As a matter of fact, I thought that life had already taken me too far beyond my everyday dimension. The *auasca* trip, followed by the two months in prison, and even the plethora of meanings attributed to my rise to the status of celebrity, everything made me dread losing my mind. In the eighties, when the diplomat and essayist Sergio Paulo Rouanet was appointed by President Fernando Collor to head the Ministry of Culture, he came to my house in Rio to apprise me of his intentions and to ask for my support. I had just read his book, *Razão cativa* (Captive Reason), and near the end of our conversation I told him: "I'm an irrationalist who's in love with reason." And he told me he was my symmetrical inverse. In 1969, at the birth of the mawkish New Age, I was struggling against irrationality.

Dedé was with me all the way. In fact she was much more genuinely averse to mysticism than I. Unlike Gil, the two of us used to go out at night. We would go with friends to a little improvised bar in the courtyard of the Cruz Vermelha Club, in Campo Grande, a poor little bar called Brasa, which offered no comfort or advantage, much less bathroom facilities. I should mention that we thought it natural that this kind of place would attract us. This bar, which served our favorite beer, also offered an atmosphere reminiscent of the tents set up in the street during Carnival, and we found it much more inspiring than the nightclubs with golden handrails and the restaurants with high-back chairs (which did not abound in Salvador anyway, even if we had been in the financial position to frequent them). As it turns out, we enjoyed, at least for a time, a careless happiness amid the oppression. Many interesting people would gather there; at Brasa we met Moraes and Galvão, two composers who later became the nucleus for the group Novos Baianos. Dedé loved to listen to their songs, sung by Moraes, who also wrote the melodies and played guitar. Later another future member of Novos Baianos began to come by and to frequent our house in Pituba. This was a very fair-skinned girl, very pretty, with long hair, who would cover her breasts with the thinnest canvas strip imaginable, cut off from the bottom of her jeans. She was called Bernardete, but Alvinho Guimarães had invented the name Baby Consuelo for a character in a film he never made, and the name stuck forever to this girl, who had been chosen to play the role.

I also used to go to the Fonte Nova stadium to watch soccer games.

These were sunny and festive outings, and it was the only period in my life when soccer played a considerable role. The press, meanwhile, being strictly censored, could not even suggest that Gil and I were in such an unusual situation, which would have made good copy. The public barely noticed our absence from the theaters and television. Vague rumors circulated about our having been arrested, but they had never been confirmed. The journalist Marisa Alvarez Lima—who had introduced me to Hélio Oiticica—came to Salvador to write a story. It would appear with a photograph of me taken with a telephoto lens, the text reporting rather mysteriously that I was in Salvador and seemed sad. Gil and I each cut a record during this time. But since we could not go to Rio or São Paulo, we recorded in a studio in Salvador (I think it was called Studio J.S.), using only guitars. The tapes were sent to São Paulo or Rio for Rogério Duprat to add bass, drums, and orchestra. Gil played guitar for all the songs on my record. There were no restrictions on broadcasting our songs. The attitude of the Brazilian authorities may have been inconsistent, but it was not ineffectual. I remember only that the record company itself decided not to release the single of a song I had recorded just before going to jail. It was a beautiful R&B-samba by Jorge Ben called "Charles, Anjo 45," a romantic homage to an out-law hero ("Robin Hood dos morros, rei da malandragem"—"Robin Hood of the slums, king of the bad boys"), of whom it was said that he had gone "to spend some holiday time, against his wishes, in a penal colony." The song celebrates an archetype that today has fallen out of fashion: the bandit with a heart of gold, whose generosity is simply a complement to his part as crusader against social injustice. Though the social causes were not Jorge Ben's main preoccupations, his Charles was a rather benign model for what today would be recognized as the drug dealer who becomes the king of the slum and takes upon himself the responsibilities that should have been handled by the civil authorities, in exchange for keeping the law out of his territory. Undeniably, this characterization made him more attractive to me than the pure and just heroes (or victims) of protest songs. At the end of the song, a big party is announced, with "batucada, feijoada, whiskey and beer, fireworks and explosions in the air . . . Before the end of his vacation, our Charles is coming back / And the whole slum will sing and be happy." Everyone thought, with reason, that the coincidence with my own prison term would sound like a provocation. But the military did not much trouble themselves about our songs; the looming shadow of anarchy, and their suspicion that we had connections with radical activists (in spite of the patent hostility the conventional Left manifested toward us)—these were their concerns. In any event, hardly anyone can live on royalties in Brazil. Unlike artists in rich countries, here we cut records only in order to create shows, and it is these shows, with long runs in the great capitals and tours throughout the rest of the country, that insure the livelihood of their stars.

The show at the Castro Alves Theater in 1969 was an unforgettable moment for many. I, however, don't have a very precise recollection of it. Rogério, as I have said, had observed that when people are imprisoned, they are imprisoned forever, and I felt myself under a heavy shadow. Roberto Santana, who had produced our shows at Vila Velha, was in charge of staging the new one. I remember only that Dedé made me a vest with bits of mirror and that someone brought from São Paulo—and graciously furnished—one of those light-show machines that projected bubbles of color, so emblematic of the late sixties and early seventies. The moment I sang "Cinema Olímpia," a new song of mine, is recorded in my memory as a very emotional one, with many faces so full of life in the sold-out orchestra section. Today I think how little it meant to me then that the show coincided exactly (and quite by coincidence) with the first landing of man on the moon. Alves and I missed this great event on television. But Gil wanted to sing "Lunik 9," a song of his then over three years old, which laments the imminent death of "romanticism" with the profanation of the moon by the space missions. The truth is that he exulted in the "conquest" of the moon, and sang those naïve, nostalgic words with sweet irony.

What stands out more vividly is the moment when Gil showed me the song "Aquele abraço" (That Embrace), which he intended to sing in public for the first time there. We were in the living room of the little house in Pituba, and this samba brought tears to my eyes. The brilliance and flow of the phrases, the evident destiny of this pop song to become a hit, its wound of love and loss, and above all its direct address to Rio de Janeiro, the city to which I feel so intimately connected because it is, as João Gilberto put it, "the city of Brazilians"—all of this had a profound effect, and I began to sob uncontrollably. During the show, the audience, too, was captivated by the song, and they sang along with Gil as though they had known it all their lives. The irony of this song—which seemed a kind of valediction to Brazil (represented, according to tradition, by Rio) but without the least rancor—is that it made us all feel up to the difficulties that lay ahead. "Aquele abraço" was, in this sense, the opposite of my state of mind, and even in such a condition, from the depths of my depression, I knew that this was the only way to keep going without being overrun. For me, this song will always have the affective power of "Chega de saudade," *La strada,* or *The Words.*

The federal police processed all the paperwork necessary for our trip as quickly as possible. We would not be exiled without a passport, as many Brazilians had been during those years. Our transit from Salvador to Rio had been choreographed in accordance with police instructions. Two agents were waiting at the airport and spent the next three days with us. They acted as though we might change our minds at any moment and run away. A comment made by Gil in one of the detention rooms is branded in my memory. He regarded Martinho da Vila's appearance as a good omen for the future of samba, and that of MPB in general. In the course of the conversation, mention was made of Milton Nascimento, whom Gil had long considered to be the greatest talent to emerge since we had begun. Gil said that Martinho was the second most important since Milton—though at a different level and for different reasons. As the police agents escorted us to the plane for Europe, one of them said: "Don't ever come back. But if you do, at least check in with us when you arrive to save us the trouble of finding you."

We got off in Lisbon the next morning without my having slept a second. Guilherme Araújo, still unable to return to Brazil from Europe since the Midem episode in which he had protested our arrest, was waiting for us at the airport with Roberto Pinho. We discussed our options at length. Guilherme had already decided on London (we would not have even dreamt of going to the United States), but he wanted us to see for ourselves. We stayed in Portugal for about a week. We had time to spend a day in Évora, to go to Sesimbra (where the reputed alchemist had offered his Sebastianist interpretation of "Tropicália"), and to hear *fado* in various Lisbon cabarets. Everything was at once touching and depressing. Portugal was now under Marcelo Caetano, the political heir to Salazar, and the impression was of a sad people thrown off the course of history in this beautiful place. From there we headed for Paris, where we felt rather restless. It was 1969, and the city was hung over from events of the previous May. The proverbial bad humor of the Parisians was palpable, and we were stopped by policemen at every corner, asking for our identification. Where Lisbon had been anachronistic, Paris was tense. London represented the opposite of both these scenarios. Stable, tranquil, and insuperably fashionable, the English capital, for all its Nordic, non-Latin strangeness and its insufferable climate, seemed our most rational solution. Be this as it may, I more nearly accepted this decision than took it, much as I pretended to weigh the pros and cons as they came up in our discussions.

london, london

hose years were a cloudy dream. In London we stayed in a small hotel in Queen's Gate in South Kensington until Guilherme found a comfortable three-story house in Chelsea and suggested we rent all three floors with him. And so we did. This was 16 Redesdale Street at the corner of Shawfield, a side street off the King's Road. A year later we moved, not to get away from the neighborhood, but to be on our own. Guilherme moved to an apartment nearby, while Gil and I decided on Notting Hill Gate, where the presence of a large number of Jamaicans made everything seem more cheerful. I lived in Elgin Crescent and Gil in Kensington Park Mews. We saw each other frequently, but it was different from living in the same house. After that I moved to West Kensington (Bassett Road), to Hampstead, and finally to Golders Green.

Curiously, all my memories of the city, of the streets, of being in London, are extremely vivid and clear, up until the move to Chelsea, after which it is my recollections of the house in Chelsea, the inside of it, that are the more indelible. Whenever I return to London, I go to look at the house in Redesdale Street and I am moved by it; but as to the other places I stayed, I don't even remember exactly where they are. It may be that during the first year, I was unable to take any interest in the city and what happened in it, and I fixed my attentions on the house and the people who lived there or frequently appeared. Or it may be that the Chelsea house was simply the best among the London houses in which we lived. There I learned to like television: I had never watched a color television, and so I decided to rent one. I marveled at the BBC documentaries and the great American classic movies. I watched *Monty Python's Flying Circus.* When I told some British friends about it, they said they had never heard of it. I thought it odd there should be such an exceptional program, to which no one paid any attention, but as it happens the show was still in its first season.

In this house, where some self-exiled Brazilian friends had come to

live, we also received a visit from Haroldo de Campos, who nicknamed
it the "Sixteen Chapel." He ended up injured in a car accident owing to
Péricles Cavalcanti's carelessness, forcing him to extend his time in
London. He stayed at our house for a few days, and sweet Péricles took
care of him with the utmost solicitude. We listened to Haroldo with
delight, and he was able to divert himself a bit as well. His friend Cabrera Infante, along with his wife, Mirian, would come over to see him,
and we would talk about Cuban and Brazilian music, American movies,
and, a little more frugally, about literature. I had read *Three Trapped
Tigers* at the height of the boom in Latin American literature and had
loved it even more than *One Hundred Years of Solitude,* although less than
anything by Borges. Cabrera Infante is such a funny man—as serious as
Buster Keaton, but in a totally different way. His bitterness toward his
ex-friend Fidel's Cuba was always noticeable but never mentioned. To
this day, whenever we are in the same city at the same time, we look
each other up and talk.

One of the most emotional visits for us was that of "the King,"
Roberto Carlos. He was very grateful for our having inspired a new
appreciation of his work, as I have said, and on his way through London
he decided to see us. When he called to arrange a time, Rosa Maria Dias
(who was then Péricles's wife, and also lived with us) could not believe
it was true, and when she realized it was, she started to cry. Roberto
came with Nice, his first wife, and we felt in him the symbolic presence
of Brazil. Like a true king, he acted and spoke for his country with
greater authority (and legitimacy) than the military government that
had expelled us, than the Brazilian embassy in London (no one there
had been in touch with us, and according to a friend who tried to locate
me through them, the expression they used was "persona non grata"),
and with greater authority as well than the many leftist intellectuals,
artists, and journalists who at first failed to understand us and now
wanted to mythologize us. Roberto Carlos was Brazil *de profundis.* As
we talked about his new record, he picked up my guitar and, confidently assuring us that we were going to like this, sang "As curvas da
estrada de Santos" ("The Turns on the Road to Santos"). Amid this
situation in which we all found ourselves, this extraordinary song sung
in Roberto's inimitable way, with only the guitar, completely overwhelmed me. I wept so much and so shamelessly that, having no handkerchief nor even the composure to go fetch one, I ended up blowing
my nose and wiping my eyes on the hem of Nice's black dress.

London represented for me a period of utter vulnerability. I took

English lessons for foreigners in one of those schools with many rooms and large classes. But I spoke Portuguese nearly all the time, living as I did in a house inhabited or frequented by Brazilians. I felt unable to take advantage of what should have been an opportunity. Gil, on the contrary, tried to make the best of the situation. He went out more, studied earnestly, met musicians, and went to lots of concerts. It is astonishing to think that, in two and a half years, I never once went to see an English play, attended not a single classical music concert, never entered a library or a bookstore. And I only went to museums (the British Museum and the Tate Gallery) the week before our return to Brazil, because I was taken by Arthur and Maria Helena Guimarães, and by the Portuguese painter and set designer Jasmim. It was the time of the "counterculture," and all roads led to rock shows and to the Electric Cinema. But what had happened to the curiosity of the boy who, back in Salvador, used to go to everything available at the MAMB, the *salão nobre de reitoria,* and the School of Theater?

The truth is that I was becoming more and more versed in pop music. My idle dreams of leaving behind what I was already doing professionally in order to study, to direct films, or to write receded with the shock of prison and exile. I simply lacked the strength even to adumbrate an act of will. The bell that had rung as I was falling asleep that morning the police had come to take me away had so deeply left its mark that I was still trembling at the sound of the doorbell in Chelsea. So it was impossible for me to dare do anything I might wish. And insofar as there was growing receptivity to what I did among my fellow professionals in London, a simple instinct for survival bound me to the activity in which I was already installed. I would stay home listening to Gil play, at times playing myself, watching television, reading, and above all conversing with people who came by. I was always chatty, but my happiness did not last even until my head hit the pillow. There was always something to feel ashamed of. And I didn't know how to get out of this.

Hélio Oiticica had been living in London since before we left Brazil. There had been an exhibition of his work, widely seen and much talked about, and the people in the Exploding Galaxy group, led by Paul Keeler and David Medalla, gathered around him and cultivated him. Guy Brett, then the art critic for *The Times,* who had written enthusiastically about Hélio as well as about conceptual artist Lygia Clark, often came to the Sixteen Chapel to join our conversations. Hélio was one of those radical artists, incredibly intelligent, and continually transform-

ing the almost unattainable singularity of his vision into luminous subjects. He had participated in the Carioca "neo-concretist" movement (a
consequence of, as much as a reaction to, the concretist movement of
the São Paulo painters), and he brought into this post-Mondrian world
not only the "organic" and the "tactile" that was supposedly missing in
those "cold" *paulistanos,* but also the extremes of pop romanticism (not
to say pop art), the explicit thematization of his personal mythology
(Mangueira samba school, the slum thugs he was friends with, rock,
sex, heavy drugs), and a commitment to be himself a conceptual work.
He moved away from the canvas toward the creation of objects
intended to be contemplated as installations—for example, "Tropicália" or the transcendental raiments that were "Parangolés" (barely
recognizable as clothes, impossible even to discern as autonomous
objects, this assemblage of cloaks, capes, scarves, and jackets made of
plastic, brocade, and netting was exhibited in such a way as to provoke
in the viewer a whirlpool of thoughts and emotions about the body,
clothing, beauty, invention, poverty, and freedom). Hélio turned himself into a kind of perambulating happening. It was very much in keeping with the spirit of the times: both Agrippino and Rogério sought to
become characters themselves, rather than merely authors of ingenious
works, and to a large extent they succeeded; let us remember that
British neo-rock in the sixties and even *tropicalismo* itself had similar
ambitions: the typically "narcissistic" political bent to ideologize intimacy and to sexualize the judgment of public acts were also of the same
nature. But Hélio took this as far as it could go, with unparalleled
sophistication and wit. To the very end he was committed to the idea of
the avant-garde, to the creation of a new design for living, one independent of the designs of poverty, oppression, and the human condition
conventionally conceived.

We followed from afar what was happening in Brazil. While I was
uncertain what might come of armed revolution, the heroism of the
guerrillas as the only response to the perpetuation of the dictatorship
earned my terrified respect. Deep down, we felt a certain romantic
identification with them, something we had never felt for the conventional Left or the Communist Party. When we heard about them, we
felt we were a little to the left of the Left. When their leader,
Marighella, was killed (he was a Bahian who had belonged to the Communist Party, and legend had it that as a student, he had written his
answers to a chemistry exam in rhyming decasyllables), the photos of
his dead body appeared on the same magazine cover as the first photos

of us in exile. Back then I used to write articles for *O Pasquim,* and as I considered the symbolic weight of the two images coinciding, painfully, on the cover (the magazine at the time had the largest circulation in Brazil), I wrote a long and bitter article that concluded: "We are dead; he is more alive than we are."

Not one person in Brazil understood what I was talking about. I received many letters meant to comfort me in the suffering of exile, and I spoke to various people who came through London and Paris: even those who mentioned Marighella's execution and my article could not even remotely relate the one to the other. I was astonished, and that made me all the more aware of the psychological distance that separated us from people who were living in Brazil. The news of terrorist activities was cause for enthusiasm and apprehension. Naturally, sweet guitar players from middle-class homes don't feel quite at ease faced with the prospect of violence. But the exchange of ambassadors from rich countries for groups of prisoners—with the assurance that those who were kidnapped had been treated humanely—seemed like glorious victories for those who fought the good fight of resistance.

When Rogério Sganzerla and Julinho Bressane arrived in London, one could see through the front windows of the Chelsea house a Brazilian flag one of us had hung to celebrate our reunions before the television was tuned to the World Cup. The British, dazzled by the soccer of Pelé, Tostão, and Jairzinho, had begun to root for Brazil, since England had been disqualified early on. But our guests, stifled by the way the dictatorship had used soccer for purposes of propaganda—something that we, being so far away, could not feel with the same intensity— these two young filmmakers seemed uncomfortable with the flag. I had left Brazil soon after the premiere of *O bandido da luz vermelha* (The Red Light Bandit), Sganzerla's first feature film, and had seen so much talent and freedom in that film that I was willing to buy all the criticisms the director might voice against Cinema Novo. Rogério and Julio had arrived in London with Helena Ignez (the beautiful actress Bethânia and I had idolized in Bahia, who had been Glauber's first wife and was now Sganzerla's), and the three of them, with their clothes, their hair, their ways, were perfect models of elegant eccentricity, without a drop of provincialism. I had been even more impressed by a film of Bressane's, *Matou a família e foi ao cinema* (Killed His Family and Went to the Movies). Today I consider it one of the most poetic of all the films made during that period, or any, in Brazil. Curiously, Cacá Diegues, who has always represented the sensible side of Cinema Novo, and has

become a kind of personification of the movement, was the one responsible for my seeing the film during a trip to Paris, and he also adored it.
Sganzerla thought it was inconsistent of me to praise Júlio's film and
give Diegues credit for introducing it to me. On the other hand,
Glauber would write me extremely violent letters, in that uncensored
style of his, practically forbidding me to make friends with the two
rebels. All this caused me some unease, and though eventually things
turned out quite well, I deplored the inability of each side to encourage
the other. Deep down they loved Glauber, and Glauber loved them.
The duo's aggression against the master had in it something of the
murder of the father leavened with some critical lucidity. It would have
been as though Gil and I decided to tar and feather Tom Jobim, accus-
ing him of having recorded an album in the United States with musical
themes similar to the so-called "nationalist" classical music, and symphonic arrangements. It was simply unthinkable. But that's because in
Brazil MPB simplifies the life of its producers in a way that film cannot
do. The ease of the production process, the vitality of the domestic market (which the international labels quickly recognized), the texture of
the tradition itself—all of this gives to the pop musician what is denied
the filmmaker. Nevertheless I knew then, as I do today, that Cinema
Novo is more vulnerable to criticism than bossa nova. (And yet, or perhaps for that very reason, we always capitalize the first while the second
does not seem to need the uppercase). Sganzerla's brilliance as a director
seemed to promise a very successful career that would establish a new
standard for Brazilian cinema, one that would have box-office appeal
and generate international attention. He prefigured much of the best in
Almodóvar and Tarantino. But the obstacles facing such a thing in
Brazil came crashing down on him heavily, and although he continued
to make films and has not lost his brilliance, he does so only at enormous intervals. Bressane, beginning shortly after the London period,
produced a long list of highly personal and erudite films, deliberately
rejecting mass-market expectations, and their solitary beauty grows
with time as he searches for answers to the most subtle of questions
about the nature of cinema as an art form. Julinho likes to tell a story
about how Tom Jobim, in reply to a girl who wanted to know if he distinguished between classical music and pop, said: "*I don't make any
distinction, but it exists.*" This always makes me ponder how one never
speaks in terms of a possible classical, as opposed to a popular, cinema: a
Carnival attraction, a technological curiosity, cinema becomes popular
as though by originary destiny; at the same time, that clear distinction

between classical and popular musicians robs the latter of the right (and obligation) to address themselves to serious cultural issues, although this is expected of filmmakers, no matter what their level of formal training.

In Rio, in the sixties, there was a running joke that Brazilian films were "shit" but the directors were "geniuses." This was aimed at the Cinema Novo filmmakers—and Glauber more than anyone—who provoked immensely sophisticated discussions about films practically no one went to see. Nevertheless, in the seventies these same filmmakers, having acquired a little more experience, made films in which intellectual ambition was tempered by teamwork and an attempt to meet the demands of the market. Thus, just as something relevant was won with the first precarious and heroic productions, so something remarkable was also achieved during the second assault. Attendance increased greatly and, as I see it, there were good moments when the films of one phase illuminated those of the other. Sganzerla and Bressane emerged precisely during this transition. The former showed himself to be quite capable of making "cinema"-type films, which the public could recognize as such, yet which would still have much to say about the language of the medium. Julinho, on the other hand, had from the very beginning assumed the radical stance of the filmmaker as poet, the sovereign author, director of experiments in the pure state with concessions neither to the creative community nor to the community of spectators. His stubborn fidelity to this position makes him the filmmaker most profoundly engaged in the dialogue with Glauber's legacy.

Gil and I didn't know what we were going to do in London. Philips, our recording company in Brazil, had sent a letter to the executives in their British branch recommending us and explaining our situation. But I did not expect—much less wish—them to respond to that request. I was afraid that if someone were to call me to record something I would embarrass myself. In Brazil the producers did not even allow me to play guitar on my own records—and I agreed with them. I sincerely hoped that Gil would establish a circle of musicians and start demonstrating the exuberance of his talent. With a little goodwill, I thought I might jump on the bandwagon as partner and adviser, once he had found work.

One night a man came to 16 Redesdale Street to listen to us. He had made arrangements with Guilherme over the phone, and we thought he was from Philips. As it turned out, he had been with Philips, and before leaving the company he had heard tell of us. Philips wasn't really interested, but he had kept our address and, now working for another label where he had a little more autonomy, he was checking us out. His name was Ralph Mace. He talked to us for a while and asked us to sing something. I was taken aback that he seemed so pleasantly surprised at everything he heard, and even more so that he would show the same enthusiasm for my songs as for Gil's. In the course of more meetings, Mace started talking about making a record with us. He was thinking of a record for each of us and proposed that I write some songs in English.

My state of mind concerning my ability to make music changed considerably because of this man. He sincerely liked us and was very thoughtful. The novelty of his being equally interested in me permitted me, for the most part, to overcome my embarrassment. I marveled to think that it was possible for someone in that place to admire my music, finding use for those aspects that in Brazil were not even taken into account. It more than made up for the fact that the British recordings would fail to capture many other elements that in Brazil would be obvious. And this was confirmed when we went into the recording studio.

Lou Reisner, an American producer living in London at the time, discovered us somehow, although not through Mace. On the contrary, the two met because Reisner wanted to produce my record. I remember going to his apartment in Knightsbridge and singing several songs. His very positive reaction was a continuous source of amazement. I'll never forget that he was the one who corrected my English in the key phrase—and title—of the song "In the Hot Sun of a Christmas Day." Everything in that tune was already as one can hear it today on that first record I did in London, except for the refrain. I sang: "In the hot sun of *the* Christmas Day." The ludicrous moment came, as he tried to suggest that I change "of the" to "of a," and I couldn't remotely fathom that word "of a." The more he repeated it, spelling it out, the more confused I became. I would hear it as "over," pronounced in the English manner (Lou was American), and thought it sounded absurd. It's not that I believed he was saying "over"—I knew he wasn't—but no other word came to mind.

language

s soon as Ralph Mace proposed making a record, I composed several songs in English. It wasn't the first time I
had done so. In São Paulo, long before I could even imagine I would
live in London one day, I composed a *marcha* bossa nova with lyrics in
English, though at the time I barely spoke the language. English was
becoming more and more international, and I thought that since we
were being bombarded with it all the time, we had the right to use it as
we could. If Brazilian radio stations played more songs in English than
in Portuguese, if products, ads, stores used English in their packaging,
slogans, and windows, we could certainly answer with our own poorly
learned English, making it the instrument of protest against the very
usage being imposed on us. At the same time we also wanted to establish a dialogue with the "outside world." It was a naïve attempt at
international communication, a way of trying to let some air into the
shuttered universe that is Brazil. I did not expect international success:
I never dreamt I would live abroad, much less in an English-speaking
country. In the album notes to my first solo recording I wrote: "When
you don't feel like going to the U.S., it's hopeless." This wasn't a han-
kering disguised as a denial. Rather it was a conscious recognition of a
sort of duty I was too indolent to fulfill. English came easily, and I was
certainly able to calculate the benefits, and yet I felt no urge to go to the
United States, bored at the prospect; I was shy and unmotivated. But I
knew that Brazil needed (needs) to engage in candid dialogues with the
world at large, if it is ever to be rid of all that has kept it closed in upon
itself like a difficult slave. So the song I wrote back then was a cry for
help in reverse: I addressed some of my imaginary interlocutors in the
world out there, and as I described the poverty and solitude of being
Brazilian, I asked for help, begging them to tell me their names so I
could tell them who I was. The song was called "Lost in the Paradise"
(note once again that definite article . . .):

My little grasshopper airplane cannot fly very high
I find you so far from my sight
I'm lost in my old green light

Don't help me, my love
My brother, my girl,
Just tell my your name
Just let me say who I am

A big white plastic finger
Surrounds my dark green hair
But it's not your unknown caress
It's not from your unknown right hand

Don't help me, my love
My brother, my girl
Just tell me your name
Just let me say who I am

I am the sun, the darkness
My name is green wave
Death, salt South America is my name
World is my name, my size
And under my name here am I
My little grasshopper airplane cannot fly very high

Now I remember. "Cinema Olímpia" was not the only unpublished song I sang at the farewell concert at the Castro Alves Theater. I also sang "Empty Boat," which I had recorded a little earlier in Salvador. This was the other song I wrote in English before leaving for—and knowing that I would go to—London. It's a very sincere song. More sincere than the previous one. Not that it's good. But in it I was telling the world that I felt empty. And that's exactly how I felt. More important, the melody and the sound of the words reproduce exactly *how* I felt that emptiness, recreating the climate in which I found myself:

From the stern to the bow
O, my boat is empty
O, my mind is empty
From the who to the how.

These blunders, born out of the notion of responding to the bombardment of the English language, would embarrass me for some time to come. Nowadays I don't care. The songs I composed in London were better: there is at least one, "Nine Out of Ten," whose lyrics still please me. But these were commissioned by a British producer, and that made them both more modest and more ambitious, since there was the possibility of their being heard by an English-speaking public. This is not to say that during the São Paulo period I did not think about such things with regard to writing songs in English, that the idea of abuse legitimated by Anglo-American domination only occurred to me a posteriori, as a justification. That would be simply ridiculous. No, I had considered it all with absolute clarity. But what should be noted is that I thought about it from a realistic perspective, mindful of pop music's relative unimportance: the "higher" pretensions would be (indeed were) destined to disappear together with the songs themselves, should the latter prove unable to make their way as such. In other words, such ambitious aims could not be charged to a song, not even in Brazil, not even in those days of "counterculture." In any event, the "higher pretensions" may seem merely laughable nowadays, but they are worth remembering if only for representing a curious turn in the history of my (our) relations with international culture as guided by the English language.

To a mind that has evolved within the circumference of Portuguese, English is as strange as any language could be to a human being. And its abiding presence, far from mitigating that strangeness, often only intensifies it: from hearing so many songs whose sounds became familiar, even as their meaning remains obscure; from seeing so many subtitled films, we become inured to English as a gibberish that is part of life, without requiring any effort on our part to make it intelligible. Later when we learn many words and some technical terms, it's still easier to "disconnect" and let these English sounds revert to their former status as a kind of grunting. Writing about my childhood earlier in this book, I recounted how to us English sounded canine. Well, even after I fell in love with the lyrics of Cole Porter, with the style of F. Scott Fitzgerald, with the diction of Frank Sinatra; even after I had read Borges's lovely tributes to the sonorous beauty of the English language; and even after coming to know Shakespeare and

Joyce and e. e. cummings, I could still, during my London exile, find in
that childish ignorance of the language a basis for my caricatures of
British and American accents as two versions of a dog's voice: Americans always bark out of one side of their mouths, while the British
alternate between intermittent howls and muffled yelps.

The fricative consonant allows for the *r*'s, unlike the *p*'s, for instance,
to be prolonged indefinitely. But whether in its properly fricative version, with the friction occurring between the tongue and the teeth (as
in Italian), or in its guttural version, with either a strong aspiration (as
in French) or one not so strong (as in Brazilian Portuguese north of Rio,
unlike that south of São Paulo, where the Brazilian *r* resembles the Italian), this prolongation is the prolongation of a sound into which the
voice does not enter. When the voice does intervene among the distinctive duration of *r,* the effect is ridiculous to us Brazilians. There is a joke
in which the narrator imitates a choir in one of those Paulista inland
towns where the voiced *r* is dominant: when the conductor signals the
end of the last bar of a song, ending with the word *"amor,"* the narrator
dwells on the note, holding on to the horrible rolling sound of the liquid and vibrant *r,* rather than the vowel *o.* Frank Sinatra (admittedly, in
a recording from the seventies or eighties) unwittingly recreates this
comical effect in a song ending with the word *"amore"* or "before." But
this is the very nature of the English language. We are inclined to find
the Scottish *r*'s somewhat inadequate, while we admire the refined
British who pronounce the intervocalic or nearly aspirated final *r*'s so
dryly—as opposed to the coarser Americans who relish chewing on
long, cavernous, supersalivated *r*'s, whatever the letter's position in the
word.

The concrete poets were aware of Pound's introduction to Ernest
Fenollosa's *The Chinese Written Character as a Medium for Poetry* and of
their passion for Chinese. From this they acquired an appreciation of
English as the language closer than any in the West to the isolating system, wherein the position of the word in the phrase is more important
than the inflection in indicating syntactical function. Thus, at the
extreme opposite of hyperhierarchical Latin one found Chinese.
English, with its placement of nouns that become adjectives and the
miracles it performs with prepositions, was closer to being, like Chinese, poetry all the time. For us it was delicious: we were used to considering the sweet southern European languages as intrinsically more
poetic than the harsh languages of the cold North, and it was surprising
to begin to conceive that English—always so practical and so unmeta-

physical—was in fact the most poetic of Western languages. And that awareness did not come down to us from the language of Shakespeare (to be precise, he would hinder rather than help this reasoning), but rather from "practical" English, the simple colloquial kind. Nowadays I feel pleasure in encountering again the baroque potential of Latin inflections softened in Italian, Spanish, and, even more so, Portuguese. I find it exciting to think that the journalistic English of Hemingway or of detective novels has turned out to be—since its transformation into the vulgar orthodoxy that has latched on to all of Western literature—a veritable stylistic distortion, venerated as though the English of Donne, Faulkner, or even Shakespeare had never existed.

Many people ask me to what extent British music influenced me during those London years. The fact is that the most profound influence of British pop had occurred before I even dreamt of going to London: it was the Beatles pre-*tropicalismo*. The many pop and rock shows I heard in England would serve more to demystify the "First World" productions on the one hand, and on the other to acquaint me with their genuine technical advances. So while I was surprised at the relative amateurishness of some prestigious venues, when I went back to Brazil two and a half years later, I missed certain basic elements, of sound and light for instance, as well as a combination of precision and spareness in performance—values that I had assimilated, however unconsciously, as I watched British shows. The greatest British contribution to my musical development, however, was the acceptance on the part of producers and listeners of my way of playing guitar. I showed Lou Reisner "London, London" and told him that for the record we would ask Gil or some British guitarist to back me. His reaction was vehement. He argued that a good studio musician would spoil the distinctive charm of the song: "He can play well, but he'll never play like you. And who says you don't play well?" When I used to play bossa nova, the untrained British (and American) ear seemed to work in my favor. The result was that I lost my sense of embarrassment, and though I still know that I don't play well, today I can lead great musicians by demonstrating what I want on the guitar, something I wouldn't have dreamt of doing before London. And though I do play guitar for shows in Brazil and throughout the world, I still don't like to hear my own recordings, particularly those in which I play. The good guitarists are João Bosco, Dori Caymmi, Djavan. To say nothing of Gil.

And even with him beside me, I can reproduce the rudiments of João Gilberto's great artistry in only the clumsiest way. But I can delineate the intention of the compositions and singing that come to me, and in the end the sound convinces many people, though it fails to satisfy many musicians.

I made one important discovery in the British show business during my stay: the Rolling Stones. This band, to which I had not paid much attention while in Brazil, and whom I only knew from recordings, swept me off my feet when I heard them live. To tell the truth, my opinion of the Stones before leaving Brazil was similar to Ned Rorem's: equally comparative and unfavorable in relation to the Beatles. In London I saw Led Zeppelin and Tyrannosaurus Rex, the Incredible String Band and Pink Floyd, John and Yoko and Hendrix, Dylan and The Who. But the performances of the Stones were Dionysian theater. They would come onstage and immediately the atmosphere they established was the most vivid demonstration of their understanding of the spirit of the times. Mick Jagger seemed like a torch of changing meanings. He was a woman, a monkey, a dancer, an athlete, a street urchin, a romantic poet, a tyrant, a sweet companion. His star quality overwhelmed that of conventional stars who, with their strategic spotlights, carefully calculated stage positions and distance from the audience. Taking further than anyone the adventure of suggesting a collusion with the multitudes, of sharing their aesthetic and behavioral audacity, he succeeded in being more of a diva than any Sinatra, any Barbra Streisand. He blended with people, with things. The group worked like an organism. Their intelligence flowed out of their pores. Keith and Mick never made songs like the Beatles, never wrote like Dylan, never sang like Steve Winwood or Paul McCartney, but onstage they represented the best and the strongest in all of them. Their repertoire, which earlier seemed confused to me, became clear. Of course "Satisfaction" had been a hit in Brazil, it was obviously a great song. But their experiments in *Their Satanic Majesties Request,* combined with the din of the rest, failed to attain a reasonable level of polish and cooled my interest. Jagger's own voice seemed to lack musicality and true savagery. I thought I had found those elements far better developed in Paul's singing than in his. But when I saw him onstage, his tone and diction revealed a singular richness that was missing in the others, something unique that I then started to recognize in the records as well. By this time they were between *Beggars Banquet* and *Let It Bleed.* Rock shows were not the gigantic affairs they are nowadays. How ironic to note that between 1969 and 1972, at the height of their popularity, the Stones played in theaters with a capacity of two or three thousand (the Lyceum, the Round House), whereas today, when one would expect them to "be history," they play to audiences of sixty, seventy, even a hundred thousand people.

elective affinities

Two people entered into my life through the door to 16 Redesdale who would prove decisive in my ideological formation: Jorge Mautner and Antônio Cícero. One was a radical irrationalist, an asystematic improviser, the living example of what Décio Pignatari had called "the new barbarian"; the other was a methodical dissecter of movements intelligible to the senses. The two have over the years profoundly influenced my political vision.

Jorge burst upon the scene as a writer in the early '60s with his first book, a torrential novel entitled *Deus da Chuva e da Morte* (God of Rain and Death). I had read an interview with him in the magazine *Senhor* in which he, looking very handsome in the photo, said some unexpected things. Anecir told me about him, stressing that Glauber had remarked how interesting the book was. (Later Glauber would say that his own title, *Deus e o Diabo na Terra do Sol,* was a deliberate echo of Mautner's.)

Mautner showed up at our house in Chelsea in the company of Arthur and Maria Helena Guimarães. To this couple, obliged as I am for so many lessons in urbanity, I owe as well my direct contact with the Mautnerian spark. Jorge had been a Nietzschean since adolescence. He turned up at the Sixteen Chapel with an umbrella and sat in the living room with the slightly suspect air of an old Chinese man, speaking very softly, as though asking questions. Emboldened by our receptiveness, he was soon howling like a Hebrew prophet. He mixed Roberto Carlos's Jovem Guarda with Mao's Red Guard and described the revolution we were undergoing as a universal cataclysm, before returning to his old dream of marrying Marx and Nietzsche; and only after limning a depressing scenario, wherein the resentment of the Third World and the arrogance of the First would end up producing an oppression even greater than we had known heretofore, he finally arrived at his more precise prophecies. Now, as though everything he'd already said had been mere rhetoric for shock effect, he changed his tone and stated that in the future political struggles would define themselves, starting in the United States, as struggles of sexual minorities, inspired by the idea of civil rights. In fact he described with great exactitude what we see today. And he was as enthusiastic about such a scenario as anyone could have been then—and as ironic about it as one could be today. At the same time he would say: "The future is ours, the old political saws— Left, Right, class struggle, Cold War, everything will come to an end. Marcuse is nothing compared to what's in store for us." Then with a diabolical smile he would add: "It's going to be utterly boring: black sadomasochist lesbians struggling for their rights with the white, Protestant, gay fathers. . . ."

Mautner's father was an Austrian Jewish intellectual (he had been a professor of mathematics and a humanist in Vienna) who while a prisoner in a Nazi concentration camp escaped with the help of his wife—Jorge's mother—a goy of Slavic descent. Jorge used to tell how she, a vivacious and instinctive woman, never stopped admiring Hitler. Apparently her Jewish husband interpreted that admiration with ironic love, and in any event it didn't alter the hatred she felt for her husband's torturers, those who followed the orders of her fascinating Führer. She reserved the same intensity for the gratitude she felt toward the country that had welcomed them after their flight: Getúlio Vargas, then Brazil's president, became for her the symbol of that hospitality. She was evidently very susceptible to charismatic leaders. Her husband, by contrast, remained exquisitely wise and ironic. Jorge played with the contradictory elements of his upbringing in a way both touching and frightening, but above all intriguing.

Mautner consistently advanced the notion that artists ought to devote all power to their imaginations but should themselves never have any real political power. Intensely and consciously, he lived his own legend, and his own demystification.

He liked to repeat: "The higher the coconut tree, the greater the fall," in emphasizing the parallel between the descent of Marx into Stalinism and of Nietzsche into Nazism. Liberal democracy appeared then as the manifestation of good sense, the only vaccine against the horror. But in that moment Mautner himself exemplified the rebellious individual who, rather than adapting to conventions and to the market, would always be its critic, enamored of dangerous thinkers and artists whose ideas should never be granted formal power. He traced his circle endlessly, always enriching our vision, but tempering everything with the disclaimer that Afro-Brazilian *batuques* had put a spell on him by way of his beloved black nanny (which also brought him closer to Getúlio Vargas).

He didn't mind seeming ridiculous and he never tried to present an image of respectability, which in his view was being offered to me on a silver platter, in spite of my scandalous public profile. When we went back to Brazil, Mautner started paying more attention to MPB, becoming a cult figure, though never a mass success. At least one of the songs he wrote, "Maracatu atômico" (Atomic Maracatu), a masterpiece composed with Nelson Jacobina, has become a classic, particularly since it was recorded by Gil. And "O vampiro" (The Vampire), a ballad he composed alone in the late fifties, would become known in a version of mine from the mid-seventies; to this day people ask me to sing it. But there are other notable songs of his, and every one has its own special charm. He is recognized today as a great presence in Brazilian culture, and remains for me an important point of reference, his critiques and prophecies continuing to enlighten me as no one else's could.

In London, my conversations with Mautner confirmed and cemented the discrepancies between the *tropicalistas* and the conventional Left that had dominated the MPB milieu before our emergence. Having already unhitched ourselves from an automatic connection and suffered no few expressions of hostility on that account, we had been wavering more or less consciously for some time between defining ourselves as the ultra-Left—the true Left, the Left to the left of the Left—or as the defenders of economic freedom and soundness of the market system. Within our own field of action, we did two things: we expanded the horizons of conduct by experimenting with forms and disseminating inventions, and at the same time sought to elevate our professional— and mercantile—competitiveness to the level of the Americans and the British. A politics of one voice, palatable and simple, was not to evolve out of this. And Mautner only exacerbated our contradictions.

By contrast, Antônio Cícero showed no apparent wish to interfere with our thinking. He spoke of our *tropicalista* adventure with restrained enthusiasm, but he was able to frame our ideas and actions so that they assumed a satisfying proportion. His was a serene realism. Without recourse to the apocalyptic tone then much in fashion, Cícero considered the weight of what had happened in popular music, and above all he felt stimulated by what we Bahians had done in Brazil. It was important to unseat populist nationalism; it was important that we regard modernity as a universal value and that we boldly take its side; it was important that something like that happen in the orbit in which we moved, that of popular music and show business.

Unlike Mautner, Cícero revealed almost nothing of his own philosophical enquiries in progress. It wasn't for lack of generosity, but rather out of modesty, and a fear of seeming importunate. It was only after I began to ask him specific questions that he felt encouraged to discuss his positions, certainties, and doubts. He also came to work in pop music after returning to Brazil, although he had not planned to do so. He had always written poetry, in addition to being a philosopher. Unlike Mautner's, his was a classically erudite poetry, without a trace of pop culture. Marina, his younger sister, a beautiful girl with curly hair and a strong personality, revealed toward the end of her adolescence—which would coincide with our return to Brazil—a talent for singing and composing songs. When she became a professional, she took one of Cícero's poems and, much to his surprise, made it into a song. Marina, who has a highly distinctive voice and a determined manner, became a national pop star. For some years she maintained the tradition of recording songs written with her brother, who was able to make a little money this way. Eventually he distanced himself from music to dedicate himself to his true passions: philosophy and poetry. Many of the songs he wrote with Marina became great popular hits—and all of them are well written.

Recently Cícero published a book, *O mundo desde o fim* (The World from the End), his first, which—despite the academy's insistence on ignoring it—is one of the greatest intellectual events to mark the end of the millennium in Brazil. It presents itself as an impertinent recapture of the Cartesian *cogito* in radical terms—which is tantamount to a scandal in the Brazilian academic environment, divided as it is between Marxist commentators of the Frankfurt school and the French post-structuralists. *If* in 1968 I read in Lévi-Strauss's *Tristes tropiques* that "the I is not simply abject, it is also impossible," and *if* I recognize in the effort to overcome the *cogito* the underlying motivation for all of our century's intellectual and philosophical pretensions, *then* I cannot help but recognize the extent of Cícero's daring. And the very tone of the book, written in an exceptionally beautiful and serene Portuguese, reveals that he arrived at this place only after pursuing with great intelligence and sincerity the essential problems that such a position entails. The book is a radical affirmation of the modernity born with Descartes—against all the anti-Enlightenment attacks that have inspired a great deal of contemporary thinking—and it imposes on Brazil the enormous responsibility of being not the great illegible "Other" that opposes European reason, but the open space for the transition from the West to the west of the West (to paraphrase Fernando Pessoa on Mário de Sá Carneiro). Which is not at all to restrict Brazil—as so many academics would do, even as they claim to resist being "folkloric"—to limit Brazil to good behavior within crystallized "Western" parameters. With this book, Cícero destroys Brazil's false choice between a strident exoticism and a modest mimicry.

For Cícero to have come to this point represents for me the validation of my profound identification with his perception of things in London. And it places him, in my imagination, not far from the Mautner of the delirious transliberalism—with *batuque*. Mautner is three years older than Gil or I, and he was, in many respects, a precursor of *tropicalismo* (we called him, with a certain irony and affection, our master), while Cícero is four years younger than we are (seven years Mautner's junior), and he was himself led to do some shunting in his thinking because of what he thought he saw in what we did, and so in a sense he is a follower of *tropicalismo*—though, of course, he did not have the same reason for calling us masters, even as a joke. But I present them here together because I attribute to both—Mautner was more influential during the London phase, and Cícero has been more so since our return—a decisive role in the organization of my thinking, precarious though it might be.

Another encounter would also prove influential from the start in the development of my thinking about politics and related matters, the one that occurred between myself and José Almino, the son of Miguel Arraes. We had spent a few hours together in Paris during my first visit in 1968. It was at the time of the show at Rhodia, before I went to prison, and I was startled by the loquaciousness, betraying both amusement and anguish, with which he discussed the events of the past May. While living in London, in late 1969 and early 1970, we would often go to Paris, especially Dedé, Guilherme, and I. Conversations at the house of his aunt Violeta were exhilarating. But it was those with Zé Almino that most captured me, no doubt because I knew they were to be consequential. I remember that during my first trip from London to Paris, he was reading an article on *tropicalismo* by Roberto Schwarz. A typewritten copy had been sent him by the author, who was a friend of his. We of course expected it to be only a more complicated and probing version of the distrustful response the Left had shown us from the beginning. But in fact Schwarz showed no hostility, nor any contempt for our movement. On the contrary: he accorded it great prominence within his scheme of the relations between culture and politics in Brazil post-1964. Indeed I thought it an honor that *tropicalismo* should receive so much and such favorable attention from a thinker who by nature would little identify with our sensibility. It was obvious, for instance, that he was more at home with film or theater than with what was happening in pop music. It impressed me that he compared Paulo Freire's literacy method to what the *tropicalistas* were doing: here his theory coincided exactly with what had happened in my life, as though he had in mind the night of the coup, when I joined Freire's group at that first meeting to plan an action. But Schwarz's reduction of the *tropicalista* "allegory" to a clash between the archaic and the modern, while it revealed connections until then unremarked, was ultimately impoverishing. Zé Almino, who understood Schwarz's reasoning better than I, showed a lovely capacity to follow (and even to anticipate) my comments. So we talked about Lévi-Strauss (as a sequel to *Tristes tropiques,* I was reading *The Savage Mind*); about Oswald de Andrade (I remember his saying that for a time he had even considered him the greatest Brazilian ever, but was now beginning to temper that judgment); about Cinema Novo, concrete poetry, the concept of the "Third World," about trying to be more anthropological (that is to say, receptive) with Europeans. He would laugh and say that Brazilian gossip had its origins in existentialism. But what touched me most deeply was hearing him say, in a lively conversation about the brilliance of the exchanges between Borges and Nelson Rodrigues, that it was essential to read authors of the Right— and it was the duty of reason to meet and welcome the irrational, not to banish it. Almino at eighteen had been his father's close confidant, when the latter was governor of Pernambuco. This collaboration in a government that was attuned like no other to popular longings had brought him face-to-face with poverty as well as the potential for greatness of the Brazilian people. And so, to witness his father's arrest and expulsion from the country—which sent him and his entire family into exile in Algeria and France—had admitted him into the tragic dimension inherent in all political conflict. The right-wing thinkers—the great ones—spoke from within that disenchantment. Zé Almino would never again nurture his hopes for social justice in any form of thought that had shown itself too naïve to comprehend that dimension. This brought him great clarity and, in middle age, melancholy. But the lesson was crucial to me. And my friendship with him remains unshakable.

love it or leave it

One day I went to Picasso's, a café in the King's Road, to buy cigarettes and look at the girls, and the waiter asked me, in his Italian-accented English, what was the name of the president of Brazil. I replied sadly: "Costa e Silva." He said: "No. The president of Brazil is not Costa e Silva." I laughed and said that he couldn't know that better than I did, since I was Brazilian. He insisted, adding that the name of the Brazilian president was Garrastazu. I said he was crazy. He laughed even more than I did and repeated: "Garrastazu Médici." I was alarmed. I could see this man was not crazy, but everything he said (that absurd name!) compelled me to think he was. This is how I first learned of our new president. Later at home I realized that the waiter at Picasso's was not mad; the name, in fact, was rather like the one he had tried to pronounce. But I could have hardly guessed that under that name we would suffer the most terrible repression, which—as though to confirm the dark fate of that part of America under Catholic colonization—would accompany what would come to be called the "economic miracle."

When my parents were to celebrate their fortieth wedding anniversary, Bethânia was able to obtain special permission from the military authorities for me to enter the country. Upon landing in Rio, I was separated from Dedé by three men who emerged from a VW parked near the stairway to the airplane. They were plainclothes military agents. They took me to an apartment on Presidente Vargas Avenue, and there they interrogated and terrorized me for six hours. Placing a tape recorder before me (where could those tapes be today?), the men who had taken me, and those already there waiting (like the others, they were plainclothes, though all identified themselves as military), demanded that I compose a song praising the Transamazon highway, the road the military government had begun to build, and which was to be one of the symbols of "Great Brazil." They listed colleagues of mine, artists they claimed were collaborating with them (even as informants, supposedly), and asked for information on my relationship with Violeta Arraes Gervaiseau and the Arraes family in exile. And once I had managed to rebuff their demand for a song on the Transamazon, they began to impose conditions on my month-long stay: I was to leave at once for Salvador, where I would remain (forbidden to go elsewhere) until my return to London; I was forbidden as well to cut my hair or to shave while on Brazilian soil (they were afraid of appearing responsible for having me shorn again); I could not refuse press interviews, but I would have to give them in writing, submitting my responses beforehand for the approval of the federal agents who would be watching me during my entire stay; and finally, I was obliged to make two television appearances, one on Chacrinha's program, and the other in *Som Livre, Exportação,* the new music show on TV Globo. The aim was to insure that "everything would look normal."

While I was undergoing this questioning (during which they reiterated several times that I might not be freed), Dedé was waiting for me at Bethânia's house, together with Glauber and Luís Carlos Maciel. Bethânia lived in Ipanema, in an apartment on Nascimento Silva Street, and when the federal police took me there (not in the VW full of military in disguise, but this time in a police van unmistakably full of policemen) we went around Alá Gardens, where through the window I saw the members of the band MPB4. They went right by without seeing me. It was my first sight since my arrival in Brazil of people I knew, and the fact that I could see them without being seen, and after so many hours of repetitive hostility, conferred on the moment a dreaminess that intensified its symbolic power. They were musicians, musicians of my generation, and so profoundly Brazilian as to have adopted the monogram MPB for the name of the group. To see them awoke in me a great love (there is no other word) for history, for fate. I loved them as we imagine the dead love the living, from the vantage of eternity. My eyes were full of tears, and I don't know whether I could have arrived at Bethânia's house psychologically intact were it not for that secret encounter.

The program *Som Livre, Exportação* was the offspring of *tropicalismo* (the phrase *"som livre,"* free sound, to say nothing of the Oswaldian notion of "export," had been coined by me in the program *Divino, Maravilhoso*) and of the music festivals, and the grandchild of *Fino da Bossa* and bossa nova. It was led by two immensely

*Caetano and Dedé's wedding, November 29, 1967. "Multitudes of girls in uniform
filled the church. Those who managed would grab snatches of my hair and some even
attacked Dedé. The nineteenth-century São Pedro church was comparatively somber,
but the teenagers seemed to multiply like lascivious angels in a Bahian baroque church."*

*Tom Zé, who arranged the wedding lunch on the beach, managed to keep it a secret.
"The day was beautiful, once everything had calmed down, and I thought only how lovely
Dedé was and how happy I was to be married to her."*

ABOVE LEFT: 2002, *Caetano and Dedé's apartment in downtown São Paulo.* "The first month went by without our deciding on furniture."

ABOVE RIGHT: *"Our apartment had an open balcony, where I could sit and look at the sky and the traffic below, feel the wind, and scare Dedé for fear that I might fall."*

LEFT CENTER: *Caetano with the producer Guilherme Araújo.* "His formula for expressing his highest praise was the expression 'Divine, marvelous,' which he not infrequently complemented with 'International!' when his enthusiasm warranted it."

LEFT: *The image from the cover of the 1968 record-manifesto* Tropicália, ou Panis et circensis.

The March of a Hundred Thousand: the protest against the murder of a student, Edson Luis, by the police. Front row, from left: Chico Buarque, Arduinho Colazanti, Renato Borghi, Zé Celso, Paulinho da Viola (facing away), Dedé, Caetano, Nana Caymmi, and Gil. June 26, 1968.

Rehearsing with Os Mutantes and the American Johnny Dandurand for TV Globo's International Song Festival (FIC) in Rio in late 1968. Caetano selected the infamous "Prohibiting Is Prohibited" to turn his entry into an event. Dandurand, the tall blond man, was to run about the stage howling and grunting when Caetano yelled, "God is loose!"

Both performances of "Prohibiting Is Prohibited" at the FIC were scandalous. "I said, 'So you're the young people who say they want to take power! If you're the same in politics as you are in music, we're done for!'" Gil joined Caetano onstage, where they were pelted with paper, plastic cups, and a chunk of wood that left Gil with a bloody ankle. "Perhaps we had touched certain deep structures in Brazilian life at great risk to ourselves. Nevertheless, I felt proud."

seja marginal
seja herói

ABOVE: *Caetano and Gil's program on TV Tupi,* Divino, Maravilhoso, *was received more warmly than their performance at the FIC and regularly featured Os Mutantes, Gal, and Tom Zé.*

RIGHT: *It was suggested that Caetano and Gil were imprisoned because they were present at the Sucata Club for a show where this banner of Hélio Oiticica's was hung. It pictures the corpse of Cara de Cavalo, a famous Carioca criminal murdered by the police, and reads "be a criminal, be a hero." A judge shut the Sucata Club down after the incident.*

BOTTOM: *Gil after his release from prison. "In jail he found the opportunity to attain a kind of asceticism; he stopped eating meat and began learning about macrobiotic food and Eastern systems of thought."*

PAULO LIMA E
ROBERTO SANTANA
APRESENTAM
CAETANO VELOSO E
GILBERTO GIL
NO TEATRO
CASTRO ALVES
20/21 JULHO 1969

ABOVE: *Onstage at the Castro Alves Theater. Four months after their release from prison, Caetano and Gil were asked to leave Brazil. They were allowed to do a concert to raise money for travel expenses.*

LEFT AND BELOW: *The program for their last show.*

FICHA TÉCNICA

CAETANO VELOSO
GILBERTO GIL
LEIF'S

Figurinos	DEDÉ VELOSO
Fotos	ARTUR IKISSIMA
Programa	SÔNIA CASTRO
Contra-regra	GATO FELIX e SANDRA GA-DELHA
Colaboração	LAIS IKISSIMA e JORGE SA-LOMAO

DIREÇÃO MUSICAL	GILBERTO GIL
DIREÇÃO GERAL	CAETANO VELOSO
PRODUÇÃO	PAULO LIMA & ROBERTO SAN-TANA
Participação	CONJUNTO FOLCLÓRICO VIVA-BAHIA
	ESCOLA DE SAMBA DO GARCIA

PROGRAMA

CAETANO
Irene
Atrás do trio elétrico
Super-bacana
Baby
Hino do Bahia
Alegria, Alegria
Cinema Olympia
Tropicália
Marcianita
Objeto não identificado.

GIL
Procissão
Domingou
Domingo no parque
Éle falava nisso todo dia
Volks Volks Wagen Blue
Cérebro Eletrônico
Frevo Rasgado
17 léguas e meia
Madalena
Aquêle Abraço
2001

LEIF'S:
Fobus in Totum
Fire
I Don't wanna save the world

ABOVE: *Exile in London. "Those years were a cloudy dream. I came truly to love the green in the parks, the calm in the crescent-shaped streets, the alleys, the mosses and flowers—in sum, there came to me there a kind of wisdom about life, in a genuine and intense way, such as I had never imagined I could find. I honored the public and the private gardens alike with sincere reverence, but every day I would steal a rose from one of them to bring to Dedé."*

CLOCKWISE FROM TOP LEFT: *Caetano and Gil; Rogerio Duprat; Gil; Caetano's brother Rodrigo calls up to Dedé at Redesdale Street; Caetano and Sandra, Dedé's sister.*

ABOVE: *In 1971, João Gilberto, who had been living in New York City, called Caetano with miraculous news: Caetano was to return to Brazil to do a TV Tupi special with him and Gal.*

LEFT: *Caetano dressed for Carnival in the mid-eighties.*

talented (and recently launched) musicians, Ivan Lins and Gonza-guinha. The truth is that those television appearances had been worked out between Benil Santos (at that time Bethânia's agent) and some military officers, according to terms entirely unknown to me. Everything about them made me uneasy, but I made my appearances openheartedly (one of them with Bethânia, who ever so beautifully sang "Janelas abertas #2" and "A tua presença, morena" [Open Windows #2 and Your Presence, Dark-Haired One]), two new songs I had composed for her). The audience, mainly young Cariocas, knew nothing of my arrest and had a pop-rock notion of my hand in the modernization of MPB. And they were well attuned to that acronym, and to how it defined itself at the moment. Just a little over a year had passed since my departure, and yet what I saw before me was plainly post-*tropicalismo:* boys naked from the waist up and girls with long, straight hair cheering my name. They left no doubt that what they expected from me was a more mature, sophisticated version of what they themselves were learning to appreciate: the fusion of British pop with carioca samba-jazz. I walked onstage alone with my guitar and sang "Adeus, batucada" (Good-bye, Batucada), the ingenious samba by Sinval Silva that had also been Carmen Miranda's most beautiful recording. Nothing could have been more true to *tropicalista* tradition: a glaring contrast with samba-jazz and fusion, the selection was also an allusion to Carmen Miranda (precisely the samba in which she, MPB's great exile, claimed to have gone "away crying, but with her heart smiling" since "she was leaving everybody who valued batucada"). The youthful audience were perplexed and disappointed. And it went entirely unnoticed that I had for the first time appeared on Brazilian television playing guitar.

will never forget the moment during my stay in Bahia when, having accepted a ride from the fiancé of Claudia, Dedé's younger sister, I got out of the car and noticed in the rear window a sticker that read BRAZIL, LOVE IT OR LEAVE IT. I felt a physical pain in my heart. Here on the car in which I was driving through the streets of Salvador for all to see was emblazoned the triumphant slogan of the dictatorship. I suppose it was an imitation of the American campaign, this advice aimed at the opposition, confounding once and for all the regime with the country. Today we get on fine, I and this fellow, who then was little more than a kid with a different political vision. But it was horribly sad to realize that my love for Brazil was a more profoundly complicated problem than I was prepared to admit. In effect, many of my dearest and most esteemed friends were either entering or exiting insane asylums and prisons, a kind of introjection of the sacred violence of those who had joined the armed resistance or of the cursed violence of those who were perpetrating the official terrorism. Rogério, for one, was committed for a long time, and I'm not at all certain he wasn't subjected to electric-shock therapy.

I returned to London truly frightened. I thought many years would pass before I could return to Brazil outright. It didn't seem likely I would be back even for a visit any time soon. In London Ralph Mace was excited by our work, and we finished the first record. Initially the producer was Lou Reisner, but he and Mace had a falling out and the latter ultimately took over the project. To this day I find the record disagreeable, too much a memento of my depression and of my personal limitations. But in Brazil it was a succès d'estime, and the track "Asa-Branca," a very personal, if harmonically poor, rendition of Luiz Gonzaga's classic, was enough to justify the record by my lights. My trip to Brazil, it turned out, had reanimated me somehow. In spite of the nightmare attending my arrival, the mere fact of seeing things, people, and places I had known before endowed the country with a certain reality that the perspective of exile had already begun to attenuate. Gal had remained in Brazil as a sort of representative of the *tropicalista* Bahianos. Her show, *Fa-Tal / Gal a todo vapor* (Fa-Tal, Gal Full Steam Ahead), conceived and directed by Waly, became the motor of Brazilian creative energies—and all artists, filmmakers, journalists, and young people in general recognized it. Bethânia was in the early stages of her partnership with Fauzi Arap. Their show, *Rosa dos Ventos,* is a cornerstone in the history of music shows in Brazil, the most successful of this exclusively Brazilian genre, a long extravaganza with a solo artist, full of songs and speeches and beautiful theatrical images, which the public attends like some great art film. Thus, in spite of everything, Brazil existed and seemed to be showing signs of recovery; so I started "rooting" for things to continue in that direction. To see real streets and places and people in Brazil was to believe in this possibility; to see shows like *Fa-Tal* was to feel encouraged. A little meant a lot then.

Macalé had written with Capinan a song called "Gotham City," and during the Globo festival in Rio (the previously mentioned International Festival of Song) he introduced it, thereby reviving—to a serenade of jeers, with journalistic accompaniment—the spirit of *tropicalista* performance. I wrote him a letter inviting him to come play with me in

London. He accepted. My idea was to form a group that could work around my particular way of playing guitar. Tuti Moreno was already living in London by then, and Áureo de Sousa had just arrived to spend some time; together they would see to the drums and percussion. I wrote as well to Moacir Albuquerque, Perinho's handsome and talented brother in Bahia, hoping to introduce a "Bahian bass" into my band. He too accepted. And so was born *Transa,* one of my favorite records. Not that I listen to it nowadays (I never listen to any of them, unless there is a special reason, and even then it isn't a pleasant labor), but merely remembering that this was my first attempt to create a sound based on my own ideas fills me with elation. I entrusted the musical direction to Macalé, who was a true guitarist, but what we devised together during the rehearsals at Art's Lab could have been created only for a work of mine. We taped everything as though for a show, in two or three sessions. Mace was enthusiastic (he is still proud to have produced it), but a phone call from João Gilberto was soon to change my life.

Violeta Arraes Gervaiseau used to keep me informed, as well as she could, about the situation in Brazil. Hopes of returning wavered. But the creation of *Transa* and my recent memories of Brazil made me more receptive to what was good about London, and I came truly to love the green in the parks, the calm in the crescent-shaped streets, the alleys, the mosses and flowers—in sum, there came to me there a kind of wisdom about life, in a genuine and intense way, such as I had never imagined I could find. I honored the public and the private gardens alike with sincere reverence, but every day I would steal a rose from one of them to bring to Dedé. I shaved my beard and stopped feeling sad all the time. With the material from *Transa,* Mace and the record label organized a show at Queen Elizabeth Hall, the theater full of Brazilians living in London and our new British friends.

One day Leslie Gould, Mace's boss at Famous Records, called us in and to my surprise began to remark upon what he called my physical beauty. He eyed me head-on, then in profile, and though there was nothing to suggest a sexual interest, he seemed happy to confirm his opinion. As it turned out, he was merely acting as executive of a company involved in a project for which I might be useful. It was a film Zeffirelli was soon to make about St. Francis of Assisi, and it would be called *Brother Sun, Sister Moon.* Gould thought I had the ideal face for the lead—and that perfectly suited the plans the record label had for me. His hope was that I would do the songs for the film (in fact Donovan had already done several, but they wanted something else), that I would sing them, and play the part of the saint. I could hardly believe he was serious. But soon after we were on our way to Rome—Dedé, Guilherme, and myself—with Gould at our side. After an astonishing first night (dazzled by Rome, where we had never been, Dedé and I went with Guilherme to the Trevi Fountain and there, probably because of my long hair, we were arrested by the police, since the Excelsior Hotel on Via Veneto had kept our passports for some hours, as is the custom in Italy: and so we were not released until daylight), we went to Zeffirelli's house on Via Apia. It was an impressive mansion, full of sculptures and beautiful *objets,* works of art and fabulous furniture, but a bit artificial. The master of the house, having welcomed us amiably, immediately started holding my face and examining it, as Gould had done, eventually concluding that I looked remarkably like Florinda Bolkan, the Brazilian actress who was then making a career for herself in Italy. But at the mansion there was already a young British boy with light eyes who was to play the role of St. Francis, and so there remained only the music to be discussed. Zeffirelli asked me to sing something and play the guitar. I sang a samba, "Escurinho" (Dark Boy) by Geraldo Pereira. Soon it was decided somehow that I would sing Donovan's songs and compose the remaining ones. I laughed to think how the guy from Paramount (Gould) was trying to propose a skinny little Brazilian mulatto for the role of St. Francis, while the film director had already chosen a conventionally pretty British boy with blue eyes. We went back to London with Donovan's songs on a tape. I actually did a first recording of "Brother Sun, Sister Moon," but not before I returned to Brazil.

João Gilberto rang late at night. We were in the apartment at Notting Hill Gate. (João had never been any kind of leftist, or shown any particular interest in politics. He had been living in New York for some years, having moved there before the coup d'état, and would not move back until 1971.) At first we could not believe it was really he. He was calling to invite me to join him and Gal in a television special that was already being taped in São Paulo.

I described for him the torments I had endured upon my return for my parents' anniversary. He assured me nothing of the sort would happen: "God is asking me to invite you. Listen to this: You are going to get off the plane in Rio, everyone is going to smile on you. You're going to see that Brazil loves you." Some months had passed since my anguished return to England, and I was not inclined to believe this, but still that gave me no right to doubt the word of João. Full of misgiving, I decided nevertheless to fly with Dedé the next day. When I landed in Rio, everything happened as João had prophesied. The customs and immigration agents treated us as though I had never had a problem in the country. Dedé looked at me, stupefied. It was as though we were reinsinuating ourselves into the world, and we arrived in São Paulo with a new prospect on the future. João and Gal were waiting for us at the television studio. I stared at João in redoubled amazement. He had always been my Brazilian hero, my favorite artist in modern MPB, but his part in my return to Brazil conferred on him an almost supernatural status. I can scarcely describe the impact of his rich art as I relived it at close range, that night and the ones to follow. There he was, singing and strumming "Retrato em branco e preto" (Portrait in Black and White) and "Estrada branca" (White Road), by Tom Jobim, and "Quem há de dizer" (Who's to Say?), by Lupicínio Rodrigues. I could not even speak. But that was mainly because he never shut up for a second: his inspiration and intelligence were as great for conversation as they were for singing and playing. All of Rogério's Heideggerian terms about Being—about being open to Being and being its guardian— seemed to be embodied in that man, who was at once madder than the mad and more lucid than the sane; that seducer who enchanted so thoroughly without possessing a drop of glamour; that artist who proved himself even more the artist when he was not practicing his art, since it was evidently that very art that had led him to arrive at himself; that demonic saint, at once the dominator and the unprotected, compassionate and sarcastic. Bossa nova had been he, *was* he, and that made him its superior. And so it followed quite naturally, that ineluctable power I ascribed to his prophecies where my return to Brazil was concerned.

When we went back to England, it was with renewed spirits. From then on life in London was luminous, and even as the recordings and shows with the band Transa got better and better, Dedé and I could think only of preparing for our definitive return to Brazil. Mace tried to persuade me to stay: why leave London just when his (our) efforts were beginning to bear fruit? But I sought only to confirm, with Violeta and other Brazilians in Paris and in Brazil, the possibility of a quiet acceptance of my presence in the country. And so we let go the rented house in Golders Green, in the north of London, and left England for good. I never felt the slightest trace of sadness, regret, or longing. I and my will to return were of a piece. This finally was the long-awaited moment of liberation from prison, the one I had so devoutly hoped for, and which, strictly speaking, had never been granted.

We arrived in Rio in January of 1972. I had decided we would do a show with Transa immediately, and the João Caetano Theater was booked for the day after our arrival. The show there ran two or three nights in a row, before we took it to São Paulo and Recife, and finally Salvador. It was more or less the same show we had done at Queen Elizabeth Hall. Even the sound equipment (which I had bought at Ralph Mace's suggestion, and under his guidance) had come with me from London, along with the sound engineer, Maurice Hughes, an Englishman who spoke not a word of Portuguese but was never to leave Brazil again. Actually, the show turned out to run longer than it had at Queen Elizabeth Hall, since there were many things I wanted to say and I missed singing at home. The audiences in general seemed impressed. But there were cases of people who, despite missing me, left before the show ended (perhaps this happened only in São Paulo), when I sang Roberto Carlos's "Quero que tudo vá pro inferno," a slowed-down version in which I repeated the refrain ("e que tudo mais vá pro inferno"—"and everything besides is going to hell") for about five minutes. But with Áureo and Tuti playing the drums in perfect unison, and the subtleties of Macalé's guitar in lovely counterpoint to mine and Moacir's sexy bass, we were all—players and spectators alike—filled with pleasure. Just as I had done in London and Paris, I would sing Caymmi's "O que é que a baiana tem" (What's the Bahiana Got?), imitating Carmen Miranda's grimaces, twisting my hands and rolling my eyes. It was an ironic imitation ("Brechtian," one would have said in Brazil at that time), with sudden interruptions and breaks to offer commentary on the situation of the exile and the relation of Brazil to the outside world. But it was an imitation all the same and as such was taken to be an antichauvinist provocation, one reinforcing as well my sexual ambiguity, which had already been commented upon before we left Brazil.

back in bahia

To be free in Salvador, in the summer, was immensely pleasant. But it was more than that. In 1968 I had composed a *marcha-frevo* celebrating the *trios elétricos,* a mode of Carnival band created in Salvador in the late forties by Dodô and Osmar. The latter was a mandolin virtuoso, and the former, in addition to also being a musician, dabbled with electronics. The Carioca Carnival *marchinhas* had always been more important than sambas in the Bahian street Carnival. The Pernambucan *frevo* is a sort of fast Carnival *marcha,* but with a richer phrasing than the *marchinhas* of Rio. This kind of music is intended to accompany a very elegant, acrobatic sort of dance cultivated by Pernambucans with supple technique. I suppose that, being neighbors of the Northeasterners, Bahians always adopted the Carioca *marchinhas* as a sort of *frevo.* Though we consider ourselves the inventors of samba, and take pride in having preserved the *samba de roda* tradition intact to this day, during Carnival we Bahians have always preferred to frolic to the fast beat of the *marchas.* Whether in the streets or in a ballroom, whenever the orchestra played a set of sambas, that was the time to rest. With the arrival in Salvador in 1948 or '49 of Vassourinhas, the great Pernambucan *frevo bloco* (whose theme song, a *frevo* by the same name, became a national hit), Dodô and Osmar discovered that if they could make themselves heard playing *frevo* on their instruments through the streets of the city, the charming sound would sweep the multitudes in their wake. They devised a way of amplifying the guitar and the mandolin, making electrified models of solid madeira wood. Dodô was acquainted with the electrified acoustic guitar but unaware that one made of a solid wood body had been developed by others elsewhere in the world—much less that it would be the instrument rock 'n' roll made famous. Notwithstanding, Dodô's solid guitar was new in Bahia and the crowds in Salvador loved it. And Osmar started composing *frevos* especially for the trio (there was now also a percussionist), which wended its way through the town on the bed of a truck. Even as the group later grew in size and many imitators appeared, the name "trio" stuck. When I was a boy in Santo Amaro, one of them would always come from Salvador. The *trios elétricos* rather clashed with the traditional *ternos,* composed of wind instruments and percussion (the Amantes da Moda and the Amantes da Folia played Carioca *marchas,* wearing colorful sequined satin clothes) and with the *batucadas* (samba bands made up exclusively of percussion, which had more admirers than followers), but we were enchanted by them all the same. Toward the late sixties, as the Carioca Carnival *marchas* (and even the sambas) were disappearing, the best composers who had emerged with (and after) bossa nova had not yet been able to find a way to adapt themselves to Carnival composition. There were several attempts to renovate the genre—all of them failed.

There is a photograph taken in 1966 of Chico Buarque, Paulinho da Viola, Edu Lobo, Torquato Neto, Gil, Capinan, and myself, along with so many others of my generation, beside Tom Jobim, Braguinha (the great composer João de Barro, then already in his seventies), and some old singers from Rádio Nacional—all of us had been gathered together at a meeting, organized by I don't know who, aimed at resurrecting the Carnival song. But not one memorable samba or *marcha* resulted from that meeting. My "Atrás do trio elétrico" (After the Trio Elétrico) broke the taboo. This quasi-*frevo* was a hit in the streets of Salvador during the 1969 Carnival, and became known all over Brazil. I, being in jail, however, was unable to enjoy that miracle. And for the two subsequent Carnivals, while in exile, I sent new *frevos* that likewise met with success. Now, back in Bahia, I found myself walking along Joana Angélica Street, toward the center of town, beside my father, and as we came closer to São Pedro Clock, the Carnival atmosphere grew more apparent from the number of people in the street and their festive aspect, and I was soon overcome with emotion: I had failed to realize until that moment that I had never expected to see all this again. Curiously, I remember having only my father beside me at the moment, which seems not very likely. It could be that he and I had wandered away from my mother, Dedé, and the others without noticing it; it could be that we left home separately as a matter of precaution or discretion, I don't know. The fact is I attached enormous importance to my father's happy pride at walking into town with me, and I even imagine (a fantasy, I suppose) that he wanted us to be alone together. We went down the *ladeira* (a sort of slope) of São Bento and then ambled into Castro Alves Square, the heart of Carnival in Salvador. From there the sea is visible, stubbornly holding the line of the horizon against the perspectival confusion caused by the steep *ladeiras.* The square, actually triangular and encircled by the *ladeiras* streaming into it, was full of people in mask and costume. There were trucks with *trios elétricos* playing, *cordão* bands squeezing people against the walls. Next to the statue of Castro Alves, the Bahian romantic poet, a rhetorical abolitionist, were our friends and family, as in years past. There we remained, drinking beer and rollicking until sundown. I was struck by the numbers of overt gays and hippies; they mixed freely and naturally with the traditional revelers: the hippies seemed right at home in a world of fanciful costumes, the gays being confounded with the cross-dressers central to Carnival tradition. Many were locals playing a double role as reveler and hippie, or as traditional transvestite and modern homosexual. Others were tourists from Rio, São Paulo, Minas, Rio Grande do Sul, or even from abroad. These diverse elements blurred definitions, and one had a sense of tremendous freedom, an impression of a triumphant pansexuality. In London I had recorded a *frevo* for *trio elétrico* called "Chuva, suor e cerveja" (Rain, Sweat, and Beer), and had been told it was even more successful than "Atrás do trio elétrico" and "Um frevo novo" (A New Frevo), which I had composed the year before. When the sun had set behind the island of Itaparica, something began to emerge from the top of the Montanha *ladeira.* I was apparently the first to spot it and asked some friends nearby what that white conical form coming up toward us might be. We could not imagine it was a *trio elétrico*—they didn't enter the square from that end, and certainly not in silence. Some jostling ensued among those trying to see the object and identify it. It looked like an airplane pointing its nose at the angle of the *ladeira.* In fact it was a truck, the one belonging to the Tapajós trio, designed to look like a space rocket. As soon as it was in full view among the revelers in the square, the lights went on and the musicians started to play "Chuva, suor e cerveja." Immediately a fierce rain began to fall, and it lasted the whole night. The crowd started singing and dancing in the rain, and I began to laugh and cry at the sight of the inscription on the side of the "rocket" that was now passing by us on its way up Chile street: CAETANAVE (Caetano + *nave,* or the spaceship Caetano). The *tropicalista* joy of punning—derived from concrete poetry, Joyce, and Godard— taken up in this simple way by the people of Bahia, touched me deeply. The image of the spaceship, carrying with it the whole mythology of space travel so prevalent at the time; the rebirth of the great Carnival song with me as its herald; the miracle of the rain; all of it seemed like a great feast of welcome that Brazil had planned for me in the depths of its imagination. Hours later, when the Tapajós trio returned from having completed their circuit to Sé Square, I got up on the truck to thank them. Roberto Pinho, my comrade in Pessoan and Sebastianist mysticism, went with me. I recall that Dedé, always much more a reveler than I, elected to stay on the ground, not to be confined within the tiny space of the truckbed, full of musicians and further diminished by the walls of the "ship." From up there I could see the drops of rain shimmering as they reflected the decorative lights on the street: looking up, we had the unmistakable sensation of vaulting swiftly through the stars into outer space. But below, on the street, I could see for the first time the Carnival crowd from a distance that revealed its power and mystery. After playing "Atrás do trio elétrico," the Tapajós played "Chuva, suor and cerveja" once more. Something struck my face that was not a raindrop. As I raised my hand to see what it was, the thing wafted onto my chest, and that's when Roberto and I realized it was an *esperança*. Despite the heavy rain, this winged green insect whose name means "hope" had flown toward the truck lights and alighted on me. I said to Roberto: "Does this mean there is hope?" And he answered with the tranquil joy of one who expects nothing less: "Of course!" We remained in the truck until the outer reaches of the Carnival festivities (today it extends to the Ondina neighborhood; at the time it extended only so far as Campo Grande). The trio stopped playing there, and the *Caetanave* continued up to Rio Vermelho (where we had rented a house) to drop me off. Gil, who didn't care for Carnival but very much believed in flying saucers, was sleeping when the truck stopped at our door. The din of the generator awakened him, immediately calling to mind something extraterrestrial. He ran to the veranda and saw his suppositions confirmed: in the middle of the night, that gigantic white craft with its blinking lights filled the whole street in front of the house. It took him a while to understand what was happening, but when he saw me descend from the strange object making the tremulous sound, he understood at once that the magical and the ordinary reality were reaffirming each other, that the symbolic and the empirical were not to be distinguished—that at this great moment, reality was pregnant with myth. The rejection of exile had not only dissipated: it was giving way to an affectionate repatriation. We the *tropicalistas,* unlike so many of our more naïve leftist friends, who seemed to believe that the military had come from Mars, had always been determined to face the dictatorship as nothing less than an expression of Brazil. That view increased our suffering, but today it also sustains what seems to be my optimism. I think and act as I do, knowing in my bones the truth of Brazil's potentialities, having entered into a dialogue with Brazil's deepest desires—and I do not conclude that we are a pure, ineluctable failure. I learned then to recognize the forces of regeneration, and even being aware of the proposition's very high risks, I am always inclined to double my wager.

It was during the last few months in London that the desire to have a child not only grew in me but insinuated itself in Dedé as well. That desire was a revolution of sorts, since Dedé and I had always been certain of never wanting children. Soon after Carnival we found out she was pregnant. We moved to a little house in Budião Square, right by the sea in the neighborhood of Amaralina. A flagstone path, worn down by the waves and covered with luminous green algae, extended beyond the sand, exposed to the wind during low tide and submerged under water when the tide was high. My return to Brazil (Gil stayed on for a few months in London) caused a certain awkwardness among those we would call today the "media." When in 1968 the military government had decreed Ato Institucional número 5 (AI5 for short), this act, the fifth in a series of "legal" decisions handed down since 1964, signaled in effect a coup d'état within the coup d'état: the right-wing hardliners in the army overpowered the more moderate forces, permitting houses to be searched without warrants, suspending habeas corpus, and so on. The public had a vague idea about the coincidence of AI5 and the exodus of artists, intellectuals, and popular singers, but since the press was censored as well, no one had the slightest notion of what had actually happened to Gil and me. Now, as a kind of spontaneous sympathy enfolded our presence in the country, the press, in a compensatory gesture, saluted us, whose suffering they could not denounce. This, however, was not to reaffirm the routine apotheosis of the *tropicalistas* that had continued during our exile. In fact, even at the moment of our arrival, one of the more exacting publications had already assumed a tone of demythification. It was just as well, considering every organ of the press—indeed, every journalist—must defend against the waves of unanimity stirred by the dream of celebrity. The newspaper *O Pasquim,* for which I had been writing in London, did a special issue on my arrival, inviting all the columnists to contribute something. I remember well Glauber saying that I was "a genius—and there's nothing we can do," and the Carioca journalist Paulo Francis confessing that while he did not believe in "iconoclasts who can't build a statue," he thought I was the kind who could, and he recalled our exchange of notes in prison. The same *Pasquim* would in time become hostile toward us, toward *tropicalismo,* and toward the fact of our being Bahians. And with a certain hypocritical suggestion of disappointment with our politics, they would betray their long-suppressed prejudices.

The Brazil to which we returned was already suffering the aftermath of the armed resistance and living the final moments of the "Brazilian miracle" of President Médici and his minister, Antônio Delfim Neto; soon it would all collapse under the blow dealt to the global economy by the Arab oil-producing states. The *desbunde,* however, had reached its zenith. This was the name the counterculture had acquired among us. *"Desbundar"* means to let oneself be led by the *"bunda"* (the bum). Here *"bunda"* is a synecdoche for *"corpo,"* the Afro-Brazilian word denoting that part of the body closest to the excremental and sexual functions (though not to be confused entirely with either)—an exuberant portion of flesh, which, notwithstanding, retains its Apollonian ritual cleanliness. Salvador, with its electric and libertarian Carnival, with its deserted beaches and its cities by the shore, its colonial architecture and its Afro-Brazilian cults, became the favorite city of the *desbundados.* But Rio had its hippie fairs and São Paulo its rocker neighborhoods. "Everyone" smoked dope and dropped acid. Luís Carlos Maciel wrote about this scene in *Pasquim* (and later in the Brazilian edition of *Rolling Stone*), interpreting it from a point of view that swung between Sartrean existentialism and eastern religion. The streets, particularly in Rio and Salvador, were full of long-haired boys and girls dressed in old lacy shirts. The most respected television newscasters, and many journalists who today proclaim contempt for the period, once had hair much longer than they'd ever had before or would ever have after. The members of the group Novos Baianos, which at the time was producing a suggestive (and abrasive) fusion of *chorinho* and rock, lived in a commune, first in the neighborhood of Botafogo in a large apartment they filled with tents and cabanas, and later in a semirural area called Jacarepaguá. Torquato, in his newspaper column, debated with Cinema Novo, leading a campaign for "marginal cinema." And even the cinéastes of Cinema Novo themselves had let their hair grow, smoked pot, and dropped acid. Gal was the muse of this universe. There was a slip of beach in Ipanema she frequented—an area where a pile of sand had been dredged up from the bottom of the ocean for the construction of a "submarine emissary"—and the spot became known as "Gal's dunes." In Salvador the *desbundados* used to gather at the beach in Porto da Barra, a perfect little bay between two colonial forts arranged before the sunset, like an amphitheater. It was a beach traditionally popular with the city, and I started going there again. There, as at Gal's dunes, boys didn't bother with swimsuits but rather sunbathed in their (somewhat transparent) underwear. And some homosexual couples (especially women) made little effort to disguise their caresses. But the hippies, properly speaking, the antitechnological and antiurban radicals, would take refuge on the more remote beach of Arembepe. I would not go to Arembepe until the eighties, by which time the scene had changed, though the remaining hippies still lived in a village nearby, between the lagoons whose water looked so golden in photographs. But I never went to that village. Zé Agrippino and Maria Esther had come back from Africa transfigured into ultra-hippies, beings of a "New Age," but somehow their way of applying themselves to these manners, combining as it did a typically profound commitment and critical detachment, did not partake of the nauseating tone that the expression connotes— and connoted for me.

I was seen as the precursor of all this—after all, I had let my hair grow long before the others, had taken *auasca* very early on, had embraced British neo-rock when all these people still rejected it, had been in prison and in exile; and even if on my return, I was a disappointment to those who expected rock 'n' roll and politics, at least I still retained the sexual ambiguity noted in my stage persona before my departure. But as the precursor I felt a bit dislocated (even if also a bit enchanted); it was just as I had felt during those festivals at the Isle of Wight, Glastonbury, or Bath: I felt myself rooted in this time but still looking ahead, seeking out the path for MPB, the path for Brazil, my own path through all this.

I was no *desbundado:* I didn't do drugs. I maintained a certain bourgeois comfort for my family and a love for what was essential in Western culture. The musicians I had met when I arrived in Rio in 1964 did do drugs to alienate themselves from the prosaic world of sensible men, to approximate the numinous, the transcendent, the free—and of course "musicality" itself. To be "crazy" was considered a privilege. People who had never "gone crazy" were contemptible.

It is curious, the term those musicians used to designate one who didn't do drugs: *"careta."* Apparently this word, which traditionally had meant "mask" or "masked person," emerged among criminals as a jocose diminutive of *cara,* which means both "face" and "person." So if one abstained from taking a mind-altering substance, it was said that he had a *"cara limpa,"* a clean face. And many times I heard musicians say that they had to deal with this or that awful situation *"totalmente de cara,"* by which they meant "completely clean," not high. In this roundabout way, through the outlaw slang of musicians, *careta* came to mean the opposite of masked or disguised. But even this "pejorative" use, referring to those who did not do drugs, ended up bringing back something of the old meaning, since to do drugs was understood as opening up to God and to music—an unmasking of oneself. *Caretas* are the bourgeois folks whose faces are always clean and who always wear a mask.

In 1972 almost everything anathema was *careta.* On this basis, Rogério had invented a nickname for me that I actually liked: Caretano. It seemed salutary, this recognition that the struggle to overcome revolutionary fanaticisms begins with humor, allowing ourselves to recognize their partial victories. We had not attained socialism, had not even found its human face; neither had we entered the Age of Aquarius or the Kingdom of the Holy Ghost; we had not overcome the West, had not rooted out racism or abolished sexual hypocrisy. But things would never be as they had been.

It is necessary to speak about sex here. But what should be said first is that there is nothing more difficult to speak about. In an interview commemorating his seventieth birthday, Jean-Paul Sartre said he had always believed all men ought to say everything: in "the realm of freedom" man, whatever he would be, will have no need to hide from his fellows. He seemed quite content with his own openness, and said he lamented only having omitted to reveal his erotic experiences. Knowing what evils attend sexual subterfuge among those starting out in life, I considered myself in perfect agreement with these ideas. Still I find nothing more disagreeable than the exposure of sexual intimacy that has since the sixties become as routine in real life as in fiction—a kind of awful consequence of the so-called "sexual revolution." There is sex in films, in ads, in books and songs; there are "revealing" interviews that lay bare sexual preferences and minutiae in every manner of magazine, and even in newspapers. It provokes in me a very specific kind of rebellion, as well as boredom: I avoid it such as I can, to protect my own emotional economy. It is not so much that what we deem petty or vulgar in the encounter of eroticism has changed: rather that the obscenities formerly shared among groups of barflies are now on display during prime time. And there is a glaring bad faith in the exercise of freedom: the talk shows on American television (which have already begun to spawn Brazilian imitators)—with their processions of "sex addicts," rape victims, and incestuous adulterers—feed an insatiable hunger for exhibitionism, voyeurism, and scandal, and these programs depend entirely on taboos that appear to have been abolished for the very sake of the broadcasts themselves. In these cases, one is left with the impression that with the advent of the sexual revolution, nothing was lost except good manners.

But then I read laments such as Mario Vargas Llosa's in which he bewails "the trivialization of the sexual act," to which he opposes a nostalgia for the bordello as a temple in which sex is celebrated as "the central mystery of life"; he deplores the diminuendo of physical love into "a passing entertainment, something very different from that other approach to the doors of heaven and hell which sex had been for my generation." It is when I encounter such views that my ties to the libertarians are renewed. It is to the "taboos, prohibitions, and prejudices" that used to surround sex that Vargas Llosa attributes the disturbing effect, for him, of a naked woman lying on a bed, while "for the average mortal, sex has become the most natural thing in the world." I, who consider sex at once the most natural and the most mysterious and transcendental of phenomena, cannot so easily accept these arguments that measure the intensity of sexual experience in relation to prohibitions operative in the day when the person formulating them came of age. I have always laughed derisively at Nelson Rodrigues's famous tirade on the subject: this highly distinctive Brazilian playwright, a wonderfully scandalous writer and also a moralist, used to say that in his youth, a man would tremble at the sight of a woman's ankle, whereas today "not even the head of an ice-cream vendor on the beach is turned at the sight of a girl in a bikini." Nothing can persuade me that for the children of the sexual revolution sex is "a passing entertainment" any more than it was for Vargas Llosa and his friends in the bordello. If sex is—as I have no doubt—the "central mystery of life," one need have no pretense of possessing it exclusively.

The discovery of orgasm through masturbation—intuited directly from the body itself and deduced from fragments of other people's conversations—was the key event of my life. In her book about old age, Simone de Beauvoir (whose *Memoirs of a Dutiful Daughter* and *The Second Sex* anticipate the "sexual revolution" and were crucial to my adolescence) writes of Lou Andreas-Salomé, for whom sexuality (which she discovered only at thirty-five) represented "a magnificent and exaltant realization of the individual." At age ten or eleven, I already felt not only fully justified in my own existence, but also entitled to justify amply the existence of the world. The illumination that was sexual experience banished the notion of sin from the realm of my privacy. It was a great manifestation of the good and the beautiful—not simply an aspect of life, one fact among others, but something that approached an absolute. I whispered God's name and asked myself in awe how it was possible that in each body, as in my own, such grace could be inscribed.

The defeat of sexual hypocrisy was destined to be a priority of mine among the wave of libertarian causes that swept the sixties, and within that crusade the case of homosexuality demanded particular attention. Offering the ideal model for the conflict between the authentic and the dissimulated, but unamenable to being framed in terms of the perversions that imply a crime or denial of someone else's freedom, homosexuality clearly posed the fundamental question concerning human sexuality, and thus the very freedom of the individual. It is no accident that homosexuality is under fire from totalitarian states—even those under construction—and from the nostalgia for a time of absolute social control.

It is not on account of my having arrived at this awareness that the topic of homosexuality has always been, is, and always will be with me. I would say rather that it is precisely because the topic has always been with me that my having arrived at this awareness was so luminous and captivating.

The sexual indeterminacy that had intrigued boys in school and which I incorporated into my public persona from the sixties onward bespeaks profound notions concerning the nature of my desires as well as my choice of roles. In *Virtually Normal,* Andrew Sullivan tells how, at age ten, when he heard a girl ask: "Are you sure you are not a girl?" he realized the meaning of this difference. As in his case, many friends I made since childhood would swoon over others of the same sex. For them the polarity male/female affirms itself definitely and is not blurred. It was not so with me. In spite of having had since before adolescence intensely sexual infatuations for girls (and at first exclusively for girls), I knew I could find neither a man nor a woman to be antierotic merely in principle. At the same time, I am sure that I would not have refused to surrender myself body and soul to a young man had I at nineteen fallen in love with one. And I have not the shadow of a doubt but that such a decision, taken clearheadedly, would have met with the affectionate acceptance of my parents. True, they were older Catholics from the interior, with a spotless married life, but they inculcated in their children a profound sense of integrity that required no particular role, whether professional, social, or sexual.

When I was twenty-three I underwent a Rorschach test, and the result revealed "latent homosexuality; female identification; idealization of women." The test was done as an experiment by a friend who was a psychology student. She herself was a lesbian (not without inner conflicts), but she told me my results had been interpreted by a professor to whom the identity of the subject was unknown. I believed it. In any event, I thought the diagnosis made sense. I was somewhat anguished—for a short time—believing that perhaps my love life would be based on some sort of self-deception, but this thought could not resist the spontaneous force of my sexual attraction to Dedé. What surprised me more in the test results was the indication of a talent for music. Since childhood I have been convinced that my verbal and visual skills are superior to my musicality: I gave up on painting but I have remained certain I would make a great filmmaker. Not being so sure about my sexual inclination, I think I would likewise make a great queer. I count among my intimates people of phenomenal musicality who nevertheless cannot obtain from music a fifth of what I can; on the other hand, there are countless indisputable heterosexuals who have far less success with women than I do. The Rorschach test concurred with fate so far as music is concerned, though both belied my intuition; as to sexuality, the test disputed fate—and my intuition has never decided with which to agree. In both respects, I consider myself more successful than I deserve to be.

So as a public figure I came close to what Andrew Sullivan called the "ubiquitous, vaguely homoerotic" climate of "the male pop groups of that period," and today I surmise that those suggestions of androgyny, polymorphism, and indeterminacy that colored the post-Beatles (post-Elvis?) pop music scene still threaten the conventions that underlie many acts of oppression. The new compartmentalization that followed that orgy of signs was inevitable. All those who were "vaguely homoerotic" without declaring themselves homosexual were assimilated as the heterosexuals of a new era. I'm inclined to reject such simplifications. Having engaged much more frequently in heterosexual than homosexual practice (including two marriages I lived as a sincere monogamist), I could say, at this point in my life, that I have defined myself as a heterosexual. But I don't. Clarity of sexual orientation is meaningless except when it manifests itself spontaneously. What does matter to me is that the paths toward a rich and intense sexual life be open.

In his *Retrato do Brazil* (Portrait of Brazil) of 1928, Paulo Prado attributes the "sadness" in our people (which he sees confused with our incapacity for social organization and economic progress) to the lechery that dominated the will of the first Europeans to arrive here: a few Portuguese men left without white women "in a radiant land" succumbed to the willingness of the native women and generated the inaugural Brazilian progeny under the sign of *mestizaje* and permissiveness. From the erotic insinuations read through Carmen Miranda's stylizations to the orgiastic promise of the Carioca Carnival, everything that in the eyes of the world stands for an alleged Brazilian happiness turns out to be nothing but a symptom of our sadness. Coming to know São Paulo (Paulo Prado's city) for the first time at the age of twenty-two, I was surprised to see couples would not kiss on the mouth or caress passionately in public. In Santo Amaro in the fifties, as in Rio or Salvador, such scenes were as common as they were in Paris. One might expect that ease in sexual mores grows in direct proportion to urban development, that a small town in the Bahian hinterland would have a more oppressive climate of public morality than a great metropolis like São Paulo. But the fact is that in this great city Dedé and I were actually admonished more than once for kissing in public. Indeed, Paris was more urban, and Santo Amaro more "Brazilian," but São Paulo was where the European immigrants had formed an industrious community devoted to clear moral principles. When I was a boy in Bahia, the traditional choice of the word *"veado"* (literally meaning "deer") to designate a male homosexual was popularly justified by the fact that this animal is hunted. And so at the least suspicion regarding someone's virility, people would yell: "Ti-bi!" (the Bahian onomatopoeia for gunshots), and generally they would add: "Go ahead and kill it, it's an animal." While there were never any cases of men actually shot in such circumstances, these symbolic shootings continued to humiliate the prey and amuse the hunters. In truth, such aggressions were thought to betray a coarseness and lack of breeding: mothers and respectable men were obliged to reprimand their sons who exhibited such vulgarity. But the boys who nowadays kill the men they go to bed with on the pretext of getting money to buy cocaine are an example of the imbalance between modern urban violence and our old, ill-concealed tolerance of homosexual practices: one could say they are the deformed (and, in a sense, inverted) image of the symbolic hunters of my childhood.

By the mid-seventies, there was a gay bar in Santo Amaro, near the market. It was not a clandestine dive, but rather a modest imitation of what supposedly existed in the great cities of the world. It was regarded by the general population with humor and without scandal, and lasted a relatively short time. It was a moment of harmony between our permissive mestizo version of Mediterranean traditions (à la Paulo Prado, sadly) and the news of the civil rights movement coming from "white" Anglophone America. An American friend of mine offered this comparison: in the United States, the father of a liberal family will fight for the right of a homosexual to live a full life, but will always remain incapable of imagining with any degree of identification a homosexual act; in Brazil, however, even the verbal hunter of queers is perfectly capable of admitting the reality of such scenes in his imagination. One cannot measure the freedom of homosexuals in Brazil by the number of participants in a gay parade. Andrew Sullivan notes, in another passage, that having lent a sense of "homosexuality" to every act between one male and another, the gay movement has done more than any institution to reduce the incidence of relationships between men in the United States.

When I returned from London in 1972, the subtle imitation of Carmen Miranda I'd woven into my performance of "O que é que a baiana tem?" amounted to a double commentary: it spoke to the meaning of Brazilian pop art in exile, and to the originality of the potential Brazilian contribution to the cause of sexual liberation. I have never abandoned the topic, though I am no longer as naïve as I was then. The other day, when I saw a young woman affecting, with utter spontaneity, those manners most deeply rooted in our sense of masculinity, I understood the hostile skepticism with which some of my gay friends receive any suggestion of a polymorphous pansexual world: the meaning of life, for them, as for the dyke I describe, depends quite clearly on the indicative signs of gender. They are opposed to the world described by Christopher Lasch as "narcissistic," what he views as the self-negating world of undifferentiation. Andrew Sullivan reaffirms the centrality of the heterosexual model by proposing that we consider homosexuality as a variant that underscores, rather than negates, the former's beauty: like redheads, albinos, and geniuses, homosexuals would be the exception that not only confirms but *honors* the heterosexual rule. I found the concept lovely but too near an analogy to lefthandedness, for instance.

Edmund White prefers to identify the image of the homosexual with that of the rebel. In any event, I know that oftentimes the hatred, fear, and repulsion inspired by homosexuality speak to its greatness more than any mere liberal acceptance could. This tension has always been present in the way the subject is approached in my work. At the moment of my return to Brazil, my life as a married man was entering a glorious period—and the topic of homoeroticism was reaching an apex of clarity in the pop music world, before it flagged and dispersed itself among the movements both salutary and reductive during the decade that was then beginning.

I have very sweet memories of that period. And the birth of my son Moreno was the greatest (sometimes I think the only) event of my adult life. Through Nando Barros (the former high school classmate in whose house in Itapuã Dedé and I had begun our relationship in earnest in 1964), we came into contact with a group of very interesting young people in post-*tropicalista* Bahia. Antônio Risério, Paulo César de Souza, the siblings Mônica and Pedro Costa and Ana Amélia (Anamelinha) de Carvalho were the main figures in this group of adolescents. Risério was an extremely active intellect who was won over to concrete poetry by *tropicalismo.* Paulo César, a great and sensitive intelligence, admired the *tropicalistas* as much as Risério did, but he defended his freedom with ironic blows against the newly elected orthodoxies, being less than charmed by the counterculture. Mônica and Anamelinha made a dazzling pair through a contrast in tonalities: the one blonde and fair, the other brown-skinned with a jet-black mane—among the most beautiful women I have ever met. My friendship with these new Bahians would become as steadfast as the one I had established with Waly, Duda, Alvinho, Roberto Pinho, and Rogério: generally speaking, it lasts to this day. I am closer to Risério and Paulo than to the others, but I see Mônica each time I go to São Paulo, where she lives, and used to see Anamelinha frequently until she died of a brain hemorrhage, still young and beautiful, leaving two daughters (she had married Tony Costa, a Carioca guitarist who played with me in the eighties). Augusto de Campos came to Bahia to finish up his research for a book he was writing on Pedro Kilkerry, the Bahian symbolist poet whose verve and originality had never been recognized in Brazilian literary histories. To this day both are friends of mine, and Risério is very knowledgeable about the essays and poems of Augusto and his concretist friends, and he himself has become a poet visibly influenced by them, as well as a rigorous essayist. Paulo César, apart from his academic historiography, has become an excellent translator of Nietzsche (with wonderful translations of *Beyond Good and Evil, Ecce Homo,* and *On the Genealogy of Morals* to his credit), Freud, and other great German authors. Mônica, who married Risério and later the Paulista poet Regis Bonvicino, also writes poetry and already has some books published. Twenty-four years ago, these future intellectuals were the demonstrably talented teenagers with whom Bahia surprised me upon my return—and who adorned our house with their beauty and vivacity.

The filmmaker Leon Hirzman had just finished shooting his adaptation of Graciliano Ramos's novel *São Bernardo,* and he asked me to do the soundtrack. During our first conversation, I mentioned the fact that Graciliano (like João Cabral de Melo Neto) didn't like music, and then recalled excitedly the ingenious solution to this predicament devised by Nelson Pereira dos Santos for *Vidas secas* (Barren Lives): the creak of the oxcart's wooden wheels served as the music in the film. And Leon agreed immediately, adding that it was with that precise idea in mind that he had asked for me, having noted the similarities between Nelson's oxcart wheels and my moans and groans in "Asa-Branca," a cut on my first London record. It was a revelation. He really wanted me to compose something for the film using only my voice, in a manner as close as possible to what I had done in "Asa-Branca," and I immediately imagined other sonoral forms organized on the basis of that material. Then he said he wanted more: that I improvise it all while watching the images projected on the screen. And that's the way we did it. I was enchanted by the result, and even more by the method. Above all I found in my collaboration with Leon a new beginning for my own work. And it is by no means a negligible fact that, once again, the path for me to follow was illuminated by cinema, and by Brazilian Cinema Novo, an experience so native to Brazil itself as to make it always an adventure, at once disconcerting and sublime.

araçá azul

The soundtrack for *São Bernardo* was recorded in Rio over two or three days' time. I returned to Salvador anxious to get back into the recording studio, believing there I could work wonders applying the same method but with vastly better technical resources. *Araçá azul* (Blue Guava) would be recorded in São Paulo in scarcely a week, though not a single track had been ready (or even roughed out) before the sessions began. Staying at a hotel next to the Eldorado studio, then the only eight-channel facility in Brazil, I began to improvise some pieces very loosely conceived. André Midani, the president of PolyGram Brazil, an incredibly intelligent (and chic) man given his position, agreed to leave me alone with the engineer and his assistant, denying access to anyone at all from the recording label.

The first track we recorded, and the first song on the record, is a vocal piece without words or melody. Born of my experience with *São Bernardo,* it consists of moans and grunts superimposed on one another: the sounds of Brazilian voices conversing with the accent retained, while the words were indecipherable. The title, "De conversa," was inspired by João Gilberto—always João!—who had recently recorded a samba by Lúcio Alves, "De conversa em conversa" (From Chat to Chat). In fact, my aim was to imitate accents from various parts of Brazil (mostly Northeastern, but also Carioca, etc.) without using a single word of the Portuguese language. To this sound I added only percussion, playing it on my own body. At the end of the piece, like some melodic and semantic revelation, surged Milton Nascimento's song "Cravo e canela" (Clove and Cinnamon). It was a salute to this great colleague, whose work was so remarkable even while being so different from our own (in fact, a sort of opposite, in some respects), but whom we had not publicly celebrated upon our return. The last line, "eu quero ver você alegre" ("I want to see you happy"), uttered at first by one voice that then joins the others in a simple harmony, is addressed to

Milton, on the personal as well as the artistic level; it was a kind of prayer that he might overcome the immense sadness that had overcome him—a prayer, I happily note today, that seems to have been answered. Do not mistake this for a fantasy of omnipotence: I meant by that last line of "De conversa" simply to acknowledge that while there was in the cult of Milton's style, in the very admiration for his work, a morbid appreciation of his sadness, there nevertheless existed in me—but obviously not just in me: in many people, but above all, in Milton himself—the desire to safeguard his capacity for life and happiness, without which his songs, even those of the most mournful beauty, would not exist.

The other tracks on *Araçá azul* partook of this same degree of unconventionality. Even the bolero "Tú me acostumbraste" was interpreted in two octaves, the second refrain being sung in a falsetto, rather as Ray Charles does with "People," but with a precarious electronic distortion—and, naturally, without the voice and musicality of the Genius. I hired Perinho Albuquerque, Moacir's younger brother, a fellow with great musical ability, whimsically self-taught, to do some of the arrangements. Once everything had been recorded, he would go to São Paulo to write the orchestral sections for *Sugarcane Fields Forever,* a long piece consisting of a series of *sambas de roda* from the Bahian *recôncavo* connected by my own interjections and instrumental interludes. But being self-taught, Perinho perhaps possessed more musical genius than musical culture, and the orchestral parts, intended to sound "modern," sounded instead like a soundtrack for an amateur short with artistic pretensions. To make matters worse, I had decided to have printed on the inside cover the phrase "UM DISCO PARA ENTENDIDOS" (A Record for Those in the Know), playing upon the ambiguity of *entendido,* which meant "to be in on something" as well as what is known today as "gay."

The public reaction was unequivocal: the album broke all records for refunds requested. *Transa* had been well received (thanks in no small measure to the new version of Monsueto Menezes's old samba, "Mora na filosofia"); and the fact of my being back in Brazil had not yet lost its novelty. There was also the show I had done with Chico Buarque at the Castro Alves Theater in Salvador: this performance, as well as the live recording, had been a huge success, much ado having been made about our joint appearance, particularly given our supposed rivalry. It was enough to drive people to the stores in search of my new record. But when they got home, most could scarcely bear even to listen to the first track all the way to the end: they would run straight back to the store, trying to return the disc. In a way, I was proud of this kind of failure. But the truth is, even I was not satisfied with the record. As for Augusto de Campos and Rogério Duprat (the latter, having sweetly accepted my invitation to orchestrate a track, did so with his customary brilliance), they were both enthusiastic about what they heard. I have never, before or since, received such impassioned praise from those two artists, and to this day I attach enormous importance to their appraisal. But finally, what made me pull back from *Araçá azul* was the realization that, in spite of my utter surrender to the project, I had not achieved anything comparable to Jorge Ben's new record, which was entitled *Ben* and would prove one of the high points of popular music in Brazil.

Jorge Ben's record came out practically at the same time as mine. So did Naná Vasconcelos's *Amazonas,* I believe—and it, too, seemed, compared to what I had done, infinitely superior as a matter of sound. None of this, to be sure, was the fault of Marcus Vinicius, my Eldorado engineer, a fine professional and excellent person, who had only been confused by my performance as "producer." Finally, there was a very realistic reaction from Zé Agrippino, who had returned with Maria Esther from Africa, where they had been living for over a year since their travels through Europe and the United States: he seemed cool to the record, criticizing the lack of depth and the plastering down of the sound. He despised the pretentious decision to sound experimental. To him, *Araçá azul* was technically and artistically underdeveloped, though, nevertheless, to be credited for not relying on the simple charm of the songs—on which account it was roundly rejected by the general public. At first Agrippino said only: "I like the songs," singling out "Júlia/Moreno," which I had done for the future baby whose sex was as yet unknown (Dedé was pregnant when I recorded the album, and there was no such thing, at least not in Bahia, as an ultrasound exam), but he was indifferent to the more avant-garde tracks. In the end he gave his opinion on these, too, with technical precision, rounding it off with a general comment on the situation of pop music and cinema in Brazil as he found it upon his return, not omitting to mention Jorge Ben and Naná. His infallible aim, going straight to the very points that had already occurred to me, reinforced my somewhat pessimistic attitude toward *Araçá azul.* It was not that Augusto's and Duprat's favor carried less weight but rather that Agrippino's disfavor was more useful. After all, I had conceived of *Araçá azul* as a bold move to break free of professional bounds: I needed to loosen up in the studio, test my limits, and extend my horizons. Inevitably I had come out of it changed, and of necessity I would do things differently afterward. But I simply could not contemplate perpetuating an experimentalist attitude born out of what seemed to me an abuse of opportunities: could I, having returned bathed in the glory of exile, laden with its attendant privileges, and having cultivated a reputation as an artist of refinement, offer a product technically beneath the standards of the very market of the underdeveloped country to which I had returned? Augusto and Duprat certainly saw things differently. For them, social issues and subtle differences among products for popular amusement counted for little as compared with the free creation of relevant artistic forms.

As for myself, I discovered that I had assumed the aspect of a spoiled boy, and reasoned I ought to have the courage to get out of it. My assignments would now be to regain humility in the studio, to pay attention to specific aspects of the craft of popular music, to contribute to the technical and mercantile advances of my professional class. I have in fact rarely managed any of this in subsequent years, but the little I have accomplished I prize enormously. Naturally I wanted to reach those aims without laying aside the motives that had led me to *tropicalismo* or to the insolent experimentalism of *Araçá azul.* Some years later, in a conversation with Augusto on the disapproval with which the record had met on the part of scholarly musicians at the University of Bahia, I heard him declare my record to be "lyrical music" of great beauty. I have always seen in Augusto's staunch approval of *Araçá azul* a determination to stand diametrically opposite those who would always fall in line with commercial convention. I saw that clearly because *Araçá azul* was, after all, in a certain way the belated birth of a record project that existed only in embryonic form when I was arrested—and which, had it come to term at that time, would have been something very much nearer the work of the concretists. Often it has occurred to me how much Walter Franco's first record (as well as Arnaldo Antunes's work in the nineties) resembles what I had in mind back then. Back home in 1972, I was trying to recapture the inventive daring of 1968. But I was bound to arrive at something very different. Suffice it to say that the record I didn't make in 1968–69 had been imagined as a radical intervention that would have enabled my impending exit from the world of pop music. But it's important to know that by the time of *Araçá azul,* my decision (however chimerical) to abandon the profession had been deconstructed by prison and exile. So *Araçá azul* appears simply as the experimental record that I was in fact capable of making, a version irreconcilable with the Paulista concretist one I would have made. But not entirely so: there is one track in *Araçá azul* inspired by a comment of Augusto's on the name of Amaralina, my neighborhood in Bahia. As he explored the formal possibilities of the word, he pointed out that *anil* (which means "indigo") was mirrored in the last syllables, finally suggesting the phonetic circle of *anilina* (aniline, the stuff of dyes). From there I invented a long word that could be read in both directions, and this palindrome, to Augusto's own surprise, proved equally reversible in the recording: *amaranilanilinalinarama (amar anil anilina li na rama)*. I intoned it in such a way as to suggest a fragment of a Hindu prayer. And in the final version I juxtaposed the normal recording with the sound of the same tape running backwards, the latter sounding almost indistinguishable from the former, producing a perfect aural mirror. It's one of the things I like the most about the record.

If I say that Agrippino's opinion was more useful at the moment of *Araçá azul*'s release, I must reiterate that I did not think it superior to Augusto's and Duprat's. After all, from a broader view, my identification with Augusto's positions and sensibility in these matters is more resilient than anything I could have shared with Agrippino. Suffice it to say that Augusto and I approached rock and pop as we did after (and because of) an adherence to João Gilberto in which Agrippino could take no part. Though concretism had been labeled the "rock 'n' roll of poetry" by the press in the fifties, Augusto and his "formalist" colleagues (a group roughly contemporary with the antiformalist American Beat Generation) quickly chose bossa nova, while Agrippino—following Mautner, who identified with the Beat poets and in his first book expressed hostility to the cool clean sound of bossa nova, praising rock and sentimental *sambas-canções* instead—would never be a bossanovista. The anti–bossa nova mask we *tropicalistas* would try on was made of that kinship with Agrippino, Mautner, rock, and the old boleros, but, like the concretists, I had been, and would always be in my heart of hearts, a lover of João Gilberto and of João Cabral de Melo Neto above all else.

Upon reflection, we had murdered *tropicalismo* several times—and from the very beginning. Several times we spoke of a "movement to end all movements." And the television special conceived by Zé Celso, which had never aired, was but another form of *tropicalismo*'s cultural suicide. Finally in *Divino, maravilhoso* we had staged the burial of the movement. Our arrest and exile represented a genuine disruption in the continuity of our work, but the adventure that began for me with *tropicalismo* has never ended. And yet I feel not the least surprised when I hear it said that *Araçá azul* marked the last stand.

path

The majority of the songs for which I am known nowadays were composed and recorded since *Araçá azul*. Apart from the phenomenon that is "Alegria, alegria," which in Brazil (and only in Brazil) is still better known than any other, today I am recognized above all as the author of some songs written in the mid-seventies and afterwards. Obviously there is a story to tell about those times. My collaboration with Perinho Albuquerque in *Jóia, Qualquer coisa,* and *Bicho* marked a memorable period. And with A Outra Banda da Terra (whose nucleus comprised Arnaldo Brandão, Vinícius Cantuária, Bolão, Zé Luís, and Tomáz Improta) I traveled through what I dare say was the happiest time of my musical life. Still recuperating from the conquest of *Transa,* I was only now beginning to find my stride in a properly professional career and to enjoy purity and freedom in my singing.

After the crazy sixties, the seventies seemed to me rather insipid: I didn't like David Bowie or progressive rock, Woody Allen or the new German films; I held no brief for Weather Report or for Earth, Wind, and Fire. Only in Bob Marley, Stevie Wonder, and some punk music did I discover encouraging novelties coming from the Anglophone world. I found the fashions (the clothes, the hair, the dances) ugly and square (*careta*), schematic recapitulations of what had been daring in the sixties. But I felt happy all the same, and Brazil was exciting. Since those years my interests have ranged, and I have become intrigued by the phenomenon of the modernization of the Brazilian soap operas (and generally by the part played by TV Globo in the education of the masses), and by the work of the theater troupe Asdrúbal Trouxe o Trombone. (This ensemble, though lacking the ambition and grandiosity of Zé Celso or Boal, has brought back to the theater a vital spontaneity and a poetry rather like the power of MPB.) Equally interesting to me have been the new waves of carioca samba that have made their way into the market (such as *pagode*), the emergence of the *blocos afros* in the streets of Salvador (Gil's song, "Filhos de Gandhi" [Gandhi's Children] did more for them than my "Atrás do trio elétrico" had ever done for the *trios elétricos*), the commercial boom of Bahian Carnival pop, the explosion of Brazilian rock bands in the eighties, the sudden demand in coastal markets for *sertaneja* music, and some of the color films made by Cinema Novo directors showing a sense of good entertainment unknown in their earlier films from the heroic phase. I also became more intimately acquainted with *candomblé*—owing to some beautiful conversations with the *ialorixá* Mãe Menininha do Gantois—and I moved to Rio in order to undergo psychoanalysis. By the mid-eighties, my marriage to Dedé had come to an end, and meeting Paula Lavigne, then a girl of thirteen who belonged to a teenage theater group, was eventually to have great consequences: we have been living together for more than ten years and we have two sons, Zeca, born in 1992, and Tom, in 1997. My attentions to things like TV Globo, *axé* music, Rock-Brasil, and even Asdrúbal Trouxe o Trombone inspired my more or less close friends to call me too quick to embrace losing propositions. But I believed I could walk on water. I loved the experimental records of Tom Zé and Walter Franco, the films of Júlio Bressane and Rogério Sganzerla, but I knew too that my place was out there in the middle of the mainstream of Brazilian mass culture, many times swimming against the current, as often just muddying the flow, at other times simply trying to clear the way. There's much one could say about all this, but the story behind the reflections bared in the book ends here.

Thirty years have elapsed between the *tropicalista* deflagration and the time when I write these last pages. Naturally, much of what here appears to be developed and considered was as yet unformed in me at the time of the events narrated. But it is also true that many other thoughts were more vividly clear in my mind in the heat of battle than they could be reconstructed now. And while many others have remained unchanged in their rhythm and form for all these years, others still are simply new to me. What is really worth noting is that what brought me to *tropicalismo* has brought me here as well.

In his *Clash of Civilizations and the Remaking of World Order,* Samuel Huntington describes the return of ancient forces of civilization that were suppressed during the Cold War, the return to a world far older and much more galvanized than the Western adventure that culminated in the United States. In particular, cultural dogmas and religious fundamentalisms command center stage. He then proposes that the United States lead the West in a mission of reaffirming its culture through the renewal of its own religion. In this scheme, "Christianity" reemerges as synonymous with "western civilization." This criterion for the classification of "civilizations" is highly questionable. There is accordingly an Islamic civilization, an Orthodox Christian one, a Chinese one, an African one, one that is western and one that is Latin American. What I find most unconvincing is his portrayal of the United States as the guardian of European civilization. I see America as a radically new stage in Western culture. Traumatically "bathed in black blood, in Indian blood," it is the aggressive antithesis of Europe. In some respects, this applies to the United States more than to the entirety of Latin countries in the New World. The violence of the U.S. mass culture and its vigorous export, since the twenties, of a "mongrel" form (to use Ann Douglas's term) defines a reality that represents not so much the crystallization of the European phase of history as its over-throw. But Huntington ends up characterizing the West as being made up of only the rich "white" countries: under the tutelage of the United States, these ought to organize themselves against "the others." And Brazil appears as the possible "nation-nucleus" of his alleged Latin American civilization.

We would find such a deliberate confusion of geopolitical blocs with "civilizations" to be simply despicable were it not for the fact that it actually strikes a sensitive chord in the Brazilian intuition of what Brazil is. Indeed to us, our country seems caught in an eternal uncertainty, being on the one hand the natural ally of the United States and its international policy and on the other the blueprint for a new civilization. Its character as a nation at once gigantic and linguistically isolated contributes equally to both impulses. And the uniqueness of its music—its beauty no less than its precariousness—follows from this as well. *Tropicalismo* derived its original energy from this tension. Books like Huntington's (or Fukuyama's *Trust,* which apparently opposes it) compel me to feel—and to think of *tropicalismo* as being—positioned clearly to the left of what would have seemed possible in 1967.

It was out of the western world that there emerged the process of the secularization of knowledge that resulted in a universally applicable science as we know it today as well as the individualist morality under-lying the concepts of "human rights." As Décio Pignatari has recently observed, atheists are a true minority in our day and age. The "revenge of God" is then a statistical fact, which cannot escape the attendant irony. But if a vigorous North American mind prescribes a frightened submission to this "revenge," the Brazilian mind cannot accept this version of restoration. Thomas Mann remarked that "there is nothing worse than the dream of restoration. An age fearful of itself seeks to restore fundamentalisms. All in vain: there is no going back." Ryszard Kapuściński concludes his book on the demise of the Soviet Union with the realization that countries of large national territories always find a means of resurgence—and he cites Brazil along with China and India as examples; Russia too, he says, will rise from the ashes of postsocialism. I see in this observation simply an acknowledgment of the ambitious self-image such countries inevitably possess. Be that as it may, let the Brazilian ambition be to take atheism, the child of the West, to its ultimate consequences. The fact that religiosity will likely be encountered again, in another stage at the end of the process, does not justify a regression into religious prescientific, prephilosophical, and prejuridical casts of thought. This is what fascinates me in Antônio Cícero's *O mundo desde o fim,* a work of philosophy that reconfigures the *cogito* as "apocrisis." And so in this sense when I speak of "a West to the west of the West" I propose not a fundamentalism respecting this particular culture, but rather a commitment to certain irreversible, historically western achievements.

Takeshi Umehara (quoted by Huntington) wrote that the "complete failure of Marxism and the spectacular disintegration of the Soviet Union are only the precursors of a collapse of Western liberalism, the main current of modernity. Far from being an alternative to Marxism and the dominant ideology at the end of History, liberalism will be the next domino piece to fall." It is this remark that leads Huntington to suggest the strategic alliance between the United States and the "Christian" European nations. But if anything, such a statement by the Japanese philosopher would lead me to pose deeper questions about the meaning of what has occurred in the West. Huntington also quotes Arthur Schlesinger, Jr.: "Europe is the source—the *unique* source—of the idea of individual freedom, political democracy, the rule of law, human rights, and cultural freedom. These ideas are *European,* not Asian, or African, or Middle Eastern, except by adoption." But as Ernest Gellner has observed, the fact that such ideas (or modern science, for that matter) emerged in the West hardly implies their ownership by white European peoples, or even that those peoples are better prepared to put them into practice or development. It is indeed obvious that liberalism will be the next domino to fall, if the self-proclaimed lovers of such western achievements—the conservatives of rich Western countries—fatally devalue this foundation as they celebrate the bankruptcy of socialism, beckoning submission with an explicit return to "faith"—and an implicit return to racist values—none of which liberal thinking would tolerate. And it will fall even as they renounce, for the moment, the shameless materialism of the age for a culture painted in deceptive romantic hues, in which there is little trust that rational ideas can produce something real in the life of societies.

The Clash of Civilizations is reminiscent of a text by Wagner that very much impressed Nietzsche; in it, Wagner cynically proposes that the masses should be led by irreligious men under the guise of religion. I am reminded here of my time in prison and of the sergeant who proudly confessed to having beaten the actors of a play supposedly disrespectful of the Virgin Mary while crudely affirming that he himself believed in none of that shit.

Huntington attributes the libertarian wave of the sixties to the growing percentage of young people in the West since the Second World War, the "baby boomers"; Eric Hobsbawm, to the world economic growth during that decade and the one before. To inquire about *tropicalismo* is to inquire about the collision of that powerful wave with the singularity of Brazil. The twentieth century has been called the "American century." Hobsbawm, who characterized it as "brief," stated that where popular culture is concerned, we were able within the dense space of that brevity to be "either American or provincial." On the periphery of the world economy, Brazil presented in the form of *tropicalismo* a model for facing this question that is only now becoming intelligible on a global scale. Something of that model is more or less replicated (though by direct influence, in the majority of cases) in the disillusionment of the best Mexican and Argentine pop and rock since the eighties.

To put it succinctly, I myself could say that I do not live my creative interests from the perspective of the "American century" but rather from the prospect of overcoming it. But I say this mainly because in the American century there still existed plenty of room to insist on making the United States the agent of a racial and religious group. There is about Huntington's book something profoundly antiwestern: he exposes the efforts of conservatives to transform the culture of Camões, Luther, Washington, and Picasso into a closed culture. It simply won't work. The great movement that carried the flame of civilization from the globe's warm regions into the cold of the northern hemisphere—thence on to Japan and the neocapitalist Asian tigers and neocommunist China—this movement is ripe for a detour. And it may have as its horizon a myth of Brazil—the American, Lusophonic, mestizo giant of the southern hemisphere. In his *O mundo desde o fim,* Antônio Cícero recalls Nietzsche's rebellion against the "moralist" thinkers who would deprecate tropical man: in favor of what, asks the German philosopher, "of the temperate zones? To the benefit of temperate men? Of what is moral? Of what is mediocre?" As a matter of fact, the Brazilian economist Eduardo Giannetti, in a book that was published at roughly the same time, also examines the opinions of some of those great moralists, precisely with a view to Nietzsche's critique. Let a quote from Kant suffice: "The excellence of thinking creatures, their quickness of apprehension, the clarity and vivacity of their concepts, in sum, the whole extension of their perfection, becomes higher and more complete in direct proportion to the distance between their inhabited space and the sun."

Though I rejected the name *tropicalismo* at first, thinking it was too restrictive, today it seems more apt than any. Precisely because I had initially preferred to emphasize our acceptance of the international pop repertoire, rather than the shock of nationalism, the moniker today sounds like an unconscious revelation of the essence of the movement. Its very elaboration, by naïve journalists guided by the suggestion of Luís Carlos Barreto himself referring to a work by Oiticica, has all the markings of meaningful chance, of the unwitting approach to a truth. That it should take responsibility for the destiny of tropical man, serve as a hidden dynamo catalyzing the historical reply to a question not unlike the one posed by Nietzsche—this was the secret motivation of what was called *tropicalismo* in Brazilian popular music. This is not a case of attributing grandiose intentions to trivial gestures: a group of young people making music for entertainment decides at last to exact a larger meaning from the evolution of their careers. I rather believe that such a meaning imposes itself despite what is small in those careers. And if it ends up feeding off the pettier aspects, it does not necessarily exalt them. I would like it if these words could be taken less as a mystical vision of history than as an effort to arrive at clarity in the face of what presented itself as the very stuff of our history, as it was being lived.

This has as its ballast the actual sound produced by João Gilberto. João takes popular music upon himself as the determinant of what truth we might be permitted and could create. I even go so far as to believe that I would have acted more responsibly had I written, instead of these reflections, the book about him I had dreamt of writing for so long. I have not completely given it up. But such a project supposes a double risk, different from this one: of supplanting my music, and, finally, of not pleasing João himself. Let my clumsy and erratic music be for now the book I cannot write about him—this is how he listens to it—and let, then, this book be an extension of his character, however distorted by my efforts. For while the music does not enchant him (though his rendition of "Menino do Rio" gives me a little hope), neither does it bore him with analyses and interpretations of that mystery he so genially defends from even (or perhaps especially) those who would mystify him. Let it be clear that the path leading to tropical truth passes through my listening to João Gilberto as redeemer of the Portuguese language, violator of Brazilian social immobility—its inhuman and inelegant stratification—as architect of refined forms and mocker of every foolish stylizing that is their diminution. With me as its intermediary, *tropicalismo* carried the reality of popular music toward its most ambitious calling, the one that proclaimed João's sound.

In the fifties, a Carioca Carnival *marchinha* ridiculed the fans of radio singers as follows:

> *She's a fan of Emilinha*
> *Can't do without César de Alencar*
> *She screams Cauby's name*
> *And after fainting dead away,*
> *Picks up* Revista do Radio *to fan herself.*
> *A photo here, a photo there,*
> *All day long she won't do a thing*
> *Meanwhile back at home*
> *I can't find a maid to cook and clean.*

The song was a great success. I was thirteen at the time and frequented the auditorium of the National Radio in Rio de Janeiro—where Emilinha and Cauby used to appear in the show *Programa César de Alencar*—and I laughed at the satire without taking offense: I fancied myself to be above the other spectators but even so I didn't think they had much to be ashamed of. They were naïve people, perhaps a little affected in their delirium, but they loved what seemed lovable to me. The audience was made up primarily of lower-class women—and the author of the *marchinha* was implying that their place was in the kitchen. Floriano Faissal, an actor and director of radio theater, had coined a sobriquet for these enthusiasts: "auditorium monkeys." The phrase caught on with startling quickness. There were a great many black women and mulattas among the fans—whenever poor people gather in Brazil, the percentage of blacks and dark-skinned rises—and as there is a well-known tendency to compare blacks and monkeys, the joke carried a racist connotation. By 1967, however, I was already hearing ladies and nice young women of the white Paulista bourgeoisie declare, with pride, that they were my "monkeys": the word "monkey" (*macaca*) had replaced entirely the word "fan." Bossa nova is chronologically situated between that moment when the expression "auditorium monkeys" as well as that *marchinha* came into being and the emergence of *tropicalismo*. Setting itself against the commercial vulgarity of the greater part of National Radio's stars was an intense struggle to create and consume a respectable kind of music. Bossa nova represented not just the culmination of this effort but also the defeat of the very anxiety that demanded it: it accomplished the most sophisticated stylization, while at the same time valuing the past, making us aware of the greatness of our tradition. When *tropicalismo* came, it endeavored to hear bossa nova with the ear of someone who had attended auditorium programs with the monkeys. Or, better put: with the capacity to recognize in João Gilberto one who took them into account. The subtleties of the social (and racial) question in Brazil—so aptly illustrated by the story of the illiterate fans who would see their sobriquet taken up affectionately by the elites of the following decade—those subtleties were understood by the genius of João Gilberto. And that is what I recognize when I read in the lovely text Tom Jobim wrote for the back cover of João's first album: "He does not underestimate popular sensibility." It's not a matter of populism, substituting the aesthetic experiment for the adulation of the unfortunate and the huckster of languages, but rather of having the courage to face the complexity of the dance by which forms move through the history of society.

I think I wrote this book, for instance, because of New York. It's a curious city. Many of its residents say it has nothing to do with the United States, that it is a world city, farther from the typical American city than from another great city anywhere else. But still everyone knows that only the United States could create a city like New York. Coming for the first time in the eighties, I felt surprisingly at ease there, as I had never felt in England or even in continental Europe, even in the Italian or Iberian parts. I soon understood why: I was—as I am in Rio or São Paulo, in Salvador or Santo Amaro—on American territory. For one who knows himself to be, however western, profoundly Catholic in a southern European way, to feel at his ease in the Anglo-

Saxon capital of the World Empire is complicatedly stimulating. An indigenous word names the island where canyons of skyscrapers rise, escaping vulgarity not merely because they seem to be, as Lévi-Strauss remarked, more topographical accidents than architecture, but also because they rise to the condition of atemporal human works: seeing them, we experience at the same time the power of a legend, as if they had been demolished many centuries ago. The word "Manhattan," which I found in the amazing "Inferno de Wall Street" (Wall Street Inferno) by the Brazilian romantic poet Sousândrade, by dint of its metric and rhyme, would sound in Portuguese like "*Manhatã*." So it comes back to mind like some Tupi word each time I walk through those canyons dotted with golden portals. Manhatã, Manhatã, I hum to myself fondly and smile at the instant understanding I am able to have of the North American adventure, of its inevitably mestiza (*mestiça*) reality.[1] The city of New York, being the capital of the world and at the same time such an intimate place to me, has persuaded me at last of the existence of the external world (until my generation, Brazilians who lived on a coast far from the borders of a giant country did not consider foreigners to have substance), and it has made me feel free to exchange a few words with that world's inhabitants. New York, the splendor of the American Empire, is also the arrow with which it points toward a future to be reaffirmed only by overcoming it.

When I went there for my record label, after my first visit, I met an obvious American waiting for me at JFK Airport. I tried to speak English to him, but he answered me in a perfectly Pernambucan Portuguese: it was Arto Lindsay, an atonal guitarist and historic figure in the music scene of the southern part of the island of Manhattan. He had spent part of his childhood and adolescence in the Brazilian Northeast, and *tropicalista* music had been very important to him. He confessed to being "star-struck" in my presence, and though it was evident he was sincerely moved to meet someone who had impressed him in his adolescence, I thought it his way of demonstrating (not without a touch of

---

1. No, no less than in Brazil: contrary to those Brazilianists who would identify in Brazil a hypocritical and therefore more noxious kind of racism than the explicit form once institutionalized in the United States, I prefer that a racist at least feel constrained to pretend he is not; the Brazilian racial confusion reveals a profound miscegenation that inevitably occurs among North Americans as well, even if they pretend—whether through their racist laws or their laws of antiracist compensation—that it does not.

humor) an independent affection he felt for an artist from the underdeveloped world. A friendship was born.

The show at the Public Theater was a disaster for me. I had just returned from a European tour that had extended all the way to Israel and had imagined that in New York (where Guilherme was taking me, fulfilling an old wish of his) we would work in technical conditions as good as any we had found in the other places, or at least on a par with those in Brazil. Americans are very affable. But I discovered that at least in New York, if you are not a star on the American level, you can't count on finding even reasonable light and sound equipment. Nothing comparable to what is offered in Paris, Brussels, or Buenos Aires. There was no shortage of kindness: I later found out that Peter Schere, Arto's partner in the group Ambitious Lovers, had been in charge of the sound. The negotiations with Guilherme had been done through Fabiano Canosa, a Brazilian friend, who was then the programmer of the film club at the Public. The woman responsible for the event was extremely sweet. But the show, which was set for ten o'clock, started after midnight because a concert by Orgasmo Adulto Escapes from the Zoo had gone on indefinitely. It angers me to think that Tom Jobim, who was in town and wanted to see me, waited two hours for the beginning of the show—he, of all people, who used to say that he would charge one million dollars to do a show and two million to watch one!

We had just released the album *Uns* and it was the basis of the show we had taken on the road. When I toured around, it was always the same show I did in Brazil. But when we took to the stage at the Public Theater to present our subpop music over the puny amplifiers under the feeble lights, the *Uns* program we performed was scarcely a centesimal of the one we knew—which, even in full, much as we loved it, wasn't all that great. But it seems that in New York the public never allows itself to be disappointed: though they appeared cool during the show—I would weep with shame for days thereafter—the newspapers were full of praises, and Bob Hurwitz of Nonesuch Records came looking for me to say he was enchanted by what he had seen and heard. Hurwitz was the man who would later make me tape a record in two afternoon sessions—it came out well notwithstanding—and, even later than that, encouraged me to do the album *Estrangeiro* with Arto and Peter. This put me in touch with instrumentalists, writers, people in the New York art world.

I think it was in 1986, during a tumultuous session of the Rio film festival, that I launched the film *O cinema falado* (Talkie)—the first and only feature I have directed. To the same festival David Byrne had brought his *True Stories*. And it was on account of that very festival that a meeting so full of subtly decisive consequences for me and for our music took place. David had arrived in Brazil a little earlier, with his wife, Bonnie, and both of them had gone on their own to Bahia before going to Rio. They came back very excited with what they had heard there on the radio. From their descriptions, I wasn't quite able to tell whether they had heard *forró* or the new Carnival music from Salvador that journalists had nicknamed (somewhat nastily, but with involuntary wit) "*axé* music." It's possible that they had heard both genres and something else. What fascinated me was David's growing interest in a type of musical production that had never attracted (nor ever would) the makers of jazz-fusion or sophisticated rock who would come to visit. The result, which I already had predicted, was that soon he would become involved as a producer of the *tropicalistas*. The first anthology of Brazilian pop he released emphasized the freedom and inventiveness of the sound of our recordings in the seventies—I was already a different kind of news coming out of Brazil. And though he asked for my opinion about a tape of his selections, I refused to give any because I believed that the purity of his first impression would give character to the record. The only comment I could not repress was that the omission of Paulinho da Viola seemed to me inexplicable and unacceptable. But David didn't touch it. Something more important, however, was about to happen: having bought a number of records of and about samba, he ended up taking in the bundle Tom Zé's *Estudando o samba* (Studying Samba); it surprised him, and he fell in love with it. The introduction he wrote for Tom Zé, first in the beautifully edited anthology and later in a production of unpublished material, was a confirmation and a deepening of the originality and aptness of his vision of our modern music. Tom Zé had been forgotten in Brazil, his experimental records from the seventies generally considered outdated and unfashionable. Byrne's attention unsettled the Brazilian press, Tom Zé's life, and ours. And it opened a new track of international dialogue for our music. Post–bossa nova MPB had arrived in the outside world with a quickness and intensity in the person of Milton Nascimento. Jorge Ben (through Sérgio Mendes) and Gil had also left their mark. Edu, Elis, Dori Caymmi—apart from the cases of musical emigration like Airto and Flora Purim—had become respected figures. Egberto Gismonti and Hermeto Paschoal are masters recognized anywhere. And Naná Vasconcelos causes people of all nationalities to feel they stand before a genius. After this, figures like Djavan and Ivan Lins attracted the attention of colleagues on a world scale. But what was established by David Byrne from the first track of the first anthology, with Bethânia and Gal singing "Sonho meu" by Ivone Lara, and which culminated with Tom Zé's records, this is something more closely related to the issues raised in this book. And so whenever I go to New York, and this happens only rarely, I look him up; and though we always see each other only briefly, and my stay in the city is never long, our conversations always bring me pleasure and stimulation.

One day at a New York nightclub called the Ballroom, where I was doing a series of shows, a fax for me arrived from the *New York Times.* They wanted an article about Carmen Miranda. The idea was to have a text written by some Brazilian connected to pop music. Someone on the editorial staff confirmed that I was the possible author suggested by a Brazilian editor and by an American literary agent who had been consulted by the staff of *Arts & Leisure* (it turns out they thought of me when their first choice, Chico Buarque, proved unavailable), and I was worth a try. Aside from the show at the Ballroom, I was recording the remaining tracks of (and starting to mix) the album *Circuladô,* so I couldn't see how I would find the time and energy to write that essay. But I ended up doing it. Between one session and the next, during the moments of waiting in the studio, which are always long, the hours stolen from recalcitrant sleep, I wrote an earnest text about Carmen. In it I focused on the small figure of the singer, the part of Brazil best known in the world, from the perspective of the *tropicalista* movement—which in turn I considered from the perspective of MPB. There were lots of names of colleagues—many of them obscure to the North American reader—and my sentences were too baroque, so I had many long conversations with the editor, negotiating words, references, the order of the paragraphs. It was all much more work than the actual writing, but the woman with whom I spoke on the phone (always on the phone) was so interesting—she sounded so much like my ideal of a refined New York woman—that this was also more pleasurable than the writing. And in the end the text came out more faithful to my first impulse than either that editor or I would have ever believed possible.

Because of what the article suggested respecting *tropicalismo,* and because of the tone in which it was done, an editor in New York thought he saw a book suggesting itself. He wrote to me about it. I was surprised and grateful, but I replied that I had no intention of writing books, and that I had already refused insistent offers to do so in Brazil.

But I agreed to meet with him and ended up capitulating. The fact is, I took the thing as a responsibility I had no right to refuse. It was a traditional respect for the odd chance that traces destiny that made me accept the task. After all, the invitation to write for the *New York Times* had come out of nowhere, and that had led a New York editor to commission the book. Perhaps this was the opportunity to provide an appreciation of the MPB experience and to situate it in global terms. But when I realized that I had accepted the task, I could see straightaway that this was also for my inmost self a pretext to write and even to read more. It was an invitation for me to fulfill my dream of drawing closer to books, before which I had always felt intimidated. I then set out with an enthusiasm that only now begins to elude me, and having made up my mind to do it, I never once thought of giving up, even if I never understood whom it could possibly interest—nor even whether its publication could in fact be useful for me and the things I hold dear. Without ever coming to a conclusion respecting any of those matters, I finished it, and as Gertrude Stein would say under Alice B. Toklas's skin, here it is.

glossary of brazilian terms

afoxé
A song form and rhythm derived from *candomblé*; groups that play *afoxé*, contemporary Afro-Brazilian Carnival music, during Carnival in Salvador (Bahia), associated with contemporary African-Bahian consciousness

agogô
Double or triple cone-shaped cowbell played with a metal or wooden stick

atabaque
Generic name for different sizes of narrow, conical single-headed drums played with the hands (similar to Cuban conga drum)

axé
Brazilian popular music genre, and the Yoruba word for the vital spiritual force of *candomblé*

baião
Binary social dance music from the Northeast of Brazil, featuring syncopated melodies, typically played by trios made up of accordion, triangle, and *zabumba* drum

bandolim
From the Italian *mandolino,* a small double-course mandolin

bateria
Percussion ensembles of Rio's samba schools; they may use a number of small, single-headed frame drums (like *tamborim*), medium-sized single-headed ones (*caixa, repique*), as well as *atabaque, cuíca,* and *surdo* drums

batucada
A drumming session or performance of a samba percussion ensemble, or the drum and percussion section of an *escola de samba*

batuque
From the Portuguese word *bater,* "to hit," an African religion and dance in some parts of Brazil, of Angolan or Congolese origin; generic name for Afro-Brazilian dances; a type of drum used in *jongo*

Beco das Garrafas
A street in Copacabana and birthplace of the style that eventually came to be associated with *O Fino da Bossa,* the television program in São Paulo that was hosted by Elis Regina

berimbau

A wooden bow with a metal string and a gourd resonator common in Bahia, of Angolan origin, used especially to accompany *capoeira*

bloco afro

Contemporary Afro-Brazilian Carnival music, often combining samba with other musical forms, such as reggae, associated with the renaissance of African-Bahian culture and contemporary black consciousness; an ensemble of players of such music

brega

The Brazilian rock of the late eighties and early nineties

BRock

Brazilian rock. "BR" is short for Brazil: federal roads are identified as such by the prefix BR: BR 324, BR 101, and so forth. Petrobras, the national oil company, has its own gas stations alongside those of Exxon, Texaco, etc., and those stations are also called BR. Ironically enough, the term "BRock" was invented by a rock-fan journalist who perfectly represents the antistate attitude of the Brazilian press, which regards Petrobras as the devil.

bumbo

Large drum

caboclo

A word of indigenous origin, *caboclo* designates an indigenous person, the mestizo offspring of Indian and European miscegenation, or simply someone who has copper-colored skin. Today a figure called Caboclo, in the form of an indigenous person, is also a central figure in some Afro-Brazilian cults.

cachaça

A somewhat bitter alcoholic drink made from fermented sugar cane

caixa

Medium-size drum

candomblé

Afro-Brazilian religion of Gegê-Nagô and Bantu derivation. Among the Afro-Brazilian religions, *candomblé,* as practiced in Bahia, comes closest to the old West African religious practices. Its ritual music utilizes three different *atabaques* (the rum, rumpi, and the lê), and pentatonic and hexatonic scales.

capoeira

An Afro-Brazilian martial arts form common to Bahia, created by slaves during the colonial period; combines dancelike movement with musical accompaniment

Carioca

A native or resident of Rio de Janeiro

choro or chorinho

Binary instrumental genre featuring rapid modulations and improvisation by lead instrument that appeared in late nineteenth century in Rio and has certain affinities to ragtime; Afro-Brazilian genre based on a polka-*maxixe* rhythm

cordão
Originally an all-male group that celebrated Carnival dancing to the accompaniment of a *batucada* that appeared in the late nineteenth century

cuíca
Small, single-headed friction drum with a thin stick inside attached to the drumskin. A moistened cloth is used to rub the stick and one hand applies pressure to the drumskin, to produce groaning or squeaking noises.

embolada
Poetic-musical form from the Northeastern coast, with a stanza and refrain structure, ¾ meter, and a fast tempo, often improvised between dueling singers, accompanied by *pandeiro,* tambourine, and *ganzá*

escola de samba
Urban samba groups and associations that organize elaborate parades during Carnival in Rio de Janeiro. It typically has other social functions as well, serving as community center in the *favelas* and poorer neighborhoods.

fado
A dance genre cultivated by the popular classes of Rio in the nineteenth century, of uncertain origin, possibly Brazilian, but fully developed in Portugal into its present form: a melancholy genre usually sung to the accompaniment of guitar

forró
A generic name for social dance music in the Northeast; a *caboclo* dance party; the accordion-based music from the Northeast derived from *baião*

frevo
A fast, syncopated Carnival *marcha* that originated in Recife, Pernambuco, played by brass band, or the electric version of the same played during Carnival in Salvador, Bahia. The Bahian contemporary version *(frevo-baiano)* incorporates a variety of styles aside from *frevo: merengue,* rock, and *ijexá.*

ijexá
Afro-Bahian culture associated with *candomblé;* the rhythm, style, and dance of *afoxé* music; also a subgroup of the Yoruba people

Integralista party
The Brazilian fascist movement, an extreme right-wing Catholic-patriotic-nationalist movement from the thirties, some of whose coreligionists supported the military government

jongo
A large drum of African origin and the folk dance in which it is used. Over time, it has evolved into a variant of samba.

Jovem Guarda
Originally a São Paulo television program, from 1965 to 1969, it gave rise to the generic term *"jovem guarda"* and to *iê-iê-iê* (from the Beatles' "Yeah, yeah, yeah"), the early Brazilian rock 'n' roll. Its most celebrated exponent is Roberto Carlos, one of the most popular ballad singers in Latin America.

lundu

Early song/dance type of Angolan origin (Bantu), derived from an Afro-Brazilian folk dance; the ancestor of many urban Brazilian song forms

maracatu

Slow, heavy Afro-Brazilian processional music and its accompanying dance from Northeastern Brazil, featuring a series of characters (king, queen, *dama de passo*); the groups that perform *maracatu* during Carnival

marcha or marchinha

Binary Afro-Brazilian form with strong accent on the downbeat and fast tempo; influenced in the 1920s by one-step and ragtime

marcha-rancho

Slower and more melodically developed variation of the *marcha*

maxixe

A fast, syncopated dance music form that emerged in the nineteenth century, a Brazilian creation from the fusion of *lundu* elements with tango, polka, and habanera

moda

Generic term for a song genre both in Portugal and Brazil

modinha

Sentimental Brazilian song style that originated in the colonial period, derived from *moda* and *lundu*

MPB

Acronym (Música Popular Brasileira) generally used to refer to the post–bossa nova music of national orientation that emerged as a result of the televised songwriters' competitions on television beginning in 1965, and which is still generically used to distinguish post–bossa nova hybridizations from rock 'n' roll, as well as to denote the generation that in different ways defined those preoccupations, particularly Chico Buarque, Caetano Veloso, Gilberto Gil, Edu Lobo, and Milton Nascimento

orixá

Brazilian spelling for the word for "deity" in Yoruba, in *candomblé* and other Afro-Brazilian religions

pagode

A party or gathering where samba is played; type of samba popularized in the 1980s by composers who gathered in Ramos, a neighborhood in Rio's Zona Norte

Paulista

An inhabitant of the state of São Paulo; related to São Paulo

quilombos

Runaway slave communities during the colonial period. The most famous and longest lasting was the Republic of Palmares, led by Zumbi.

rancho

Early Carnival associations, made up of blacks, mulattos, and the unskilled white laborers who danced in the streets to the rhythm of percussive instruments singing in responsorial form to the improvised verses of a leader. They are, with the *cordão,* the precursors of the *escolas de samba* and of Carnival music.

samba

Generic term designating a wide variety of musical and dance styles, musically characterized by ¾ meter and interlocking, syncopated lines in melody and accompaniment

samba-canção

Slower, softer type of samba in which the melody and lyrics are emphasized over the rhythm (plural: *sambas-canções*)

samba breque

"Break samba," a choppy, almost reggae rhythm

samba de breque

Type of samba with a "break" in which the singer dramatizes a situation or improvises dialogues

samba de gafieira

The type of samba favored by the large urban dance halls patronized by the urban working classes, often jazz-inflected, as seen in the use of instrumental and horn arrangements

samba de morro

The term used by the Brazilian media in the forties and fifties to designate the kind of samba that maintained the essential characteristics of the style developed by *estácio* (i.e., morro) composers, such as Ismael Silva and Bide; also used to distinguish this type from others, such as *samba-canção* or *sambolero*

samba de pagode

A good-time soaring dance rhythm exemplified by Agepe, Clara Nunes, and Alcione, and the Raa Negra band (which first hooked David Byrne)

samba de roda

Circle dance samba, accompanied by hand-clapping and *batucada*

(samba de) partido alto

A type of samba usually sung/played only by the (Afro-Brazilian) specialists, relying on improvisation of long verses between refrains

samba-enredo

A samba that evolved from the theme-based parades of the *escolas de samba* beginning in the 1930s

sambolero

Fusion of samba and bolero

sertaneja

Brushland of Brazil's Northeastern interior; someone or something from rural or hinterland areas of Brazil

surdo

Double-headed drum played with a wooden stick topped by velvet-covered wooden head used in many genres of Brazilian music. Surdos come in three sizes and function as the bass in the samba *bateria*.

tamborim

A small tambourine with a plastic or metal frame, without jingles, played with a stick

terreiro

The temple for Afro-Brazilian religious worship

trio elétrico

Bahian electric guitar trio accompanied by a small percussion group typical of Salvador Carnival. It originated in the 1960s when Dodô and Osmar, who began performing *frevos* on treble (*guitarra baiana*), tenor (*triolim*), and bass electric guitars (*pau-elétrico*), backed by a small percussion group (cymbals, snare drum, *zabumba, surdo*), who blasted their music from the back of a pickup truck as they drove through the streets. The term also applies to the musicians who play the electric instruments, as well as to the decorated trucks on top of which they perform during Carnival in Salvador.

viola

Brazilian plucked and strummed instrument of Iberian origin, with double courses of strings (can have five, seven, eight, ten, twelve, or fourteen strings, depending on the region). It is a staple of *caipira* music, among other genres.

violão

Brazilian guitar, the common six-stringed guitar

xote

Northeastern slow *caboclo* dance, a genre based on the schottische

zabumba

Large, double-headed bass drum; also the name sometimes given to the *bandas de pífanos*

Zona Norte

Northern area of Rio de Janeiro that includes neighborhoods such as Estácio, Tijuca, Vila Isabel, and Ramos. Some of the poorer areas of the city are located here.

Zona Sul

Southern part of Rio de Janeiro, it is the area closer to the beaches; it includes the neighborhoods of Flamengo, Botafogo, Copacabana, Ipanema, Leblon, Jardim Botânico, and Gávea. It is inextricably linked to the development of bossa nova.

index

textual permissions

Grateful acknowledgment is made to the following for permission to reprint previously published material:

Terra Enterprises: Excerpts from "Genipapo absoluto," "O leaozinho," "Lost in the Paradise," "The Empty Boat," and "Irene," all written and copyrighted by Caetano Veloso, reprinted by arrangement with Terra Enterprises, Inc.

Warner Bros. Publications U.S. Inc.: Excerpt from "Paisagem útil" by Caetano Veloso, copyright © 1968 (renewed) Warner Chappell Edições Musicais Ltda (UBC). All rights administered by Warner-Tamerlane Publishing Corp. (BMI); excerpt from "Tropicália" by Caetano Veloso, copyright © 1968 (renewed) Warner Chappell Edições Musicais Ltda (UBC). All rights reserved. Used by permission of Warner Bros. Publications U.S. Inc., Miami, Florida 33014.

illustration credits

Sônia Castro: design of program for Caetano and Gil's show at the Castro Alves Theater

Rogerio Duprat's personal archive: Duprat playing the cello; Duprat with Big Ben

Folha Imagem: rehearsal for *É proibido proibir*

Gilberto Gil's personal archive: Gil without his shirt

Arthur Ikissma: photo on program for Caetano and Gil's show at the Castro Alves Theater

Rita Lee's personal archive: Os Mutantes walking down the street

Projeto Hélio Oiticica: *Tropicália* installation; Oiticica lying on floor; *Seja marginal, seja herói* poster

Paulo Salomão/Abril Imagens: on the set of *O Fino da Bossa;* Roberto Carlos on Chacrinha; Caetano and Dedé on the balcony; on the set of *Divino, Maravilhoso*

Manchete Press: Caetano and Dedé's wedding; Caetano and Dedé on the beach after their wedding; Caetano sitting on floor of São Paulo apartment; the March of a Hundred Thousand; Caetano and Gil on stage at the Castro Alves Theater in 1969; Gil at entrance to the Underground; Gil and Caetano in Trafalgar Square

Mario Sampaio's personal archive: covers of Gilberto Gil's, Maria de Graça's, Maria Bethânia's, and Caetano Veloso's 1966 albums; program for Caetano and Gil's show at the Castro Alves Theater

J. Ferriera da Silva/Abril Imagens: Gil and Nana Caymmi

Clara Veloso's personal archive: Gal Costa in 1964

Mabel Veloso's personal archive: the Veloso family in Santo Amaro

Rodrigo Veloso's personal archive: Sandra and Caetano on the street in London; Rodrigo and Dedé in London

a note about the author

Caetano Veloso was born in 1942 in Santo Amaro da Purificação, Bahia, Brazil. He lives in Bahia and Rio de Janeiro.

a note on the type

The text of this book was set in Garamond No. 3. It is not a true copy of any of the designs of Claude Garamond (c. 1480–1561), but an adaptation of his types, which set the European standard for two centuries. It probably owes as much to the designs of Jean Jannon, a Protestant printer working in Sedan in the early seventeenth century, who had worked with Garamond's romans earlier, in Paris, but who was denied their use because of Catholic censorship. Jannon's matrices came into the possession of the Imprimerie Nationale, where they were thought to be by Garamond himself, and were so described when the Imprimerie revived the type in 1900. This particular version is based on an adaptation by Morris Fuller Benton.

Composed by North Market Street Graphics, Lancaster, Pennsylvania

Printed and bound by Berryville Graphics, Berryville, Virginia

Designed by Iris Weinstein